the Reich

Battles on Germany's Western Frontier 1944–1945

Into the Reich

Battles on Germany's Western Frontier 1944–1945

James R Arnold · Stephen Badsey
Ken Ford · Steven J Zaloga

First published in Great Britain in 2002 by Osprey Publishing,
Elms Court, Chapel Way, Botley, Oxford OX2 9LP, United Kingdom.
Email: info@ospreypublishing.com

Previously published as Campaign 75: *Lorraine 1944 Patton Vs Manteuffel*, Campaign 24: *Arnhem 1944 Operation Market Garden*, Campaign 5: *Ardennes 1944 Hitler's Last Gamble in the West* and Campaign 74: *The Rhineland 1945 The Last Killing Ground in the West*

ISBN 1 84176 617 8

Series Editor: Lee Johnson
Editor: Sally Rawlings
Index by Alan Rutter

Printed in China through World Print Ltd.

02 03 04 05 06   10 9 8 7 6 5 4 3 2 1

FOR A CATALOGUE OF ALL BOOKS PUBLISHED BY
OSPREY MILITARY AND AVIATION PLEASE CONTACT:

The Marketing Manager, Osprey Direct UK
PO Box 140, Wellingborough,
Northants, NN8 2FA, United Kingdom
Email: **info@ospreydirect.co.uk**

The Marketing Manager, Osprey Direct USA
c/o MBI Publishing, 729 Prospect Avenue,
Osceola, WI 54020, USA
Email: **info@ospreydirectusa.com**

www.ospreypublishing.com

FRONT COVER: Men of the 2nd Gordon Highlanders, and the parish church and stone tower of Goch. (© Imperial War Museum)

BACK COVER: Troops moving over frozen ground on 21 January 1945. (© Imperial War Museum)

CONTENTS

ARDENNES 1944

THE RHINELAND 1945

THE STRATEGIC SITUATION

In September 1944, Hitler sensed the opportunity to deal the Allies a crushing blow. Patton's Third Army was spearheading the Allied advance eastward, and as his forces attacked into Lorraine, they seemed on the verge of penetrating the Westwall defenses into Germany itself. However, Patton's right flank was exposed while the US 6th Army Group moved northward along the Swiss frontier, having landed a month earlier in southern France. So by massing several of the newly formed Panzer brigades, Hitler prepared for a major armored counteroffensive in Lorraine. His aim was to encircle and destroy Patton's forces. To lead this audacious attack and head up the Fifth Panzer Army, he chose one of his youngest and most aggressive tank commanders, Gen. Hasso von Manteuffel. This would be the largest German panzer counterattack on the Western Front and one of the largest tank versus tank battles fought by the US Army in World War II. The tank battles in Lorraine in September 1944 are the focus of this book.

Alsace-Lorraine had been a warpath between France and Germany for centuries: taken by Germany in the wake of the 1870 Franco-Prussian War, it was recovered by France after 1918 and then reabsorbed into

During August, Patton's Third Army raced across France as the Wehrmacht retreated in disorder. Here, on 21 August 1944, an M4 tank of the 8th Tank Bn., 4th Armd. Div. fires on German troops across the Marne River, trying to destroy one of its bridges. The 4th Armd. Div. was usually Patton's spearhead, and would play the central role in the September tank fighting in Lorraine. (US Army)

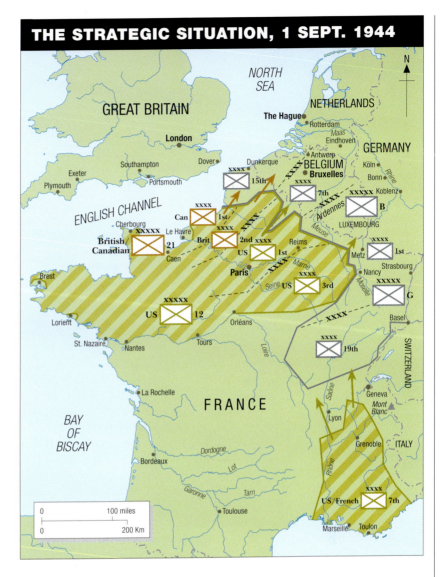

THE STRATEGIC SITUATION, 1 SEPT. 1944

Germany after 1940. As a traditional invasion route between the two countries, the area has also been fortified over the centuries with great fortress cities such as Metz. The "Charmes Gap" figured in French war plans in 1914, and the nearby Verdun forts were the center of the fighting in 1916. The French side of Lorraine was the site of portions of the Maginot Line, mirrored on the German frontier by the Westwall which was also called the Siegfried Line.

At the beginning of September 1944, the Allies were optimistic the war might soon be won. In August, German forces in northern France had been encircled and smashed in the Falaise Gap. German casualties had exceeded 300,000 killed and captured, and a further 200,000 had been trapped in the Atlantic ports and Channel Islands. For nearly a month, the Allied armies had advanced with little opposition, surging past Paris and into Belgium. In the east, the German forces had suffered an equally shattering setback with the destruction of Army Group Center in Byelorussia as a result of the Red Army's Operation Bagration. A subsequent offensive through Ukraine had pushed the German forces

completely out of the Soviet Union and into central Poland along the Vistula River. While the central region of the front had stabilized by the beginning of August, the Red Army had poured into the Balkans. Germany's eastern allies – Finland, Romania, Hungary, and Bulgaria – were on the verge of switching sides, and Germany's main source of oil in the Romanian fields near Ploesti was soon to be lost. On 20 July 1944, German officers attempted to assassinate Hitler, and some believed that this signaled the beginning of a German collapse, similar to that experienced by the German Army in the autumn of 1918.

The Anglo-American forces under Gen. Dwight Eisenhower comprised three main elements. Gen. Bernard Montgomery's 21st Army Group on the left flank was advancing from the regions of Dieppe and Amiens towards Flanders. The 21st Army Group consisted of the First Canadian Army, on the extreme left, and the Second British Army to its right. The main American element was Gen. Omar Bradley's 12th Army Group, consisting of Hodges' First Army, moving to the north-east into central Belgium, and Gen. George S. Patton's Third Army moving through the Argonne into Lorraine. In addition, Gen. Jacob Devers' 6th Army Group, consisting of the US Seventh Army and the French First Army, had landed in southern France and was advancing northward along the Swiss border towards the Belfort Gap.

German forces in France lost most of their armored equipment in the Normandy campaign and the ensuing envelopment at Falaise. Of the 1,890 tanks and assault guns available on D-Day, about 1,700 were lost. This is a salvage yard in Travières, France, on 4 September 1944, showing some of the captured equipment. In the foreground are two tank destroyers based on captured French chassis, while to the right are three Panther tanks. (US Army)

OPPOSING PLANS

GERMAN PLANS

From the German perspective, the strategic situation was an unrelieved disaster. The Wehrmacht was in headlong retreat from France, and the immediate tasks were to reconstitute German forces in the west and hold back the Allied forces while defenses in depth were strengthened along the Westwall. In the wake of the attempted military coup in July, Adolf Hitler was extremely suspicious of German military leaders, and he imposed an even tighter control on all military operations down to the tactical level. Hitler remained contemptuous of the Anglo-American armies, and was convinced that bold operations could derail the Allied advance. In spite of the utter failure of his panzer counteroffensive at Mortain a month earlier, Hitler was entranced with the concept of cutting off and destroying the lead elements of the Anglo-American forces. He expected that his panzer forces could win great encirclement battles in the west as they so often had on the Eastern Front. Not surprisingly, he selected veterans from the Eastern Front to conduct his offensive in Lorraine.

At the beginning of September, German forces in the west were under the command of Generalfeldmarschall Gerd von Rundstedt. These included Generalfeldmarschall Walter Model's Army Group B, with four armies from the North Sea to the area around Nancy, and the much smaller Army Group G, under Generaloberst Johannes Blaskowitz, with only a single army covering from Nancy southward to the Swiss frontier.

Hitler believed that a violent panzer attack against Patton's Third Army was both the most necessary and the most promising option. Patton's Third Army had advanced the furthest east, and its momentum towards the Saar suggested that it would be the first Allied force to enter Germany. Besides blunting this threatening advance, a panzer counterattack towards Reims would have the added benefit of preventing the link-up between Devers' 6th Army Group advancing from southern France and Bradley's 12th Army Group in northern France. On 3 September 1944, Hitler instructed Rundstedt to begin planning this attack. Under Hitler's initial plan, the attack would be carried out by the 3rd, 15th, and 17th SS Panzer Grenadier Divisions, the new Panzer Brigades 111, 112, and 113, and with later reinforcements from the Panzer Lehr Division, 11th and 21st Panzer Divisions and the new Panzer Brigades 106, 107, and 108. The Fifth Panzer Army headquarters would be shifted from Belgium to Alsace-Lorraine to control the panzer counteroffensive. On 5 September 1944, the newly appointed commander of Fifth Panzer Army, Gen. Hasso von Manteuffel, flew in straight from the fighting on the Eastern Front to be

11

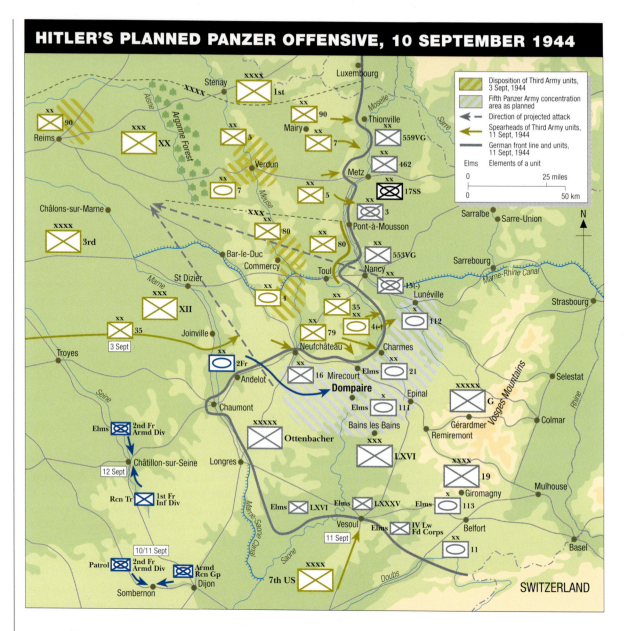

personally briefed by Hitler on the objectives of the counteroffensive. The date of the counterattack was initially set for 12 September 1944, but events soon overtook these plans.

ALLIED PLANS

The dilemma facing Allied planners in September 1944 was very different. Towards the end of August 1944, many Allied military leaders had begun to wonder whether the Germans might completely collapse, as they had done in 1918. Under such circumstances, a continuing string of bold advances could best take advantage of the German plight. Yet there remained the nagging doubt that the Germans might prove resilient and that their resistance might stiffen as the prewar German frontier was attacked.

The advance through France in August 1944 had seen the Allied forces achieve far more than was originally planned: they had expected to be on the Seine River in early September when in fact they were now 150 miles beyond. Indeed, Patton's Third Army was at the phase line expected for April 1945. The most immediate consequence of the unexpectedly speedy advance was that the Allied forces were beginning to experience serious logistical difficulties. Supplies landed on the Normandy beaches had to be trucked forward, since the French railroad network had been shattered by pre-invasion bombing. Shortages in fuel and ammunition would become a critical determinant of combat capabilities in the autumn of 1944. Ideally, a port closer to the front was needed. The most likely candidate was Antwerp, which was large enough to handle the necessary volume of supplies. This was in the British sector, and Montgomery's 21st Army Group was given the vital assignment of securing it.

Beyond the short-term need to improve the supply situation before pressing on into Germany, there remained controversy over how best to conduct operations. In May 1944, the SHAEF (Supreme Headquarters Allied Expeditionary Force) had completed studies which recommended a broad front advance with two main axes of attack. The main drive would take place through Belgium, north of the Ardennes forest, then swing behind the Rhine River to eliminate Germany's industrial heart in the Ruhr. This would involve Mongomery's 21st Army Group and the US First Army. The secondary axis of attack would be through Lorraine towards Frankfurt, to take the Saar industrial region and win bridgeheads over the Rhine into central Germany. This would involve Patton's Third Army and the 6th Army Group.

The supply problems of September 1944 led to questions about these plans, especially from the commander of the British forces, Gen. Bernard Montgomery. In early September, Montgomery argued that the lack of sufficient supplies would make a broad front attack impossible. Instead, he urged that the resources be directed to his 21st Army Group, which could make a bold thrust through the Netherlands. Montgomery contended that Germany was on the brink of defeat and that his forces could race to Berlin, bringing about a swift end of the war. As September progressed and German resistance began to stiffen, Montgomery stuck with his single-thrust strategy, arguing that it was still the best alternative to close on the Ruhr and end the war through industrial strangulation. Underlying this debate was an unstated recognition that Britain was losing its once-dominant position in the Allied coalition. The British Army had committed all of its ground forces, and as the war continued, the US Army would play an increasingly important role in the fighting. Montgomery's championing of British leadership in the assault on Germany was an attempt to push off his inevitable loss of influence as the British forces shrank as a proportion of the Allied armies.

Montgomery's position was vehemently contested by US Army leaders, especially by his American counterpart, Gen. Omar Bradley. The US Army commanders had lost confidence in Montgomery following his conduct in the prolonged armored offensives to take Caen during the Normandy campaign, and they were skeptical of his ability to achieve the rapid offensive he proposed. The American leadership was suspicious of Montgomery's motives, feeling that he was prompted more by his desire for British forces to play the predominant role in the European campaign than by realistic tactical advantage. Bradley wanted to continue Patton's advance through Lorraine, in the hope of being able to seize Rhine crossings towards Frankfurt should German resistance continue to be weak. Montgomery's plan would force Patton's Third Army to halt before breaching the Moselle River line and before joining up with Devers' 6th Army Group.

The supreme Allied commander, Gen. Dwight Eisenhower, attempted to mediate, with little appreciation from either side. Montgomery was openly contemptuous of Eisenhower's ability as a field commander, while Bradley felt that he was overly solicitous to Montgomery's exorbitant demands. The importance of seizing Antwerp led to Eisenhower granting Montgomery priority in the allotment of supplies on 4 September, but arguments continued through early September over how much priority 21st Army Group would in fact receive. The key issue remained the Allies' perception of the condition of the German forces. Was the Wehrmacht on the brink of collapse, or was it on the brink of recovery? If on the verge of collapse, then bold ventures were worth the risk, but if on the verge of recovery, then steps were needed to ensure that the Allied armies would be ready to conduct well-prepared operations into Germany in the ensuing months. The Allies were reaching the end of the logistical possibilities of the Normandy harbors, and the supply question needed attention.

On 3 September 1944, Montgomery first mentioned to Bradley plans for a proposed operation called Market-Garden, with an aim to seize a bridgehead over the Rhine with airborne forces at Arnhem as the first stage of a northern Ruhr envelopment. Bradley was opposed to the plan, feeling that it was impractical and too risky. In a cable to Eisenhower on 4 September, Montgomery continued to urge "a powerful and full-blooded thrust towards Berlin." The issue finally came to a head at a 10 September meeting. Montgomery again demanded a thrust on Berlin, but it became evident that Eisenhower would not consider any such operation until the port of Antwerp was functioning. By mid-September, Eisenhower had lost his late-August optimism about Germany's imminent collapse and was becoming more convinced that the Germans were rallying. Montgomery then presented his daring Market-Garden plan. Eisenhower approved Market-Garden as a less fanciful and less disruptive alternative to the Berlin adventure.

Eisenhower's decision to approve Market-Garden shaped the subsequent conduct of Allied operations in September. The broad front strategy had not been given up, but realistically the supply problem would limit the amount of offensive operations the Allies could conduct. Eisenhower gave priority to the northern thrust, including both the 21st Army Group's Market-Garden operation and a supporting drive by the US First Army in Belgium to protect the British right flank. Patton's advance in Lorraine was not yet frozen, but its potential was severely circumscribed by the likelihood of supply cut-offs. The debate over the Berlin dagger-thrust and Market-Garden had also distracted the Allied leaders from concentrating on the need to secure Antwerp by clearing the Scheldt estuary. Montgomery's preoccupation with offensive operations led to serious delays in devoting resources to the Scheldt, and as a result, Antwerp was not ready to begin receiving supplies until the

Commander of the Fifth Panzer Army, General der Panzertruppe Hasso von Manteuffel, on the left, confers with the Army Group A commander, Gen. Walter Model (right) and the inspector of the panzer force on the Western Front, Gen. Lt. Horst Stumpff (center). (US Army MHI)

end of November 1944. This would prove to be one of the most critical Allied blunders of the autumn campaign.

The Germans did not expect so bold a venture as Market-Garden from the Allies, especially not from so cautious a commander as Montgomery. As a result of both sides' misperceptions of the other's strategic intentions, the contest between Patton's Third Army and Manteuffel's Fifth Panzer Army was more equal than it otherwise might have been. The German forces in Lorraine received priority in supplies and equipment because of Hitler's planned panzer offensive, while their American opponents were being constrained in their operations by supply limits. Patton's forces in Lorraine still enjoyed some significant firepower advantages over the Wehrmacht, but the unusually rainy weather in September restricted the amount of air support that was possible. The Germans enjoyed the advantage of the formidable defensive possibilities presented by the Metz fortified area, as well as the natural defenses of the Moselle valley.

OPPOSING COMMANDERS

GERMAN COMMANDERS

Adolf Hitler

While the main focus of this assessment is on the tactical commanders, it is impossible to detail the German side without considering Adolf Hitler, who had played an unusually active role in directing German military operations even before the failed military coup of 20 July 1944. After the unsuccessful assassination attempt, Hitler became even more suspicious of the commitment of the German generals to the war, and he insisted that the Wehrmacht "stand and hold" every inch of territory, thereby robbing the commanders of their tactical flexibility. Hitler's suspicions led to an extremely high degree of centralization, with commanders having to obtain permission from higher headquarters for any significant tactical decision. Senior generals were not trusted, and there was considerable turmoil in the upper ranks of the Wehrmacht as Hitler frequently replaced commanders. A large portion of the senior officers taking part in the Lorraine fighting in 1944 were brought in from the Eastern Front, as Hitler regarded them as less defeatist.

Wilhelm Keitel

The supreme German command nominally rested in the hands of the OKW (Oberkommando der Wehrmacht), headed by Generalfeldmarschall Wilhelm Keitel. Although the power of the OKW was circumscribed by Hitler's paranoia, it still retained an important function, since it could shape the Führer's views of the battle, and all subordinate commanders had to reach Hitler through the OKW structure.

Gerd von Rundstedt

SHAEF's German counterpart was the OB West (Oberbefehlshaber West), headed by Generalfeldmarschall Gerd von Rundstedt. He took over command of the Western Front on 1 September 1944, having given up the post in June 1944 after a confrontation with Hitler over the response to the Normandy invasion. Rundstedt remained the last of the undefeated German field marshals, with the stunning victories of 1939-40 to his credit, but his powers that September were severely restricted by Hitler and the OKW; and he later complained that he really only commanded the guards at his headquarters. Rundstedt had been brought back to act as a symbol of stability and to inspire confidence after the summer disasters.

Walter Model

Army Group B was commanded by Generalfeldmarschall Walter Model, who had been in charge of the entire Western Front until the OB West headquarters was reinstituted on 1 September 1944. Although Army Group B commanded most of the forces in Lorraine at the beginning of

September, a reorganization on 8 September shifted First Army to the neighboring Army Group G. Model was a favorite of Hitler – a brash, young officer better known as a trouble-shooter who could protect German fortunes in the face of staggering defeat than for his skills in conducting successful offensive operations.

Johannes Blaskowitz

The commander of Army Group G, Generaloberst Johannes Blaskowitz. (USNA)

Army Group G, near Nancy, was the centerpoint of the subsequent Lorraine panzer offensive. Army Group G had originally been organized to manage the German defense of southern France. Generaloberst Johannes Blaskowitz was a traditional German commander, more in the mold of Rundstedt than Model. East Prussian and non-political, he had commanded Eighth Army since October 1940 and had spent most of the war in command of First Army occupying France. At Rundstedt's insistence, Blaskowitz had been assigned command of Army Group G on 10 May 1944. Blaskowitz developed the reputation as an excellent organizer and capable commander, and the well-executed withdrawal of Army Group G from the Bay of Biscay and southern France to the Nancy sector was widely regarded as further evidence of his professional ability. Blaskowitz was unpopular at OKW due to his lack of enthusiasm for the Nazi regime, and was especially unpopular with the SS. A religious man, he had protested against SS atrocities in the Polish campaign in 1939 and ran into trouble again in early September 1944, when he queried Himmler's order for the creation of a defensive line behind his sector in the Nancy-Belfort area that was not under his control. His lack of interest in politics shielded him from the repercussions of the July military coup, and he retained the support of Rundstedt.

Otto von Knobelsdorff

The commander of the German First Army, General der Panzertruppe Otto von Knobelsdorff. (US Army MHI)

As of 8 September 1944, Army Group G consisted of the First Army and the Nineteenth Army. The First Army was commanded by General der Panzertruppe Otto von Knobelsdorff who had taken over after the army's retreat across France earlier in the summer. Knobelsdorff had distinguished himself as a panzer corps commander in the attempts to relieve Stalingrad. He was personally appointed by Hitler because of his bravery and unflinching optimism. Senior commanders felt that his tactical skills were unimpressive, and he was in poor physical shape after grueling service on the Eastern Front.

Friederich Weise

The Nineteenth Army commander was General Friederich Weise, who had been an infantry officer in World War I and, after serving in the police in the Weimar Republic, had returned to the army in 1935. Weise had advanced to divisional command in the autumn of 1942 and corps command a year later. He had been assigned to army command in France in June 1944, and his conduct of the retreat from southern France had acquainted him with the different battle style of the Western Front. He was a capable if unexceptional commander.

Hasso von Manteuffel

The most prominent tactical commander in the Lorraine fighting in September 1944 was General der Panzertruppe Hasso von Manteuffel,

The commander of the 47th Panzer Corps, General der Panzertruppen Heinrich Freiherr von Luttwitz. (US Army MHI)

another brash young officer, whose bravery and tactical skills had attracted Hitler's personal attention. Manteuffel had served as a cavalry officer in World War I, including duty at Verdun. He had remained a junior cavalry officer in the army after the war, switching to the new panzer branch in 1934. He had commanded an infantry battalion in Rommel's 7th Panzer Division in France in 1940, and had taken over regimental command in October 1941, during the fighting in the Soviet Union. He had been awarded the Knight's Cross for his action in seizing a bridgehead during the Moscow fighting in November 1941. Manteuffel had commanded a brigade in the North Africa campaign and while still a colonel formed an improvised division in Tunisia. (General von Arnim described him as one of his best divisional commanders in Tunisia.) Hitler had personally assigned him to command the 7th Panzer Division in June 1943 and transferred him to lead the élite Grossdeutschland Panzer Grenadier Division later in the year after he had been decorated with the Oakleaf for the Knight's Cross. Manteuffel's battlefield reputation and personal contacts with Hitler had led to his steady advancement, and on 1 September 1944 he was called to the Führer's headquarters and ordered to take command of Fifth Panzer Army, leapfrogging the ranks to army commander in a single step and bypassing the usual stage as a panzer corps commander. Manteuffel did not have the training or experience for the position, and would be further handicapped by the awkward deployment of the Fifth Panzer Army in sectors of the First and Nineteenth Armies.

ALLIED COMMANDERS

Unlike the Wehrmacht in the autumn of 1944, the US Army command structure was decentralized. Although Eisenhower, as SHAEF commander, made broad strategic decisions, he was seldom involved in any decisions below army level. His involvement in the actual Lorraine campaign was mainly in connection with the running debate over broad versus narrow front, and the allocation of supplies. Almost without exception, the senior US Army leaders were West Point graduates, part of a small but distinguished group of officers who had weathered the arid interwar years in regular army service as mid-ranking officers, and many of whom were personally acquainted with one another through long years of service.

Omar Bradley

The commander of the 12th Army Group was Gen. Omar Bradley, a fellow graduate of the West Point Class of 1915 with Eisenhower. Also like Eisenhower, Bradley had seen no overseas combat posting in World War I, but had earned a reputation in the interwar years as a quiet, hard-working staff officer. In 1940 he had commanded the Infantry School and later led the 82nd and 28th Divisions in succession. In early 1943, Eisenhower had required a deputy to serve as a trouble-shooter in North Africa. This position was short-lived, as the poor performance of the II Corps at Kasserine Pass had led to the relief of the corps commander and his replacement by Gen. George S. Patton. The latter did not want Bradley as an emissary from Eisenhower, and had asked that

General Omar Bradley commanded the US First Army in Normandy, and after the addition of Patton's Third Army in August, was promoted to lead the 12th Army Group. Here he is seen visiting with an M4 tank crew of Co. B, 34th Tank Bn. in November 1944.

he be appointed as deputy corps commander instead. Patton and Bradley had made an able team in re-forming the US Army in North Africa after the Kasserine defeat and Bradley became the II Corps commander when Patton was assigned to plan the US role in the invasion of Sicily as commander of the Seventh Army. Bradley's corps served under Patton during the Sicilian campaign, and Bradley won the respect of Eisenhower for his calm competence and a better grasp of logistics than Patton. Due in part to Patton's self-destructive behavior, Bradley became the obvious choice to lead the US First Army in Normandy. When the US Army in France expanded in July 1944, Bradley had taken command of 12th Army Group, with Lt. Gen. Courtney Hodges in command of First Army and Lt. Gen. George S. Patton in command of the Third Army. Bradley had a sound working relationship with Eisenhower, based on friendship and mutual respect.

George S. Patton

Gen. George S. Patton was a study in contrast to the other two US commanders. Bradley and Eisenhower were from Midwestern farm families with little military tradition. Patton was from a wealthy Southern family and the descendant of a long line of soldiers who had graduated from the prestigious Virginia Military Institute. His grandfather and namesake had been a distinguished commander in the Confederate Army during the US Civil War. Graduating from West Point six years before Eisenhower or Bradley, Patton had commanded the infant US tank force in combat in France in 1918, where he won the Distinguished Service Cross. He had been a prominent cavalry officer during the interwar years, shunning the staff positions in Washington at which both Eisenhower and Bradley excelled. His tank and cavalry experience had led to his command of the new 2nd Armored Division in 1940, at a time when mechanization of the army was a central concern. He had

Commander of the US Third Army, Lt. Gen. George S. Patton, visits the Lorraine battlefront with the XII Corps commander, Maj. Gen. Manton S. Eddy. (US Army)

Patton discussing the conduct of the campaign with the XII Corps commander, Maj. Gen. Manton S. Eddy. After the XX Corps thrust stalled at Metz, Patton placed the emphasis in Lorraine on Eddy's corps, leading to the Arracourt tank battles. (US Army)

attracted national attention for the exploits of his tank units in pre-war exercises, even gracing the cover of *Life* magazine. Patton had been a natural choice to lead the I Armored Corps in North Africa in 1942, and when it came time to replace the II Corps commander after the Kasserine débâcle, Patton had been selected. His inspirational leadership gave the troops confidence, and Eisenhower had selected him to lead the US Seventh Army in the campaign in Sicily. There, his leadership was mixed: he was, if anything, too impetuous and aggressive, and he did not pay sufficient attention to logistics in a war where logistics were often key. His flamboyant style was very different from Bradley's, and his extravagant behavior got him into serious trouble when, during two visits to field hospitals on Sicily, he slapped soldiers with battle fatigue. In an army of citizen-soldiers this would not do, and it had cast a shadow over Patton's future. Eisenhower still valued his aggressiveness and facility with mobile forces, but his impetuousness and impolitic style both on and off the battlefield and his lack of patience for the mundane but essential chores of modern war had limited his rise to army command. He was widely regarded as the US Army's most aggressive and skilled practitioner of mobile warfare, a reflection of his cavalry background. In spite of his reputation as a tank expert, he was not as familiar with tank technology as with mobile tactics. Gen. Bruce Clarke later remarked, "Patton knew as little about tanks as anybody I ever knew."

Patton's Third Army had two corps committed to the Lorraine fighting at the beginning of September, and a third corps still committed to mopping up German coastal pockets in Brittany. The XII Corps had been commanded since 19 August 1944 by Maj. Gen. Manton S. Eddy, a World War I veteran who had commanded infantry divisions in North Africa, Sicily, and Normandy. The XX Corps was commanded by Maj. Gen. Walton Walker, West Point Class of 1912 and a veteran of World War I.

OPPOSING ARMIES

THE GERMAN ARMY

The German Army in Lorraine at the beginning of September 1944 was in a shambles, but was beginning to coalesce around defensive lines along the Moselle River. As the month went on, additional units were brought into the area to stabilize the front and to carry out Hitler's planned counteroffensive. By 1944, the Wehrmacht had become a hollow force. The enormous demands of the Eastern Front and Germany's dwindling manpower reserves had led to formation of large numbers of divisions that were often understrength. The sheer size of the force meant that German divisions were not as well equipped as their American opponents. The average German infantry division depended on horse transport and had no armored vehicles. The average US infantry division was motorized and had attached tank or tank destroyer battalions, making it comparable to German panzer grenadier divisions in capability.

The principal formations of the German Army in Lorraine were infantry divisions of three types: divisions shattered in earlier fighting, new Volksgrenadier divisions that had only recently been raised, or divisions withdrawn more or less intact from southern France. As a result, the infantry formations were of very mixed quality. The 16th Inf. Div., for example, was one of the better units. Earlier in 1944, it had been deployed

The main technical advantage enjoyed by the German units in Lorraine was their Panther tank. The thick frontal armor of the Panther was almost unaffected by the most common US tank gun of the period, the 75mm gun, but it was also virtually impervious to the more powerful 76mm guns found on later production M4 medium tanks, M10, and M18 tank destroyers. This captured Panther was subjected to 76mm gun fire in a trial and none of the rounds fully penetrated. As a result, US armored vehicles had to maneuver to hit the thinner side armor, or use other tactical ploys such as white phosphorous smoke rounds to blind the gun sights. (US Army)

A pair of Panther Ausf. G tanks of Pz. Brig. 111 during operations near Parroy in late September 1944. It was a common practice at this stage of the war to cover the tanks heavily in foliage in an attempt to protect them from aircraft attack. (USNA)

on occupation duty near the Bay of Biscay and had retreated eastward in August, losing the equivalent of two infantry battalions in fighting with French partisans. By early September, it had a strength of about 7,000 men, above average for the units in Lorraine. Many of the other infantry divisions retained the names and numbers of earlier formations, but were in fact nearly entirely new formations, rebuilt from scratch. The Volksgrenadier divisions were a last-minute attempt by Hitler to mobilize every able-bodied man for a final, desperate effort to defend Germany. This was really scraping the bottom of the barrel: they came from schools, Luftwaffe units, naval units, static fortress units, and support formations. Some were better than others. For example, the 462nd Volksgrenadier Division contained a regiment drawn from a school for young lieutenants who had earned battlefield commissions on the Eastern Front. In nearly all cases, however, the infantry divisions were very weak in anti-tank guns and field artillery.

The Wehrmacht had a very different replacement policy from the US Army, and divisions remained in the field at strengths far short of the tables of organization and equipment. As a result, the order of battle for the two opposing sides in the campaign is somewhat deceptive, since so many German units were substantially understrength while all US divisions were near strength. No German division on the Western Front was rated by the high command as Kampfwert I – that is, able to carry out an all-out attack. The best infantry divisions in the west were graded as Kampfwert II – capable of limited offensive operations. By the middle of September, German forces in the Lorraine region amounted to the equivalent of eight divisions in the main line of resistance, with a further six division-equivalents in reserve.

While much is often made of "battle experience" when evaluating the combat potential of units, there is a point at which battle experience becomes battle exhaustion, and enthusiasm for combat is replaced by an overwhelming urge for self-preservation. Many German units in Lorraine had the worst of all possible combinations: inexperienced troops mixed with veterans who only weeks before had experienced the nightmare of the Falaise Gap slaughter or the harrowing experience of the destruction of Army Group Center in the east. If there was any common thread holding together the Wehrmacht in September 1944, it was the protection of German soil from the imminent threat of invasion.

The German forces in Lorraine were particularly weak in artillery. The Nineteenth Army had lost 1,316 of their 1,481 artillery pieces during the retreat from southern France. Although artillery was not as central to tactics as in World War I, it was still the dominant killing arm on the battlefield. Much of the field artillery in infantry divisions was horse-drawn, and there were frequent shortages of ammunition due to transportation bottlenecks resulting from Allied fighter-bomber interdiction of the roads and railroads. The German lack of firepower was a decided disadvantage.

Technological innovation in the Wehrmacht had also stagnated in other fields, such as communication. Infantry regiments deployed a signals platoon at regimental level, with field telephones and four radio sections. These sections could be deployed at company level. Most communications were done with field telephones, especially in defensive fighting, but in mobile operations, the Wehrmacht was at a disadvantage. The standard German man-pack field radio was old and cumbersome, requiring two soldiers to carry it, and it relied on AM transmission that was more subject to static than the FM radios used by the US infantry. Although the Wehrmacht did deploy forward artillery observers, their communication net was not as widespread or robust as in the US Army, so attacking German formations could not count on artillery fire support to the extent of their American opponents.

The panzer and panzer grenadier divisions in Lorraine were a very mixed lot. The 17th SS Panzer Grenadier Division "Goetz von Berlichingen" had been thoroughly smashed by the US Army during Operation Cobra near St. Lo in early August. It was re-formed around two SS panzer grenadier brigades brought in from Denmark and fleshed out with Luftwaffe troops and Volksdeutsche from the Balkans. Like all of the

German field artillery was of high quality, but during the Lorraine campaign it was not available in large numbers, and there were frequent ammunition shortages. This is a Rheinmetall 150mm Kanone 18, the standard Wehrmacht fieldpiece for corps level artillery units. This particular example was captured with several others and used by the US Army's 344th Field Artillery Battalion during the Lorraine fighting until the ammunition ran out. (US Army)

panzer grenadier divisions in this sector, it had little armor: four Pz IV/70 tank destroyers, 12 StuG III assault guns, and 12 FlakPz 38(t) anti-aircraft tanks. The 3rd and 15th Panzer Grenadier Divisions had been stationed in southern France, and had withdrawn in good order into Lorraine. Both divisions were up to strength in troops, and both had a battalion of the new Pz IV/70 tank destroyers. The 15th Pz. Gren. Div. had a battalion of 36 PzKpfw IV tanks, while the 3rd Pz. Gren. Div. had a battalion of StuG III assault guns.

The 11th Panzer Division was widely regarded as the best tank unit in German service in this sector. Like the two panzer grenadier divisions, it had withdrawn from southern France in good order, but in the process had lost much of its tank strength. Starting with about 60-70 tanks, by the time it was committed to the fighting in Lorraine in mid-September, it was down to 50 tanks, of which 30 were Panthers. The 21st Panzer Division had been heavily committed to the fighting in Normandy and after suffering stiff losses had not been brought back up to strength. It had no tanks at the beginning of the month, though its StugAbt 200 (assault gun battalion) had several StuG III assault guns by mid-month.

As of 20 August 1944, there were only 184 tanks and assault guns on the entire Western Front. This would change by the middle of September as more armor was rushed forward. The plan was to increase the strength in the west to 712 tanks and assault guns by early September in order to carry out Hitler's directives for a Lorraine counteroffensive. Tank production in Germany reached record levels in 1944, thanks to the belated industrial rationalization of Albert Speer. At the same time, however, fuel and manpower shortages meant that there were not enough trained crews or trained tank unit officers to replace the heavy losses in experienced troops. The quality of German tank crews fell steadily in 1944, especially after the summer 1944 disasters. The problem was not the lack of tanks but the lack of tank crews.

The bulk of the German tank strength in Lorraine was located in the new panzer brigades. They had been organized earlier in the summer on Hitler's personal instructions and against the advice of the inspector of the panzer forces, Gen. Heinz Guderian. These brigades were given priority in assignments from the summer's tank production instead of replacing losses in the regular panzer divisions. Most were formed around the remnants of units that had been destroyed in the débâcle on the Eastern Front in June and July, when Army Group Center had been destroyed.

The first batch of these brigades, numbered from 101 to 110, were in fact closer to a regiment in strength, with only a single tank battalion. Equipment included 36 Panthers, 11 Pz IV/70 tank destroyers and four Flakpanzers for air defense. The later brigades, numbered above 110, had two tank battalions: one of PzKpfw IV and one of PzKpfw V Panthers. Three of the four brigades used in the Lorraine fighting were of this heavier configuration. On paper at least, these were formidable formations, with 90 tanks and 10 tank destroyers—much more armor than most German panzer divisions of the time possessed. But they were slapdash formations suffering from poor organization and inadequate training. The panzer brigades were intended to be used on the Eastern Front as a potent mobile reserve which could staunch gaps in the line. As a result, they were not well-balanced combined arms forces like normal panzer divisions, but were heavy in tanks and weak in infantry, artillery, reconnaissance, and support. The brigade staff was completely inadequate and the brigade commanders had a difficult time communicating and directing their units. As was the tendency on the Eastern Front, anti-tank weapons had been given more attention than field artillery, and the brigade lacked field artillery fire-support. In addition there was little in the way of reconnaissance units in the brigades; this would become evident in the Lorraine fighting. The brigades also suffered from a lack of tank recovery vehicles and maintenance equipment, which exacerbated their losses in combat, since damaged vehicles could not easily be recovered and were often abandoned.

The brigades were raised in various locations across Germany, and the brigade commanders seldom met their subordinate commanders or their component units until they disembarked from trains in the staging areas leading into Lorraine. Manteuffel later wrote that the panzer brigades would have been effective units on the Eastern Front, an interesting comment considering his extensive experience in that theater. In the west, against a very different opponent, they would prove to be a major disappointment.

Part of the problem of the German forces in the Lorraine counter-offensive was the "Eastern" outlook of many of the units. Manteuffel himself had been brought in from Poland only days before the start of the attack, and the new brigade commanders and many of their troops were veterans of the Eastern Front. While quite prepared to deal with the Red Army, they were unfamiliar with the US Army and its very different tactics and fighting abilities. This would quickly become evident in their use of armor. On the Eastern Front, it was not unusual to use tank formations as a shock force to punch through the emaciated Red Army infantry formations. The Red Army was poorly provided with modern anti-tank weapons and had very limited capability to call in either artillery support or close-air support. This was not the case with the US Army, as would become apparent over the following month.

The Luftwaffe would not prove to be of any use in the ensuing battles. The fighter and fighter-bomber force in France was under the control of Jagdkorps II, while fighters in neighboring Germany deployed for defense of the Reich were controlled by Jagdkorps I. On 29 August 1944, the advance of Allied forces had obliged Jagdkorps II to order all remaining fighter-bomber units out of France and into western Germany. At the beginning of September, there were about 420 fighters and fighter-bombers in this force, of which about 110 covered the Nancy-Metz area of Lorraine.

Unlike the US Army, the Wehrmacht received very little air support during the Lorraine fighting. As with the tanks, this was not so much from lack of aircraft production as from a shortage of trained pilots. The Luftwaffe had suffered massive losses in air battles over the Reich since the spring of 1944, and this had been further accelerated by the summer fighting. To make matters worse, a fuel crisis in August further curtailed training. German aircraft production reached record levels in the summer of 1944, but this did not translate into a readily useful force. US aircraft encountered the Luftwaffe in large numbers on only two occasions during the Lorraine fighting in September, and found that the pilots were inexperienced and vulnerable. Besides the sheer lack of experienced pilots, the Luftwaffe's fighter-bomber force had atrophied badly by 1944, due in part to the heavy concentration on fighter aviation for defense of the Reich. There was no standardized means for ground direction of close-air support, and despite frequent army calls for air support, none was forthcoming except for a few rare occasions when key bridges were attacked.

The geography of Lorraine held mixed opportunities for both sides. From the German perspective, the Moselle valley formed a natural defense line, since the river has a high rate of flow, many potential crossing sites are wooded, the river banks have a high gradient, and most crossing sites are covered by hills on the east bank. It was particularly formidable in the northern portion of the sector, and likely river crossings were covered by the artillery in the Metz fortresses. Germany had controlled the area around Metz from 1870 to 1918 and again after 1940, so the most modern defenses faced west. The Metz-Thionville Stellung was the major defensive obstacle in Lorraine. The traditional capital of Lorraine, Nancy, has not been fortified in modern times, but the river lines and the plateau of the Massif de Haye on its west bank serve as a significant natural obstacle. The ground most suitable for mobile operations was in the southern sector between Toul and Epinal. This region, known to French planners as the Trouée de Charmes, or the Charmes Gap, had been a traditional battlefield, most recently, three decades before when the German Army had been defeated there in the opening phases of World War I. The area held by Nineteenth Army was notionally located within the defenses of the so-called Kitzinger Line, which had been constructed starting in early August. In reality, there were no substantial new defenses. The weather slightly favored the Germans: September 1944 was unusually wet and foggy, which would severely limit Allied close-air support.

THE US ARMY

Patton's Third Army entered the Lorraine campaign with two corps; its third corps was laying siege to German garrisons at Brest, on the coast. In September 1944, the US Army was in excellent shape after a triumphant dash across France the previous month. The divisions in Patton's Third Army were generally in better condition than those in Hodges' First Army, which had experienced the brutal close-country bocage fighting in June and July 1944. In marked contrast to the German units, which were seldom at full organizational strength, the US Third Army had not yet encountered the personnel shortages that would afflict them in the late autumn. Unit cohesion, training, and morale were generally excellent.

German and American infantry tactics differed in significant ways. The German infantry squad was trained to use their MG 42s as the centerpiece of their tactics, based on World War I experiences which emphasized the importance of machine-guns in infantry combat. In a platoon action, one of the squads would often be equipped with the headquarters' machine-gun, allowing it to serve as the focal point. US tactical doctrine placed emphasis on the individual rifleman, armed with the semi-automatic M1 Garand rifle, rather than the BAR squad automatic rifle. Although the US M1 Garand had a higher rate of fire than the bolt-action German 98k rifle,

The workhorse of the US divisional artillery batteries was the M2A1 105mm howitzer. This weapon could fire a 33lb high-explosive round to a range of about 12,000 yards. Each infantry division had 54 of these plus 12 of the heavier 155mm howitzers. Of these, 36 105mm howitzers were found in the divisional artillery, while six 105mm howitzers were deployed in a cannon company in each infantry regiment. (US Army)

US infantry squads were seldom able to achieve firepower superiority over their German opponents due to the lethality of the German machine-gun tactics.

Nevertheless, US infantry formations often enjoyed significant firepower advantages over their German opponents. What the squad and platoon lacked in organic firepower was made up in artillery support. While German and American artillery divisions had similar artillery strength on paper, in reality the US divisions were more likely to actually have their establishment of weapons – and more often had adequate ammunition supplies. However, the real advantage in infantry combat was communications, especially in mobile operations. The US infantry had far better and more lavish radio equipment than the Germans. At platoon level, the US Army used the SCR-536 "handie-talkie", a small hand-held AM transceiver. At company level, they used the man-pack SCR-300 "walkie-talkie" FM transceiver to communicate with the battalion and higher headquarters. The German Army had no platoon radios, and their older AM man-pack radios were deployed no lower than at company level. The widespread use of dependable radios meant that US infantry could call for fire support during mobile offensive operations much more easily than their German counterparts.

In another important tactical innovation, the US Army in Europe regularly deployed an artillery forward observer team with forward infantry companies. The officer was equipped with a man-portable radio linked to the artillery net, and was assigned both to call in and to correct fire. American units in key sectors also enjoyed the added firepower of corps artillery, and infantry divisions often had additional artillery battalions allotted to their support for special missions. US infantry also

The US Army enjoyed advantages in communications, with more advanced equipment like the SCR-300 "walkie-talkie" radio. This was the first widely used FM infantry radio, and offered better performance than the German AM radios. It is seen here in use near Vagney, France, on 17 October 1944. (US Army)

had better armored support, often having a tank battalion and tank destroyer battalion added to each division.

The German infantry tended to hold a disparaging view of American infantry, judging them to be less aggressive in close-combat tactics. This was in part a reflection of the stagnation in German infantry tactics. Experienced US infantry units, painfully aware of their firepower shortcomings when up against German infantry squads, were perfectly happy to use the killing power of artillery when it was available instead of suffering needless casualties. This difference in outlook was in part a cultural clash: the pragmatism of the GI versus the romantic fighting spirit of the German *Landser* (fighting man).

The US armored divisions were far better equipped than their German counterparts in September 1944, being close to establishment strength, and they fought differently. US doctrine held that the penetration of the enemy main line of resistance would be carried out by infantry backed by separate tank battalions and artillery. US armored divisions were held in reserve for exploitation after the penetration had been achieved. German panzer divisions were frequently used to win the penetration, a tactic that had proven increasingly costly as the war went on and infantry anti-tank tactics and technology improved. As a result, US armored divisions were not generally employed like the panzer brigades in Lorraine as a shock force to overcome enemy infantry formations. In this respect, the US was closer to the Red Army's tank corps in doctrine than to the German practices. US armored divisions were true combined-arms teams, especially when compared to the tank-poor German panzer divisions and tank-heavy panzer brigades. It is often forgotten that each US armored division had the same number of artillery and armored infantry battalions as tank battalions – three each. In addition, US armored divisions were often reinforced with additional infantry or artillery for specific missions.

The US Army had a significant advantage over the Wehrmacht in artillery, both in terms of quantity and quality. US heavy artillery was mechanized, using fully tracked tractors like this M4 high speed tractor towing an 8-in. howitzer of the 999th Field Artillery Battalion (Colored) near Nantes-Gassicourt on 20 August 1944. (US Army)

The primary US combat unit was the combat command. Each combat command was tailored to the tactical mission but generally included a tank battalion, an armored infantry battalion, and an armored field artillery battalion. Other units could be added from division or corps. For example, during part of the Lorraine fighting, the 4th Armored Division's Combat Command A had three artillery battalions at its disposal. Each division normally employed three combat commands, CCA, CCB, and CCR. In some divisions, all three combat commands were in combat at one time. The 4th Armd. Div., which bore the brunt of the Lorraine tank fighting, used its structure in the intended fashion, with the CCR serving as a reserve. Battle-weary battalions would periodically be cycled through the CCR to prevent the corrosive effects of battle exhaustion.

In terms of weaponry, the German panzer force enjoyed a significant technological advantage with its Panther tank. US tank design had stagnated during the war years because of the failure of the Army Ground Forces and the armored force to absorb and learn from the advances in tank technology. As a result, the armored divisions in Lorraine were using essentially the same M4 medium tank as had been standard in Tunisia two years before. New M4 medium tanks were becoming available with the newer 76mm gun, but they were not numerous, their armor was not improved, and their armor penetration capability was inferior to the German Panther's long 75mm gun. The M4 with 76mm gun was disparaged by Patton, and was not initially popular in the 4th Armored Division. Tankers felt that the 75mm gun was more versatile than the 76mm gun, which was optimized for tank fighting only. In a head-to-head tank fight at normal combat ranges, the Panther was impervious to the M4 tank's 75mm gun, but the Panther could destroy the M4 tank frontally at any reasonable combat range. The main advantage enjoyed by US tankers compared to German panzer crews in 1944 was superior training. German fuel supplies were so low and training time so short that the quality of German tank crews had declined precipitously since the glory days of 1939-42. German tanks were still very dangerous because of their technological advantage, or when used from defilade, but in Lorraine, the US tankers usually prevailed. Innovative tactics played an important part. A popular tactic in experienced US tank battalions when encountering Panthers was to strike them first with white phosphorous smoke rounds. Inexperienced German crews would sometimes be forced out by the acrid smoke, drawn in through the tank's ventilator. Even if these tricks did not work, the smoke prevented the Panthers from locating their opponents, giving the M4 tanks time to maneuver to the flanks or rear, where their 75mm gun could penetrate the Panther's armor. This tactic was standard operating procedure in some units, including CCA, 4th Armored Division. Some US tank units preferred to fire high-explosive rounds at the Panther, finding that inexperienced German crews would simply abandon their tank.

US tankers enjoyed the same communications advantage as the US infantry. Their tanks used modern FM radios, and better radio communications meant that tank companies could call for artillery fire support, and in some cases close-air support, to carry out their mission. This was often the case when a column was stopped by hidden German armor in defilade position, which could not be easily eliminated by direct tank fire. Each tank battalion had a platoon of M4 tanks with

105mm howitzers in the headquarters company, and most combat commands had at least one battalion of self-propelled M7 105mm howitzer motor carriages for each tank battalion, sometimes more. US armored divisions had advantages in less recognized areas as well. Armored units were better supplied with engineer equipment, which was essential in mobile operations for river crossing. An important innovation was the engineer's treadway bridge, which could be broken down into loads small enough to fit into standard $2\frac{1}{2}$-ton trucks. Coincidentally, it was the commander of Patton's spearhead formation, Col. Bruce Clarke, an engineer by training, who had been the army's prime advocate for the development of rapid bridging equipment for the armored force.

The US Army had the greater number of tanks in the Lorraine sector. German strength was never more than 350 tanks, even at the peak of the tank fighting in the third week of September. The Third Army started out the campaign with about 165 M5A1 light tanks, 596 M4 (75mm) and 76 M4 (76mm) medium tanks, and about 450 M10 and M18 tank destroyers. About 40 percent of the tanks were in separate tank battalions supporting the infantry, and the remainder were in the armored divisions.

If there was one combat arm in which the US Army had unquestioned superiority over the Wehrmacht, it was the artillery. This was not simply a question of quantity. The US field artillery battalions were more modern than their German counterparts in nearly all respects. While their cannon were not significantly different in capability, the US field artillery battalions were entirely motorized, while German field artillery, especially infantry division units, was still horse-drawn. US heavy artillery was mechanized, using fully tracked high-speed tractors. The high level of motorization provided mobility for the batteries, and also ensured supply.

The US field artillery also enjoyed a broader and more modern assortment of communication equipment. Another US innovation was the fire direction center (FDC). Located at battalion, division, and corps level, the FDC concentrated the analog computers and other calculation devices alongside the communication equipment, permitting prompt receipt of messages and prompt calculation of fire missions. This level of communication allowed new tactics, the most lethal of which was TOT or "time-on-target." Field artillery is most effective when the first few rounds catch the enemy out in the open. Once the first few rounds have landed, enemy troops take cover, and the rate of casualties to subsequent fire declines dramatically. The aim of TOT was to deliver the fire on the target simultaneously, even from separate batteries. TOT fire missions were more lethal and more economical of ammunition than traditional staggered fire-strikes, and effective communication meant that the batteries could switch targets rapidly as well.

Another firepower advantage enjoyed by the US Army in the Lorraine fighting was air support. The US Army Air Forces tactical air commands (TAC) were structured to operate in direct support of a single army. As a result, Patton's Third Army had Brig. Gen. Otto Weyland's XIX TAC attached. US tactical air units were more tightly integrated than in any other army, and Weyland's command was co-located with Patton's headquarters. The XIX TAC generally had about 400 aircraft available, usually organized into two fighter wings, each organized into groups with an average of three fighter squadrons per group. A fighter squadron had 25 aircraft; a squadron mission typically employed 12 fighters; and a group mission used 36. At the beginning of September, XIX TAC had seven fighter groups and one photo reconnaissance group. The majority of the XIX TAC squadrons were equipped with the P-47 Thunderbolt fighter-bomber to provide close support and interdiction using heavy machine-gun fire, bombs, napalm, and rockets. There were also one or two squadrons of P-51s, which were used to provide tactical air cover as well as "fast reconnaissance," including spotting for the corps' heavy 240mm guns. The XIX TAC conducted a larger proportion of close-air support missions out of their total combat missions than any other TAC in Europe.

The XIX TAC deployed 20 radio teams with the ground units: one team per corps and infantry division headquarters, two with each armored division (with each combat command), and one with each cavalry group when they were performing key screening or holding missions. The team was based around a radio crew that linked the division to the XIX TAC headquarters by means of a SCR-624 radio installed in the division's truck-mounted SCR-399 "doghouse." The tactical air liaison officers (TALO) operated from "veeps" – jeeps with a rack-mounted SCR-522 VHF aircraft radio. They deployed forward with advancing units so that they could vector attacking fighter-bombers onto targets much in the same fashion as artillery forward observers.

The effectiveness of close-air support in World War II remains controversial. Both the Allies and the Germans tended to exaggerate its power: the US air force in its post-war struggle to become a separate service, the Germans as an excuse for poor battlefield performance. Wartime and post-war operational studies have concluded that the ability of fighter-bombers to knock out tanks on the battlefield was greatly exaggerated. In a post-battle survey after the Ardennes fighting in 1945 of a XIX TAC sector, it was found that aircraft had knocked out about six armored vehicles of the 90 claimed. The munitions of the day – unguided rockets, bombs, and heavy machine-guns – were not sufficiently accurate or sufficiently powerful to destroy many tanks. On the other hand, fighter-bombers had an enormous psychological impact, bolstering the morale of GIs and terrifying the average German soldier. German field commanders spoke of the fear instilled by close-air attack in much the same way as they spoke of the "tank panic" of the 1939-41 blitzkrieg years, and as in the case of tank panic, the psychological effects of close-air attack lessened quickly through experience.

The most effective employment of close-air support was to attack supply columns, storage areas, and other soft targets. Even if not particularly effective against the tanks themselves, fighter-bombers could severely limit the mobility of panzer units by forcing them to conduct road marches only at night. Furthermore, the avaricious demand for fuel and ammunition in modern armies made them very vulnerable to supply cut-offs. A panzer brigade could be rendered as ineffective by destroying its trucks and supply vehicles as by destroying the tanks themselves. The commander of CCA of the 4th Armd. Div., Col. Bruce Clarke, later remarked, "We were certainly glad to have [close-air support] but I would say their effect was certainly not decisive in any place."

Besides the fighter-bombers, US divisions had organic aviation in the form of L-4 (Piper Cub) and other liaison aircraft, popularly called "Flying Grasshoppers." These were primarily used to correct field artillery and conduct artillery reconnaissance. Col. Clarke flew ahead of his advancing tank columns in one, enabling him to direct the columns with precision.

GERMAN ORDER OF BATTLE, 16 SEPTEMBER 1944*
Army Group G: Generaloberst Johannes Blaskowitz

First Army: General der Panzertruppe Otto von Knobelsdorff

80th Corps	**General der Infanterie Dr. Franz Bayer**
5th Fallschirmjaeger Division	Generalmajor Ludwig Heilmann
Panzer Lehr Division (battlegroup)	
82nd Corps	**General der Artillerie Johann Sinnhuber**
19th Volksgrenadier Division	Generalleutnant Karl Wissmath
36th Volksgrenadier Division	Generalmajor August Welln
559th Volksgrenadier Division	Generalmajor Baron Kurt von Muhlen
13th SS Corps	**Generalleutnant der Waffen-SS Herman Priess**
3rd Panzer Grenadier Division	Generalmajor Hans Hecker
15th Panzer Grenadier Division	Generalleutnant Eberhard Rodt
17th SS Panzer Grenadier Division	
"Goetz von Berlichingen"	Oberst Eduard Deisenhofer
462nd Volksgrenadier Division	Generalleutnant Vollrath Lubbe
553rd Volksgrenadier Division	Oberst Enrich von Loesch
106th Panzer Brigade	
"Feldherrnhalle"	Oberst Franz Bake

Fifth Panzer Army: General der Panzertruppe Hasso von Manteuffel

47th Panzer Corps: General der Panzertruppen Heinrich Freiherr von Luettwitz	
21st Panzer Division	Generalleutnant Edgar Feuchtinger
111th Panzer Brigade	Oberst Heinrich von Bronsart-Schellendorf
112th Panzer Brigade	Oberst Horst von Usedom
113th Panzer Brigade	Oberst Erich von Seckendorff

Nineteenth Army: General der Infanterie Friederich Weise

66th Corps	**General der Artillerie Walter Lucht**
16th Infantry Division	General der Infanterie Ernst Haechel
Kampfgruppe Ottenbacher	Generalleutnant Ernst Ottenbacher
Elements of 15th Panzer Grenadiers, 21st Panzer	
64th Corps	**General der Pionere Karl Sachs**
716th Infantry Division	Generalleutnant Wilhelm Richter
189th Reserve Division	Generalmajor Bogislav von Schwerin
85th Corps	**Generalleutnant Baptist Kneiss**
11th Panzer Division	Generalleutnant Wend von Wietersheim
4th Luftwaffe Field Corps	**Generalleutnant Erich Petersen**
338th Infantry Division	Generalleutnant Flottmann
159th Reserve Division	Generalleutnant Albin Nake
198th Infantry Division	Generalmajor Otto Richter

* German Order of Battle only lists those units opposite the US Army's Third Army in Lorraine

US ARMY ORDER OF BATTLE*

12th Army Group: General Omar Bradley

Third Army: Lt. Gen. George S. Patton

XX Corps	Maj. Gen. Walton Walker
2nd Cavalry Reconnaissance Group	Col. W. P. Withers
7th Armored Division	Maj. Gen. Lindsay Silvester
5th Infantry Division	Maj. Gen. Stafford Irwin
90th Infantry Division	Maj. Gen. Raymond McClain
XII Corps	Maj. Gen. Manton S. Eddy
106th Cavalry Reconnaissance Group	Col. Vennard Wilson
4th Armored Division	Maj. Gen. John Wood
6th Armored Division	Maj. Gen. Robert Grow
35th Infantry Division	Maj. Gen. Paul Baade
80th Infantry Division	Maj. Gen. Horace McBride
XV Corps	Maj. Gen. Wade Haislip
79th Infantry Division	Maj. Gen. Ira Wyche
French 2nd Armored Division	Maj. Gen. Jacques Leclerc
XIX Tactical Air Command	Brig. Gen. Otto P. Weyland
100th Fighter Wing	
303rd Fighter Wing	

*US Army Order of Battle only lists those units in the US Army's Third Army in Lorraine

OPENING MOVES

Approaching the Moselle

At the beginning of September 1944, Patton's Third Army had halted after having crossed the Meuse River. Priority for supply in Bradley's 12th Army Group went to Hodges' neighboring First Army, to support its drive towards Aachen, which covered the right flank of Montgomery's 21st Army Group. By 4 September, Montgomery's forces were well over the Seine and German reserves in Belgium had been enveloped by Collins' VII Corps near Mons. Eisenhower decided that under such favorable circumstances the original SHAEF conception of a two-axis thrust towards Germany could be supported, so Third Army would receive equal support priority to Hodges' First Army. While this did not end the supply crisis, it allowed the Third Army to resume offensive operations on a limited scale.

"Reconnaissance-in-force" operations were planned to see if bridgeheads could be secured over the Moselle before the Germans could erect sufficient defenses. The objectives of Walker's XX Corps

The terrain in Lorraine consisted of rolling farmland, with many hills. Here, officers of the 80th Inf. Div. have set up an observation post on a hill overlooking the countryside around Montsec on 3 September 1944. (US Army)

Reconnaissance was a vital requirement in the Lorraine fighting, and the hard-pressed cavalry squadrons seldom enjoyed the recognition they deserved for their dangerous and demanding assignment. They were equipped with M8 light armored cars, like the one seen here, and machine-gun armed jeeps. Here, the crew of an M8 armored car of the 80th Division's reconnaissance troop enjoy some snacks from an American Red Cross worker near the Moselle River on 8 September 1944. (US Army)

opposite the fortified city of Metz proved the most difficult. Walker hoped that a Moselle bridgehead could be secured with a rapid armor thrust, as had already worked on the Marne and the Meuse in August, but probes by cavalry squadrons on 5 September made clear that the Germans would not easily be pushed aside. Attacks by the 7th Armd. Div.'s CCB finally reached the banks of the Moselle south of Fort Driant in the early hours of 7 September, followed by CCA's drive to the river north of Arnaville. On the corps' left flank, north of Metz, the 90th Inf. Div. began moving from Etain towards Thionville on the Moselle River.

Although the German forces had been holding the Moselle River line successfully for most of the day, the new German First Army commander, Gen. Knobelsdorff, wanted more vigorous action. He contacted the Führer headquarters with a plan to stage a spoiling attack by turning the flank of Walker's XX Corps with a tank attack from the west bank of the Moselle. He intended to use Pz. Brig. 106, which had been reserved for use in the forthcoming Lorraine counteroffensive, so the effort required Hitler's direct approval. This was granted late on 7 September, with the proviso that the brigade could be used for only 48 hours before being returned to the reserve.

Pz. Brig. 106 had been formed around remnants of the Panzer Grenadier Division Feldherrnhalle that had been encircled and destroyed in July 1944 in Byelorussia during Operation Bagration. It was commanded by one of the most distinguished Wehrmacht tank commanders, Col. Dr Franz Bake. He had won the Iron Cross First and Second Class as an infantryman in World War I, and had commanded a PzKpfw 35(t) company in France in 1940. He had also led a panzer battalion in the climactic tank encounter at Prokhorovka during the 1943 Kursk battles, and then the legendary Heavy Panzer Regiment Bake on the Eastern Front in 1944. He had been decorated with the Knight's Cross in January 1943 and the Oak Leaves in August 1943, and was only

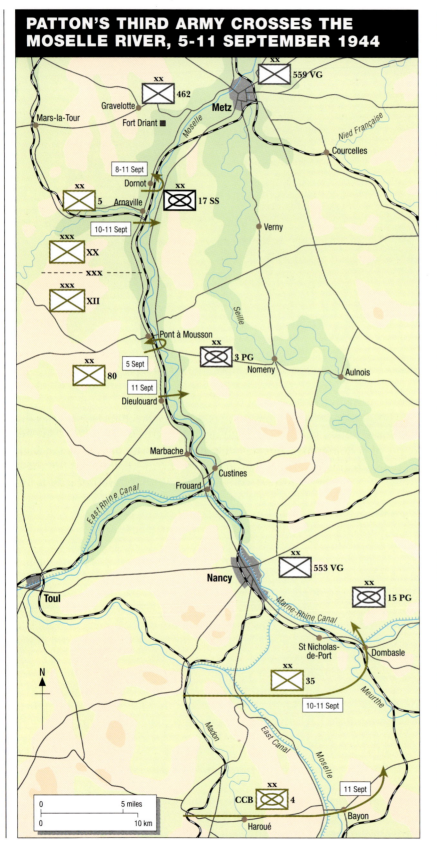

PATTON'S THIRD ARMY CROSSES THE MOSELLE RIVER, 5-11 SEPTEMBER 1944

Mars-la-Tour

Gravelotte

462 xx

Metz

559 VG xx

Fort Driant

Moselle

Nied Française

Courcelles

8-11 Sept

Dornot

Arnaville

5 xx

17 SS xx

10-11 Sept

Verny

XXX XX

XXX XII

Seille

Pont à Mousson

3 PG xx

Nomeny

Aulnois

80 xx

5 Sept

11 Sept

Dieulouard

Marbache

Custines

Frouard

East Rhine Canal

Toul

Nancy

553 VG xx

15 PG xx

Marne-Rhine Canal

St Nicholas-de-Port

Dombasle

35 xx

10-11 Sept

Meurthe

N

Macon

East Canal

Moselle

11 Sept

0   5 miles
0   10 km

CCB 4 xx

Bayon

Haroué

ABOVE **An M1 57mm anti-tank gun covers an intersection in Algrange during the fighting between the 358th Infantry of the 90th Division and the 559th Volksgrenadier Division on 10-12 September. The 57mm gun was a license copy of the British 6-pdr anti-tank gun and was the standard anti-tank weapon of infantry divisions in 1944. There were 18 in each regiment, three per battalion. The 90th Division also had an attached towed**

3-in. tank destroyer battalion to supplement their firepower. (US Army)

BELOW The town of Mairy is surrounded by hills on all sides. This is a view looking north into the town from route D145 from Mainville, as would have been seen by the panzer grenadiers entering the town from this direction during the 8 September attack. (S. Zaloga)

the 49th German soldier of the war to receive the Swords to the Knight's Cross, in February 1944. He had been assigned command of Pz. Brig. 106 when it was raised near Danzig in July 1944. The brigade had received its Panther tanks in early August, but lack of fuel had meant that there had been little tactical training. The brigade had one of the most experienced cadres of any of the new units, with other Knight's Cross holders – Erich Oberwohrmann commanding the Panther regiment and Ewald Bartel serving as the brigade adjutant.

The target of the panzer attack was the 90th Inf. Div., who called themselves the "Tough Ombres" after their divisional insignia – a superimposed "T" and "O" symbolizing their recruitment area in Texas and Oklahoma. The division had a bad reputation due to its poor combat performance in Normandy. Within six weeks of landing, it had lost the equivalent of 100 percent of its strength and some rifle companies had suffered casualties the equivalent of 400 percent of their establishment strength. The original divisional commander had been sacked and his replacement was a National Guardsman, a banker from Oklahoma, Brig. Gen. Raymond McLain. It was unusual for National Guard officers to receive divisional command, and the appointment was a testament to McLain's earlier achievements in the Mediterranean theater. Under new leadership, the division's performance improved markedly during the fighting for the Falaise Gap, and by September, it was a well-led, combat-hardened unit. The 90th Inf. Div. was the northernmost division of XX Corps, positioned on its exposed left flank as it moved towards Thionville.

Pz. Brig. 106 was equipped with 36 Panthers, 11 Pz IV/70 (V) tank destroyers, and 119 armored half-tracks. The attack was ordered for the night of 6 September, but was delayed by the late arrival of the 59th Infantry Regiment. There was no space in the half-tracks for these troops, so they rode into action on the Panther tanks. After a foray on

A GI from the 90th Inf. Div. inspects some of the German equipment captured by the division during the fighting with Pz. Brig. 106 near Mairy. These are both armed versions of the standard German Hanomag SdKfz 251 Ausf. D armored infantry half-track. An SdKfz 251/21 anti-aircraft vehicle with a triple MG151 30mm cannon mounting is seen to the left. Pz. Gren. Bn. 2106 had ten of the SdKfz 251/9 Stummel assault gun armed with a close support 75mm howitzer, seen on the right. (US Army)

the afternoon of 7 September, in which they failed to locate US forces, they were ordered to stage a second attack later in the evening in support of the 19th Volksgrenadier Division. Due to the fluid nature of the lines, the unit began its attack from the north of the advancing American forces, against their exposed flank. Late on the night of 7/8 September, Pz. Brig. 106 began its move southward from Audun-le-Roman towards Briey in two columns, the Stossgruppe 1 (attack group 1) advancing via Mont-Bonvilliers, and the Stossgruppe 2 via Trieux. The attack was preceded by little or no reconnaissance, and at about 0200 the main column split in two near Murville, part of the force moving down the main route N43 and the other moving along a small country road towards the villages of Mont and Mairy.

The headquarters of the 90th Inf. Div. was bivouacked on a wooded hill south-east of Landres, flanked by roads on either side. Columns from Stossgruppe 1 of Pz. Brig. 106 began moving down these same roads around 0200. The area is hilly and wooded, and the German armored column moved past the scattered headquarter units without either side noticing until 0300. The crewman on a M4 medium tank guarding the divisional artillery HQ realized that the column was German and fired at the trailing vehicle. The German half-track exploded in flames, but the fire illuminated the American tank, which was then brought under fire from the lead Panther tanks. The US tank exploded, and casualties among the artillery staff were heavy. Stossgruppe 1 continued to move south-eastward towards Briey, but much more cautiously. The divisional headquarters personnel, supported by some tanks from the 712th Tank Bn., began attacking the tail-end of the German formation while at the same time warning the neighboring infantry battalions. The nearby 712th Tank Bn. was dispersed, but the tankers were reluctant to fire in the dark for fear of fratricide.

In the pre-dawn darkness, the Panther tanks and panzer grenadiers became spread out across the countryside as the Americans rallied. Instead of retreating in the face of a surprise night-attack, as the

ABOVE **The attack on Mairy was broken up with support from the 607th Tank Destroyer Battalion. This unit was equipped with the M6 3-in. anti-tank gun, as seen here during training exercises with the 614th Tank Destroyer Battalion (Colored) on 23 September. (US Army)**

RIGHT **The 90th Inf. Div. was the northernmost of Patton's divisions during the attempts to cross the Moselle, and was the subject of the first panzer attack near Mairy on the night of 7/8 September. After crushing this attack, the division continued to move towards Thionville. These troops are from the division's 358th Infantry Regiment and are taking shelter in a trench leading into an old German bunker with the inscription *Viel feind, viel Her* ('Many enemies, much honor'). (US Army)**

Germans had expected, the American infantry began methodically to attack the intruder. After daybreak, the left wing of Stossgruppe 1 began an attack on the village of Mairy, occupied by the 1st Battalion, 358th Infantry, which was supported by a platoon of towed 3-in. anti-tank guns from the 607th Tank Destroyer Battalion. Mairy is in a depression surrounded by hills. The Panther spearhead began firing at the village from the high ground near Mont around 0700, but they were brought under fire from the anti-tank guns and two German tanks were knocked

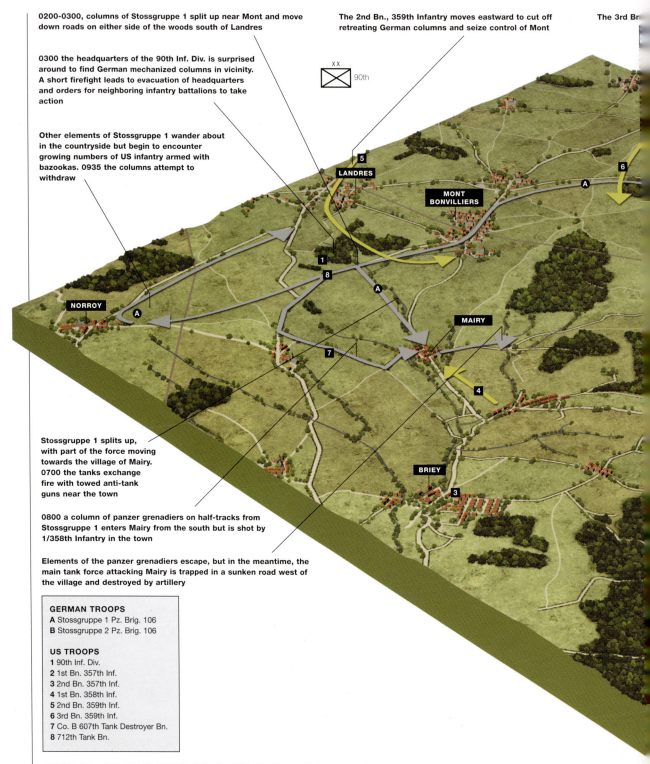

0200-0300, columns of Stossgruppe 1 split up near Mont and move down roads on either side of the woods south of Landres

The 2nd Bn., 359th Infantry moves eastward to cut off retreating German columns and seize control of Mont

The 3rd Br

0300 the headquarters of the 90th Inf. Div. is surprised around to find German mechanized columns in vicinity. A short firefight leads to evacuation of headquarters and orders for neighboring infantry battalions to take action

Other elements of Stossgruppe 1 wander about in the countryside but begin to encounter growing numbers of US infantry armed with bazookas. 0935 the columns attempt to withdraw

Stossgruppe 1 splits up, with part of the force moving towards the village of Mairy. 0700 the tanks exchange fire with towed anti-tank guns near the town

0800 a column of panzer grenadiers on half-tracks from Stossgruppe 1 enters Mairy from the south but is shot by 1/358th Infantry in the town

Elements of the panzer grenadiers escape, but in the meantime, the main tank force attacking Mairy is trapped in a sunken road west of the village and destroyed by artillery

90th

LANDRES
MONT BONVILLIERS
NORROY
MAIRY
BRIEY

GERMAN TROOPS
A Stossgruppe 1 Pz. Brig. 106
B Stossgruppe 2 Pz. Brig. 106

US TROOPS
1 90th Inf. Div.
2 1st Bn. 357th Inf.
3 2nd Bn. 357th Inf.
4 1st Bn. 358th Inf.
5 2nd Bn. 359th Inf.
6 3rd Bn. 359th Inf.
7 Co. B 607th Tank Destroyer Bn.
8 712th Tank Bn.

THE DESTRUCTION OF PANZER BRIGADE 106, 8 SEPTEMBER 1944

In an attempt tp prevent Walker's XX Corps reaching the Moselle River, Gen. Knobelsdorff used Pz. Brig. 106 to launch a spoiling attack. This was driven back by the US 90th Inf. Div.

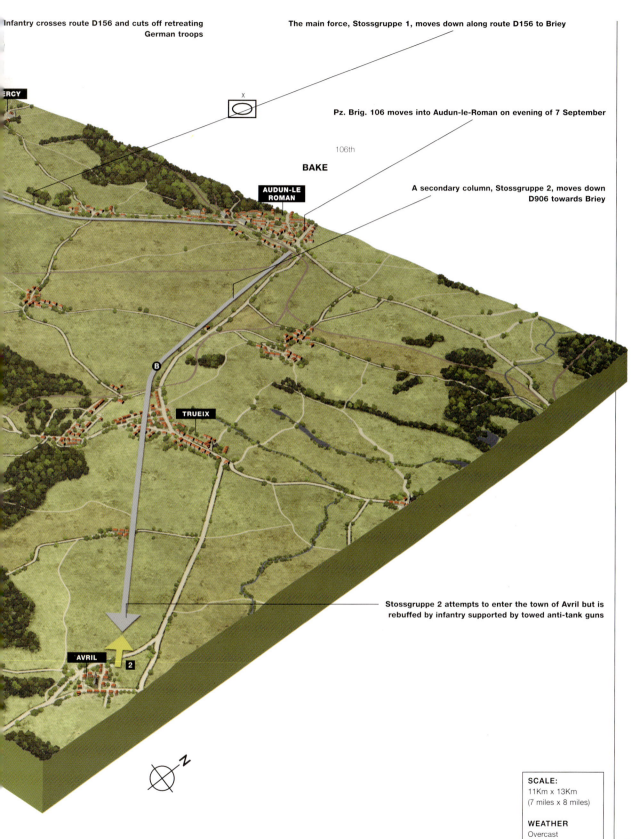

Infantry crosses route D156 and cuts off retreating German troops

The main force, Stossgruppe 1, moves down along route D156 to Briey

Pz. Brig. 106 moves into Audun-le-Roman on evening of 7 September

106th

BAKE

A secondary column, Stossgruppe 2, moves down D906 towards Briey

ERCY

X

AUDUN-LE ROMAN

B

TRUEIX

Stossgruppe 2 attempts to enter the town of Avril but is rebuffed by infantry supported by towed anti-tank guns

AVRIL

2

N

SCALE:
11Km x 13Km
(7 miles x 8 miles)

WEATHER
Overcast

OPPOSITE, TOP **This Panther Ausf. G tank from Pz. Brig. 106 was left abandoned west of Metz after the Mairy fighting. It was left by the roadside with a small sign to serve for vehicle recognition by passing troops. This team from the 5th Division is preparing to remove it in October 1944. (US Army)**

OPPOSITE, BELOW **On 10 September a patrol from the French 2nd Armored Division, the southernmost unit of Patton's Third Army, linked up with a patrol from the 6th Army Group, marking the link-up of the Allied forces from the North Sea to the Mediterranean. Here, a French crew from an M20 armored utility car shake hands with an American crew from an M8 armored car of the US Seventh Army in the streets of Autun. (US Army)**

BELOW **US troops inspect a knocked-out column of armor from the 4th Armd. Div. west of Nancy, France, on 10 September during the initial stages of the Moselle River operations. The M3A1 half-track has been hit by a high explosive round which has caved in the side armor and set the vehicle on fire. (US Army)**

out. A panzer grenadier company attempted to outflank the anti-tank defenses, barreling into the town from the south along the Mainville road on 11 SdKfz 251 armored half-tracks around 0800. Two were blown apart at close range by the US infantry supported by the 105mm howitzers of their cannon company, two more were knocked out by bazooka fire from the tank destroyer platoon, and four more were lost to 3-in. anti-tank guns as they tried to retreat out of the town to the north. A portion of the main column led by Panther tanks attempted to infiltrate towards the village down a sunken farm road around 0850. The lead Panther was disabled by an infantry team, and before the column could extract itself from the gully, a forward observer from the 949th Field Artillery directed fire on it. Over 300 rounds of 155mm howitzer fire pummeled the column, knocking out five Panthers and 20 half-tracks. The fighting around Mairy cost Pz. Brig. 106 seven Panther tanks and 48 half-tracks.

While this fight was taking place, the 2nd Battalion, 359th Infantry was sealing off escape routes behind the German advance. With the left column shattered in its ill-fated attack on Mairy, the scattered right wing was being trapped. The 90th Division HQ was reinforced with tanks from the 712th Tank Bn., while the 3rd Battalion, 359th Infantry occupied the town of Bonvillers and placed roadblocks on the road from Audun to Langres.

At 0935, the commander of Stossgruppe 1 requested permission to withdraw. This was granted, and Stossgruppe 1 was promised the support of Stossgruppe 2, which had yet to encounter any US forces. This column soon ran into the 1st Battalion, 357th Infantry near Avril, supported by a platoon of towed 3-in. anti-tank guns. An attack by panzer grenadiers supported by armor was quickly broken up after two Pz IV/70 tank destroyers and two half-tracks were knocked out. The column withdrew.

Stossgruppe 1 was now trapped as the US infantry closed in. In a series of disjointed attacks, the remnants of the column were destroyed. By the end of the afternoon, Pz. Brig. 106 had been reduced to a quarter of its manpower strength, mostly in Stossgruppe 2, which had seen little

combat. A total of 764 men had been captured, including the commanders of the Panther regiment and the panzer grenadier battalions, and many more had been killed. The brigade had lost most of its equipment, including 21 of its tanks and tank destroyers, 60 of its SdKfz 250 and 251 half-tracks, and more than 100 support vehicles. Only nine of the tanks and tank destroyers of the original 47 were operational after the fighting. Over the course of the next few days, a total of 17 tanks and nine Jagdpanzer IVs were recovered or escaped back to German lines, along with a portion of the panzer grenadiers. Tactics that might have worked on the Eastern Front had proven ineffective in the west, and the brigade was largely destroyed without any appreciable effect on its intended target.

German unit records show complaints about the lack of effective reconnaissance, but Bake appears to have lost effective control of the brigade by early morning as the various columns became scattered in the hilly farmlands. US artillery forward observers reported that the Germans were suffering from communications problems, and that they could see panzer crews running from tank to tank to carry messages, even in the midst of artillery strikes. What is equally remarkable was the American reaction to the attack: the divisional history brushes off the destruction of a panzer brigade as an ordinary encounter and devotes more attention to the bloody street fighting in Thionville later in the month; in fact the fighting around Mairy essentially eliminated one of the four panzer brigades committed to the Lorraine counteroffensive.

Pz. Brig. 106 attacks Mairy, 8 September 1944, as SdKfz 251 Ausf. D armored half-tracks of the Pz. Gren. Bn. 106 move down the road towards Mairy.

Further south, a shallow bridgehead over the Moselle was made by the 5th Inf. Div. at Dornot on 8 September but was stopped in the shadow of Fort St. Blaise. In the face of intense German pressure from the 17th SS Panzer Grenadier Division, it was finally withdrawn on 11 September, but by this time, a broader and more useful bridgehead had been seized opposite Arnaville. Engineers attempting to erect a bridge across the Moselle to support the bridgehead faced a difficult time as the river was in range of German artillery less than three miles north, at Fort Driant. On 13 September, the Fort Driant artillery sank a ferrying raft, partially demolished the treadway at the river ford, and broke up a pontoon bridge that was nearly completed. Patton hoped that the 7th Armd. Div. could still push across the river to the south of the fortress city, and envelope it by a drive to the north-east. However, the 7th Armd. Div. attack stalled due to stiff German resistance, the timely destruction of key bridges, the effective use of fortifications, and the onset of rainy weather which lessened the mobility of the tanks in the slippery clay mud.

Tony Bryan. 03/00

ACROSS THE MOSELLE

While Walker's XX Corps was bogged down in its efforts to secure usable bridgeheads near Metz, Eddy's XII Corps was having more success around the other major Moselle river city, the provincial capital at Nancy. Eddy decided against a direct attack on Nancy. The city was not fortified, but the Forêt de Haye and the heights of the Grand Couronne on the city's western approaches would make it a difficult objective. Instead, the intention was to secure crossings north and south of Nancy and attempt a concentric envelopment. North of Nancy, a regimental combat team from the 80th Inf. Div. tried to take control of a crossing near Pont-à-Mousson on 5 September. Although a bridgehead was seized, a counterattack by the 3rd Panzer Grenadier Division overwhelmed the small force. The Germans still held the west bank of the Moselle at many points, and for the next few days, the 80th Inf. Div. attempted to push them over to the east bank in preparation for river crossing operations. The defense by the 92nd Luftwaffe Field Regiment and 3rd Parachute Regiment was tenacious, and the German troops did not withdraw until 10 September.

The difficulties of the 80th Inf. Div. north of Nancy prompted Eddy to shift his emphasis south of the city using the 35th Inf. Div. The plan was to inject the 4th Armd. Div. to envelope Nancy once the bridgehead was gained. This decision was a controversial one, since the area south of the city was laced with additional rivers and canals. The attack was launched on 10 September, and 134th Infantry Regiment managed to

The 134th Infantry, 35th Division ford across the Madon River at Pierreville, five miles from the Moselle. Curiously enough, the regiment's 57mm anti-tank guns are being carried in their 3/4 ton trucks rather than being towed. (US Army)

The first successful crossing of the Moselle was conducted by the 137th Infantry, 35th Division, which overcame the defensive positions of the 104th Pz. Gren. Rgt. at Neuviller-sur-Moselle, south of Bayon, late on the afternoon of 11 September. The engineers later erected a pontoon treadway bridge at the site, and it is seen here the following day with an M10 tank destroyer crossing. (US Army)

An artillery forward observer team huddles in a small stone farm building at Pont St. Vincent on 11 September 1944 during the river crossing operations near Bayon. The 134th Infantry held the left flank of the river crossing operation at Pont St. Vincent, where the Madon River runs into the Moselle. (US Army)

push a battalion across an undamaged bridge in the early evening. The Germans attempted to bomb the bridge, and finally succeeded in dropping the span with artillery in the early morning hours of 11 September. A counterattack by elements of the 15th Panzer Grenadier Division crushed the bridgehead. In the meantime, the 137th Infantry seized several other small bridgeheads during the course of the day. The 4th Armd. Div.'s CCB (Combat Command B) made its own attempt near Bayon, and the tanks of the 8th Tank Bn. managed to create their own crossing over the Bayon Canal and four streams of the Moselle. On the evening of 11/12 September, the 137th Infantry linked up with the armor near Lorey. A battalion from the 15th Panzer Grenadier Division attempted a counterattack with tank support, but was trapped and destroyed.

On Wednesday 12 September, both Hodges and Patton were called to Bradley's headquarters at Dreux. The supply situation had again reached a critical point, and Bradley warned his subordinate commanders that it would inevitably mean a slow-down in operations. Hodges estimated that he had supplies for ten more days of strenuous fighting, and the following day his 7th Corps broke across the German frontier on the way to Aachen. Patton estimated he had four days of ammunition, but enough fuel to "roll on to the Rhine" after having captured some German stocks. Bradley warned Patton that he would only have two more days to cross the Moselle in force in the Nancy-Metz region, and that if he was unable to do so, the Third Army would have to go over to the defensive from Nancy to the Luxembourg border. While fuel deliveries to the Third Army had averaged 400,000 gallons through the second week of September, by late September, they would fall to 270,000 gallons, in spite of the addition of another corps.

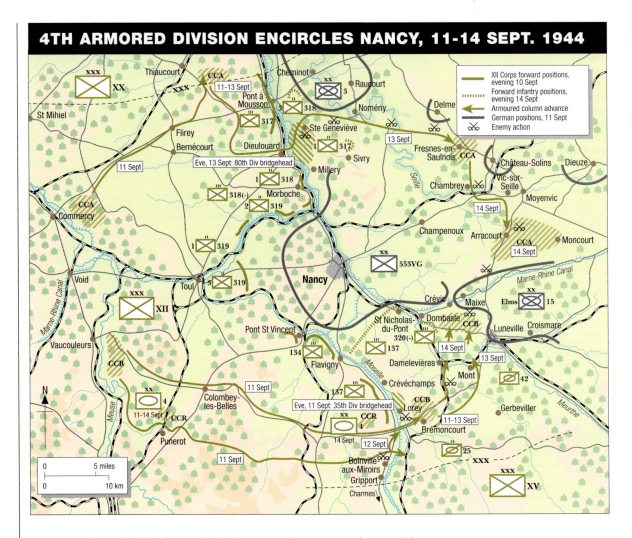

With Walker's XX Corps tied down on the approaches to Metz, Patton placed his hopes on XII Corps and the hard-charging 4th Armd. Div. The supply line had again been stretched, and the situation now reached a critical point; Bradley warned Patton that Montgomery was pressing for a higher priority of resources to the northern 21st Army Group, and that supplies would likely become scarcer. The meeting led Patton to press Eddy to complete the encirclement of Nancy.

With the bridgeheads south of Nancy secured, Eddy's XII Corps put more effort into taking northern bridgeheads. After being rebuffed near Pont-à-Mousson, his attention shifted to a crossing site near Dieulouard. Like many of the sites along this stretch of the river, this crossing was overlooked by a plateau. The military significance of the crossing site was obvious from the remains of Celtic earthworks, a Roman fort, and a medieval church-fortress. Before dawn on 11 September, two battalions from the 80th Inf. Div. crossed the river and took the high ground overlooking the river. The Germans counterattacked at 0100 on 13 September with a battalion from the 3rd Panzer Grenadier Division backed by ten StuG III assault guns. In a vicious night-time battle, the attack pushed the GIs back to within 100 yards of the bridges by 0500, but in the meantime, a company of M4 medium tanks from the

48

Tankers of the 8th Tank Bn., CCB, 4th Armd. Div. found some suitable fords across the Bayon canal and so were able to cross without bridges. The 8th Tank Bn. used foliage camouflage much more extensively than other tank battalions of the 4th Armd. Div., as is evident on this M4 medium tank. (US Army)

An M4A1 medium tank of the 8th Tank Bn. crosses the Bayon canal through a shallow but muddy ford on 12 September 1944. The crossing was made possible when a tank platoon used their 75mm guns to reduce the steep banks of the canal on the opposite shore. (US Army)

702nd Tank Bn. had moved forward, engaging the German armor at a range of only 200 meters. The bridgehead came very close to being overrun, but the area near the crossing site was stoutly defended by the engineers who had erected the bridges. In the face of growing American resistance, the German attack lost its momentum.

Prior to the German counterattack, Maj. Gen. John P. Wood of the 4th Armd. Div. had decided to push the CCA over the river at Dieulouard to begin the second arm of the envelopment of Nancy started by CCB near Bayon. At the head were the M8 armored cars of D Troop, 25th Cavalry Recon. Squadron, which reached the western end of the bridges around 0400 while the fighting on the east bank was going on. The regulating officer would not let the cavalry across until 0615 because of concerns about artillery coordination. After crossing the bridge, the armored cars fought their way through the German infantry before finally being forced to stop by some entrenched StuG III assault guns. A council of war had formed on the west bank, including the corps commander, Gen. Eddy, and the CCA commander, Col. Bruce Clarke. Eddy had some doubts as to whether it was sensible to deploy a large mechanized force in such a small bridgehead, especially in light of the unexpectedly fierce German attack. Clarke turned to the pugnacious commander of the 37th Tank Bn., Lt. Col. Creighton Abrams, who replied, "That's the shortest way home!" So the exploitation phase began in spite of the German action.

The German defensive line in the sector was thin, and CCA bulldozed its way through the attacking German infantry near Dieulouard with few losses. Once past the German main line of resistance, the tanks raced deep into the enemy rear towards Chateau-Salins, destroying 12 German armored vehicles, 85 other vehicles, and some artillery in the process. By the end of the day, the armored force was deep behind German lines and threatening to complete the envelopment of Nancy. The division log noted, "The rapid drive of

The 8th Tank Bn. crossing of the Bayon Canal was made possible by the low water level in several sections. This is evident here as several of the barges are left high and dry in the mud. The M4 exiting the canal is one of the newer M4 medium tanks armed with the long 76mm gun. These were not in widespread service in the 4th Armd. Div. at the time, since Patton did not feel that they were necessary. (US Army)

CCA through the enemy lines has so disrupted the enemy forces that small groups have been apprehended wandering, almost aimlessly, through their bivouac areas."

The German response

Blaskowitz recognized the threat posed by this armored breakthrough and began moving forces forward to crush the bridgehead and cut off CCA. Intense fighting raged in the forests and on the hills near the bridgeheads as the 3rd and 15th Pz. Gren. Div. attacked in force over the next two days. These attacks were repulsed by the 80th Inf. Div., and by 16 September, the Germans had suffered too many casualties to continue the fight. Rather than risk losing the substantial forces trapped in Nancy, Blaskowitz gave permission for units in Nancy to begin to

The Wehrmacht responded to the Bayon crossing by a series of counterattacks, including a brief tank attack by PzKpfw IVs of the 15th Panzer Grenadier Division near Mehoncourt, in which one M4 medium tank of the 8th Tank Bn. was knocked out. It can be seen in the background while a medic tends to a wounded tanker in the foreground. (US Army)

RIGHT **The northern crossing of the Moselle took place near the town of Dieulouard. The area is laced with small tributaries of the Moselle which complicated the crossing. Here an M4 bulldozer tank is used to create a roadway across a narrow tributary of the river on 12 September. (US Army)**

RIGHT, BELOW **Troops of the 80th Inf. Div. cross the Moselle near Dieulouard on 12 September via an improvised bridge. The next day, the engineers had erected a pontoon treadway bridge elsewhere on the river to enable heavy traffic to cross. (US Army)**

evacuate on the evening of 13 September, and the loss of the bridgeheads at Dieulouard and Bayon led to the complete abandonment of the city over the next few days. It was occupied by the 80th Inf. Div. with the support of the FFI French resistance forces on 15 September.

Plans for Hitler's panzer offensive in Lorraine had been steadily delayed through the first two weeks of September. His original scheme had been to launch the attack from the area of Pontarlier on the Swiss border north-west towards the Plateau de Langres, cutting off US forces advancing towards the Belfort Gap and preventing a link-up of the US Third and Seventh Armies. The attack would have involved three panzer grenadier divisions and three panzer brigades, with three more panzer divisions and three more panzer brigades as reinforcements. An initial attack date had been set for 12 September, but this had proved

impossible, and by the second week of September, the German retreat and the approach of the two US armies near Dijon, overrunning the areas from which the offensive would have been staged, had disabled Hitler's plans still further.

On 10 September, Manteuffel was again called to the Führer headquarters. Hitler's revised plan envisioned an attack from the Plateau de Langres and Epinal towards Reims, with an aim towards cutting off Patton's Third Army when it was entangled in the battles along the Moselle River. The American advances threatened to create a breach between the German First and Nineteenth Armies which would allow the American tank columns to race ahead into the Saar basin across the German frontier. Although the notional aim of the counteroffensive was to cut off the Third Army, the more realistic officers at Blaskowitz's

RIGHT **The bridgeheads south of Metz in the XX Corps sector proved even more difficult than those around Nancy, with the crossing sites under fire from the artillery of Fort Driant. On 12 September, a heavy bridge was finally completed near Arnaville, allowing the 7th Armd. Div.'s CCB to send reinforcements to the beleaguered infantry on the west bank. This is an M32 armored recovery vehicle crossing the bridge on 13 September. (US Army)**

BELOW, RIGHT **The Germans destroyed most of the bridges over the Moselle. However, in the days following the first crossings, engineers began to use the pilings of the bridges to create improvised crossings, like the one at Arnaville in use by medical teams on 21 September. (US Army)**

headquarters hoped that the attack would at least prevent a rupture between the First and Nineteenth Armies and cover the Vosges mountain area while a new "Vosges Outpost" defensive line was created.

Manteuffel arrived at Army Group G headquarters on 11 September and was briefed on the local situation. Fifth Panzer Army existed more in Hitler's imagination than in reality, and Manteuffel felt that the counteroffensive plan was "beyond all hope." To make matters worse, the US First Army attacking from Belgium were approaching Aachen, the first major German city to be threatened on the Western Front. Rundstedt was stripping forces from all over the theater to reinforce this sector. Two of the panzer brigades slated for the Lorraine offensive, Panzer Brigades 107 and 108, were being sent towards Aachen instead,

ABOVE **With the CCB of 4th Armd. Div. and 35th Infantry over the Moselle, the tanks began moving on to encircle the regional capital of Nancy. Here, an M4 medium tank of the 737th Tank Bn. fires on buildings near Dombasle, along the left flank of the advance on 15 September 1944, in support of the 320th Infantry, which was crossing a nearby canal at the time. (US Army)**

LEFT **A couple of GIs of the 35th Inf. Div. enjoy coffee and donuts at a Red Cross station outside Nancy on 19 September 1944. Task Force Sebree from the division entered the city on 15 September and found that it had been abandoned by the Germans. (US Army)**

The fighting during late September 1944 in Lorraine was characterized by rain and mud. It was one of the wettest Septembers on record, and the fields soon turned to glutinous mud, as shown here with a jeep from the 134th Infantry, 35th Division near Nancy. (US Army)

and the date for the offensive was postponed to 15 September. However, Hitler was adamant that it should start no later than that, even if only some of the allotted forces were ready.

The units assigned to the Fifth Panzer Army included: the 21st Panzer Division from OB-West's reserve, which was refitting in Molsheim; the 15th Panzer Grenadier Division, which was already heavily committed to the fighting in the First Army sector; and Panzer Brigades 106, 111, 112, and 113. The Fifth Panzer Army was organized into the 47th Panzer Corps headquartered at Remiremont, and the 57th Panzer Corps, activated on 18 September, at Languimberg. Command and control of the army was made more difficult by the fact that it did not control its own sector of the front, sharing control with the First and Nineteenth Armies. There were not enough telephone lines to support separate headquarters, and the Fifth Panzer Army took a back-seat to the existing formations. After the decimation of Pz. Brig. 106 in the attack on 90th Inf. Div., Hitler ordered that none of the units intended for his offensive be used for frontal attacks on the Americans but only for the planned counterattack. However, before Hitler's revised plan could be put into effect, Allied attacks in a new sector threatened the staging area for the panzer attack.

DISASTER AT DOMPAIRE

hile Hodges' and Eddy's corps fought for the Moselle bridgeheads, Patton's Third Army was reinforced by a third corps, Maj. Gen. Wade Haislip's XV Corps. This had been taken from the Third Army during the Seine crossing operation and was being returned to Patton's forces in Lorraine to cover his exposed right flank. During the push into Lorraine, the right flank had been ignored due to the weakness of the Wehrmacht. But in the meantime, the 6th Army Group was advancing northward after its landings in southern France and was already moving up along the Swiss border towards the Belfort Gap. As the 6th Army Group closed on Third Army, German forces would be pushed forward into the gap between the two Allied armies, requiring more attention to the flank. A patrol from the French 2nd Armored Division, the southernmost unit in XV Corps, linked up with a patrol from the 6th Army Group late on 10 September to the west of Dijon, marking a continuous line of Allied forces from the North Sea to the Mediterranean.

On 11 September, Haislip's XV Corps began moving forward to push the weak German 64th Corps back over the Moselle. The spearhead of XV Corps was the French 2nd Armored Division, commanded by the legendary Jacques Leclerc. This division was the first Free French division formed, and the only one to operate separately from de Lattre's 1st French Army in the 6th Army Group. The division had originally served under Haislip's XV Corps in Normandy. Leclerc had appreciated

Mines were a constant menace and accounted for about a quarter of the US tanks knocked out during the war. This M4 (76mm) of the 749th Tank Bn. was disabled near Charmes on 12 September during the fighting between the US 79th Division and the German 16th Infantry Division. While the US forces kept the Germans occupied, the French 2nd Armored Division sent a combat command deep behind German lines, precipitating the tank battle at Dompaire. (US Army)

the aggressive command style of the French-speaking Haislip, but had had problems when shifted to Maj. Gen. L. T. Gerow's V Corps for the liberation of Paris. De Gaulle had wanted Leclerc's division to remain in Paris as a counterweight to the Communist-dominated resistance, or transferred to de Lattre's 1st French Corps, but Leclerc had been unhappy being subordinated to a former Vichy general like de Lattre and had finally won permission to return to Haislip's XV Corps. Haislip had been equally pleased, as Leclerc's division was easily the best of the Free French divisions, being composed mostly of volunteers from the tough African colonial units. While the US 79th Inf. Div. pinned the German 16th Inf. Div. by frontal attack, the French 2nd Armored Division sent its GTL (*Groupement Tactique Langlade*, Combat Command Langlade) through the gap between the weak Kampfgruppe

The RBFM (*Régiment Blindé de Fusiliers Marins*, Armored Regiment of Naval Riflemen) was the tank destroyer battalion of the French 2nd Armored Division. Its platoons were usually spread out among the various battle-groups to provide added firepower to the tank companies when encountering German Panthers. The battalion was formed in North Africa in 1943 from volunteers from the French fleet, and the crews retained their sailor's cap. Here, French Minister of the Navy Jacquinot visits crews who distinguished themselves during the fighting at Dompaire. (US Army)

RIGHT *Siroco*, an M10 of the 3rd Platoon, 4th Squadron of the RBFM, was the highest scoring tank destroyer of the battalion, credited with nine German tanks including three Panthers at Dompaire. The tank destroyers were named after pre-war French warships. *Siroco* was preserved after the war and is currently on display at the Saumur tank museum in the Loire region of France, near the French Army cavalry school. (S. Zaloga)

Ottenbacher and the 16th Inf. Div. (The French combat commands were named after their leader, in this case, Col. Paul Girot de Langlade.)

The French armored columns were soon behind the German positions and threatened to encircle them. In spite of Hitler's orders to conserve the panzer brigades for the planned offensive, Blaskowitz felt it was more important to keep the defensive line intact than hoard precious tank formations for a doomed offensive. He ordered Manteuffel to send some of his forces into the area west of Epinal to prevent the collapse of the entire 64th Corps. The plan was to use Col. von Usedom's Pz. Brig. 112 and a combat group of the 21st Panzer Division to clear out the rear areas of the French intruders. The panzer brigade moved out of Epinal in two groups: the Panthers of I/Pz. Rgt. 29 reached the town of Dompaire in the early evening of 12 September and the PzKpfw IV tanks of Pz. Rgt. 2112 moved towards Darney.

GTL Langlade had excellent intelligence about the strength and location of the German forces from the local French villagers. By late evening of 12 September, I/Pz. Rgt. 29 was strung out in a poorly chosen bivouac in a shallow valley from the village of Dompaire to the west and through its neighboring hamlets of Lamerey and Madonne to the east. Langlade decided to attack this formation first, even though it was larger than his own forces.

GTL Langlade consisted of mechanized infantry from the *Régiment de Marche du Tchade* (RMT) and companies from two tank battalions, the 12e *Régiment de Chasseurs d'Afrique* (RCA), and the 501e *Régiment de Chars de Combat* (RCC). Langlade's force was composed of three battlegroups: Group Putz near Darney, and Groups Massu and Minjonnet near Dompaire. Each group had 15 M4A2 medium tanks with 75mm guns,

one M4A2 with a 76mm gun, three to four M10 tank destroyers, and one or two companies of infantry. The total strength of GTL Langlade was inferior to Pz. Brig. 112, at less than half the number of tanks and infantry, but Langlade had the advantage of better positions, as well as artillery and air support which the Germans lacked completely.

Group Massu took up positions in the hills overlooking Dompaire from the west and north-west, and Group Minjonnet towards the center of the town, with clear fields of fire to the east. Group Massu was the first to encounter the Germans: during a probe towards Dompaire on the evening of 12 September, they had a short firefight with Panther tanks on the south-western side of the town. The French M4 tanks withdrew into the woods above the town after each side had lost a tank.

The terrain held by the French was a plateau a few kilometers south of Dompaire, separated by gradually sloping farm fields and scattered woods. This provided excellent fields of fire against the town below and clear vantage points from which to direct artillery fire. The French troops were more experienced and better trained than their German adversaries. For example, the 12e RCA, previously commanded by Langlade, had fought against the Afrika Korps in the Tunisian campaign on Somua S-35 tanks before being re-equipped and retrained by the US Army in 1943-44 on M4A2 tanks. The other units had been drawn mostly from French-African units. Curiously enough, the M10 tank destroyers were manned by volunteer sailors from the RBFM (Armored Regiment of Naval Riflemen).

Like most other panzer brigades, Pz. Brig. 112 was new, poorly trained, and untested in combat. A French villager who watched the column of Panthers move through Lamerey towards Dompaire the evening before the battle recalled that the crews "seemed almost like children." The French expected the Germans to conduct rigorous night patrols to reconnoiter their positions. Instead, the Germans sat out the rainy night in comfort in the villages while the French endured the rain in muddy farm fields, preparing for the next day's battle. A German officer who participated in the battle later recalled that before the battle, the Germans had seriously underestimated the combat skills of the French tankers.

The fighting began along the eastern side of the town. Panther tanks began to try to infiltrate south out of Lamerey by using the hilly terrain and woods. A pair of M10 tank destroyers in hull-down position stopped the initial advance, further emphasizing the point by calling in an artillery strike of 250 rounds from a battery of 105mm howitzers. Group Minjonnet sent a company of light tanks towards Damas, to the south of Dompaire, to try to force out entrenched German infantry, and faced a stiff fight.

The previous night, Langlade had arranged to receive American air support, and around 0800, Col. Tower, the TALO (tactical air liaison officer) from the XIX TAC, moved up in a radio-equipped M4 tank to the command post of Group Massu in the hills above Dompaire. He directed an air strike from P-47s of the 406th Fighter-Bomber Group against the Panther tanks strung out in the hamlets of Lamerey and Madonne. The I/Pz. Rgt. 29 was raked with rocket fire, bombs, and machine-guns; the Germans responded with ineffective 20mm fire. A French tanker recalled that it was "the most impressive and terrifying

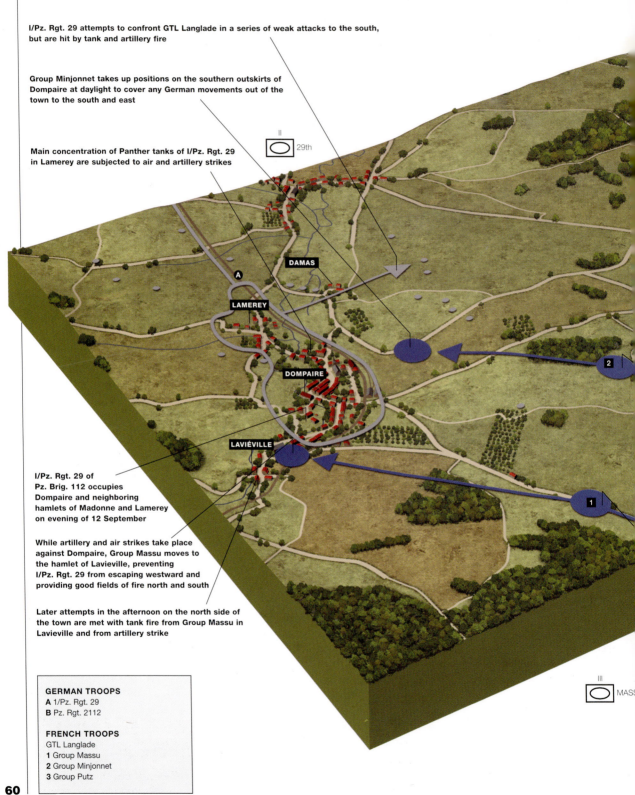

I/Pz. Rgt. 29 attempts to confront GTL Langlade in a series of weak attacks to the south, but are hit by tank and artillery fire

Group Minjonnet takes up positions on the southern outskirts of Dompaire at daylight to cover any German movements out of the town to the south and east

Main concentration of Panther tanks of I/Pz. Rgt. 29 in Lamerey are subjected to air and artillery strikes

DAMAS

A

LAMEREY

DOMPAIRE

LAVIÉVILLE

2

1

I/Pz. Rgt. 29 of Pz. Brig. 112 occupies Dompaire and neighboring hamlets of Madonne and Lamerey on evening of 12 September

While artillery and air strikes take place against Dompaire, Group Massu moves to the hamlet of Lavieville, preventing I/Pz. Rgt. 29 from escaping westward and providing good fields of fire north and south

Later attempts in the afternoon on the north side of the town are met with tank fire from Group Massu in Lavieville and from artillery strike

29th

III MASS

GERMAN TROOPS
A 1/Pz. Rgt. 29
B Pz. Rgt. 2112

FRENCH TROOPS
GTL Langlade
1 Group Massu
2 Group Minjonnet
3 Group Putz

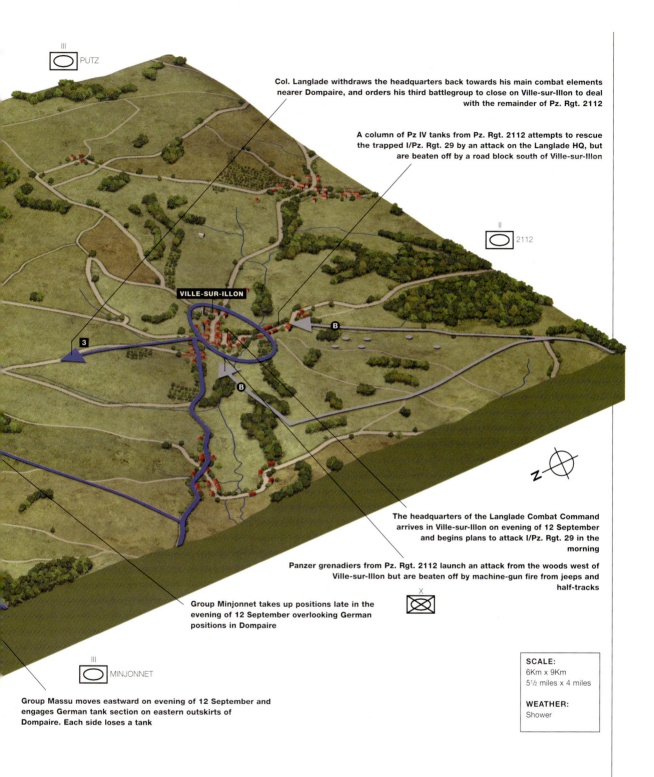

III
PUTZ

Col. Langlade withdraws the headquarters back towards his main combat elements nearer Dompaire, and orders his third battlegroup to close on Ville-sur-Illon to deal with the remainder of Pz. Rgt. 2112

A column of Pz IV tanks from Pz. Rgt. 2112 attempts to rescue the trapped I/Pz. Rgt. 29 by an attack on the Langlade HQ, but are beaten off by a road block south of Ville-sur-Illon

II
2112

VILLE-SUR-ILLON

B

3

B

The headquarters of the Langlade Combat Command arrives in Ville-sur-Illon on evening of 12 September and begins plans to attack I/Pz. Rgt. 29 in the morning

Panzer grenadiers from Pz. Rgt. 2112 launch an attack from the woods west of Ville-sur-Illon but are beaten off by machine-gun fire from jeeps and half-tracks

X

Group Minjonnet takes up positions late in the evening of 12 September overlooking German positions in Dompaire

III
MINJONNET

Group Massu moves eastward on evening of 12 September and engages German tank section on eastern outskirts of Dompaire. Each side loses a tank

Z

SCALE:
6Km x 9Km
5½ miles x 4 miles

WEATHER:
Shower

THE DESTRUCTION OF PANZER BRIGADE 112 AT DOMPAIRE, 13 SEPTEMBER 1944

GTL Langlade encircled the weak German units to prevent a counter-offensive and severely reduced the German panzer force.

spectacle imaginable." The French observers estimated that eight tanks had been knocked out, but the smoke and fire in the villages made it difficult to be precise. Under the cover of the air attack, the French columns began moving into position to trap the Germans in the villages and prevent their movement down neighboring roads. French M4 medium tanks entered the west side of Dompaire through the hamlet of Lavieville and moved up the hill towards Bouzemont to take up positions on the hills behind the Germans. They were followed later in the morning by a platoon of M10 tank destroyers. The Panthers were now hemmed in on three sides.

Around 1100 a second flight of six P-47 Thunderbolts arrived overhead, this time in bright sunlight and clear skies. There was some confusion due to the infiltration of French tanks into the villages, and the German use of Allied air recognition panels on some of their tanks. After consultation with the TALO, the air strike commenced. French villagers later reported that the strike had terrified the inexperienced German tank crews and that a number of crews had deserted and tried to steal civilian clothes in order to escape. The commander of I/Pz. Rgt. 29 requested assistance from the brigade's other tank battalion, Pz. Rgt. 2112 in Darney, when it became clear that the Germans were trapped.

Langlade's command post was in the village of Ville-sur-Illon, on the plateau south of Dompaire. Around 1330, he received a phone call from a woman in an outlying house south of his position warning him that she had seen 300-400 German panzer grenadiers and some tanks moving towards the town. This was the spearhead of the rescue party from Pz. Rgt. 2112 that had been requested a few hours earlier. The force consisted of a battalion of panzer grenadiers and a number of the regiment's 45 PzKpfw IV tanks, and the advance posed a serious risk to the entire French battlegroup. It not only threatened to overrun the French command post, but it could also sandwich Group Minjonnet against the German tanks in Dompaire. However, the German infantry halted abruptly after finding and drinking a large cache of kirsch liquor in a garage along the route. In the meantime, Langlade organized a hasty defense of his command post by setting up a roadblock along route D6 using a handful of tanks, M10 destroyers, and towed anti-tank guns.

By the third week of September, German units in Lorraine were faced by additional Allied forces when Devers' 6th Army Group linked up with Patton's Third Army. Here, an M4A1 medium tank of the 191st Tank Bn. crosses the Moselle near Arches on 21 September 1944, part of the drive which undermined the German 64th Corps. (US Army)

About a dozen PzKpfw IV tanks moved within range of the roadblock. The lead two were destroyed by M4 medium tanks at 200-300 meters, and three more were wiped out later by concealed M10 tank destroyers. The German infantry, delayed by their earlier drinking, finally arrived from the west against the right flank of the French position. This area was defended by only two jeeps armed with .30 caliber machine-guns. They opened fire, and then boldly raced out into the forest clearing, raking the panzer grenadiers with machine-guns. This put a temporary halt to this threat as the German troops retreated into the nearby woods. A pair of half-tracks from an engineer platoon were rushed in to assist and managed to capture a few prisoners. When the size of the German force became evident from prisoner interrogations, Langlade evacuated his command post to more defensible positions closer to the bulk of his battlegroup near Dompaire.

While the fighting was taking place on the plateau, at 1530 a third air strike by a flight of six P-47s began against Lamerey. This attack was partly wasted on burnt-out tanks due to difficulties in establishing a radio link with the TALO. The I/Pz. Rgt. 29 in Dompaire staged a series of weak, intermittent attacks through the afternoon, usually consisting of two or three Panthers trying to find weak points in the French positions. This was a futile exercise as the French had carefully established camouflaged hull-down positions around the village and were able to destroy the more heavily armored Panthers with flank shots at close range. One probe in the early afternoon nearly found a gap, in a position protected only by an exposed 57mm towed anti-tank gun, but a barrage from a battery of 105mm howitzers put an end to the attack. German prisoners made it quite clear that they feared the artillery even more than the air strikes. Due to the excellent observation positions

A German casualty is evacuated by a stretcher team from the 45th Division near Archettes after the 7th Army crossed the Moselle near Arches on 21 September. One of the stretcher bearers is a German prisoner-of-war. (US Army)

afforded by the plateau, the French were able to bring down precision artillery strikes all day long, regardless of the changing weather, and a fourth air strike around 1500 left many of the Panthers in the hamlets east of Dompaire burnt or abandoned.

After a day of weak and futile probes against the plateau to the south and east, I/Pz. Rgt. 29 began to stage an attack to the north-east, towards the French blocking positions on the hills behind Dompaire. An initial foray of three Panthers proved half-hearted after the lead vehicle was struck ineffectively at 1,600 meters by M10 fire. Two more platoons of Panthers, accompanied by panzer grenadiers, appeared next. Several were put out of action by the M10 tank destroyers. This temporarily broke up the attack, which resumed about 1830 for the loss of two more Panthers. By evening, the attacks had petered out, and by the end of the day, Pz. Brig. 112 was a shambles. The I/Pz. Rgt. 29 had been virtually wiped out, losing 34 of its Panther tanks and having only four operational. Pz. Rgt. 2112 had only 17 of its original 45 Pz. Kpfw IV tanks operational and had lost many infantry in the woods near Ville-sur-Illon.

The following morning, Group Massu occupied the eastern end of Dompaire, finding four abandoned Panther tanks in the streets of the town. A Kampfgruppe, made up mostly of the 192nd Pz. Gren. Rgt. under Col. von Luck from the 21st Panzer Division, was sent west from Epinal to reinforce the attack, but by the time it arrived, on 14 September, Langlade had been reinforced near Ville-sur-Illon by his third battlegroup, Group Putz. Von Luck's battlegroup, consisting of 17 tanks and 240 infantry, made an attack on Group Minjonnet from the east, near Hennecourt, attempting to prevent the complete annihilation of 1/Pz. Rgt. 29 in Dompaire. It was brought under fire by divisional artillery and stopped after an hour of fighting. The German 47th Panzer Corps headquarters decided that any further attacks would be futile. Von Luck and the surviving elements of Pz. Brig. 112 were ordered to withdraw towards positions west of Epinal, hoping that these remnants might be used later in the planned counteroffensive. The hapless survivors of Pz. Brig. 112 were put under 21st Panzer Division command. In less than two days of fighting, the brigade had been reduced to only 21 operational tanks of its original 90. Casualties were estimated to be 350 dead and about 1,000 wounded. Of the 33 tanks found in Group Massu's sector, 13 had been knocked out by tank or tank-destroyer fire, 16 by aircraft attack, and four had been abandoned intact. French losses were five M4A2 medium tanks, two M5A1 light tanks, two half-tracks and two jeeps; 44 were killed, and a single P-47 was shot down.

The decimation of Pz. Brig. 112 on 13 September, less than a week after the defeat of Pz. Brig. 106, substantially reduced the tank strength available to Manteuffel for the planned counteroffensive. Fifth Panzer Army was now down to only two panzer brigades, the demoralized remnants of brigades 112 and 106, and the understrength and tank-less 21st Panzer Division. By the night of 17 September, the German 64th Corps had collapsed and had retreated over the Moselle, with most of the 16th Inf. Div., trapped by the Americans and French. All of Patton's three corps were now lined up along the Moselle. On 19 September, Haislip's XV Corps crossed the river and advanced towards the Mortagne River, reaching the area south of Luneville.

THE TANK BATTLES FOR ARRACOURT

The American and French advances in the XV Corps sector forced Blaskowitz to inform Rundstedt that the proposed panzer counteroffensive along the west side of the Moselle was no longer feasible since the Wehrmacht had lost the Plateau de Langres from which it was to be launched. Not wishing to display a lack of the "offensive spirit" that Hitler took to be a measure of loyalty to the regime, Blaskowitz suggested a more feasible, though more limited, offensive. This would emanate from the Epinal area to the north-east, seize a base of operations at Luneville, and then cut off the lead elements of Patton's armored spearhead, the 4th Armd. Div., around Arracourt. Blaskowitz planned to use the Fifth Panzer Army attack to accomplish the more limited tactical objective of closing the gap between the First and Nineteenth Armies, though the plan had to be couched in more ambitious terms to mollify Hitler's predilection for the grandiose.

Rundstedt knew better than to approve the change in Hitler's plan on his own authority, so sent the proposal to OKW in Berlin. The OKW approved the plan, reinforcing Manteuffel's force with the 11th Panzer Division and noting that Panzer Brigades 107 and 108 would be added to the attack once Hitler's intuition told him it was the right moment. In fact, both brigades were committed later to the Aachen fighting instead.

The panzer offensive was now scheduled to begin no later than 18 September 1944, even though it was unlikely that the 11th Panzer Division would be available. Rundstedt did win a concession from the inspector of the panzer forces on the Western Front, Gen. Lt. Horst

A column from the 106th Cavalry Group passes a PzKpfw IV with its turret blown off on a road near Luneville on 20 September. This is probably a tank from Pz. Brig. 112, which was incorporated into the 21st Panzer Division after its disaster at Dompaire and employed with little success against the XV Corps advance on Luneville a week later. (US Army)

A lieutenant from the 79th Division calls in mortar fire during the fighting around Luneville on 21 September. The city of Luneville remained a source of contention even after it was occupied by US forces since the German 15th Pz. Gren. Div. could launch attacks on it from the neighboring Parroy forest. (US Army)

Stumpff, that priority in new tanks would be given to units assigned for the attack, especially the depleted 21st Panzer Division. However, this never materialized. On 16 September, detailed orders were issued for the offensive. Manteuffel protested that the Fifth Panzer Army was not strong enough to conduct such an ambitious attack, but he was told in no uncertain terms that he would attack on 18 September regardless of his opinion.

The objectives were to eliminate the US Army XII Corps from the east bank of the Moselle by seizing Luneville as a base of operation, then crush the bridgehead at Pont-à-Mousson. The 58th Panzer Corps would attack westward along the north bank of the Marne-Rhine canal against the US 4th Armd. Div. using Pz. Brig. 113 and the 15th Panzer Grenadier Division. The 47th Panzer Corps would strike towards Luneville using

The tank fighting in late September centered around the small town of Arracourt, seen here in the upper center of an aerial photo taken shortly after the war. The most intense fighting took place around Hill 318, in the center of the photo, immediately to the right of the Benamont Woods seen on the left. In an aerial photo like this, the area appears flat, but in fact the terrain slopes downward towards the bottom of the photo, to the south-east. (David Isby)

Pz. Brig. 111, the remnants of Pz. Brig. 112, and the 21st Panzer Division.

The initial objective for Luttwitz's 47th Panzer Corps was the town of Luneville. The situation near the town was fluid. Two squadrons from "Patton's Ghosts", the 2nd Cavalry Group, had tried to enter the town on 15 September but were beaten off by elements of the 15th Pz. Gren. Div. The next day, the 42nd Cav. Sqn. again moved on Luneville, reinforced with tanks of CCR of the 4th Armd. Div. The German infantry withdrew. The 42nd Cav. Sqn. did not occupy the town, but set up a line of outposts to the south-east. On the evening of 17 September, German infantry again infiltrated the town and reported that it was in their hands. When the panzer attack began early on the morning of 18 September 1944, Luttwitz

An M18 tank destroyer from the 603rd Tank Destroyer Battalion, CCB, 7th Armd. Div. guards the intersection at Rue Carnot in Luneville, facing towards Frambois, on 22 September. Vehicles from this unit took part in the tank fighting in Luneville with Pz. Brig. 111 on 18 September. (US Army)

was under the impression that Luneville was in friendly hands. Instead, the lead column of Panther tanks from Pz. Brig. 111 ran into an outpost of the 42nd Cav. Sqn. The squadron's M8 75mm howitzer motor carriages (HMC) rushed forward to provide fire support for the lightly armed M8 armored cars. However, the little howitzers on these light armored vehicles were completely ineffective against the thick frontal armor of the Panthers. Three of the six M8 HMCs were quickly destroyed, and the German tanks pressed ahead. However, a tenacious defense by dismounted cavalry troops delayed the panzer grenadiers until 1100. The commander of the 42nd Squadron was killed and the commander of the 2nd Cavalry Group was severely wounded in the ensuing fighting. Although badly outnumbered, the cavalry force managed to delay the German advance long enough for the 2nd Cavalry Group to withdraw through Luneville and to call for reinforcements. CCA of 4th Armd. Div. rushed a task force to the scene, along with elements of CCB of the 6th Armd. Div. A close-range firefight developed

Fifth Panzer Army commander Hasso von Manteuffel had a bitter exchange with Col. Heinrich von Bronsart-Schellendorf, commander of Pz. Brig. 111, on 22 September. Schellendorf was killed by machine-gun fire during the fighting later in the day near Juvelize. (USNA)

inside the town between the 603rd Tank Destroyer Battalion and lead German armor elements. The most potent American reinforcements were two battalions of M7 105mm HMC and the 183rd Field Artillery Group which began to pummel the German troops. The intense artillery fire forced the Germans behind the rail line in the southern section of the town. Manteuffel ordered Pz. Brig. 111 to disengage from the town and proceed to Parroy for the continuation of the main attack.

At the end of the first day of the panzer offensive, the Germans had made few gains, holding on to parts of Luneville, and even before the southern thrust had accomplished much of anything, Luttwitz found that his left flank was threatened by the continuing advance of the US Army XV Corps. There was also pressure from Hitler and the OKW to press the attack. The objective was again redefined, with Nancy now being the initial objective instead of Chateau Salins, to rescue trapped German forces. (Hitler would throw away entire divisions due to careless decisions, and then become obsessed with rescuing a few encircled battalions in another sector.)

Manteuffel was forced to reorganize his plans yet again. Luttwitz was ordered to take up defensive positions using the 15th Pz. Gren. Div., 21st Pz. Div., and Pz. Brig. 112, while Pz. Brig. 111 was taken away and assigned to the 58th Panzer Corps, which would now bear the brunt of

PREPARING FOR THE ASSAULT: German panzer grenadiers climb aboard the Panther tanks and half-tracks of Pz. Brig. 113 as they prepare for their assault towards Arracourt.

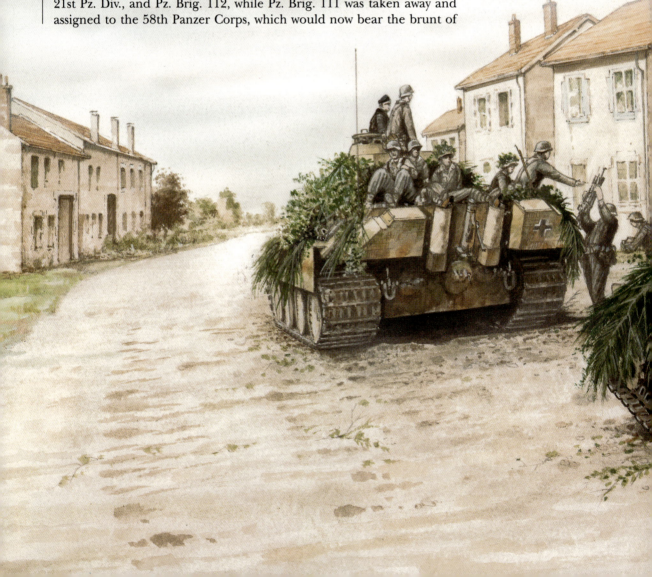

Tony Bryan. 03/00

Two prominent combat leaders of CCA, 4th Armd. Div. were Lt. Col. Creighton Abrams, commander of the 37th Tank Bn., seen here to the left, and Lt. Col. Harold Cohen, commander of the 10th Armored Infantry Battalion, seen to the right. The close cooperation between the tanks and half-track infantry was one of the reasons for the success of this fighting force. (J. Leach collection, Patton Museum)

the offensive mission. At midnight, Manteuffel telephoned the 58th Panzer Corps commander, Gen. Kreuger, and told him that Pz. Brig. 113 must be ready to conduct offensive operations towards Arracourt or he would suffer the direst consequences. The disorganized condition of the German panzer forces and persistent demands for action from Berlin forced Manteuffel into a ragged and piecemeal commitment of his forces. The 2nd Cavalry Group had prevented German reconnaissance units from determining much about the dispositions of the 4th Armd. Div. around Arracourt, and the Luftwaffe had also proven to be useless in this regard. Manteuffel was operating in an intelligence void, exacerbated by the tendency of the Eastern Front veterans to launch tank attacks without any scouting.

It was not immediately apparent to Patton that a major panzer offensive had begun. There was no signals intelligence on German intentions, and the attack on Luneville was so weak and disjointed that it was presumed to be a minor local action. Patton's plan for 19 September was for the 4th Armd. Div. to continue its attack towards the German border. CCB was to push from Delme towards Saabrucken, while CCA would attack from Arracourt towards Saareguemines. On the night of 18/19 September, there were numerous reports along the frontlines of the sounds of German tracked vehicles.

The early morning attack had been planned as a two-brigade assault, with Pz. Brig. 113 attacking the eastern spearhead of the CCA forces near Lezey while Pz. Brig. 111 attacked the center near Arracourt. This would have given the Germans more than a four-to-one advantage in armor in this sector. In the event, Pz. Brig. 111 became lost during the night road march, allegedly after receiving bad instructions from a French farmer, but even without Pz. Brig. 111, Pz. Brig. 113 still had more than a two-to-one advantage.

Panther Ausf. G tanks of Pz. Brig. 111 maneuver on the outskirts of Bures on 20 September. Bures was one of the small towns between the Parroy forest and the base of the Arracourt hills, and so was a favorite staging area for the German attacks. (USNA)

The morning of 19 September dawned as it had for the previous few days with a thick fog in the low-lying areas. Around 0730, Capt. W. Dwight, a liaison officer moving between his platoons in a jeep, ran into the rear of a German tank column near Moncourt. In the thick fog, he went unnoticed, and he escaped to Arracourt, reporting to the 37th Tank Bn. commander, Lt. Col. Creighton Abrams, by radio. An outpost of M5A1 light tanks from Company D, 37th Tank Bn. encountered the same group, but were able to withdraw in the thick fog and report back.

The German column was a company of Panther tanks spearheading the eastern column of the Pz. Brig. 113 attack. A platoon of M4 medium tanks from Co. C, 37th Tank Bn. were holding an outpost when they heard the lead tanks moving towards their position. A group of Panther tanks emerged from the fog about 75 yards from their position. Quickly engaging them, three Panthers were knocked out in rapid succession. In shock, the German column broke off to the south-west. The US tankers enjoyed a greater familiarity with the local terrain, and Capt. Lamison raced a platoon of M4 medium tanks to a commanding ridge west of Bezange-la-Petite to trap the withdrawing panzer column. As the eight surviving Panthers appeared, four were quickly knocked out at close range from the flanks. Before the Germans could respond, the M4 tanks moved behind the cover of the reverse slopes. In the dense fog, the Panther crews had no idea where the American tanks were located, and seconds later, the M4 tanks reappeared from behind the ridge and destroyed the remaining four Panthers.

In the meantime, Capt. Dwight had reached Arracourt and was ordered to take a platoon of M18 tank destroyers to reinforce the outpost near

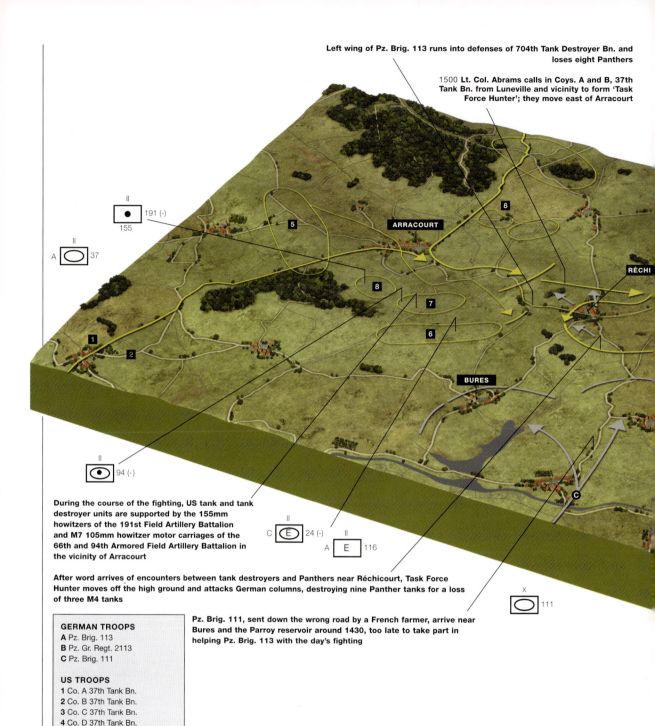

Left wing of Pz. Brig. 113 runs into defenses of 704th Tank Destroyer Bn. and loses eight Panthers

1500 Lt. Col. Abrams calls in Coys. A and B, 37th Tank Bn. from Luneville and vicinity to form 'Task Force Hunter'; they move east of Arracourt

191 (-)
155

A 37

ARRACOURT

8

5

8

7

6

RÉCHI

BURES

94 (-)

During the course of the fighting, US tank and tank destroyer units are supported by the 155mm howitzers of the 191st Field Artillery Battalion and M7 105mm howitzer motor carriages of the 66th and 94th Armored Field Artillery Battalion in the vicinity of Arracourt

C 24 (-)

A E 116

C

After word arrives of encounters between tank destroyers and Panthers near Réchicourt, Task Force Hunter moves off the high ground and attacks German columns, destroying nine Panther tanks for a loss of three M4 tanks

X
111

Pz. Brig. 111, sent down the wrong road by a French farmer, arrive near Bures and the Parroy reservoir around 1430, too late to take part in helping Pz. Brig. 113 with the day's fighting

GERMAN TROOPS
A Pz. Brig. 113
B Pz. Gr. Regt. 2113
C Pz. Brig. 111

US TROOPS
1 Co. A 37th Tank Bn.
2 Co. B 37th Tank Bn.
3 Co. C 37th Tank Bn.
4 Co. D 37th Tank Bn.
5 704th Tank Destroyer Bn.
6 66th Armd. Field Arty. Bn.
7 94th Armd. Field Arty. Bn.
8 191st Armd. Field Arty. Bn.

TANK BATTLE AT ARRACOURT, 19 SEPTEMBER 1944

Under pressure from Berlin, Manteuffel sent Pz. Brig. 113 to destroy the dispositions of the US 4th Armd. Corps around Arracourt.

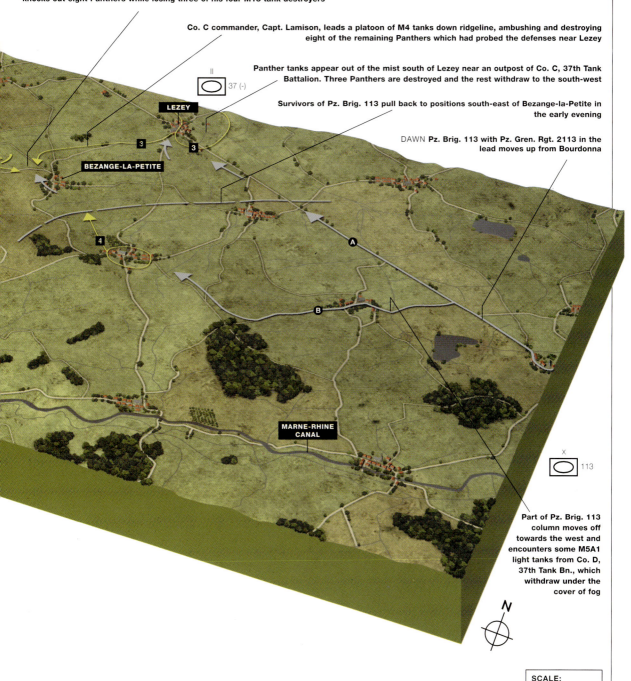

0730 Capt. William Dwight, who first encountered the German columns, returns to Arracourt and collects a platoon of M18 tank destroyers which he leads eastward. Near Bezange, he encounters the left wing of Pz. Brig. 113 and in the ensuing duel knocks out eight Panthers while losing three of his four M18 tank destroyers

Co. C commander, Capt. Lamison, leads a platoon of M4 tanks down ridgeline, ambushing and destroying eight of the remaining Panthers which had probed the defenses near Lezey

Panther tanks appear out of the mist south of Lezey near an outpost of Co. C, 37th Tank Battalion. Three Panthers are destroyed and the rest withdraw to the south-west

Survivors of Pz. Brig. 113 pull back to positions south-east of Bezange-la-Petite in the early evening

DAWN Pz. Brig. 113 with Pz. Gren. Rgt. 2113 in the lead moves up from Bourdonna

LEZEY

BEZANGE-LA-PETITE

MARNE-RHINE CANAL

37 (-)

113

Part of Pz. Brig. 113 column moves off towards the west and encounters some M5A1 light tanks from Co. D, 37th Tank Bn., which withdraw under the cover of fog

N

SCALE:
10Km x 20Km
6 miles x 12 miles

WEATHER:
Foggy

Lezey. On the way to Lezey, near Bezange-la-Petite, the platoon
encountered the lead elements of the western spearhead of Pz. Brig. 113.
Unnoticed in the thick fog, the M18s deployed in a shallow depression
and began engaging the German tanks at a range of only 150 yards from
hull-down positions. In the sharp firefight that ensued, seven German
tanks were knocked out, but three of the four M18 Hellcats were put out
of action as well. The German column retreated.

Pz. Brig. 113 continued its attack towards Réchicourt-la-Petite.
Another platoon of M18 Hellcats of the 704th Tank Destroyer Battalion
struck at one of the German columns, knocking out eight Panthers and
causing the attack to falter. By mid-afternoon, the tank destroyers had
knocked out 19 tanks but had suffered significant casualties, including
the battalion commander, who was killed by mortar fire.

As the tank fighting intensified, Abrams radioed his scattered tank
companies, ordering them to rally near Arracourt. In the early afternoon,
Cos. A and B were united under Task Force Hunter and sent to counterattack near Réchicourt. The ensuing tank battle led to the destruction of
nine more Panther tanks, at a cost of three M4 medium tanks.

Patton visited Arracourt late that day and talked with Gen. Wood, the
divisional commander. Wood indicated that his units had destroyed 43
enemy tanks during the fighting, mostly factory-fresh Panthers, at a cost
of six killed and three wounded, plus three M18 tank destroyers and five
M4 tanks knocked out. Patton believed that the German strength in the
area had been spent, and he ordered Wood to continue the advance on
Saareguemines the next day.

The opportunity to hit the 4th Armd. Div. with a concentrated blow
by two panzer brigades was foiled by poor map-reading. Pz. Brig. 111 did

not reach the Arracourt area until the middle of the afternoon, and played no role in the day's fighting. The 58th Panzer Corps commander estimated that his units had lost 50 tanks destroyed or damaged during the day's fighting. Blaskowitz was furious at the failure of the 58th Panzer Corps and ordered Manteuffel to continue the attack the next day regardless of the casualties.

In the early morning of 20 September, CCA of 4th Armd. Div. moved out from the area near Lezey on their planned offensive. They had reached Dieuze when the division's rear elements near Arracourt reported that the German tanks were attacking again from the Parroy woods towards the town. This time, it was the tanks of Pz. Brig. 111 which had missed the previous day's battle. About eight German tanks had appeared out of the mist about 1,000 yards from the 191st Field Artillery Battalion as it was preparing to limber up and move out. The 155mm howitzers were quickly swung around and began to take the tanks under fire at point-blank range. A small number of tanks and tank destroyers from other units showed up, and the panzer attack was beaten off under intense fire.

Col. Abrams ordered the 37th Tank Bn. back towards Lezey to clear the area of German tanks once and for all. In the meantime, Capt. Junghannis's PzKpfw IV company, supported by anti-tank guns, took up ambush positions on the approaches to the area where the earlier fighting had taken place. When Co. C, 37th Tank Bn. crested the rise, they were hit with a volley from the tanks and anti-tank guns below, losing a half-dozen M4 tanks in a few seconds. The Americans pulled back over the rise and waited for Co. B to reach them. After forming up, the two companies maneuvered to gain a better position and in the ensuing tank fighting, knocked out 11 German tanks while losing

A medic from the 37th Tank Bn. tends to a wounded tank crew while the fighting rages in the field above, near Arracourt on 24 September 1944. Several tanks are silhouetted against the skyline. (US Army)

another six themselves. A further five Panthers were knocked out later in the afternoon when the American task force reached Bures.

While CCA, 4th Armd. Div. was fighting with the panzers for most of 20 September, CCB was attacking near Chateau Salins, threatening to drive a wedge between Manteuffel's Fifth Panzer Army and the First Army to the north.

Blaskowitz was becoming increasingly frustrated by Manteuffel's failures and accused him of limiting his units to defensive action. Pz. Brig. 113 had remained largely inactive during the fighting on 20 September, and Pz. Brig. 111 had managed to put only a couple of companies of tanks into action during the whole day, having bungled their part in the previous day's attack. Manteuffel, in turn, complained about the poor combat value of the panzer brigades, but he was lectured by Blaskowitz on tactics. When American tanks pushed German troops out of Moncourt later in the evening, Manteuffel used it as an excuse to request a general withdrawal of the 57th Panzer Corps east of the Parroy woods. Outraged, Blaskowitz ordered him to counterattack again the next day.

TANK DUEL: Panthers emerge from the early morning mist near Arracourt and are taken under fire at close range by M4 medium tanks of Co. C, 37th Tank Bn., 4th Armd. Div.

Hitler was furious to learn that the carefully husbanded panzer brigades had been squandered with so little effect and that his plans for an early and quick victory over Patton had been frustrated. On 21 September, he sacked Blaskowitz and replaced him with General Hermann Balck, who that same day ordered a shift in plans. The focus was now coming north of Arracourt, from around Chateau Salins. A combined operation by First Army and Fifth Panzer Army would aim at seizing the key road junction at Moyenvic. This confused the effort even more, since most of the German armor was south of Arracourt. As a result, there was little fighting on 21 September while the Germans shuffled their command.

The German attack on the morning of 22 September got off to a late start due to the tardy arrival of an infantry battalion. The northern flank of CCA, 4th Armd. Div. was screened by elements of 25th Cav. Sqn. In the thick morning fog, the German columns managed to get close to the cavalry outposts before being observed. A series of skirmishes broke out, in which seven M5A1 light tanks of Co. F were knocked out while desperately trying to fend off attacks by the much more powerful German tanks. The German attack was blunted when it ran into a thin

screen of M18 Hellcat tank destroyers of Co. C, 704th Tank Destroyer Battalion. This knocked out three German tanks. The late start of the attack meant that the fog was starting to lift, and this made the German columns vulnerable to air attack. For the first time in several days, the P-47 Thunderbolts of the XIX TAC came roaring over the battlefield, strafing and bombing the German columns.

While the cavalry screen delayed the German attack, Abrams reoriented the 37th Tank Bn. northward and occupied a hill near Trois Crois which looked down into the valley east of Juvelize, where the German reinforcements were moving forward. Co. A, 37th Tank Bn. took the German tanks under fire at ranges of 400 to 2,000 yards as well as calling in field artillery fire on them. During the fighting, the Pz. Brig. 111 commander, Col. Heinrich von Bronsart-Schellendorf, was killed by machine-gun fire. Some of his officers felt that he had given up hope after another tongue lashing earlier in the morning from Manteuffel, and had carelessly exposed himself to hostile fire.

The retreating German columns were pounded by artillery fire from M7 105mm HMCs and by the continued attacks of P-47 Thunderbolts. After the Luftwaffe refused his pleas for air support, Manteuffel committed his last armored reserve – the surviving tanks from Pz. Brig. 113. This had no perceptible effect. By the end of the day, Pz. Brig. 111 was down to seven tanks and 80 men from an original strength of over 90 tanks and 2,500 troops. The following day, the Pz. Brig. 113 commander, Col. Erich von Seckendorf, was killed when his half-track command vehicle was strafed by a P-47 from the 405th Group.

In the three days of fighting from 19 to 22 September, the 4th Armd. Div.'s Combat Command A had lost 14 M4 medium and seven M5A1 light tanks as well as 25 men killed and 88 wounded. In return they had effectively shattered two panzer brigades.

Any thoughts of reinforcing the Fifth Panzer Army with more armor were rejected by Hitler due to the significant shifts in the strategic situation in late September. The Lorraine panzer offensive had been planned in early September, when Hitler had thought that Patton's thrust would be the first to reach German soil. By late September, it was becoming obvious that the Allies had other plans. On 17 September, two days before the Lorraine panzer attacks had started in earnest, the Allies had staged Operation Market-Garden, a massive airborne operation in the Netherlands combined with a tank thrust by the British 21st Army Group aimed at seizing the Arnhem River to strike into the Rhine from the north. This was supported by an intensified attack by Hodges' First Army in Belgium. Furthermore, on 15 September, the US 3rd Armd. Div. had punched a hole through the Westwall, threatening the German city of Aachen. By 24 September, after the first series of Lorraine tank battles had ended, Rundstedt was pleading with Hitler to shift the surviving armor northward to prevent an American entry into Aachen. Although Hitler would not provide any more reinforcements, neither would he abandon his plans in Lorraine. The belated arrival of the 11th Pz. Div. marked a new stage in the Lorraine tank fighting.

Bradley contacted Patton on 23 September and informed him that due to a lack of supplies, the Third Army would have to take up defensive positions. The 6th Armd. Div. was being taken away from him, so the armored forces needed for a drive on the Rhine would not be available. Furthermore, Haislip's XV Corps would be shifted to the 6th Army Group at the end of the month, removing a second armored division and leaving Patton with only two. The next day, Patton met with his three corps commanders, Walker, Eddy, and Haislip, and they agreed on a line that could be defended by the remaining forces.

The German attacks resumed on 24 September. Based on Balck's new plan, the focus shifted to the formations of the German First Army, mainly the 559th Volksgrenadier Division supported by remaining tanks of Pz. Brig. 106. The CCB of 4th Armd. Div. was holding a screening position in front of the 35th Inf. Div. near Chateau Salins when the Germans began the attack with a heavy concentration of artillery around 0830. Two regiments of infantry attacked the CCB positions, combined with a tank attack on the right flank. The 80 percent cloud cover made flying inadvisable, but two squadrons of P-47s were vectored into the area using radar. Around 1000, the P-47s found a gap in the clouds and made a skip-bombing attack on the Panthers from an altitude of about 15 feet, then returned to strafe. Within 15 minutes, the German attack had collapsed and they withdrew, leaving behind about 300 dead and 11 tanks. Patton recommended the Medal of Honor for the pilot who led the attack.

As Balck quickly realized, First Army did not have the resources to attack the American positions. Once again the focus shifted to Fifth Panzer Army. By the following day, Manteuffel had managed to scrape together about 50 tanks, including 16 from the newly arrived 11th Pz. Div. By this stage, the panzer brigades had been decimated and were no longer fit for operations. Manteuffel received permission to merge their tanks and troops with the divisions which could utilize their remaining resources. Pz. Brig. 111 went to the 11 Pz. Div.; Pz. Brig. 112 to 21 Pz. Div.; and Pz. Brig. 113 to 15 Pz. Gren. Div. Manteuffel did not want a repeat of the 22 September fighting and had troops scout the US lines in advance of the attack. Reconnaissance indicated that the crossroads town of Moyenvic was unoccupied on the evening of 24 September, so this became the initial objective of the attack. A quick and largely uncontested advance in the morning convinced Manteuffel to continue the offensive, and attacks were launched all along the salient held by CCA, 4th Armd. Div. The attacks were all beaten back, as the Americans held the high ground and had an advantage in both tanks and artillery.

As a result of the 24 September decision to shift Third Army over to the defensive, on 25 September, the CCA was ordered to withdraw about two miles from its exposed positions around Juvelize, back towards Arracourt to create a more defensible line. The CCA commander, Col. Bruce Clarke, selected the Arracourt region as the hills around the town gave his unit a good vantage point, looking down on German positions in the neighboring area. The withdrawal was also marked by a shift in the composition of the forces. Abrams' 37th Tank Bn. was pulled back to rest and refit, and the line was now held by three of 4th Armd. Div.'s armored infantry battalions. Realignment was completed on 26 September, and the German attacks would now be faced by dismounted armored infantry dug in along the crest of the hills to the south and east of Arracourt.

Manteuffel used the uncontested withdrawal by Clarke's CCA to claim a local victory, and Fifth Panzer Army occupied Juvelize and Coincourt.

On 27 September, the German attacks resumed. By this time, the armored forces in the sector consisted of 24 Panthers, six PzKpfw IVs, and some assault guns. Manteuffel sought to secure two hills on the southern

JABO STRIKE: An aerial view of P-47 D-25 Thunderbolts of the 405th Fighter Group, XIX TAC as they go out on a tank-hunting mission over Lorraine.

flank of the 4th Armd. Div. positions which overlooked the Fifth Panzer Army positions. The aim of the attack was to seize the camel-back plateau of Hills 318 and 293. He ordered Gen. Wietersheim to concentrate a battlegroup in an attack from Bures towards Arracourt. Kampfgruppe Hammon consisted of the remnants of Pz. Brig. 113 and the division's reconnaissance battalion with about 25 tanks. From his experience on the Western Front, Wietersheim was opposed to concentrating all the armor, feeling that it would be too vulnerable to air and artillery attack; based on his Eastern Front experience, Manteuffel was equally adamant that the armor be concentrated and not committed piecemeal.

The assault started with a diversionary advance by the rest of the division on the eastern end of the salient which seized Lezey and Ley, while Pz. Gren. Rgt. 111 supported by a few tanks occupied the village of Bezange-la-Petite below the positions of the 10th Armd. Inf. Bn. on Hill 265. The German infantry clawed their way to the top of Hill 265, but in bitter fighting were finally pushed off the hill. Lt. James Field received the Medal of Honor for gallantry in the clash. The position on Hill 265 was reinforced by a platoon of tank destroyers and a platoon of engineers, and another German attack at 2150 that night was successfully pushed back. On the north-east flank, Pz. Gren. Rgt. 110 moved into Xanrey, but while regrouping around 1600, it was hit by a counterattack by M4 tanks of the 35th Tank Bn., losing 135 grenadiers and being forced to retreat.

The main attack by the German battlegroup began around 1000 but moved only 1,800 yards when brought under intense fire from six field artillery battalions supporting Clarke's CCA. The German attack was halted and the panzers withdrew. Gen. Wietersheim shifted the 2nd battalion of 110th Pz. Gren. Rgt. to support the southern sector, and the next day the attack resumed. The panzer grenadiers infiltrated past the farm at the base of Hill 318, and after bitter fighting, Kampfgruppe Hammon reached the top of the hill and the edge of the neighboring woods. The crest of Hill 318 became the focus of the fighting over the next few days.

The crew of a PzKpfw IV command tank, the company commander in the center, from Pz Abt 2111 of Pz. Brig. 111 shortly before the tank fighting around Arracourt in late September. The tank has the armor skirts around the turret and the command radio antenna is evident over the shoulder of the second tanker from the left. The captain is decorated with the Iron Cross First and Second Class and also wears the insignia for those who served in the Crimea campaign on the Eastern Front in 1942. (USNA)

The panzer grenadiers of Pz. Brig. 111 check their weapons prior to another attack on Arracourt in late September 1944 while French townspeople look on. (USNA)

Manteuffel's orders for the next day were blunt: "Take Hills 293 and 318, then press farther toward the north-west in the direction of Arracourt." At dawn on 28 September, the 51st Armd. Inf. Bn. retook the forward slope of Hill 318, but the fighting surged across the crest during the day. There were 107 fighter-bomber sorties in the fighting, with the P-47s leveling the village of Bures and badly disrupting the German reinforcements concentrated there. After pushing back three more German attacks, the GIs retook Hill 318 around noon. The German grenadiers had received little artillery support, since the batteries had moved to new positions during the night and their forward observers were not in place until later in the day.

A GI inspects one of the StuG III assault guns knocked out during the fighting around Luneville. The side Schurzen, or armor shields, dubbed "bazooka pants" by the GIs, are missing, but their attachment rails are evident. Although widely believed to be a form of protection against bazookas, PIATs, and other shaped-charge anti-tank weapons, they were in fact used as protection against Soviet anti-tank rifles, and so were often removed on the Western Front, where they had no defensive value. Indeed, they would enhance the penetration of a bazooka warhead by optimizing the stand-off distance to the main armor. (US Army)

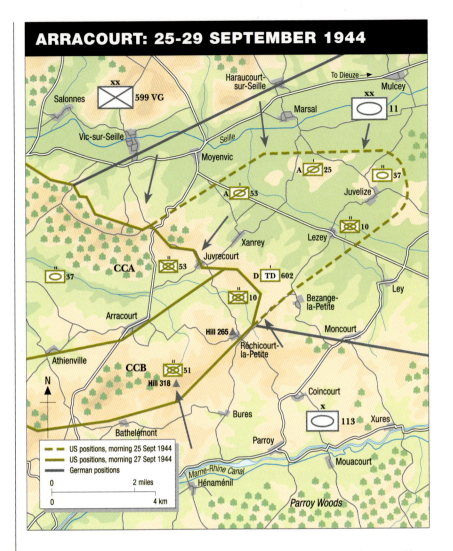

Salonnes · 599 VG · Vic-sur-Seille · Haraucourt-sur-Seille · Marsal · To Dieuze → · Mulcey · 11 · Seille · Moyenvic · A 25 · 37 · A 53 · Juvelize · 10 · Lezey · Xanrey · Juvrecourt · CCA · 53 · 37 · D TD 602 · 10 · Ley · Bezange-la-Petite · Arracourt · Hill 265 · Moncourt · Réchicourt-la-Petite · Athienville · CCB · 51 · Hill 318 · N · Coincourt · Bures · 113 · Xures · Bathélemont · Parroy · Mouacourt · Marne-Rhine Canal · Hénaménil · Parroy Woods

- - - US positions, morning 25 Sept 1944
——— US positions, morning 27 Sept 1944
——— German positions

0 ___ 2 miles
0 ___ 4 km

A final German daylight attack was broken up by American artillery fire before it could reach its objective. After dark, the Germans sent in another assault force, supported by tanks, which secured the south face of the hill. The 51st Armored Infantry withdrew to the north slope, but were hit by a heavy German artillery barrage. The 4th Armd. Div. responded by a four artillery battalion fire-strike on the south slope, followed by a 51st Armored Infantry counterattack which secured the southern high ground around midnight.

The fighting on neighboring Hill 265 was nearly as intense. At 1900, a German infantry attack against Co. A, 10th Armd. Inf. Bn. forced one of its platoons to pull back, but the attackers were brought under intense American artillery fire. Wietersheim requested to Manteuffel that his troops be allowed to break off the attacks to get some rest or they would simply lose their combat effectiveness. Manteuffel refused and, under extreme pressure from Berlin, he insisted that the attacks continue.

By dawn of 29 September, the 11th Pz. Div. had reinforced its units opposite Hills 265 and 318 from other sectors. Massing near the smoldering ruins of Bures, its forces included the reconnaissance regiment of the 11th Pz. Div., a battalion from Pz. Gren. Rgt. 110, an

A German StuG III assault gun lies in ruins, its engine deck blown off, in the outskirts of Luneville on 27 September 1944. The StuG III was used primarily to provide direct fire support for German infantry formations, but its 75mm gun was also effective against Allied tanks. This is probably one of the StuG IIIs from Pz. Brig. 111 lost in the fighting there. (US Army)

armored engineer company, and the remaining armor of Panzer Brigades 111 and 113. The armored strength in the sector included 18 PzKpfw IVs, 20 Panthers, and 11 Flakpanzer IVs. Another attack on Hill 318 pushed the 51st Armd. Inf. Bn. back about 500 yards, and the Germans had reoccupied the forward crest of the hill by 1015.

Given the heavy casualties suffered by the 51st Armd. Inf. Bn., Col. Clarke ordered forward a company of M4 medium tanks from the 8th Tank Bn. They reached the beleaguered infantry during the morning, and in the course of the day's fighting were credited with knocking out eight more panzers. As the morning fog lifted, a tactical air liaison officer with the group directed P-47 Thunderbolt strikes on the panzers in the field below Hill 318, where they were massing for another attack. Without the fog for protection, the troops were exposed. The initial air attacks were ineffective, as the fighter-bombers were diverted from a planned mission over Metz armed only with propaganda leaflets. However, during the course of the day, the 405th Fighter Group carried out several low-altitude air strikes against the German forces preparing to assault the hill. Besides knocking out tanks with bombs and rocket fire, the air strikes managed to drive a number of German tanks out of the cover of woods, where they were then struck by artillery fire.

By the middle of the afternoon, the German troops were in full retreat. After three days of intense fighting, with little sleep and heavy casualties, many of the German units had disintegrated, and the commander of Kampfgruppe Bode suffered a nervous breakdown. The German staging area at the base of the plateau had the Marne Canal at its back, and many of the troops feared that the Americans might charge down off the plateau and trap them against the water. The 15th Pz. Gren. Div. was forced to set up a straggler line with tanks near Parroy in an attempt to restore some order. The surviving Flakpanzers were positioned in Parroy and Bures in an attempt to ward off the continuing air attacks, but they were almost completely ineffective. The corps commander's report to Manteuffel was blunt: "Hill triangle lost. Troops exhausted, need rest." A total of 23 tanks and several armored half-tracks had been knocked out, according to German accounts of the fighting. Only four tanks remained operational by the end of the day, though

The crew of an M4 medium tank, commanded by Sgt. Timothy Dunn of the 37th Tank Bn., bed down for the night in a field to the north-east of Arracourt on the evening of 26 September 1944. The crewman at the front of the tank is removing the Culin device, a set of steel prongs designed to cut through the thick hedgerows found in Normandy.

stragglers continued to filter back to German lines over the next day. Tanks that had been abandoned were attacked and burned out by P-47 fighter-bombers.

The fighting on neighboring Hill 265 was mainly directed against the right flank held by Co. A, 10th Armd. Inf. Bn. The GIs were finally pushed back to the reverse slope of the hill, but held their positions at nightfall. Exhausted, the German infantry withdrew into the town of Bezange below. Some German units remained trapped on the hills between Hills 265 and 318 but escaped under the cover of darkness when it became apparent that the other battlegroups were withdrawing.

The attack on 29 September represented the last major attempt by Fifth Panzer Army to cut off the Third Army's spearhead near Arracourt. The last four days of attacks on CCA, 4th Armd. Div. had already cost the Fifth Panzer Army about 700 killed and 300 wounded, as well as 14 PzKpfw IVs and 22 Panther tanks. Of the 262 tanks and assault guns deployed by the German units in the week of fighting near Arracourt, 86 were destroyed and only 62 were operational at the end of the month. The 4th Armd. Div., which had borne the brunt of the Arracourt tank fighting, lost 41 M4 medium tanks and seven M5A1 light tanks during the whole month of September. Casualties were 225 killed and 648 wounded.

On 29 September, while the fighting was still raging on the hills south of Arracourt, the new Army Group G commander, Gen. Balck, visited the Western Front commander, von Rundstedt at his HQ in Bad Kreuznach. Balck told the field marshal that if his forces did not receive reinforcements with at least 140 tanks and more artillery, it would be impossible to continue any offensive actions. Von Rundstedt replied that reinforcements were out of the question, and he tacitly accepted that the Lorraine panzer offensive would come to an end without fulfilling Hitler's objective. At 2300 hours, Balck told Manteuffel to call off the attack. The battered 11th Pz. Div. would be pulled out of the line and defensive positions secured. Hitler, preoccupied with the airborne assault at Arnhem and the penetrations of the Westwall near Aachen, ignored yet another defeat of his preposterous schemes.

STALEMATE

By the end of September, the Lorraine fighting had ended in stalemate. Deprived of units and supplies, Patton's Third Army was in no position to plan further offensives. Yet September had seen real accomplishments. Patton's aggressive actions during the month, in spite of frequent supply shortfalls, had pushed his Third Army over the formidable barrier of the Moselle. Under a less aggressive commander, the Third Army would not have crossed the river and would have faced the daunting task of making the crossing in winter against a more firmly established German line. The Lorraine operations in September 1944 placed the Third Army in a firm position for later operations against the Saar and was instrumental in Patton's ability to conduct the rescue of Bastogne two months later, during the Ardennes fighting.

The controversies surrounding Eisenhower, Bradley, and Montgomery over strategic issues have obscured the role played by the Third Army in the broader context of Allied operations in September. In Normandy, the British forces had acted as a magnet, attracting German panzer forces and allowing the US offensive at St. Lo. In September, Patton's aggressive actions in Lorraine attracted the bulk of the panzer forces, permitting the British forces to conduct their bold Market-Garden offensive relatively unhindered by tank attack. Without Patton's actions in Lorraine, Market-Garden would have had even less chance of success and other Allied actions in Belgium would have faced stiffer resistance.

Patton's ambitions to push his forces beyond the Westwall and into the Saar in September proved impossible. This was not due to any

A tanker of the HQ company of 37th Tank Bn., Private Kenneth Boyer, on board his M4 (105mm) assault gun on 26 September 1944 during the Arracourt fighting. The M4 105mm assault gun resembled the normal M4 tank, but instead of a 75mm gun, it had a 105mm howitzer. These assault guns were attached to the headquarters companies of tank battalions to provide direct and indirect fire support.

tactical failure: the strategic planning of SHAEF placed greater emphasis on operations north of the Ardennes and allotted vital supplies accordingly. The Metz fortress prevented the advance of XX Corps, and the attacks by Fifth Panzer Army in late September derailed a narrow thrust by XII Corps. It is quite possible that Patton would have been able to push beyond the Westwall had the Fifth Panzer Army counterattacks not taken place or had he been allotted additional forces and supplies. The chief of staff of Army Group G, Col. Frederich von Mellenthin, later argued that Patton could have penetrated into Germany in mid-September if he had had the resources, since German reserves in the area were so weak. Distracted by the debates over the broad versus narrow front, and the resulting compromise decision to stage Operation Market-Garden, Eisenhower opted for the safe course in Lorraine and instructed Patton to cool his heels on the eastern bank of the Moselle. An opportunity in Lorraine and the Saar was given up for a riskier but potentially more lucrative gamble in Holland.

Total Third Army armored vehicle losses in September included 49 light tanks and 151 medium tanks and tank destroyers. A total of 392 tanks were issued in September, so by the end of the month, Third Army had more than replaced all of its losses.

From a German perspective, the Lorraine fighting had mixed results. Fifth Panzer Army had been shattered and was incapable of any further attacks. Hitler's plans to cut off Patton's forces were grossly unrealistic given the disparity in forces in the region. While offensives by German panzer forces at near parity strength to their adversary may have been successful on the Eastern Front, they were not possible against the US Army in 1944. Both German panzer counteroffensives in the late summer of 1944 had failed – the August attack by the 47th Panzer Corps and the 1st SS Panzer Corps at Mortain, and the September operation by

One of the heaviest field artillery weapons in US Army service during the war was the M1 240mm howitzer. It could fire a 360lb high explosive round to a range of about five miles. This weapon from the 278th Field Artillery Battalion is in support of Third Army operations in Lorraine on 29 September 1944. (US Army)

the Fifth Panzer Army near Arracourt. In both cases, the German forces had enjoyed advantages in armored vehicle strength in the attacking sector but had been unable to exploit these advantages due to US superiority in firepower and the declining offensive skills of the German forces. Even someone as deluded as Hitler drew the appropriate lessons from these two failed counteroffensives. Mortain and Arracourt were to Hitler's later Ardennes offensive as Dieppe was to the Allied Normandy offensive: a clear reminder that half-hearted operations against a skilled opponent had no chance of success. In late September, with the prospects for success in Lorraine evaporating, Hitler began plans for Operation Wacht-am-Rhein, the Ardennes counteroffensive. No longer underestimating the US Army, he planned a breakthrough operation by 26 German divisions against four American divisions.

Although the panzer counteroffensive against Patton had failed, this can obscure the more important consequence of German operations. In late August 1944, Allied leaders had believed that Germany was on the brink of collapse. By late September 1944, they were not so optimistic. After the catastrophic defeats in the summer of 1944, the Wehrmacht had recovered and re-established a firm defensive position along the western German frontier. The September recovery is appropriately called "the miracle in the west" in German histories. Commanders like Blaskowitz seldom attract attention in the same way as the more flamboyant leaders such as Model and Manteuffel, but his skilled and patient efforts were instrumental in re-establishing a firm German defensive line in front of the Westwall. While these actions reaffirmed the reputation of the Wehrmacht for its tenacity in adversity, the strategic

The US Army continued to locate disabled and abandoned equipment from the Arracourt fighting for weeks afterwards. Here, a GI is seen in the commander's cupola of a PzKpfw IV medium tank near Grandvillars on 18 October 1944. The turret is traversed to the rear to discourage US troops from firing on it. (US Army)

consequences for Germany were tragic, ensuring a further seven months of war and millions of additional civilian casualties, mostly in Germany itself.

Of the 616 tanks and assault guns committed to the Lorraine fighting in September, there were only 127 still operational by 1 October. Losses had amounted to 101 PzKpfw IVs, 118 Panthers, and 221 assault guns and tank destroyers. A further 148 armored vehicles were on hand but were damaged and in need of repair. German losses in men and equipment in Lorraine were far higher than those of the Americans – and far more difficult to replace.

The popular myth of the superiority of German tanks in combat in north-west Europe is belied by the record of their actual performance. In an engagement of the type seen around Arracourt, with both sides in an offensive posture and neither side enjoying particular numerical advantage, panzer units were overcome by superior American training and tactics. While airpower played an important role in some encounters, such as Dompaire, most of the fighting took place under rainy and foggy conditions where airpower could not intervene to a significant extent. German tanks and anti-tank guns could still exact a painful toll against American tanks when skillfully employed from defensive positions, as would be evident in the remaining months of the war. However, the same was true of American tank and tank destroyer units, as was seen in the difficult opening weeks of the Ardennes offensive, when the panzer offensive was stopped in its tracks far short of its objectives. Unlike the Eastern Front, there were very few meeting engagements or offensive panzer operations in north-west Europe in 1944-45, so perceptions of the relative merits of German and Allied armoured unit performance is skewed by the natural advantages enjoyed by a force fighting almost exclusively on the defensive. The German tank units of 1944-45 were only an emaciated reflection of their glory days in 1939-43.

THE BATTLEFIELD TODAY

Like most World War II battlefields, there are few signs of the conflict in Lorraine in 1944. Lorraine may be a traditional warpath between Germany and France, but it is also a natural trade route which has prospered in the half-century since World War II. Its rivers, roads, and canals, and its proximity to French and German industrial regions have made it a natural business center. Traces of war disappear quickly from the countryside, but the farmlands where the battles were fought are certainly closer to their wartime appearance than the towns and cities.

There are no major museums to the Lorraine campaign in the area. This is not surprising, given the relative scale of military events in the region over the past several centuries, such as at neighboring Verdun. Indeed, World War I memorials outnumber World War II memorials by a large measure, and it is hard to find a town without a remembrance of the valiant poilus of 1914-18. However, many of the towns in the area have small memorials to the September fighting. For example, in the hamlet of Mairy, there is a street named Rue de 8 Septembre 1944 after the fighting there between Pz. Brig. 106 and the 90th Infantry Division, and most towns have small plaques identifying historical sites.

The most extensive memorial is to Gen. Jacques Leclerc and the French 2nd Armored Division. It is located appropriately enough between the towns of Dompaire and Lamerey. There is an M4A1 on display at the site in the markings of *Corse*, the command tank of Adjutant-Chef Titeux of the 3rd Platoon, 2nd Squadron of the 12e Régiment des Chasseurs d'Afrique. However, the tank named *Corse* that fought at Dompaire was an M4A2 serial number 420050 and the M4A1 tank on display may have been the one that replaced it in 1945.

Not surprisingly, tanks have proven to be one of the most popular forms of memorial to the fighting in Lorraine. In the town of Arracourt, opposite a World War I memorial, is an M4A4 medium tank in the markings of Co. A, 37th Tank Bn., 4th Armd. Div. This tank has battle damage on the left side, but is an ex-French Army vehicle, since the US Army seldom used the M4A4 in combat and 4th Armd. Div. at the time was equipped with the M4 version of this tank series. Another M4 is preserved in Ville-sur-Illon to commemorate the fighting by the GTL Langlade HQ. There is an M4A1 (76mm) in US Army markings on display in the Place Stanislas at Laxou outside Nancy, but it is not clear whether this tank was an actual veteran of the fighting or an ex-French Army tank. An M8 75mm HMC in French 2nd Armored Division markings is preserved at Andelot as a memorial to the fighting on 11/12 September 1944, and an M4A1 medium tank is preserved at Dijon to celebrate the link-up between Patton's Third Army and Devers' 6th Army Group.

Remarkably enough, at least four more armored vehicles have survived from the Lorraine fighting, though they are located elsewhere. Two of the

Panther tanks that were recovered by the French 2nd Armored Division in Dompaire were sent back to Paris in 1944 to celebrate the victory. For many years, they sat outside the gates of the Invalides military museum in central Paris, emblazoned with the division's Cross-of-Lorraine insignia on their glacis plate. About a decade ago, they were removed to the tank museum at the French Army cavalry school at Saumur. The hull of a third Panther was fished out of the Parroy lake, where it had become trapped in 1944, and this too ended up in Saumur. Finally, an M10 tank destroyer of the RBFM which fought at Dompaire, named *Siroco*, was also preserved and is currently on display in Saumur. Commanded by Second-maitre Krokenberger and serving with the 3rd Platoon, 4th Squadron of the RBSM, *Sirocco* was credited with knocking out three Panther tanks during the fighting at Dompaire as part of Group Massu.

Memorials to the Lorraine fighting have also taken other forms. Two of today's most modern main battle tanks are named after tank commanders who first made their reputations in the Lorraine campaign. The US Army's current tank, the M1 Abrams, was developed in the 1970s when Creighton Abrams was the army chief-of-staff. After having personally experienced the struggle of the US Army's inadequate M4 medium tank against the German Panther at Arracourt, Abrams was determined that the new M1 tank would be superior to any it opposed. Following his death in 1974, the M1 tank was named in his honor. France followed a similar tradition, when its new main battle tank entered service in the early 1980s, naming it the Leclerc, after the commander of the French 2nd Armored Division.

A GUIDE TO FURTHER READING

This book was prepared largely through the use of superb library and archival records of the Military History Institute (MHI) of the US Army War College at Carlisle Barracks, Pennsylvania. Besides its extensive collection of records and unit histories of the US Army in Lorraine in 1944, the MHI is also the repository for a large collection of interviews with senior German commanders collected after the war by US Army historians. These include several hundred pages of interviews about the Lorraine fighting with many of the major German figures, including Manteuffel, his aide, and many other army, corps, and division commanders.

To list all the books, articles, and documents used in the preparation of this book would take many pages. Instead, the focus here is on the essential and more readily available accounts.

Omar Bradley, *A Soldier's Story* (Henry Holt, 1951). Bradley's memoirs are more detailed than Patton's on many of the controversies, and this book has been reprinted in several different editions.

H. M. Cole, *The Lorraine Campaign* (US Army, 1981). This is the official US Army account of the Lorraine campaign by the Third Army's historian and remains the best and single most essential volume on the subject. It is still in print by the US Government Printing Office.

David Eisenhower, *Eisenhower at War 1943-1945* (Random House, 1986). One of the best accounts of the 1944 Eisenhower-Montgomery controversy from Ike's perspective, written by one of his grandsons.

Carlo D'Este, *Patton: A Genius for War* (HarperCollins, 1995). An assessment of Patton by one of the younger generation of American military historians.

Ian Gooderson, *Air Power at the Battlefront: Allied Close-air Support in Europe 1943-45* (Frank Cass, 1998). An intriguing new look at the effectiveness of close-air support.

Thomas Jentz, *Panzertruppen*, Vol 2 (Schiffer, 1996). A detailed look at the organization, unit strength, tactics and other aspects of the panzer force, based on archival records.

Ronald McNair, 1944: *Les Panzers en Lorraine* (Heimdal, 1984). This is a bound edition of articles appearing in the French historical journal 39-45. It is one of the best treatments of the Arracourt tank battles from the German perspective. A shorter English treatment is available in the British journal After the Battle, No 83.

Jacques Salbaing, *La Victoire de Leclerc à Dompaire* (Muller, 1997). This short French book provides a detailed examination of the destruction of Pz. Brig. 112 at Dompaire by the French 2nd Armored Division.

George S. Patton Jr, *War As I Knew It* (Houghton-Mifflin, 1947). Patton's personal account of his role in World War II; available in many different editions.

Russell Weigley, *Eisenhower's Lieutenants: The Campaigns of France and Germany 1944-45* (Indiana Univ Press, 1981). A critical assessment of the performance of the US Army in north-west Europe, and still one of the best overviews of the US Army in the ETO.

WARGAMING OPERATIONS IN LORRAINE 1944

The campaign in Lorraine offers both a strategic situation for a high-level operational game, and a series of engagements between armored forces with widely differing morale, equipment and tactical doctrine, for a low-level battle game. It has been assumed that readers wishing to wargame this campaign will follow Hitler's original plan of operations, rather than devise and play through different plans which might be suggested by hindsight.

The View From Headquarters: Operational Map Games

If the game organizer wishes the players to take the roles of Army Group, Army or Corps commanders, he must endeavor to recreate their headquarters, devising systems that will provide incoming information about their own forces and those of the enemy, and determine the outcomes of the players' orders. A 'closed' map game, in which separate teams or individual players submit orders, based upon subjective map displays of the strategic situation and intelligence reports, to an umpire or group of umpires who maintain a central, objective campaign map, and resolve movement, logistics, combat and report back to the players, is a tried and tested structure for a successful operational wargame.

This simple structure can be adapted to most levels of the chain of command, by adjusting the volume and detail of incoming information, both from above and below, and giving players appropriate pre-game briefings. In the case of Manteuffel, this briefing could take the form of a recreation of the meeting on 5 September 1944 with Hitler, role-played by the game organizer or an umpire, who would explain the objectives of the counteroffensive and the forces available to him.

The World War II general's perspective is, in terms of his surroundings and equipment, relatively simple to recreate using large-scale maps upon which intentions and intelligence can be marked; numerous paper documents, ranging from detailed orders of battle and personal files on his subordinate commanders, to current intelligence reports. Two aspects of life at headquarters are, however, much harder to recreate. The first is the sheer volume and depth of intelligence concerning both one's own forces and enemy formations received each day; the second is the professional training and experience of the general and his staff.

Map Kriegsspiel

A more stylized version of the headquarters game for a smaller number of players, who will portray the various army or corps commanders, can be devised on the assumption that the game organizer or umpire will act as their staffs, filtering out irrelevant or unreliable information, summarizing combat and intelligence reports to present them with an

At least three of the Panther tanks participating in the Lorraine fighting have survived, including this Panther Ausf. G preserved at the French tank museum at Saumur. It was captured from Pz. Brig. 112 during the fighting with the French 2nd Armored Division at Dompaire. (Hilary Doyle)

appropriate appreciation of the current situation. An umpire moves formations according to the players' orders, resolves combat, determines expenditure of ammunition and fuel to update the logistic situation, and reports back in accordance with the degree of accuracy appropriate to each side's communication systems. Some attempt should be made to reflect the command styles of individual generals – Patton, for example, insisted upon visiting forward areas to show himself to the troops and assuage his sense of guilt at not sharing the danger of combat.

Each player must specify how his character's time will be spent during the next 24 hours, either by placing counters, labeled "Write Orders", "Inspect Troops", and "Sleep", for example, at the appropriate times of day, or by writing his actions in on a copy of the day track. Should some unforeseen event, or the arrival of fresh intelligence, require him to react, then he may change his plans for the remainder of the day (but not what he has already done), before the umpire judges he would have become aware of the situation. Less experienced or inadequate staffs, such as those of the panzer brigades, will process information more slowly, so there will be delay between events and intelligence of them reaching the general, than will be the case in an efficiently run, experienced headquarters.

The combat results table is governed by the points awarded for ammunition and fuel usage. The average of the ammunition and fuel points could determine the combat effectiveness of an armored formation in attack; but the ammunition points alone represented the strength of a unit engaged in static defense.

Each turn represents one day. The game could be played in scaled-down time with all players present, perhaps in different rooms, while the umpire updated a master map on the dining table. Alternatively, players could telephone or e-mail their initial orders and actions for the next game-day to the umpire early each evening, and receive situation reports and intelligence later that night, where there would have been time to react that day in reality, or wait until their return home the following day for the situation at the close of that game-day.

"Back-to-Back" Wargames

In a "closed" game structure, using duplicate miniature terrain displays and forces, the players move small-scale troops, vehicles and tanks of their own side on their individual displays. An umpire resolves questions of visibility, calculates the effects of artillery, tank and small-arms fire, and updates both displays by placing upon them only that which would, in reality, be visible, or known by radio communication. This has been called "back-to-back" wargaming, because such a seating arrangement, around the umpire's central model or map, prevents players observing each other's displays. It would, for example, be possible to represent GTL Langlade, or one of its battlegroups, and I/Pz. Regt. 29 quite cheaply for a scenario based upon the action at Dompaire on 13 September.

A multi-player variant of this style of game has been devised by Andy Grainger, in which players take the roles of individual M4 Sherman tank troop commanders, communicating out loud with their own tanks, and with the squadron commander. Each player has a separate table, with a simple model of the terrain immediately around his own tanks, which is updated by one of a team of umpires, who control the pre-programmed German opposition. This could be adapted very easily to portray the French perspective at Dompaire, or that of the Americans at Arracourt.

Another option is for a group of players to portray the members of the crew of one tank – M4, PzKpfw. IV or Panther. The game organizer provides precise details of the crew numbers, their responsibilities in combat, the amount and type of ammunition carried on board, and a plan of the interior of the tank. Those in the turret sit on stools so that they are above the driver and other crew members in the hull of the tank, who sit immediately in front of them, facing a detailed miniature terrain, scaled to 15mm, 20mm or 25mm model figures, upon which is a model of their own tank. The driver has a set of "flash cards", which he displays at each turn to indicate how he is controlling the tank; the gunner and/or loader have a set to show what type of ammunition is being used and a "Fire!" card; the tank commander has cards listing his duties and possible personal actions, but must communicate with his crew only by speech and physical prompts.

Ideally, all tank crew should wear personal stereos, playing deafening music to recreate the effect of motor noise within the crew compartment. Players could also wear cardboard "spectacles", with narrow slits to simulate the view through a periscope, removing them only when they put their heads up through open hatches, thus obtaining a better view of the terrain, but risking being hit by shrapnel or small-arms fire.

Each turn, the players display the appropriate flash cards to indicate their actions. An umpire moves the model of their tank accordingly, resolves questions of visibility and fire, using very simple rules to maintain the speed and tension of play, and gives the players feedback as necessary. Should their tank be hit, and the commander give the order to bale out, those in the turret must climb upon the commander's stool and jump off, while those inside the hull exit by jumping off, their own chairs – unless the umpire announces that a hatch cover has jammed, when they must exit by an alternative route. Crew members who fail to leave the tank within a specified time will be deemed to have been killed. Several tanks on the same side can participate in this type of game, provided there is an umpire familiar with the rules to monitor each tank. **96** The enemy is best pre-programmed, or controlled by another umpire.

THE ORIGINS OF THE BATTLE

The Battle of Arnhem, known by its Allied codename of Operation 'Market-Garden', was the largest airborne battle in history, and the only attempt in the Second World War by the Allies to use airborne troops in a strategic role in Europe. It was a battle of Army Groups numbering hundreds of thousands of men – 21st Army Group under Field Marshal Sir Bernard Montgomery against Army Group B under Generalfeldmarschall Walther Model – but repeatedly its outcome hinged on the actions of small forces and individual battalions at crucial points. Rather than a set-piece battle with a tidy beginning and end, it began on 17 September 1944 from a confused and daily changing pattern of events, and ended ten days later as the only major defeat of Montgomery's career, and the only Allied defeat in the campaign in North-West Europe.

The direct origin of the Battle of Arnhem was actually Montgomery's greatest victory, the Battle of Normandy (described in *Normandy 1944: Allied Landings and Breakout*, Campaign Series 1). The destruction of the original Army Group B (Seventh Army and Fifth Panzer Army) in the Falaise Pocket in August 1944 at the end of the battle was a disaster for Adolf Hitler's Third Reich. Of 38 German divisions committed to Normandy, 25 were completely destroyed, with at least 240,000 men killed or wounded, and a further 200,000 taken prisoner. Generalfeldmarschall Model, appointed on 18 August as both Commander-in-Chief West (Oberbefelshaber West or OB West) and commander of Army Group B, found himself managing the rout of his shattered forces across northern France into Belgium and Holland.

In the planning before D-Day on 6 June, the Allies had assumed that they would advance steadily inland, with General Dwight D. Eisenhower, commanding Supreme Headquarters Allied Expeditionary Forces (SHAEF), taking over the land

The Allied Pursuit, 26 August to 10 September 1944

North Sea

Kiel Canal
Kiel
Lübeck
Cuxhaven
Hamburg
Wilhelmshaven
Lüneburg
Emden
Elbe
Groningen
Bremen
Aller
Den Helder
Zuyder Zee
XXXXX
CHRISTIANSEN
Armed Forces Netherlands
Hanover
Rheine
Osnabrück
Wesser
XXXX
14 US
Amsterdam
HOLLAND
The Hague
XXXXX
Arnhem
XXXXX
MODEL
B
Paderborn
Leine
Harz Mts
XXXX
15
Rotterdam
Nijmegen
Kleve
Wesel
Hamm
Dortmund
XXX
4 BR
VON ZANGEN
Tilburg
Eindhoven
RUHR
Düsseldorf
GERMANY
Channel ports remain in German hands
9 Sept: Liberated
Ostend
Antwerp
XXXX
1
Kassel
Calais
Dunkirk
Brussels
STUDENT
Cologne
4 Sept: First Parachute Army formed
Boulogne
Maastricht
Aix
Bonn
XXXXX
OB WEST
Lille
Liège
Rhine
Remagen
ept: erated
Mons
XXXX
7
Koblenz
VON RUNDSTEDT (from 4 Sept)
ieppe
Maubeuge
Eifel Mts
EBERBACH/ BRANDENBERGER
Frankfurt
XXXX
Rouen
Amiens
ARDENNES
XXXXX
Mainz
XXXXX
G
XXX
1 CDN
XXXX
2 BR
XXXX
1 US
THE SAAR
XXXX
1
BLASKOWITZ
RAR
DEMPSEY
HODGES
Luxembourg
Mannheim
XXXXX
Seine
Rheims
XXXX
3 US
VON DER CHEVALLERIE/ VON KNOBELSDORFF
Karlsruhe
25 Aug: Liberated
Paris
PATTON
Verdun
Metz
Stuttgart
Châlons-sur-Marne
Marne
Nancy
XXXX
5
Moselle
Strasbourg
Ulm
XXXXX
12
Troyes
DIETRICH
Augsburg
BRADLEY
Yonne
Epinal
Vosges Mts
Colmar
Danube
Orléans
XXXX
19
Mulhouse
ire
XXXXX
WIESE
Basel
XXXX
1 FR
Dijon
XXXX
7 US
XXXXX
6
XXXX
DE LATTRE DE TASIGNY
11 Sept: Link between 12AG & 6AG at Dijon
PATCH
SWITZERLAND
AUSTRIA
DEVERS
Berne

▶ *As part of the creation of First Allied Airborne Army, Major General Matthew Ridgway of the 82nd ('All American') Airborne Division was promoted to command the new US XVIII Airborne Corps and succeeded by his deputy, Brigadier General James 'Slim Jim' Gavin. This picture shows the handover ceremony on 10 August. Left to right on the saluting base are Gavin, Eisenhower, Ridgway and Brereton, who is still wearing his 9th Air Force shoulder patch.*

▲ *General Eisenhower with the senior officers of Bradley's 12th Army Group, taken in May 1945 at the end of the war in Europe. Front row left to right are Lieutenant General William H Simpson commanding Ninth US Army, Patton, General Carl Spaatz commanding US Strategic and Tactical Air Forces, Eisenhower, Bradley, Hodges, and Lieutenant General*

Leonard T. Gerow, commanding Fifteenth US Army (not formed in September 1944). Standing between Eisenhower and Bradley is Lieutenant General Walter Bedell Smith, Eisenhower's chief of staff, and next to him (with peaked cap) is Lieutenant General Hoyt S. Vandenberg, who replaced Brereton commanding 9th Air Force on 7 August 1944.

battle from Montgomery after a few weeks and directing the advance of his three Army Groups – Montgomery's 21st Army Group, 12th Army Group under Lieutenant General Omar Bradley, and 6th Army Group under Lieutenant General Jacob Devers coming from southern France – on a broad front against a strong German defence. Instead, the Battle of Normandy had been weeks of hard-fought virtual stalemate followed by a sudden German collapse resulting in the Falaise pocket.

The very size of this victory was Montgomery's undoing. Success in Normandy had depended on cooperation between the various Allied members and services. Now, with the unexpected destruction

of Army Group B, many on both sides believed that history was repeating itself, and that August 1944 in France was August 1918 once more, with Germany virtually defeated and bound to surrender before the year ended. Senior Allied commanders, taught to regard a successful war as just one episode in their developing careers, began to display openly the self-interest and concern for their own futures they had kept buried during the battle.

After some delay, Eisenhower was due to assume command from Montgomery on 1 September, establishing SHAEF Headquarters at Granville in western Normandy. On 13 August, as Army Group B's encirclement was being completed, Montgomery first raised with Eisenhower the idea of changing Allied strategy to a 'single thrust' advance by his own 21st Army Group, supported by First US Army under Major General Courtney Hodges, through northern France and the Low Countries and into Germany. Montgomery's point was that German opposition against him was negligible, but that there was not enough transport to keep all three Army Groups advancing at full stretch over 500km (300 miles) from Normandy. Even the fleets of Allied transport aircraft intended to mount airborne operations were being committed to ferrying supplies to 21st and 12th Army Groups. Montgomery asked Eisenhower to appoint a ground commander to execute the

'single thrust', even offering to serve under Bradley if necessary, as long as the forces to the south gave up their supplies.

Whatever the merits of this argument, it was firmly opposed by Bradley, for whom Montgomery's conduct of the Battle of Normandy had been profoundly suspect, and who was one of several American commanders who believed that they had won Normandy *despite* Montgomery, and not *because* of him. With final victory in sight it was time for American prowess to display itself, and Montgomery and the British were no longer a factor. Montgomery's plan would also have meant halting the American troops that had advanced farthest towards Germany, Third US Army under Lieutenant General George S. Patton Jr, Montgomery's old rival.

On 23 August, Montgomery at last pressured Eisenhower into agreeing that 21st Army Group's thrust into northern France should have priority in supplies (which Montgomery chose to interpret as absolute priority), to free the English Channel ports for Allied supply ships and overrun the launch sites for the V-1 'buzz-bombs' attacking southern England. Bradley's principal mission was to support this thrust with First US Army, sending most of its divisions north of Aachen. Instead, Bradley quietly connived at Patton's continuing southern thrust towards Germany, holding First US Army back and

directing it increasingly south, away from 21st Army Group. At the end of August, as Third US Army's drive began to halt at the gates of Germany from lack of fuel, relations between Montgomery and the American generals could hardly have been worse.

Allied victory in the Battle of Normandy had also depended very heavily on massive air support for the ground troops, a duty imposed for Eisenhower on the often reluctant airmen by Allied Expeditionary Air Forces (AEAF) under the unpopular Air Chief Marshal Sir Trafford Leigh-Mallory. On 15 August, Leigh-Mallory, also believing that the war in Europe was won, started to close down AEAF Headquarters and plan for his next posting. The Allied heavy bomber forces of RAF Bomber Command and USAAF 8th Air Force went back to their preferred strategy of bombing German cities, while the SHAEF tactical air forces split along national lines, with USAAF 9th Air Force supporting 12th Army Group and RAF 2nd Tactical Air Force supporting 21st Army Group. Since the Luftwaffe (German Air Force) in the west barely existed, and the Allies enjoyed unquestioned air supremacy, this appeared not to matter.

Before D-Day, SHAEF staff had identified the need for a new headquarters to coordinate the various Allied airforces for airborne operations, and as part of the disbanding of the AEAF Eisenhower created Combined Airborne Forces Headquarters on 2 August under Lieutenant General Lewis Brereton, the highly controversial former commander of 9th Air Force, who was disliked by Bradley. On 16 August this name was changed to First Allied Airborne Army as part of the Allied deception plan based around the fictitious First US Army Group (FUSAG), which had fooled the Germans for months.

Under pressure from Washington, where Army Chief of Staff General George C. Marshall and General Henry 'Hap' Arnold, commanding the Army Air Forces, both wanted a major airborne operation mounted in Europe before the end of the war, Eisenhower placed First Allied Airborne Army under 21st Army Group control. As the Allied supply crisis and dispute over strategy worsened, it was from this tangle of conflicting interests that an airborne solution, Operation 'Market-Garden', started to emerge.

THE OPPOSING COMMANDERS

The Allied Commanders

On 1 September, Eisenhower formally took command of the ground battle from Montgomery. Next day, after conferring with Bradley, Hodges and Patton, he issued his own interpretation of priority for Montgomery, a compromise 'two thrust' strategy from north and south including Third US Army's drive in the plan. Communications from SHAEF Headquarters at Granville were very poor, with top priority messages like this taking three days or more to reach Montgomery and Bradley. On the same day Eisenhower was immobilized with a twisted knee, while political demands on his time increased when on 5 September Winston Churchill and the British Chiefs of Staff sailed for Quebec for a major strategy conference with President Roosevelt and his military advisers. In these circumstances, Eisenhower could exercise little control over the land battle or his own quarrelling subordinates.

Montgomery, as was his custom, remained at 21st Army Group Tactical Headquarters, relying on his chief of staff, Major General Francis 'Freddy' de Guingand, to represent him at SHAEF. Unfortunately, on 9 September de Guingand collapsed from exhaustion, and Montgomery sent him home to rest for a week. Montgomery regarded the 'two thrust' strategy as nothing more than the original broad front advance – which could not be sustained. Despite several meetings between Bradley and Montgomery, physical separation and communications problems compounded this breakdown in relations between 21st Army Group and the Americans.

With the activation of SHAEF, Montgomery was promoted from a general commanding all 43 SHAEF divisions to a field marshal commanding

◀ *Lieutenant General Brian Horrocks, taken in Normandy in July 1944, a few days before his collapse. Horrocks had been injured by German aircraft fire while commanding XIII Corps in Italy in June 1943, and never properly recovered. Note the very clear 'Running Boar' formation sign of XXX Corps on his shoulder. (IWM photograph B9532)*

▶ *A Cromwell tank of 1st (Armoured) Battalion of the Coldstream Guards, the Guards Armoured Division, receiving a rapturous welcome in the centre of Brussels on 4 September. The leading troops of the division reached Brussels as darkness fell on the previous day. The rapid advance of XXX Corps from the Seine came as a complete surprise to Montgomery's critics, who thought of him as a slow-moving commander, and transformed the argument for the 'single thrust' strategy. (IWM photograph BU480)*

the fourteen divisions of his own 21st Army Group: in practice, with First Canadian Army occupied clearing the Channel ports, this meant the three Army Corps (eight divisions and four armoured brigades) of Second British Army under Lieutenant General Sir Miles 'Bimbo' Dempsey. As the effective ground commander for 'Market-Garden', Dempsey remains a complete enigma, entirely under the shadow of his illustrious and autocratic superior, for whose mistakes he seemed happy to shoulder the blame.

In Normandy, Montgomery had relied for his major offensives on the talented commander of British VIII Corps, Lieutenant General Sir Richard O'Connor. However, at the start of August, Montgomery brought out an old protégé, Lieutenant General Brian Horrocks ('Jorrocks' to everyone) who was still recovering from wounds, to command British XXX Corps. On 20 August, Horrocks' health collapsed, and he fell ill with fever. Montgomery concealed this fact while Horrocks recovered, and on 26 August he placed XXX Corps at the head of Second British Army's victorious

advance north from the Seine. Horrocks commanded from a tank for the next two weeks as XXX Corps drove forward almost unopposed for 300km (200 miles), liberating Arras on 1 September, Brussels on 3 September, and Antwerp on 4 September, followed by British XII Corps under Lieutenant General Neil Ritchie. Unable to sustain all of Second British Army at this speed, Montgomery ordered VIII Corps to give up its transport and halt on the Seine, where the pragmatic O'Connor began to organize another posting for himself.

At Antwerp, XXX Corps halted, largely from exhaustion and lack of fuel. Although its sudden advance had trapped most of German Fifteenth Army under General Gustav von Zangen between the coast and the River Scheldt (Schelde) estuary, Horrocks failed to advance the short distance north of Antwerp to complete the trap. Instead, after a two-day pause, XXX Corps began to spread out eastward, trying to force the Albert and Meuse-Escaut Canals and press into Holland. On 8 September the first launch of German V-2 rockets

◀ *Frederick Arthur Montague Browning, shown with (left) Major General Stanislav Sosabowski, commanding 1st Polish Parachute Brigade which came under his command. Aged 47 in 1944 and a former Grenadier Guards officer, Browning had won the Distinguished Service Order in the First World War, and had first met Churchill when they shared a dugout together in 1916.*

against southern England from sites in northern Holland gave extra impetus to the need for Second British Army's advance.

Meanwhile, Lieutenant General Brereton was at SHAEF Headquarters seeking a role for First Allied Airborne Army. A hard-living, hard-drinking former First World War pilot with a remarkable ability to prosper from defeat, Brereton saw his role entirely as an organizer of air power, rather than as an Army commander. He was determined to fulfill General Arnold's wishes by using all three airborne divisions assigned to First Allied Airborne Army in one operation.

Brereton's Deputy Commander for First Allied Airborne Army was also the commander of British I Airborne Corps, Lieutenant General F. A. M. 'Boy' Browning. A dashing figure, he had been appointed by Churchill to command British Airborne Forces in 1941 and had built them up by political and administrative manipulation of the British military establishment as a protégé of Admiral Lord Louis Mountbatten. Disliked and distrusted by the Americans as a 'supercilious English aristocrat', Browning was anxious to lead the troops he had created into battle before the war ended.

Repeatedly during August, airborne operations had been planned and then cancelled as the speed of the Allied advance made them unnecessary. On 2 September a drop by all three divisions near Lille and Courtrai, for which Second British Army halted its own advance, was cancelled at the last moment when Bradley diverted First US Army to liberate the area instead. Matters came to a head next day when Brereton agreed with SHAEF on a new drop to be mounted on 4 September, only to discover that Browning had agreed an entirely different operation with 21st Army Group, using only I Airborne Corps to support an advance northward into Holland by XXX Corps on 6 September. Browning threatened to resign to stop Brereton's plan, leaving relations between the two men very poor. From Eisenhower to Browning and Horrocks, the Allied command chain for 'Market-Garden' was in disarray.

The German Commanders

Since 1941, Adolf Hitler had exercised direct control over German military operations from Oberkommando der Wehrmacht (OKW) Head-quarters at Rastenburg in eastern Germany. On 14 July 1944, a bomb plot to kill Hitler at Rastenburg by German Army officers had only narrowly failed, and senior German officers fought the rest of the war under a cloud of suspicion in which retreat or failure could bring arrest for treason.

▶ *Generalfeldmarschall Gerd von Rundstedt (on the far left) with (gesturing) Obergruppenführer Josef 'Sepp' Dietrich, briefly commander of Fifth Panzer Army. Von Rundstedt commanded Army Group B from 10 March 1942 until 2 July 1944, being dismissed for insubordination after his criticism of Hitler's conduct of the Battle of Normandy. He nevertheless presided over the German Army 'Court of Honour' following the assassination attempt against Hitler, and felt unable to decline Hitler's recall to active service again in September.*

▶ *Generalfeldmarschall Otto Moritz Walther Model. Aged 53 in 1944, Model had won the Iron Cross First Class and Knight's Cross with Swords in the First World War. Despite his humble origins, he always tried to appear as a Prussian aristocrat, even down to his habitual monocle. True to his own view of German military tradition, in April 1945 Model committed suicide rather than face surrender. (IWM photograph MH12850)*

The shock of Second British Army's advance brought an immediate change in the German command in the west. On 3 September, Generalfeldmarschall Gerd von Rundstedt, an elderly aristocrat whose loyalty was unquestionable, was recalled to take over OB West from Generalfeldmarschall Model, largely as an administrator, freeing Model to concentrate on Army Group B and the defence of Holland and north-west Germany. Model, a Prussian of non-aristocratic background, had earned his reputation on the Eastern Front as 'the Führer's fireman', able to take charge of a rout and turn it into a counter-attack, which was precisely the challenge he now faced. He at once signalled Rastenburg that he needed a further 25 divisions to stop the Allied drive. Next day, while Model organized the escape of Fifteenth Army across the Scheldt estuary, OKW alerted

General Kurt Student, former commander of the German airborne forces and the leading expert on their use, to take command of a new First Parachute Army under Army Group B, to be formed east of Fifteenth Army with its head-quarters at 's Hertogenbosch in central Holland. Model also ordered II SS Panzer Corps of two armoured divisions, which had been virtually destroyed in the Falaise fighting, to rally close to his own headquarters at Arnhem. The commander of II SS Panzer Corps, Obergruppenführer Wilhelm 'Willi' Bittrich, like Brereton a former pilot and a specialist in defence against airborne operations, had taken command of the Corps on 28 July and led it through the Falaise rout.

▶ *Kurt Student, shown after his promotion to Generaloberst and command of Army Group H following 'Market-Garden'. Born in 1890 of minor Prussian nobility, Student pioneered the use of German airborne forces and commanded them in France in 1940 and in the capture of Crete in 1941, the only completely successful strategic airborne operation of the war. Partly because of the high cost in casualties, the Germans mounted no further major airborne operations after Crete, and Student's career languished until September 1944. (IWM photograph MH6100)*

▶ *Left to right, Major General Allan Adair commanding the Guards Armoured Division, Montgomery, Horrocks, and Major General G. P. B. 'Pip' Roberts commanding 11th Armoured Division, which was transferred from XXX Corps to VIII Corps for 'Market-Garden', taken near the Albert Canal on Friday 15 September. Although Montgomery went to great lengths after 'Market-Garden' to distance himself from the battle, the photographic record suggests that he was heavily involved down to divisional level. Both Horrocks and Montgomery are wearing a type of sleeveless leather jerkin popular with senior British officers, the latter with an RAF flying jacket. (IWM photograph B9973)*

THE OPPOSING ARMIES

The Allied Forces

By September 1944, Second British Army had overcome most of the amateurism that marked British forces earlier in the war and was a victorious army at the height of its abilities. Even so, and although its artillery and engineers were excellent and its infantry almost unbreakable in defence, it had a reputation for slowness and poor coordination when attacking. Having borne the brunt of the heavy fighting in Normandy followed by the pursuit across France, it was also exhausted, with battle fatigue casualties running at epidemic proportions. It was badly short of troops, and to keep it up to strength Montgomery was forced to break up one division in early September. Those troops that were left, believing the war was virtually won, were increasingly reluctant to risk their lives in battle.

Second British Army had also outrun its own supplies, its tactical Intelligence, and most of its air support. Almost half of 2nd Tactical Air Force was tied up with First Canadian Army, and the rest was searching for suitable airfields in Belgium. As German resistance stiffened, Lieutenant General Dempsey became deeply concerned at the weakness of the proposed northern thrust into Holland, and Montgomery agreed to a delay until 10 September. On that day, the Guards Armoured Division under Major General Allan Adair captured an intact bridge, promptly named 'Joe's Bridge', over the

▲ *The C-47 Dakota (officially named the 'Skytrain' by the USAAF), the workhorse Allied transport aircraft of the war. This particular aircraft is in USAAF IX Troop Carrier Command service for 'Market-Garden' in September 1944. The markings on its fuselage show that it has made three paratroop drops,* *five casualty evacuation flights, and fourteen cargo flights (the 'camel' symbol). The commandeering of their aircraft for supply flights in this way was a constant source of trouble for the airborne forces. With the paratroops (probably Poles) in front of the Dakota is one of its crew, in flying jacket and baseball cap.*

Meuse-Escaut Canal (50ms wide) near Neerpelt, and became the natural choice to lead the advance of XXX Corps under the still sickly Horrocks.

Like other British armoured divisions, the Guards Armoured had abandoned its formal organization in Normandy, adopting a 'group' structure that paired an armoured battalion with a trucked battalion of the same regiment. Guardsmen were specially selected, and the division had a high reputation; but, as with other British divisions, the infantry shortage had forced it to reduce some battalions from three to two companies, and many of its recent replacements had come from other formations such as anti-aircraft artillery batteries. In all, the Guards Armoured Division probably numbered about 13,000 men and 200 tanks. After taking 1,400 casualties during two months in Normandy, it had lost a further 600 men in ten days' fighting along the Belgian canals, leaving it with few illusions about German fighting intentions.

Exact figures for higher formations have little meaning, but XXX Corps numbered at least 100,000 troops, and Second British Army more than 800,000 in total.

Also on 10 September, the still-crippled Eisenhower flew out to Brussels with his deputy, Air Chief Marshal Sir Arthur Tedder, to meet Montgomery at last. This highly charged meeting produced another change of plan. In return for the promise of more supplies from Eisenhower, Montgomery would delay his drive northwards into Holland in order to use the whole of Second British Army and First Allied Airborne Army together. The plan was codenamed 'Market-Garden', and if it

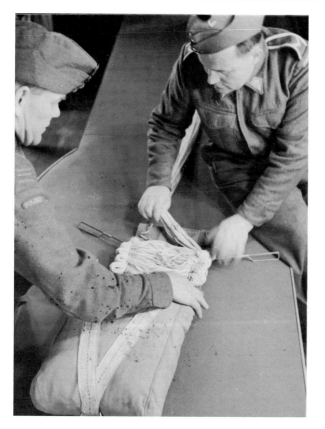

▲ *Aircrew of 1st Polish Parachute Brigade, which used British equipment, packing a parachute. Made of silk, nylon or a type of cotton, the British 'X-Type' parachute was meant to be virtually foolproof, and no reserve parachute was carried (American paratroops carried two T-5 type parachutes).*

▲ *An American paratrooper helps shoulder an equipment-carrying 'parapack' into position on board his aircraft. The man is wearing the new M1943 uniform with a US flag 'invasion patch' but no divisional patch on his other sleeve, suggesting a training exercise just before 'Market-Garden'. The wearing of a first aid pack or field dressing on the front of the helmet was common practice.*

succeeded Montgomery hoped to use it to force Eisenhower into accepting the 'single thrust' north.

During September, Lieutenant General Brereton increased First Allied Airborne Army's staff from 323 officers and men to 1,385. Its air component was about 1,300 C-47 Dakota aircraft, and 250 Albemarles, Halifaxes and Stirlings of the RAF, together with about 2,000 gliders. Transport pilots were regarded as non-combatants by the USAAF and generally ranked well below fighter and bomber crews. Unlike the Americans, British glider pilots and pathfinders were trained to fight as infantry in their own units once on the ground.

The ground element of First Allied Airborne Army was about 35,000 combat troops who would fly into action, plus a 'seaborne tail' to follow later.

US XVIII Airborne Corps Headquarters under Lieutenant General Matthew Ridgway was complete by September, but Lieutenant General Browning was still busy turning his British Airborne Forces administrative headquarters into British I Airborne Corps Headquarters. In particular, Browning's signals section was only created on 2 September, and he had no direct liaison with 2nd Tactical Air Force or other Allied airforces. Attempts very late in the planning of Operation 'Market-Garden' to provide air liaison officers resulted in failure. Like Horrocks at XXX Corps, Browning also had no Dutch liaison officer at his headquarters; however, all the airborne divisions

had Dutch liaison officers for 'Market-Garden'.

The 82nd US Airborne Division and 101st US Airborne Division each had three regiments (each three battalions strong) of parachute infantry, who were all volunteers, and one of airlanding infantry in gliders, who were not. Each division had 36 field guns, twice as many as a British airborne division. All these troops were specially trained and of the highest quality, and both they and their commanders had recent battle experience. The two divisions were busy absorbing more than 10,000 replacements for casualties suffered in Normandy.

◀ *A Sergeant Pilot of the Glider Pilot Regiment, wearing his rank badges and pilot's wings (with an enclosed letter 'G' identifying him as a Second Pilot) on the Denison smock, and armed with a Mark IV Short Magazine Lee-Enfield rifle. The other man, carrying the standard Bren light machine-gun, may belong to any of the British Airborne units at Arnhem as unit and rank badges (except for NCOs) were not normally worn on the smock. He wears an early-pattern helmet with black leather straps, and has tied his face veil as a cape over his shoulders.*

▶ *British paratroop kit being explained to King George VI at an inspection in May 1944. On display is the British version of the 'leg bag' carrying the soldier's equipment. This was released during descent to dangle beneath the paratrooper on a restraining rope to minimize the danger of injury on landing. This bag holds a PIAT (Projector Infantry Anti- Tank), with an effective range of about 50m. (IWM photograph H36712)*

ALLIED ORDER OF BATTLE

SUPREME HEADQUARTERS ALLIED EXPEDITIONARY FORCES (SHAEF)
Supreme Commander: General Dwight D. Eisenhower
Deputy Supreme Commander: Air Chief Marshal Sir Arthur Tedder
Chief of Staff: Major General Walter Bedell Smith

12th ARMY GROUP
Lieutenant General Omar N. Bradley

FIRST US ARMY (from 24 September)
Lieutenant General Courtney H. Hodges

XIX US CORPS
Major General Charles H. Corlett

2nd Armored Division
30th Infantry Division
7th Armored Division (from 27 September)
29th Infantry Division (from 27 September)
113th Cavalry Group

21st ARMY GROUP
Field Marshal Sir Bernard Montgomery
Chief of Staff: Major General F. W. de Guingand

SECOND BRITISH ARMY
Lieutenant General Sir Miles Dempsey

XII CORPS
Lieutenant General N. M. Ritchie

7th Armoured Division
Major General G. L. Verney

15th (Scottish) Division
Major General C. M. Barber

53rd (Welsh) Division
Major General R. K. Ross

VIII CORPS
Lieutenant General Sir Richard O'Connor

11th Armoured Division
Major General G. P. B. Roberts

3rd Division
Major General L. G. Whistler

4th Armoured Brigade
Brigadier R. M. P. Carver

1st Belgian Brigade
Colonel B. Piron

XXX CORPS
Lieutenant General B. G. Horrocks

2nd Household Cavalry Regiment

Guards Armoured Division
Major General A. H. S. Adair
5th Guards Brigade (Grenadiers/Irish)
32nd Guards Brigade (Coldstream/Welsh)

43rd (Wessex) Division
Major General G. I. Thomas
129th Brigade: 4 SLI, 4, 5 Wilts
130th Brigade: 7 Hamps, 4, 5 Dorsets
214th Brigade: 7 SLI, 1 Worcs, 5 DCLI
Machine Gun Battalion: 8 Middlesex

50th (Northumbrian) Division (to VIII Corps
18 September)
Major General D. A. H. Graham
69th Brigade: 5 East Yorks, 6, 7 Green Howards
151th Brigade: 6, 8, 9 DLI
231st Brigade: 2 Devons, 1 Hamps, 1 Dorsets
Machine Gun Battalion: 2 Cheshires

8th Armoured Brigade
Brigadier E. G. Prior-Palmer

Royal Netherlands Brigade 'Prinses Irene'
Colonel A. de Ruyter van Steveninck

FIRST ALLIED AIRBORNE ARMY
Lieutenant General Lewis H. Brereton
Deputy: Lieutenant General F. A. M. Browning

AIR ELEMENT

USAAF IX TROOP CARRIER COMMAND
Major General Paul L. Williams
52 Wing: 61, 313, 314, 315, 316, 349 Groups (Dakota)
53 Wing: 434, 435, 436, 437, 438 Groups (Dakota)
50 Wing: 439, 440, 441, 442 Groups (Dakota)
Total: 60 Squadrons 1,100 aircraft

RAF 38 GROUP
Air Vice Marshal L. N. Hollinghurst
190, 196, 295, 299, 570, 620 Sq (Stirling)
296, 287, 298, 644 Sq (Halifax/Albemarle)
Total: 12 Squadrons 240 aircraft

RAF 46 GROUP
Air Commodore A. L. Fiddament (to 15 Sept)/
Air Commodore L. Darvall
48, 233, 271, 437 (RCAF), 512, 575 Sqn (Dakota)
Total: 6 Squadrons, 279 aircraft

GROUND ELEMENT:

XVIII US AIRBORNE CORPS (HQ secondary role only in battle)
Major General Matthew B. Ridgway

82nd ('All American') Airborne Division
Brigadier General James Gavin
504th Parachute Infantry Regiment
505th Parachute Infantry Regiment
508th Parachute Infantry Regiment
325th Glider Infantry Regiment
376th Parachute Field Artillery Battalion
319th Glider Field Artillery Battalion
320th Glider Field Artillery Battalion

101st ('Screaming Eagles') Airborne Division
Major General Maxwell Taylor
501st Parachute Infantry Regiment
502nd Parachute Infantry Regiment
506th Parachute Infantry Regiment
327th Glider Infantry Regiment
377th Parachute Field Artillery Battalion
321st Glider Field Artillery Battalion
907th Glider Field Artillery Battalion

I BRITISH AIRBORNE CORPS
Lieutenant General F. A. M. Browning

1st Airborne Division
Major General R. E. Urquhart
1st Parachute Brigade: 1, 2, 3 Para
4th Parachute Brigade: 10, 11, 156 Para
1st Airlanding Brigade: 1 Border, 2 South Staffs,
7 KOSBs
1st Airlanding Light Regiment, Royal Artillery

1st Polish Independent Parachute Brigade
Major General Stanislav Sosabowski
1, 2, 3 Parachute Infantry.

52nd (Lowland) Division (airportable)
Major General E. Hakewell-Smith
155th Brigade: 7/9 Royal Scots, 4 KOSB, 6 HLI
156th Brigade: 4/5 R Scots Fusiliers,
6 Cameronians, 1 Glasgow Highlanders
157th Brigade: 5 KOSB, 7 Cameronians, 5 HLI
Machine Gun Battalion: 7 Manchesters
79, 80, 186 Field Regiments, 1 Mountain
Regiment, 54 Anti-Tank Regiment Royal Artillery

AIR FORCES

RAF SECOND TACTICAL AIR FORCE
Air Marshal Sir Arthur Coningham

RAF 83 GROUP
Air Vice Marshal H. Broadhurst
39 (RCAF) Reconnaissance Wing (Spitfire)
121, 122, 123, 143 Wings (Typhoon)
125, 126 (RCAF), 127 (RCAF) Wings (Spitfire)
Total: 29 Squadrons, 350 aircraft

RAF 2 GROUP
Air Vice Marshal B. E. Embry
136, 138, 140 Wings (Mosquito)
137, 139 Wings (B–25 Mitchell)
Total: 13 Squadrons, 160 aircraft

RAF 84 GROUP (not involved in the battle)
Air Vice Marshal E. O. Brown

AIR FORCES INVOLVED ON 17 SEPTEMBER:

RAF AIR DEFENCE OF GREAT BRITAIN (FIGHTER COMMAND)
Air Marshal Sir Roderic Hill

RAF BOMBER COMMAND
Air Chief Marshal Sir Arthur Harris

RAF COASTAL COMMAND
Air Chief Marshal Sir Sholto Douglas

USAAF 9TH AIR FORCE
Lieutenant General Hoyt S. Vandenberg

USAAF 8TH AIR FORCE
Lieutenant General James H. Doolittle

A Sergeant (1st Class) of 2nd (Dutch) Troop, 10th (Inter-Allied) Commando, members of which were dropped with the British at Arnhem. He also wears British battledress and equipment (note the rubber boots) including a British Commando's green beret with a black-backed 'Lion' badge, and the sleeve badge of British Combined Operations above the Dutch national badge. His shoulder titles are '10 Commando' on the left side, and 'Commando' on the right.

1st British Airborne Division consisted of two brigades of the Parachute Regiment, all volunteers from other units, and an airlanding brigade of infantry battalions, plus the attached 1st Polish Parachute Brigade under Major General Stanislav Sosabowski. Many of its battalions had considerable previous combat experience and, like the Americans, its troops were of the highest quality. But it had never fought before as a division, nor under its current commander, Major General R. E. 'Roy' Urquhart. Waiting in reserve was 52nd (Lowland) Division, a British infantry division organized to be airportable in C-47 Dakotas once airfields were provided for it, together with two small specialist airfield engineer units, one British and one American.

The German Forces

On 1 September OB West reported that it possessed the equivalent of nine infantry divisions and two weak armoured divisions north of the Ardennes, and was outnumbered ten to one in tanks, three to one in artillery, and absolutely in aircraft. The capture of Antwerp on 4 September provoked 'Mad Tuesday' next day, as German rear-area troops of Armed Forces Command Netherlands fell back in chaos throughout Holland. In these circumstances, any accurate count of German forces opposing 'Market-Garden' was impossible, but Allied estimates suggest no more than 15,000 troops and 250 tanks by 7 September. Model's great achievement was his organization of a coherent defence in just ten more days from this. Altogether 82,000 men, 46,000 vehicles and 530 guns of Fifteenth Army escaped across the Scheldt estuary by 23 September, and some were able to reinforce First Parachute Army by the time 'Market-Garden' started. Other troops came virtually untrained from reserve units, or were grouped together in improvised formations.

The basic German fighting unit for 'Market-Garden' was the Kampfgruppe (battlegroup), an improvised formation of no fixed size or strength. Some were smaller than battalions, but those that played an important role in 'Market-Garden' are best regarded as wrecked and reconstituted divisions, very weak in infantry but

GERMAN ORDER OF BATTLE

The German order of battle for 'Market-Garden' changed daily. These are the main formations involved .

REICHSFUHRER HAUPTQUARTIER (RFH)/ OBERKOMMANDO DER WEHRMACHT (OKW)
Commander in Chief: Adolf Hitler
Chief of Staff: Generalfeldmarschall Wilhelm Keitel   Chief of Operations: Generaloberst Alfred Jodel

OBERBEFELSHABER WEST (OB WEST)
Generalfeldmarschall Gerd von Rundstedt

ARMED FORCES COMMAND (AFC) NETHERLANDS

General der Flieger Friedrich Christiansen

II SS Panzer Corps (to Army Group B 17 September)
Obergruppenführer Wilhelm Bittrich

SS-Kampfgruppe 'Hohenstauffen'
Obersturmbahnführer Walther Harzer

SS-Kampfgruppe 'Frundsberg'
Brigadeführer Heinz Harmel

'Hermann Goering' Division Training Regiment
Oberstleutnant Fritz Fullreide

Kampfgruppe 'Von Tettau'
Generalleutnant Hans von Tettau

ARMY GROUP B

Generalfeldmarschall Walther Model

FIFTEENTH ARMY
General der Infanterie Gustav von Zangen

LXVII Corps
General der Infanterie Otto Sponheimer

346th Infantry Division
Generalleutnant Erich Diester

711th Static Division
Generalleutnant Josef Reichert

719th Coastal Division
Generalleutnant Karl Sievers

LXXXVIII Corps
General der Infanterie Hans Reinhard

Kampfgruppe 'Chill'
Generalleutnant Kurt Chill

59th Infantry Division
Generalleutnant Walter Poppe

245th Infantry Division
Oberst Gerhard Kegler

712th Static Division
Generalleutnant Friedrich-Wilhelm Neuman

FIRST PARACHUTE ARMY
General der Fallschirmstruppen Kurt Student

LXXXVI Corps
General der Infanterie Hans von Obstfelder

176th Infantry Division
Oberst Christian Landau

Kampfgruppe 'Walther'

6th Parachute Regiment
Oberstleutnant Friedrich Freiherr von der Heydte

107th Panzer Brigade
Major Freiherr von Maltzahn

Division 'Erdmann'
Generalleutnant Wolfgang Erdmann

II Parachute Corps (from 19 September)
General der Fallschirmtruppen Eugen Meindl

XII SS Corps (from 29 September)
Obergruppenführer Kurt von Gottberg

180th Infantry Division
Generalleutnant Bernard Klosterkemper

190th Infantry Division
Generalleutnant Ernst Hammer

363rd Volksgrenadier Division (from 5 October)
Generalleutnant Augustus Dettling

Continued overleaf

GERMAN ORDER OF BATTLE *CONTINUED FROM OVERLEAF*

WEHRKREIS VI

CORPS 'FELDT' (from 18 September)
General der Kavalerie Kurt Feldt

406th Landesschützen Division
Generalleutnant Scherbening

LUFTWAFFE WEST

(directly under **LUFTFLOTTE REICH**)

Approximately 300 Bf 109, Fw 190 and Me 262 fighters, 120 Ju 87 and Ju 88 bombers, very low on fuel.

strong in artillery and assault guns, with a size and combat power roughly equal to an Allied brigade. Kampfgruppe 'Walther', defending against XXX Corps, changed its structure daily, including troops from the Army, Navy, Luftwaffe and Waffen-SS, and existed for less than a month (its commander's full identity has not survived). Kampfgruppe 'Chill' was formed by Generalleutnant Kurt Chill from the remains of his own 85th Infantry Division together with 84th and 89th Infantry Divisions. Even ordinary German formations in 'Market-Garden' were rarely at full strength. Generalleutnant Walter Poppe's 59th Infantry Division was barely 1,000 men, 30 guns and eighteen assault guns, while 6th Parachute Regiment was without one of its battalions. Commanding or coordinating attacks between these improvised formations was extremely difficult, and they varied greatly in quality.

After its retreat from the Falaise pocket, II SS Panzer Corps claimed on 12 September to have only twelve functioning tanks. By this date 9th SS Panzer Division had formed itself into SS-Kampfgruppe 'Hohenstauffen' under its senior surviving officer, Obersturmbannführer Walther Harzer. After sending troops to Kampfgruppe 'Walther', this consisted of a company of PzKpfw IV and PzKpfw V Panther tanks, two batteries of Jagdpanther IV assault guns, a reconnaissance battalion, a weak panzergrenadier regiment, and an artillery battalion (twelve guns). SS-Kampfgruppe 'Frundsberg', formed from 10th SS Panzer Division under Brigadeführer Heinz Harmel, had only a few PzKpfw IVs and Jagdpanthers, its reconnaissance battalion and panzergrenadier regiment, but two artillery battalions. The total force was probably no more than 3,000 men with a high proportion of heavy infantry weapons and machine-guns. Like the Allied airborne troops, they were of the highest fighting quality.

Exhausted, routed or untrained, the Germans were indeed prepared to fight, although most were perfectly aware that the war was lost. Some, particularly in the Waffen-SS, had little wish to survive to face disgrace and possible war crimes trials. As the Allies pushed closer to German soil, most were ready to defend their homeland against an invader who demanded unconditional surrender, and whose attacks were visibly weakening.

▶ *The bridge over the River Maas (Meuse) at Grave, with nine spans measuring 600m in length across a river 250m wide, was a substantial object-ive for 82nd Airborne Division. Its ominous name (usually pro-nounced to rhyme with 'Marv') led to some late attempts on the part of American staff officers to call it 'Gravey bridge'. This picture was taken on 27 September at the end of the battle. (IWM photograph B10347)*

THE OPPOSING PLANS

The Allied Plan

Immediately after Montgomery's conference with Eisenhower, Dempsey ordered Browning to start planning I Airborne Corps' part in the battle. One later version of this meeting had Browning telling Montgomery that his troops could hold Arnhem bridge for four days, but that this might prove 'a bridge too far'. There is no evidence for this unlikely story, and planning was based on a general estimate of Second British Army reaching Arnhem in two to five days rather than to a fixed timetable.

Montgomery issued formal orders for Operation 'Market-Garden' on 12 September, after briefing Horrocks. The plan called for First Allied Airborne Army to assist Second British Army in a rapid advance from the Meuse-Escaut Canal all the way to Nunspeet on the Zuider Zee (IJsselmeer) almost 160km (100 miles) away, before turning east into Germany. The airborne troops would capture bridges over the major rivers and canals at three

towns, each with a population in 1944 of about 90,000: Eindhoven, about 20km (13 miles) from the start line, Nijmegen 85km (53 miles) away, and Arnhem 100km (64 miles) away.

The tree-lined double track road along which XXX Corps was to advance ran through countryside that was almost entirely flat, partly of sandy soil and partly *polder* or drained bogland, broken by orchards, copses, small streams and ditches, all making opposed cross-country movement very difficult for vehicles. North of the line from 's Hertogenbosch to Nijmegen the ground was almost all *polder*, veined with hundreds of small drainage ditches. The drained *polder* between the River Waal north of Nijmegen and the Lower Rhine (or Lek), filled with orchards and laced with waterways, was known locally as the *Betuwe* or 'island', with roads running along causeways up to 3m above the surrounding fields. North of the Lower Rhine at Arnhem the soil was sandy heathland, rising away north of the town past Apeldoorn to the Veluwe

Market-Garden, The Plan 17 September 1944

heights, at 100m the highest ground in Holland.

Browning returned to I Airborne Corps Headquarters at Moor Park near London after his meeting with Dempsey, and notified First Allied Airborne Army at Ascot that an air plan was required. Brereton also produced this plan, Operation 'Market', by 12 September. For simplicity, as far as possible all paratroops were to be carried by USAAF aircraft and all gliders towed by RAF aircraft, regardless of the nationality of the troops. Despite predictions of up to 40 per cent aircraft losses, Brereton wanted to prove that a major air assault could be mounted in daylight (there was no moon in the target period, ruling out a night drop), and sided with his pilots by allowing only one major lift each day. As a result, the 'Market' plan would take at least three days to fly the complete airborne divisions to their targets. The fourth day would be spent on resupply, and 52nd (Lowland) Division would be flown in north of Arnhem over the next two days. In order to prevent

◀ *OPERATION 'MARKET', THE AIRBORNE PLAN. On 17 September, First Allied Airborne Army drops three airborne divisions along a corridor north of Eindhoven. 101st US Airborne Division secures bridges from Eindhoven to Veghel. 82nd US Airborne Division secures bridges from Grave to Nijmegen and the Groesbeek heights. 1st British Airborne Division secures Arnhem bridge and the high ground to the north.*

OPERATION 'GARDEN', THE GROUND PLAN. Simultaneous with 'Market' on 17 September, Second British Army drives northwards from the Meuse–Escaut Canal on a very narrow front, led by XXX Corps, which links up with each of the airborne divisions in turn. Flanking attacks by XII Corps and VIII Corps on either side protect this drive. Once north of Arnhem, XXX Corps establishes the Guards Armoured Division on the Zuider Zee with a bridgehead over the River Ijssel at Zwolle, and 43rd Division with a bridgehead at Deventer. Once Apeldoorn is secure, 52nd Division is flown in to reinforce this position and secure a bridgehead at Zutphen.

With four divisions established north of the Lower Rhine, XXX Corps leads Second British Army east towards Osnabruck and/or south-east towards Hamm to encircle the Ruhr, possibly in conjunction with First US Army from the south. Meanwhile, First Canadian Army clears the remainder of the Netherlands and the V-2 sites.

◄ *An aerial view looking west.of the River Waal flowing through the centre of Nijmegen, taken by an RAF reconnaissance aircraft on the evening of 22 September at the height of the battle, The road bridge (bottom of picture) and railway bridge, both about 650m long, can be clearly seen (note the shadows showing the shape of both bridges). Although Browning's plan gave no priority to capture of the railway bridge, Allied engineers could convert such a bridge to take armoured vehicles within a day. (IWM photograph CL1203)*

confusion over the target, Brereton also ruled that while his flights from England were in the air 2nd Tactical Air Force must remain grounded rather than flying into the same airspace. Allied meteorologists predicted at least two days of clear weather starting on Sunday 17 September, which became 'D-Day' for the battle.

Brereton agreed that Browning's I Airborne Corps would command all three divisions of First Allied Airborne Army, with XVIII Airborne Corps relegated to an administrative role. Browning's plan was for each of the first wave to land as a formed body in open country about 10km (6 miles) from its main objective, and then advance to capture it. If everything worked, each of the three complete divisions would finish after three days holding an all-round perimeter of at least 40km (25 miles) while the ground forces arrived.

These distances and timescales only made sense if the German troops were not in fact going to fight. Although handicapped by poor coordination between SHAEF, 21st Army Group and First Allied Airborne Army, the Allied picture of German forces in the 'Market-Garden' area was reasonably clear. Browning's plan estimated the Germans at Arnhem as one broken panzer division, or the equivalent of 3,000 infantry with a few tanks, which was exactly right. Allied Intelligence had tracked II SS Panzer Corps Headquarters back from France to the Eindhoven-Arnhem area before losing it on 4 September, and had identified First Parachute Army Headquarters near 's Hertogenbosch and Army Group B near Arnhem itself by 16 September. The only significant Allied error was a SHAEF belief that II SS Panzer Corps might have retreated to the Kleve area, east of Nijmegen, rather than north.

In Browning's plan, 101st Airborne Division under Major General Maxwell Taylor was to drop north of Eindhoven, to capture the bridges over the River Aa and the larger Willems Canal (30m wide) at Veghel, over the minor River Dommel at St Oedenrode, and over the Wilhelmina Canal (35m wide) at Son, and then go on to capture Eindhoven by nightfall. Originally, Browning had wanted Taylor to secure the road from Eindhoven to Grave, a perimeter of 65km (40 miles). Taylor protested, and Dempsey overruled Browning, allowing 101st

Airborne to halt at Veghel and leave a gap of about 20km (13 miles) in the Allied deployment. Even so, Taylor planned to take all three of his parachute infantry regiments on the first day, believing that artill-ery support would soon arrive from XXX Corps.

Brigadier General James Gavin, Ridgway's successor commanding 82nd Airborne Division, also believed that Browning had set him too large a task, but chose not to protest. Because of the expected threat from the Kleve region, Browning made Gavin's first priority the capture of the Groesbeek heights, an area of wooded hills about 100m high and 12km (8 miles) long to the east of Nijmegen, followed by the bridges over the River Maas (Meuse) at Grave (250m wide) and over the Maas-Waal Canal (60m wide). Only then was 82nd Airborne to try for the road bridge over the Waal (300m wide) in the centre of Nijmegen. Gavin took a mixed force of infantry and artillery on his first lift, realizing that he might have to fight alone for some time.

The landing zones for 1st British Airborne Division under Major General Urquhart were on the heathland west of Arnhem. But Browning specified that Urquhart's main objective was to be the road bridge over the Lower Rhine (100m wide) in the town centre, together with the railway bridge and a nearby pontoon bridge (discovered late on 16 September to have been dismantled by the Germans). Urquhart's troops, joined by 1st Polish Parachute Brigade, would then secure the high ground just north of Arnhem. Urquhart decided to lead with his airlanding troops, and take half his artillery and anti-tank guns on the first lift. Suggestions that a small party of paratroops or glider troops could land directly on Arnhem bridge from the south came too late to change the plan.

On 16 September at Leopoldsburg (Bourg Leopold) about 20km (13 miles) south of Joe's Bridge, Horrocks briefed XXX Corps' senior officers on 'Garden', the ground plan. The Guards Armoured Division would lead XXX Corps' drive northward, codenamed the 'Club Route', aided by flank attacks from XII Corps on the left and VIII Corps (which had just begun to move from the Seine) on the right. As XXX Corps linked up with each airborne division it would take them under command from I Airborne Corps, handing off its troops further south to VIII Corps as it did so.

If the main bridges at Grave, Nijmegen or Arnhem were destroyed, the Guards Armoured would secure the river bank and 43rd (Wessex) Division following would mount an assault crossing. Both divisions were issued rations for four days and fuel for 400km (250 miles). Horrocks' main concern was breaking through the German defenders between Joe's Bridge and Valkenswaard, believed to be six battalions and 20 armoured vehicles. In fact Kampfgruppe 'Walther' had ten weak battalions (including 6th Luftwaffe Penal Battalion in tropical uniforms) and ten assault guns defending the bridgehead. Once this German 'crust' was broken, Horrocks expected easy going.

The German Plan

Strictly, there was no German plan for 'Market–Garden'. Some form of Allied advance from the Meuse-Escaut Canal was expected, but German tactical Intelligence was so bad that Kampfgruppe 'Walther' believed that it was facing Canadians, while during the battle SS-Kampfgruppe 'Frundsberg' identified the Guards Armoured Division as Americans.

At the highest level, German defensive plans were based on two assessments of Allied intentions. One threat was an amphibious landing by the (completely fictitious) Fourth British Army on the Dutch coast to cut off the remaining troops of Fifteenth Army. The other was a drive north-east towards Wesel by 21st Army Group as part of a pincer move to encircle the Ruhr. The Germans expected landings by First Allied Airborne Army to support either of these operations, and Generalfeldmarschall Model deployed the meagre forces of Student's First Parachute Army in central Holland to cover them both, exactly in the path of 'Market-Garden'. Model's personal headquarters was the Hartenstein Hotel in Oosterbeek, just east of 1st British Airborne's planned landing sites.

II SS Panzer Corps was not part of Model's defence, coming under Armed Forces Command Netherlands while it rested. Obergruppenführer Bittrich's own headquarters was at Doetinchem, 25km (15 miles) east of Arnhem, with his troops spread out between Arnhem and Deventer. On 12 September SS-Kampfgruppe 'Hohenstauffen' was ordered to start entraining for Siegen near Koblenz in Germany, where it would be refitted. The last of its vehicles were due to leave on 17 September, after which SS-Kampfgruppe 'Frundsberg' was to move to Aachen to refit. On 16 September Bittrich sent Brigadeführer Harmel by car to SS Headquarters in Berlin to plead in person for reinforcements, while Obersturmbahnführer Harzer continued to train his troops. The Allied landings next day would come as a complete surprise.

◀ *British paratroops of 1st Parachute Brigade boarding a C-47 Dakota of USAAF IX Troop Carrier Command on the morning of Sunday 17 September. The soldiers are wearing their parachutes and harness over the sleeveless version of the parachute smock or 'jump jacket' introduced in 1944. Modelled on the German version, this zip-fronted gabardine garment was worn over the Denison smock and discarded on landing. (IWM photograph K7588)*

THE AIR ARMADA, 16 TO 17 SEPTEMBER

What was to become the Battle of Arnhem began an hour before midnight on Saturday 16 September (British Summer Time, equal to GMT plus one hour but an hour behind local time in Holland) as 200 Lancasters and 23 Mosquitos of RAF Bomber Command dropped 890 tons of bombs on four German fighter airfields in northern Holland, including one for Me 262 jet fighters. This was the start of Brereton's plan to deliver the ground troops safely to the target by suppressing the German defences, estimated as including 112 light and 44 heavy anti-aircraft guns. Over the next 24 hours, 1,395 bomber sorties and 1,240 fighter sorties were flown in support of Operation 'Market-Garden'.

The bombing continued at 0800 next day as 822 B-17 Flying Fortresses of 8th Air Force with 161 P-51 Mustangs in escort bombed all 117 identified German anti-aircraft positions along the 'Market-Garden' route, together with airfields at Eindhoven, Deelen and Ede. These were backed up by 54 Lancasters and five Mosquitos of Bomber Command, while another 85 Lancasters and fifteen Mosquitos attacked the anti-aircraft positions on Walcheren island. Two Flying Fortresses, two Lancasters and three Mosquitos were lost. Such was Allied air superiority that these attacks scarcely registered as unusual with the Germans. To coincide with Operation 'Market-Garden', the Dutch Government in exile in London called for a general strike of transport workers throughout the Netherlands.

Sunday 17 September, D-Day for 'Market-Garden', dawned as a beautiful late summer day, slightly cloudy with good visibility. In England, the airborne troops started to board their aircraft. The slower glider tugs, which cruised at 120mph, took off first at 0930, followed by the C-47 Dakota paratroop carrier aircraft at 140mph. The pathfinders, who would arrive first, took off at 1025. Crossing north-east of London, the sky train

A Sergeant Glider Pilot (identified as a First Pilot by the crown at the centre of his pilot's winged badge) wearing MRC body armour, developed by the British Medical Research Council in 1941. Arnhem was probably the only occasion on which MRC armour was worn in action. In theory, MRC armour was worn under the battledress, but the method shown was more comfortable.

◄ Lieutenant General Browning poses for a photograph with Air Chief Marshal Tedder and an American brigadier general on the morning of Sunday 17 September, a few hours before Browning's glider took off. Although the senior Allied airman in the European theatre, Tedder like Montgomery distanced himself from 'Market-Garden' after its failure. (IWM photograph CH13856)

► Top: The pathfinders of 1st British Airborne Division's 21st Independent Parachute Company waiting to take off from RAF Fairford on the morning of Sunday 17 September. Behind them are their transport aircraft, Short Stirlings of 620 Squadron, RAF 38 Group. Employed to mark the landing sites with lights, panels and radar homing beacons for the approaching aircraft, pathfinders were regarded as an élite. Unlike their American equivalent, who were drawn from their own parent units, the men of 21st Independent Parachute Company

resolved itself into two streams, with 101st Airborne Division on the southern route into Holland, and both 82nd Airborne Division and 1st British Airborne Division on the northern route. I Airborne Corps Headquarters took off in gliders behind 82nd Airborne, including Browning's personal chef and wine cellar.

Before boarding his own Horsa glider, Urquhart told his chief staff officer, Lieutenant Colonel Charles Mackenzie, that in the unlikely event of both himself and Brigadier Gerald Lathbury, commanding 1st Parachute Brigade and 1st British

Airborne's senior brigadier, being killed or captured command of the division should pass to Brigadier P. H. W. 'Pip' Hicks, commanding 1st Airlanding Brigade and flying in that day, rather than to Brigadier J. W. 'Shan' Hackett of 4th Parachute Brigade, who was senior to Hicks but not due to arrive until 18 September. Urquhart preferred the elderly and solid Hicks to Hackett, a 33-year-old cavalryman with a background in special forces.

By 1135 the last aircraft had left the ground. The two columns of the sky train each stretched for 150km (94 miles) in length and 5km (three miles) in

trained and fought as a unit. (IWM photograph CL1154)

▼ *Below: Fully laden paratroopers of 101st Airborne Division board their C-47 Dakota on the morning of Sunday 17 September. The jump goggles of the soldier far left were not standard issue, and many paratroopers carried non-regulation or semi-regulation items of equipment into battle. The tape or ties below the knees of the uniform trousers were standard practice.*

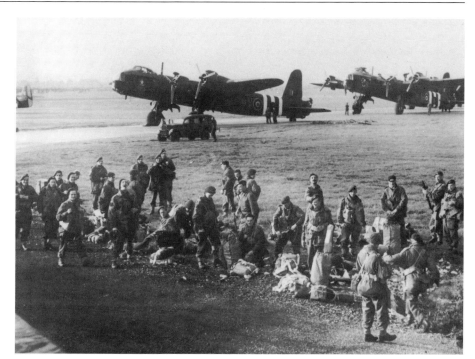

breadth. On the southern route, 101st Airborne was carried by 424 Dakotas and 70 glider/tug combinations. On the northern route, 82nd Airborne travelled in 482 Dakotas and 50 glider/tug combinations, followed by the 38 glider/tugs (enough for an infantry battalion) of I Airborne Corps Headquarters. 1st British Airborne led as planned with 1st Airlanding Brigade and its artillery and divisional troops in 358 glider/tugs, with 1st Parachute Brigade following in 145 Dakotas. The total was 1,051 troop carrier aircraft and 516 glider/tug combinations, or 2,083 aircraft in all, flying at an average height of 1,500ft (500m). Escort

on the northern route came from 371 Spitfires, Tempests and Mosquitos of Fighter Command, with 548 P-47 Thunderbolts, P-38 Lightnings and P-51 Mustangs of 8th Air Force on the southern route. Average flight time was between 90 and 150 minutes to target.

At about 1200 local time, all 117 German anti-aircraft positions along the 'Market-Garden' route were bombed and strafed once again by 212 Thunderbolts of 9th Air Force, while 50 Mosquitos, 48 Mitchells and 24 Bostons (the RAF version of the A-20 Havoc) of RAF 2 Group bombed German barracks and airfields at Nijmegen, Deelen, Ede and

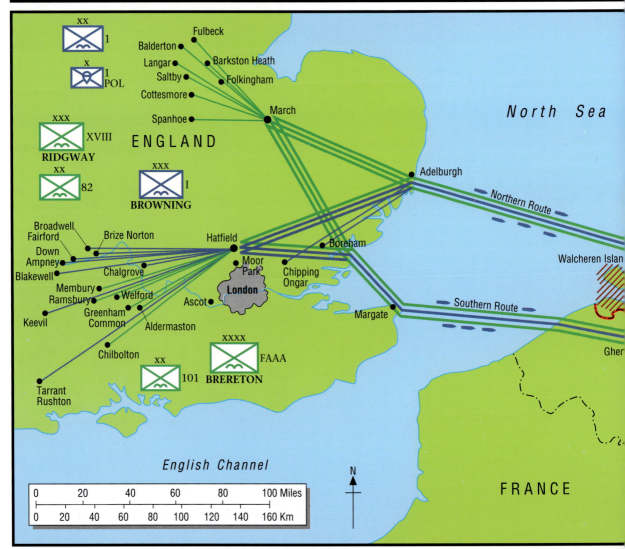

Operation Market: The Allied Fly-in, 17 September 194

Kleve. Allied pilots reported German anti-aircraft crews abandoning their positions before the aircraft attacked. At 1240, twelve RAF Stirlings dropped the British pathfinders of 21st Independent Parachute Company to the west of Arnhem. At the same time, four USAAF Dakotas released the pathfinders of 101st Airborne north of Eindhoven, and two more put the pathfinders of 82nd Airborne down near Grave bridge. The main drop of 82nd Airborne on to the Groesbeek heights would go in without pathfinders to achieve surprise, directly on top of the anti-aircraft batteries.

Meanwhile, the two great columns of transport

▲ Lieutenant General Browning designed his own uniform as commander of British Airborne Forces and wore it into action for 'Market-Garden'. Made of barathea, it had a false Uhlan-style front and a zip opening at the neck, displaying a regulation shirt and tie, and was worn with medal ribbons, collar patches and rank badges on the shoulders. The highly polished brown 'Sam Browne' belt and swagger stick are correct for a Guards officer. For 'Market-Garden' Browning also wore grey kid gloves. The only indication that he is in Airborne Forces is the famous red beret (which he introduced), with the cap badge correct for his rank. (IWM photograph H21248)

aircraft had crossed into enemy airspace. The Dakotas, without armour, guns or self-sealing fuel tanks, slowed to 110mph and descended to 500ft (160m) for the drop. The average time over the German anti-aircraft positions was about 40 minutes. On the southern route, Brereton and Ridgway each watched from a Flying Fortress with the 101st Airborne. Of 75 German fighters scrambled, about 30 reached the sky train, but were seen off by its escort. The only dogfight was over Wesel, where seven out of fifteen Me 109s were lost for one American fighter. The anti-aircraft defences were least damaged over Eindhoven, where 101st Airborne lost 33 Dakotas and Brereton's own aircraft was holed. Some gliders failed to complete the trip, or broke up in mid-air. In total 68 Allied aircraft and 71 gliders were lost from all causes in

ALLIED AIR TRANSPORT

AIRCRAFT	Cruising/ towing speed (mph)	Range (miles)	Payload Troops	Payload Supplies/ Equipment (lb)
British				
ALBEMARLE	120	1,350	10	4,000
HALIFAX	130	3,000	10	6,000
STIRLING	120	3,000	12*	6,000
American				
C-47 SKYTRAIN (British name DAKOTA)	140	1,500	20*	6,000

All these aircraft, normally unarmed, were capable of towing one glider at maximum range, or two at shorter ranges, or of carrying the payload shown. A 6,000lb supply load is the equivalent of two large pieces of equipment, e.g., a jeep, trailer or small artillery piece.

*For parachute drops only. For air transport the C-47 could carry up to 28 troops, and the Stirling up to 40 troops.

GLIDERS	Max towing speed (mph)	Stalling speed (mph)	Payload Troops	Payload Equipment/ Supplies (lb)
British				
HORSA	160	60	28	6.900
HAMILCAR*	150	65	–	17,000
American				
CG-4A WACO (British name HADRIAN)	125	38	15	3,750

*The Hamilcar could only be towed by four-engined aircraft such as the Halifax and Stirling. It was designed as a large cargo carrier only, and carried larger calibre artillery pieces or bulldozers. All the gliders had a crew of two pilots.

▲ *British paratroops of 1st Parachute Brigade inside a C-47 Dakota, either about to take off or in flight, on Sunday 17 September. This picture gives some idea of the amount of equipment carried into battle by the paratroops. In addition to*

the flight, including two RAF and eighteen USAAF fighters.

At 1300 the first gliders of 1st Airlanding Brigade skidded to earth west of Arnhem, followed by Urquhart's artillery and divisional troops. Of 319 gliders, 35 failed to arrive, of which 21 landed in England and flew in to Holland next day. The only serious loss was two gliders each carrying a 17pdr anti-tank gun. Meanwhile, Major General Taylor jumped with 6,769 men of 101st Airborne north of Eindhoven. 501st Parachute Infantry Regiment landed correctly on its drop zone south of Veghel, except for 1/501st which was dropped by a fortunate error at Heeswijk, 5km (three miles) to the north-west on the wrong side of the Willems Canal and the River Aa. 502nd Parachute Infantry and 506th Parachute Infantry landed together with 101st

their leg bags, two of the men have special weapons cases, probably to protect machine-guns. Note the quick-release ring at the centre of the parachute harness on each man's chest. (IWM photograph K7586)

ALLIED AIRLIFT REQUIREMENTS

Formation	C-47 Dakotas (carrier)	Gliders/Tugs (all kinds)
Parachute battalion (British/American/Polish)	35	–
Parachute brigade/regiment (British/American/Polish)	120-140	20-40
Airlanding battalion	–	60-70
Divisional artillery* (British)	–	160
Field artillery battalion* (American)	–	95
Parachute artillery battalion* (American)	60	
Airborne division	400	700
Airportable division	2,000 (transport only)	

These are approximate figures only.

*A British light artillery regiment and anti-tank regiment was twelve 75mm guns, six 105mm guns, twelve 6pdr A/T guns, and six 17pdr A/T guns. An American field artillery battalion was twelve 75mm guns or parachute artillery battalion.

Airborne Headquarters just north of the Sonsche forest. At the same time, 6,527 men of 82nd Airborne dropped successfully for the loss of two Dakotas south of Nijmegen, Brigadier General Gavin jumping from the lead aircraft as was his custom. Of these, 2,016 men of 504th Parachute Infantry landed at Grave, including a company of 2/504th dropped deliberately west of the bridge, while 505th Parachute Infantry and 508th Parachute Infantry dropped on to the Groesbeek heights just north and south of the village. The drop included the first ever parachute deployment of artillery into battle by the 544 men of 376th Parachute Artillery Battalion, jumping with their twelve disassembled 75mm howitzers from 48 Dakotas. At about 1330, Browning's I Airborne Corps Headquarters landed near Groesbeek village, without two of its gliders. Finally at 1353, 1st Parachute Brigade jumped west of Arnhem to complete the British landing. By 1408, some 20,000 combat troops, 511 vehicles, 330 artillery pieces and 590 tons of equipment had been safely landed.

As the sky train climbed to 3,000ft (1,000m) for the return journey, Brereton flew back to IX Troop Carrier Command Headquarters at Eastcote (near Moor Park) to oversee the preparations for the second wave next day together with Tedder and Ridgway. Brereton was delighted to have proved that heavy enemy anti-aircraft defences could be overcome to mount a major daylight airborne operation. The whole 'Market' deployment from England was already fixed, and when the second wave flew out next day his role in the battle would effectively be over. There was no one in England to coordinate the land battle with the air plan, and no reserve.

▼ *Men of 1st Airlanding Light Regiment, Royal Artillery, unloading a jeep and trailer from a Horsa glider on Landing Zone 'Z' near Wolfheze, just after touchdown on Sunday 17 September. The tail section of the Horsa was made to detach for ease of unloading. On the left, with red beret, is Lieutenant Colonel W. F. K. 'Sherrif' Thompson, commanding the regiment. Note the signaller in the jeep behind Thompson, already trying to establish a radio net with his 22 radio set, and the wingtip damaged by the glider on landing. (IWM photograph BU1164)*

▶ *Top right: CG-4A Waco gliders of 101st Airborne Division circling and landing north of the Sonsche forest, Sunday 17*

September. This picture gives a good idea of the flatness of the Dutch countryside on either side of the path of XXX Corps' advance. Note that one glider, far right, appears to have ploughed in on landing, breaking its left wingtip and leaving a plume of disturbed earth. (IWM photograph MH2071)

▼ The C-47 Dakotas of the skytrain turn for home as the last troops of 1st Parachute Brigade land on Drop Zone 'X' near Wolfheze, alongside Horsa gliders that have already been unloaded and abandoned. Note in the background the woods which covered part of the heathland forming 1st British Airborne Division's landing zone. (IWM photograph BU1163)

THE ALLIED ATTACK, 17 SEPTEMBER

At 1400, with fighter-bombers of RAF 83 Group waiting overhead, Lieutenant General Horrocks' XXX Corps opened its bombardment at Joe's Bridge with eleven field artillery regiments and six medium regiments, a total of 408 guns. After 35 minutes, the Irish Guards Group led off for the Guards Armoured Division along the Club Route up the Eindhoven road, with infantry from 231st Brigade of 50th (Northumbrian) Division keeping pace on either side of the road to widen the bridgehead. Despite Horrocks' fears, the break-through went well, as Kampfgruppe 'Walther' was overwhelmed by the weight of Allied firepower. But Major General Adair, commanding the Guards Armoured, stuck strictly to orders and halted at Valkenswaard at 1930, having lost nine tanks. At the same time, XII Corps under Lieutenant General Ritchie attacked with 15th (Scottish) Division north

from Aart and 53rd (Welsh) Division north from Lommel against Kampfgruppe 'Chill'. Attacking across country without the air support of the Guards, these troops made little progress. Nevertheless, the German defensive crust had been broken, and Field Marshal Montgomery reported to London that XXX Corps would be in Arnhem next day.

North of Eindhoven, 101st Airborne reached most of its objectives by 1600. 501st Parachute Infantry secured the rail and road bridges at Hees-wijk and Veghel, and 502nd Parachute Infantry captured the St Oedenrode bridge against light opposition. But at Son, a handful of trainees from the Luftwaffe's Division 'Hermann Goering' blew the bridge over the Wilhelmina Canal as 506th Parachute Infantry arrived, and a weak push by a

◀ *Soldiers of 231st Infantry Brigade, 50th (Northumbrian) Division, moving up in support of the Guards Armoured Division along the road to Eindhoven from Joe's Bridge on Sunday 17 September. Note the abandoned German 88mm Flak gun by the roadside. Following their retreat, the Germans often lacked the heavy cross-country movers to position these guns properly, and dropped them in exposed positions along the length of the road. This made them easier to overcome, but reinforced the British belief that the Germans had mined the roadside verges, which they had been able to do in only a few places. (IWM photograph B9982)*

company of 2/502nd Parachute Infantry towards an alternative bridge south of Best was checked by part of Parachute Battalion 'Jungwirth' (of Kampf-gruppe 'Chill'), producing a stalemate. Until bridg-ing equipment from XXX Corps arrived at Son, there was no way forward. Taylor sent foot patrols south towards Eindhoven, but like Adair he made no effort to enter the town.

In response, General Student, watching the landings from his personal headquarters at Vught, redirected 59th Infantry Division from Fifteenth Army, moving eastward by train through Tilburg, to reinforce LXXXVIII Corps at Best. Later that afternoon Student received what he subsequently described as a complete set of plans for 'Market-Garden' from a crashed Allied glider, almost certainly missing from Browning's headquarters. General Hans Reinhard of LXXXVIII Corps ordered Kampfgruppe 'Chill' to hold to the last man, while LXXXVII Corps under General Otto Sponheimer moved 719th Coastal Division eastward to Turnhout in support.

Further north still, 82nd Airborne's attempt to capture its bridges also met with mixed fortune. 505th and 508th Parachute Infantry established themselves on either side of Groesbeek village, while 504th Parachute Infantry secured Grave bridge. But two of the three bridges over the Maas-Waal Canal were blown by their German defenders before more troops from 504th and 505th Parachute Infantry arrived on foot. This closed the direct road from Grave to Nijmegen, leaving only the bridge nearest Heumen in American hands. Not until after dark was a single company of 1/508th Parachute Infantry sent into Nijmegen to investigate the road bridge across the River Waal, with the aid of some PAN (Dutch resistance) workers. This was stopped well before the bridge by Kampfgruppe 'Henke', an improvised battalion of soldiers, airmen and railway guards defending Nijmegen.

As the first reports of the landing at Wolfheze came in at 1300, Generalfeldmarschall Model quickly abandoned the Hartenstein Hotel, moving Army Group B Headquarters from Oosterbeek to Terborg, some 50km (30 miles) to the east. At 1330 Obergruppenführer Bittrich at Doetinchem, calling for Brigadeführer Harmel's immediate return from

Market-Garden: Area of Operations, 16-26 Sept 1944

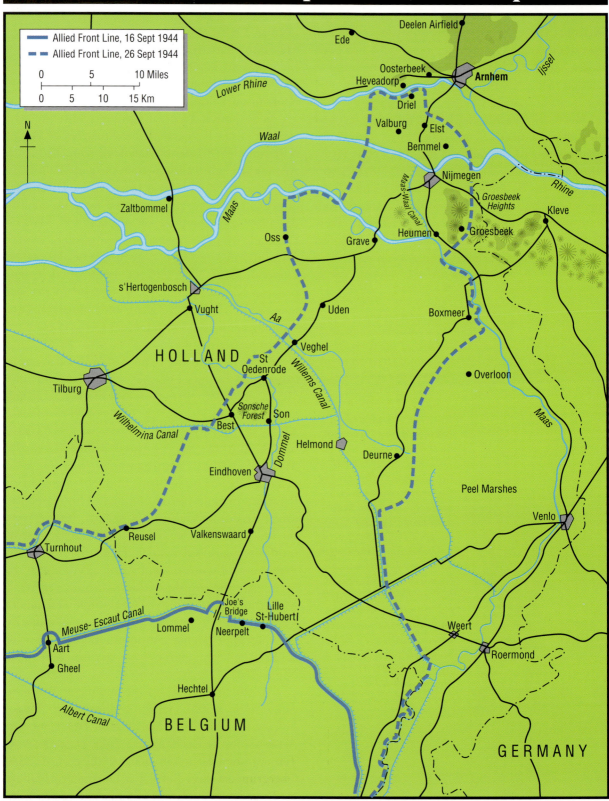

Allied Front Line, 16 Sept 1944
Allied Front Line, 26 Sept 1944

N

Deelen Airfield
Ede
Lower Rhine
Oosterbeek
Heveadorp
Arnhem
IJssel
Driel
Valburg
Elst
Bemmel
Waal
Maas-Waal Canal
Nijmegen
Rhine
Zaltbommel
Maas
Groesbeek Heights
Kleve
Oss
Grave
Heumen
Groesbeek
s'Hertogenbosch
Uden
Boxmeer
Vught
Aa
HOLLAND
St Oedenrode
Veghel
Willems Canal
Overloon
Tilburg
Sonsche Forest
Son
Best
Helmond
Maas
Wilhelmina Canal
Dommel
Deurne
Eindhoven
Peel Marshes
Reusel
Valkenswaard
Venlo
Turnhout
Joe's Bridge
Lille St-Hubert
Meuse-Escaut Canal
Lommel
Neerpelt
Weert
Aart
Roermond
Gheel
Hechtel
Albert Canal
BELGIUM
GERMANY

Berlin, ordered his men on to full alert, and SS-Kampfgruppe 'Hohenstauffen' started unloading its remaining vehicles from the trains. At 1500 Model arrived at Doetinchem and assumed direct command of II SS Panzer Corps from Armed Forces Command Netherlands, much to Bittrich's annoyance.

Nevertheless, Model and Bittrich agreed that the key to the battle was not Arnhem, but Nijmegen road bridge. If the Allied drive could be stopped on the Waal, any success farther north became irrelevant. Bittrich wanted to destroy both Arnhem and Nijmegen bridges at once, but Model refused, more aware of Hitler's suspicions and claiming that he needed the bridges for a counter-attack.

At Rastenburg, Hitler was stunned and shaken by the Allied airborne assault. In response to Model's signals he agreed to give the defeat of 'Market-Garden' absolute priority, ranking even above the defence of Germany. Over 300 fighters were promised for next day, virtually the entire Luftwaffe frontline strength in western Europe. Model also obtained the troops in training from Wehrkreiss VI, the military district of Germany immediately east of the Netherlands, together with all those in transit or on leave in the Wesel area, at least 3,000 men formed into improvised march battalions. General Friedrich Christansen in Amsterdam also promised reinforcements from Armed Forces Command Netherlands under his chief training officer, Generalleutnant Hans von Tettau. More importantly, the armour, artillery, ammunition and replacement troops that II SS Panzer Corps badly needed would start to arrive within 48 hours.

The Battle of Arnhem was exactly the kind of military improvisation at which Model excelled, and three hours after the Allied landings his defence plan was ready. General Student was to handle operations near Eindhoven, sending Kampfgruppe 'Chill' against XII Corps and XXX Corps, and 59th Infantry Division together with 107th Panzer Brigade (promised by Generalfeldmarschall Rundstedt at OB West) against 101st Airborne. The forces from Wehrkreiss VI under General Kurt Feldt were to recapture the Groesbeek heights from 82nd Airborne, with II Parachute Corps being rushed from Cologne to assist. SS-Kampfgruppe

'Frundsberg' was to move across Arnhem bridge to Nijmegen that evening and prevent any Allied crossing, while SS-Kampfgruppe 'Hohenstauffen' held the British west of Arnhem. During the battle, Model visited Obersturmbahnführer Harzer's headquarters every day to ensure that reinforcements were getting through.

By 1500, while 1st Airlanding Brigade secured its defensive perimeter around the landing zones west of Arnhem, the British were already in action against 16th SS Panzergrenadier Depot Battalion (440 strong) under Haupsturmführer Sepp Krafft, which had been training on the heath. The SS NCO Training School 'Arnheim' at Wolfheze also formed a scratch force, as did Kampfgruppe 'Weber' of Luftwaffe troops from Deelen. The 3rd Dutch SS Police Battalion was also on its way from the north. The first 47 prisoners the British took came from 27 different parent units.

At about 1540, 1st Parachute Brigade started to move towards Arnhem by three routes, 3rd Battalion of the Parachute Regiment down the main Oosterbeek highway (the 'Tiger' route) with the brigade headquarters, led by 28 jeeps of 1st Airborne Reconnaissance Squadron under Major C. F. H. 'Freddie' Gough along the line of the railway, 1st Battalion to the north ('Leopard') and 2nd Battalion to the south ('Lion'). Most of 1st British Airborne's radios were working, but as expected there were problems in maintaining contact, and divisional headquarters could not reach Gough or Lathbury, who were about to come under heavy fire from Krafft's troops near Oosterbeek. The powerful Luftwaffe transmitter at Deelen, calling for help from all directions, added to the problem.

At about 1600 a false rumour reached Urquhart that most of the gliders carrying Gough's reconnaissance force had failed to arrive. Leaving his headquarters, Urquhart set out to find Gough and check on his division, driving off in his jeep down the 'Lion' route. Reaching part of 2nd Battalion, he failed to find its commander, Lieutenant Colonel John Frost, and swung northwards, meeting Lathbury with 3rd Battalion but away from his own brigade headquarters.

The first part of the paratroops' advance had been almost a triumphal procession beside grateful Dutch civilians. Now, among the trees and buildings on the outskirts of Oosterbeek, they encountered increasing numbers of German snipers and mortar teams, and Urquhart's own jeep was hit. 1st Battalion to the north was having equal trouble as Obersturmbahnführer Harzer assembled his blocking force, SS-Kampfgruppe 'Spindler' (barely two battalions) which gradually absorbed Krafft's troops into a solid line by midnight, cutting off 1st Parachute Brigade from Arnhem bridge and the high ground. As darkness fell, Urquhart radioed to his headquarters that he and Lathbury were spending the night with 3rd Battalion.

Meanwhile, Major Gough had heard that he was wanted and, returning to divisional headquarters, found that Urquhart had gone. He set out once more towards Arnhem. At about 1900 one of

▼ The body of General-major Kussin in his bullet-ridden staff car, caught in a hail of fire by men of 3rd Battalion of the Parachute Regiment at Wolfheze crossroads, taken by a member of the Army Film and Photographic Unit on the evening of Sunday 17 September. Two of Kussin's aides who were with him in the car also died. (IWM photograph BU1155)

Gough's patrols notified 1st British Airborne Headquarters of the existence of a ferry at Heveadorp, but with Urquhart elsewhere no action was taken to secure the ferry.

On the German side, at about 1800 Generalmajor Kussin, the Arnhem Town Commandant who was responsible for the defence of its bridges, was killed by paratroops of 3rd Battalion at Wolfheze crossroads after driving to confer with Krafft. As Frost's 2nd Battalion approached the railway bridge at about 1830 it was blown in their faces, and the pontoon bridge was found to be dismantled as expected. But at Arnhem road bridge itself the small guard of German pioneer troops had abandoned their posts, and the bridge was undefended. Approaching at dusk, the paratroops watched 30 vehicles of 9th SS Reconnaissance Battalion drive on to the bridge from the north, and keep going: the battalion was on loan to SS-Kampfgruppe 'Frundsberg', and its orders were to drive to Nijmegen. At 1930 the first of Frost's men moved completely unopposed into position among the buildings at the northern end of the bridge. Within half an hour the first troops of the 'Frundsberg' heading for Nijmegen tried to cross the bridge from the north and found their way blocked.

Bittrich at once secured the southern end of the bridge with armoured cars of 10th SS Reconnaissance Battalion. Frost did not have enough troops to hold the entire bridge, and a speculative night attack with flamethrowers on a German pillbox at the northern end did little but set most of the structure alight. But before night fell, Frost notified divisional headquarters and Urquhart that his end of the bridge was secure.

During the night Major Gough reached the bridge with two of his jeeps, and other troops of 1st Parachute Brigade managed to get through to Frost before dawn. By morning his force was about 600 men, mostly from his own 2nd Battalion, including four 6pdr anti-tank guns plus mortars and anti-tank mines. More importantly, at 0800 the headquarters of 1st Parachute Brigade arrived (without Lathbury), giving Frost radio contact with 1st British Airborne Headquarters and artillery support from one of the three troops (four guns each) of the division's 75mm howitzers.

THE ALLIED FAILURE, 18 SEPTEMBER

The Allied meteorologists were one day out in their predictions, and on Monday (D plus 1) the autumn weather closed down. Heavy fog in the morning was followed by heavy rain in the afternoon and evening. In England, the take-off of the second airborne wave, due for dawn at 0600, was delayed. The fog also grounded the Allied aircraft in Belgium and northern France for the morning. Lieutenant General Ridgway flew out to Brussels in an effort to join his troops but was unable to land because of the weather. Farther north in Holland and western Germany the airfields cleared just as the Luftwaffe started its maximum effort. Together with Browning's failure to arrange RAF and USAAF liaison officers with his troops, and Brereton's stipulation that the aircraft in Belgium remain

grounded while his own were flying, this meant that 82nd Airborne received only 97 close-support sorties from RAF 83 Group, and 1st British Airborne received none, compared with 190 Luftwaffe fighters committed to the area. German air attacks took place as far south as Joe's Bridge, which was narrowly missed by a fighter-bomber raid. 'Market-Garden', a plan based on air power, was the only battle of the entire campaign in North-West Europe fought with Allied air inferiority, a large part of it self-inflicted.

At 0600, with the armoured cars of the 2nd Household Cavalry Regiment reconnoitring ahead, the Guards Armoured advance resumed, leaving 231st Brigade to hold Valkenswaard. Halfway to Eindhoven the Grenadier Guards Group took over

▶ *Humber armoured cars of 2nd Household Cavalry Regiment driving through the streets of Eindhoven, Monday 18 September. A composite unit made up from the Life Guards and the Royal Horse Guards, the Household were known in radio communication by their collective regimental nickname of the 'Stable Boys', and acted as the reconnaissance battalion for XXX Corps during the battle. (IWM photograph B10127A)*

the lead, with the Welsh Guards Group opening up the second Heart Route axis towards Helmond. During the morning, 506th Parachute Infantry cleared Eindhoven of a single German company and secured the bridges over the River Dommel east of the town. By the evening, the Guards Armoured had passed around east of Eindhoven and reached the destroyed bridge at Son, where work on a Bailey bridge began. The Welsh Guards' attempt to strike out across country had bogged down against Kampfgruppe 'Walther' in the flat terrain, and Major General Adair ordered it to rejoin the main axis at Son.

During the day, German LXXXVI Corps arrived from the east under General Hans von Obstfelder with 176th Infantry Division (7,000 trainees and semi-invalids) and Division 'Erdmann' (3,000 recruits for the planned 7th Parachute Division), strengthening the German position between Weert and Helmond. Meanwhile, after a strong attempt by 2/502nd and 3/502nd Parachute Infantry to capture Best bridge, it was finally blown at 1100 by 59th Infantry Division. The British advance now depended entirely on the speed at which the Bailey bridge at Son was completed.

With dawn at Nijmegen, Gavin ordered 1/508th and 3/508th Parachute Infantry to try again for the road bridge. Three times during the day the paratroops reported that the bridge was theirs, but each time the German defence held. Blocked at Arnhem bridge, SS-Kampfgruppe 'Frundsberg' began the slow process of ferrying troops and vehicles across the Pannerden Canal, the canalized stretch of the Lower Rhine east of Arnhem. The first troops reached Nijmegen on bicycles, followed by four PzKpfw IV tanks, the vanguard of SS-Kampfgruppe 'Reinhold'. Brigade-führer Harmel, who had driven flat-out from Berlin, set up headquarters next day at Doornenburg 9km (six miles) north of Nijmegen to coordinate the defence.

Also at dawn, the first troops of Corps 'Feldt' from Wehrkreis VI, about 3,400 barely trained men in four groups under 406th Landesschütz Division, started to attack on the Groesbeek heights, finding gaps in the thin American line. During the day, the PAN warned Gavin of more Germans massing in the Reichswald. Taking this to heart,

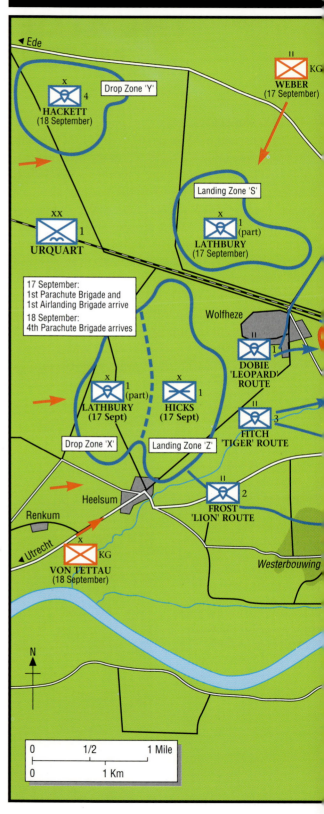

Arnhem: British

t Airborne Division Operations, 17-21 September 1944

XXX IISS (elements)
BITTRICH

Deelen

Apeldoorn

ding Zone 'L'
September:
lish gliders land

Supply Drop Zone 'V'

GOUGH

SS KG **SPINDLER** (17-18 September)

ARNHEM

x SS KG HOHENSTAUFFEN (elements)
HARZER (17-18 September)

16 SS
KRAFFT

Hartenstein Hotel

Model's HQ, later 'Urquhart's HQ

Oosterbeek

19 September: Attempted breakthrough by 1st Parachute Brigade fails

Pontoon Bridge (disabled)

17 September: 2nd Parachute Battalion reaches bridge

Arnhem Bridge

eadorp

Ferry

Lower Rhine

17 September: Ferry missed by British

17 September: Railway Bridge blown by Germans

Elden

SS KG **FRUNDSBERG** (elements)
HARMEL (18-21 September)

x 1 POL
SOSABOWSKI

Driel

x 1 POL
SOSABOWSKI

21 September: 1st Ind. Polish Parachute Brigade arrives at Driel

19 September: Proposed drop zone for 1st Polish Parachute Brigade

Nijmegen

◀ *Men of 'C' Troop of Major Gough's 1st Airborne Reconnaissance Squadron near Wolfheze station on Monday 18 September, with their jeeps just visible beyond the railway line. The soldier in the foreground is armed with a PIAT. This picture gives a good idea of the woodland between the British landing zones and Oosterbeek. (IWM photograph BU1144)*

▼ *The result of the attack by 9th SS Reconnaissance Battalion of the 'Hohenstauffen' across Arnhem bridge into*

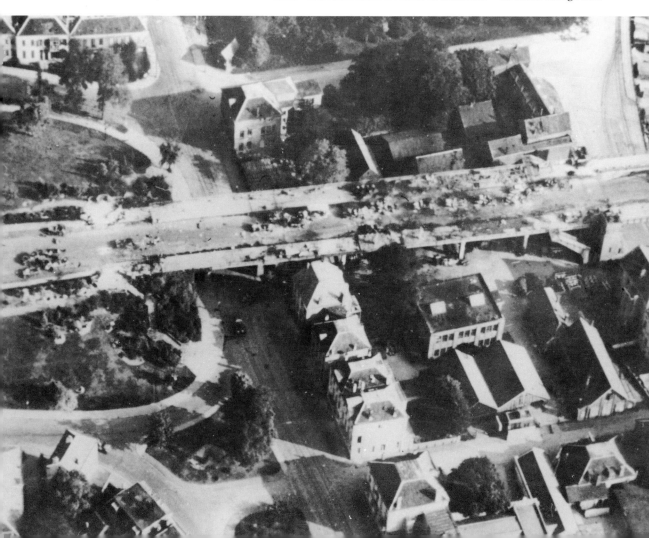

Frost's position, taken by an RAF reconnaissance aircraft on Monday 18 September, looking east. The picture shows the raised section of the main road leading on to the bridge itself (to the right of the picture). Over twenty destroyed German half-tracks and reconnaissance vehicles can be seen. Haupsturmführer Viktor Grabner, commanding the battalion, who had received the Knight's Cross from Obersturmbahnführer Harzer at noon on the previous day, was killed in the attack. (IWM photograph MH2062)

▼ *Lieutenant Colonel John Frost was the most experienced battalion commander in 1st British Airborne Division, having commanded 2nd Battalion of the Parachute Regiment since October 1942 and led it through battles in North Africa and Sicily. Like all British paratroops, he was a volunteer. He is shown here as a major in the uniform of his parent regiment, the Cameronians (Scottish Rifles), after receiving the Military Cross for leading the Bruneval Raid of 27 February 1942, the Parachute Regiment's first Battle Honour.*

82nd Airborne and Browning with them fought the rest of the battle for Nijmegen bridge looking over one shoulder, preparing to defend against an expected armoured drive by II SS Panzer Corps across the Groesbeek heights which never came.

At Arnhem, both sides attacked before dawn. Kampfgruppe 'von Tettau' (including 224th Panzer Company with French Renault tanks) moved against 1st Airlanding Brigade from Renkum to the west, gradually absorbing all other German forces west of Oosterbeek in a firefight that lasted most of the day. Meanwhile, 3rd Battalion of the Parachute Regiment resumed its advance towards Arnhem bridge against SS-Kampfgruppe 'Spindler', with Lathbury and Urquhart in attendance.

As 3rd Battalion's advance pushed to within 2,000m of the bridge, the British and Germans became intermingled in confused street fighting. Urquhart's party was cut off, and shortly before noon Lathbury was wounded and had to be left in a nearby house. As the Germans closed in, Urquhart accompanied by two captains was forced to take refuge in a sympathetic householder's attic while enemy troops patrolled the streets below. With Urquhart and Lathbury both missing, Brigadier Hicks officially took over the division at 0915, sending 2nd Battalion of the South Staffordshire Regiment (two companies strong) to reinforce 1st Parachute Brigade's increasingly fragmented drive.

At Arnhem bridge itself, Frost was still in a strong position, with at least as many troops as SS-Kampfgruppe 'Knaust' of the 'Hohenstauffen', which attacked from the north. The Germans soon discovered that the airborne troops were a formidable enemy, and that infantry assaults achieved little against them. Artillery and armour were needed to blast Frost's men out of their houses, and two 100mm guns began the process just after dawn. At 0930 about 22 vehicles of 9th SS Reconnaissance Battalion returned from Nijmegen and tried to charge across the bridge and into Frost's position, only to be destroyed by British mines, anti-tank guns and grenades. But Frost had rations only for 48 hours, and was forced to restrict ammunition during the day. Meanwhile, 1st Parachute Brigade was checked by SS-Kampfgruppe 'Spindler' still short of the bridge. Over the next two days the replacement tanks and guns demanded by Model

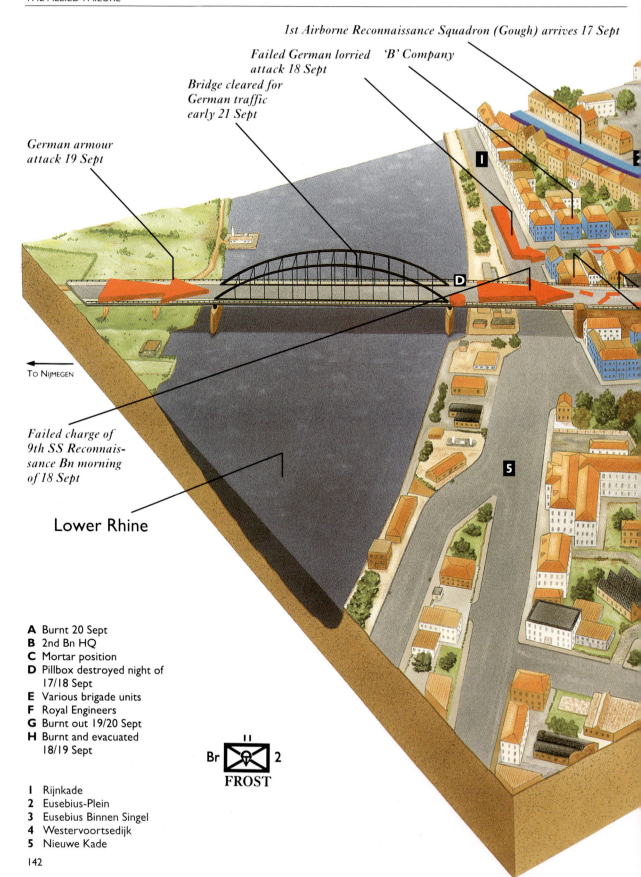

1st Airborne Reconnaissance Squadron (Gough) arrives 17 Sept

Failed German lorried
attack 18 Sept

'B' Company

Bridge cleared for
German traffic
early 21 Sept

German armour
attack 19 Sept

To Nijmegen

Failed charge of
9th SS Reconnais-
sance Bn morning
of 18 Sept

Lower Rhine

A Burnt 20 Sept
B 2nd Bn HQ
C Mortar position
D Pillbox destroyed night of
17/18 Sept
E Various brigade units
F Royal Engineers
G Burnt out 19/20 Sept
H Burnt and evacuated
18/19 Sept

Br 2
FROST

1 Rijnkade
2 Eusebius-Plein
3 Eusebius Binnen Singel
4 Westervoortsedijk
5 Nieuwe Kade

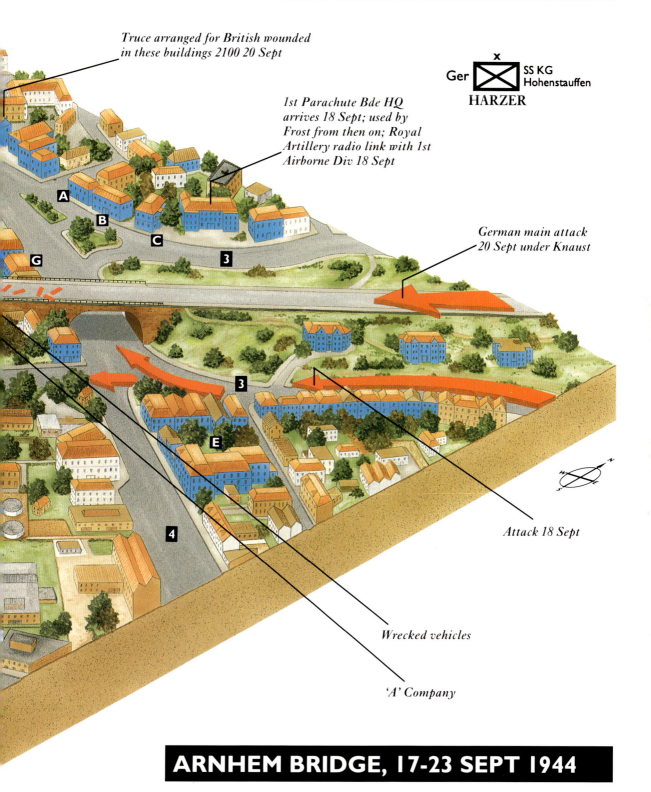

Truce arranged for British wounded
in these buildings 2100 20 Sept

1st Parachute Bde HQ
arrives 18 Sept; used by
Frost from then on; Royal
Artillery radio link with 1st
Airborne Div 18 Sept

Ger ⊠ SS KG
Hohenstauffen
HARZER

A

B

C

G

3

German main attack
20 Sept under Knaust

3

E

4

Attack 18 Sept

Wrecked vehicles

'A' Company

ARNHEM BRIDGE, 17-23 SEPT 1944

**Frost's men held the northern part of the bridge, denying the
Germans a crossing place, until the night of 20/21 Sept. The
last British resistance near the bridge ceased 23 Sept**

started to arrive at Arnhem from all over Germany, including Flak Brigade 'Von Swoboda' from Luftwaffe West equipped with 70 anti-aircraft guns (33 x 88mm, 29 x 20mm and 8 x 37mm) in five battalions.

All this was unknown to Browning and his staff, who were rapidly discovering the difference between an administrative headquarters and an Army Corps command. There was endless trouble with radio communications, for which Browning later blamed his signals section. In fact the GHQ Liaison Regiment ('Phantom') unit with 1st British Airborne was in touch with London through its specialist radio equipment, as was a BBC reporting team with a VHS set (later in the battle, newspapers carrying their first reports were dropped to the troops at Arnhem), and the division had direct contact with Frost on Arnhem bridge. 1st British Airborne was also speaking to I Airborne Corps Rear Headquarters at Moor Park, which was in intermittent contact with Browning. The PAN, using a private telephone system belonging to the regional electricity company, also sent coded messages between Arnhem and Nijmegen warning 82nd Airborne that 1st British Airborne was in

trouble, and the same telephone system reached south to 101st Airborne at Son. The failure was not principally one of communications, but of staffwork and experience at Browning's headquarters. Next morning I Airborne Corps asked Moor Park for copies of 1st British Airborne's signals, and that afternoon firm radio contact was established. But for the vital first two days of the battle, Browning was never in proper command.

At 1000 in England, the glider/tug combinations of the delayed second airlift took off, followed by the paratroop carriers at 1200, all in one stream on the northern route escorted by 867 fighters of 8th Air Force and Fighter Command. In the bad weather, 91 out of 904 gliders taking off failed to arrive or were lost over Holland. At 1300 two battalions of 327th Glider Infantry Regiment and some divisional troops, a total of 2,656 men, 146 jeeps, 109 trailers and two bulldozers, reached 101st Airborne safely in 428 gliders, and Major General Taylor ordered his deputy, Brigadier General Gerald Higgins (at 34, the youngest general in the US Army) to take over the western flank of his defences. Within the hour, 502nd Parachute Infantry reinforced by British tanks from 8th

◀ *The British Army's backpacked 68P radio set (shown here being worn by a Polish paratrooper) was used for speech over a range of about 5km (three miles). The two jeep-mounted sets, the 22 set and the 19HP set, had ranges of 8km (five miles) and 40km (25 miles) respectively. Beyond this, the 76 Morse key set with a range of 500km (300 miles) was used. Throughout the war, radio communications were intermittent in all battles, and likely to fail altogether at night.*

▲ *Receiving neither jump pay nor flight pay, American glider troops were sensitive to their undeserved image as inferior to the paratroopers with whom they shared equal dangers. Here troops of* *327th Gilder Infantry Regiment, 101st Airborne Division, attempt to clear the bodies and wreckage from a CG-4A Waco glider after a particularly heavy landing near Son on Monday 18 September.*

Armoured Brigade attacked 59th Infantry Division's positions at Best and took more than 1,400 prisoners; the village itself remained in German hands. Farther north, a probe by 59th Infantry Division towards Veghel was beaten off by the Americans.

On Groesbeek heights the morning attack by Corps 'Feldt' had overrun part of 82nd Airborne's landing zones, which were cleared in a rifle charge by 505th Parachute Infantry just as 385 gliders landed with 1,782 men and the remainder of the division's artillery (twelve 75mm guns, twelve 105mm guns and eight 57mm anti-tank guns) at 1300, almost capturing General Feldt himself. As the tug aircraft departed, 135 B-25 Liberators of 8th Air Force dropped resupply to 82nd Airborne (80 per cent of which was recovered) and a further 117 Liberators dropped resupply to 101st Airborne (50 per cent recovered), losing eleven aircraft. At 1700 Browning ordered Gavin to plan for a night attack on Nijmegen bridge, then changed his mind and cancelled the attack.

West of Arnhem the British second wave arrived at 1500 to heavy German anti-aircraft fire which set fire to the heath below them. Hackett's 4th Parachute Brigade, in 124 Dakotas, dropped from 800ft (250m) right on top of 3rd Dutch SS Police Battalion, which was skirmishing with 1st Airl-anding Brigade, causing the Dutch SS to rout. The remainder of the South Staffordshire Regiment and the rest of the divisional troops also landed in 296 gliders, a total of 2,119 men. Only one Dakota was lost, but 20 escorting fighters were shot down holding off 90 Luftwaffe aircraft.

This landing was followed by 145 Stirlings and

Dakotas of RAF 38 and 46 Group on resupply. But the intended supply drop zone was still in German hands, and the Germans copied the British recognition signals. Most of the aircraft were hit by anti-aircraft fire, and of 87 tons dropped only twelve tons reached 1st British Airborne, for the loss of thirteen aircraft.

On landing, Hackett was surprised to be told by Mackenzie that Hicks was commanding the division, and was taking away 11th Battalion of the Parachute Regiment and the South Staffordshires to reinforce 1st Parachute Brigade's attack. Hackett arrived at the Hartenstein Hotel, now established as 1st British Airborne's headquarters, shortly before midnight, where Hicks ordered him to send his remaining two battalions at once up alongside 1st Parachute Brigade towards Arnhem. Hackett protested that he needed a plan, and that his brigade should attack towards its original objective of the high ground. A heated exchange followed in which Hicks accused Hackett of trying to take the division from him, but finally agreed to a delay.

The absence of the commander of 1st British Airborne at this point was critical. What mattered was a bridgehead over the Lower Rhine. If Hicks had given up the original objective of Arnhem

bridge he could have secured the Heveadorp ferry and the ground on either side, dug in and waited for XXX Corps. But this would have meant disobeying Browning's orders, and abandoning Frost.

With the junction between XXX Corps and 101st Airborne complete, Major General Taylor came under Horrocks' command. In turn, 50th (Northumbrian) Division was passed to VIII Corps under Lieutenant General O'Connor and began to move up towards Eindhoven. Just on midnight, VIII Corps began its delayed supporting attack with an assault crossing of the Meuse-Escaut Canal at Lille St Hubert by 3rd Division, part of which was still on the road from Brussels.

After two days, the battle was starting to swing against Montgomery. Despite breaking through the German defences, XXX Corps was checked at Son while the two flanking Army Corps had yet to make an impact. I Airborne Corps had lost any advantage of surprise from its airborne assault and had fallen into disarray. There was little information available to 21st Army Group on which to base an assessment, and no British reserve with which to influence the battle.

On the other side, Model's counter-attack was now ready.

◄ *Brigadier 'Pip' Hicks, taken at his headquarters at the Hartenstein Hotel on Monday 18 September. Hicks, who celebrated his 49th birthday during the battle (the same age as Lieutenant General Horrocks), was probably the oldest brigade commander in the British Army. He had led 1st Airlanding Brigade since April 1943, including its first major battle in the liberation of Sicily. (IWM photograph BU1152)*

THE GERMAN COUNTER-ATTACK, 19 SEPTEMBER

On Tuesday (D plus 2) the weather continued with fog in the morning and rain all day. The third wave of flights from England, due to take off at 1000, was fogbound until 1300 when the last battalion of 327th Glider Infantry took off with 101st Airborne's artillery in 385 gliders, of which 189 were lost or turned back. The 428 gliders carrying 82nd Airborne's reinforcement, chiefly two battalions of 325th Glider Infantry, remained grounded all day. The 114 Dakotas of 1st Polish Parachute Brigade were also grounded, but the brigade's small component of 35 gliders took off alone.

News of these changes was not passed by First Allied Airborne Army to 2nd Tactical Air Force in Belgium, which continued to fly support according to the original timetable. As a result, the airborne troops in Holland received no close air support, compared to 125 Luftwaffe fighter sorties. During the day, 43 Allied aircraft and 73 gliders were lost. Considering his job complete, Lieutenant General Brereton flew to Brussels with Ridgway and drove on to Eindhoven, wearing his dress uniform complete with medals, to watch the victory.

At 0330 in the dark and fog at Arnhem, 1st Parachute Brigade started its attack eastward along the line of the Lower Rhine, while 4th Parachute Brigade (10th and 156th Battalions of the Parachute Regiment) moved north-east across the railway line towards the high ground. 1st Parachute Brigade made about 400m towards the bridge before the fog lifted shortly after dawn, when it found itself caught in a German crossfire on the river road, between 20mm multi-barrelled anti-aircraft guns firing from the southern bank and SS-Kampfgruppe 'Spindler' from the embankment to the north. By 1000 the British attack had collapsed and been routed. At the

▶ *Paratroops of 1st Polish Parachute Brigade waiting beside their grounded C-47 Dakota at an airfield in eastern England, probably Tuesday 19 September. In Browning's plan, all German anti-aircraft defences to the south of Arnhem bridge would have been overcome by this date, making it safe to land paratroops. Major General Sosabowski made little effort to hide his lack of enthusiasm for this plan, or his belief that his troops were being misused by Browning.*

◀ *Men of the 2nd Battalion of the South Staffordshires moving down the main road from their landing zone through Oosterbeek to Arnhem on the morning of Tuesday 19 September, together with a 6pdr anti-tank gun towed by a jeep. Like all British airlanding troops, the South Staffordshires were a line battalion that had received special training in gliders. Note the woodland on either side of the road, which both sides found perfect for ambushes. (IWM photograph BU1091)*

end of the day, 1st Battalion of the Parachute Regiment numbered 40 unwounded men, while 3rd Battalion escaped with 116 men.

The attack through the town by 11th Battalion of the Parachute Regiment and 2nd Battalion of the South Staffordshires also met little success, reducing them to about 150 and 200 men respectively in the day's fighting. But by 0715 they had driven SS-Kampfgruppe 'Spindler' back far enough to free Major General Urquhart from his attic. Urquhart reached the Hartenstein minutes later by jeep, and began to reorganize what remained of his division. Hackett's attack north-east was reinforced by 7th Battalion of the King's Own Scottish Borderers from 1st Airlanding Brigade, leaving only 1st Battalion of the Border Regiment in reserve. Warnings were broadcast to 1st Polish Parachute Brigade not to land on its planned zones, which were under German control. Urquhart also ordered Colonel Hilary Barlow, deputy commander of 1st Airlanding Brigade, to take command of the street battle in Arnhem. Barlow set off towards the fighting and was never seen again, alive or dead. Years later, his battered cigarette case was found less than 1,000m from Arnhem bridge.

At Son, the Bailey bridge was complete, and the Guards Armoured resumed their advance at dawn. By 0820 the Household Cavalry reached Grave bridge, where Browning and Gavin were waiting for Horrocks, with the Grenadiers arriving two hours later. The journey of 85km (53 miles) from Joe's Bridge to Nijmegen had taken the Guards Armoured 42 hours and 130 casualties.

The arrival of XXX Corps put 82nd Airborne under Horrocks, who was increasingly unwell, and left Browning commanding only 1st British Airborne, with which he was barely in contact. The two Army Corps commanders, with Gavin and Adair, set up a joint HQ near Heumen and proceeded to command by a form of mutual agreement.

With 325th Glider Infantry delayed, Gavin had organized 450 of his glider pilots into an improvised battalion and was grateful for support from 8th Armoured Brigade and the Guards Armoured. An attack by 2/505th Parachute Infantry with the Grenadiers at Nijmegen began that afternoon but again failed to reach the bridge. Gavin proposed an assault crossing of the Waal to take the bridge from both ends, and Horrocks ordered XXX Corps' assault boats forward from Hechtel, through the

▶ *A 75mm pack howitzer of 1st Airlanding Light Artillery Regiment in action at Oosterbeek, Tuesday 19 September. Of American manufacture, the howitzer had an effective range of approximately 9,500m and a weight of 500kg (1,200lb). The radio communications and fire support of these guns were vital to Frost's defence of Arnhem bridge. (IWM photograph BU1094)*

rest of the traffic strung out on the highway.

East of Son, 107th Panzer Brigade (a battalion of PzKpfw V Panther tanks and a regiment of panzergrenadiers) arrived for Student's planned pincer attack with 59th Infantry Division from Best. This was pre-empted early in the afternoon by a renewed attack by 101st Airborne and 8th Armoured Brigade which routed 59th Infantry Division north of Best, securing 1,400 prisoners. 107th Panzer Brigade attacked by itself later in the afternoon from the east across the difficult country and almost overran 101st Airborne's headquarters at Son before Taylor could improvise a successful defence. While this was happening, 196 gliders landed with half Taylor's expected artillery and 1,341 out of 2,310 troops, followed by 60 Dakotas which delivered only 40 out of 256 tons of stores on target.

At Arnhem, by mid-afternoon the fighting had been continuous for 48 hours, and 1st British Airborne's attack was being ground down by lack of supplies, high casualties and sheer exhaustion. More German armour and artillery were arriving all the time, including 208th Assault Brigade (Sturmgeschütz IIIs) from Denmark and the first guns of Flak Brigade 'Von Swoboda'. Neither Generalleutnant von Tettau to the west nor Obersturmbahnführer Harzer to the east had a clear picture of the battle, or could coordinate their own forces, but 4th Parachute Brigade found its drive north-east firmly blocked.

Under fire from SS-Kampfgruppe 'Krafft' and threatened from the west, Hackett began to pull his brigade back south of the railway line at 1600. Just at this moment the Polish gliders arrived without an escort and landed between the British and German forces on their planned landing zone, having failed to receive Urquhart's warning. Only two Polish anti-tank guns and a handful of men survived to join the British. By the end of the day, Hackett's three battalions each numbered about 250 men. Resupply aircraft of RAF 38 and 46 Group following the Poles, 63 Dakotas and 100 Stirlings, dropped only 31 out of 390 tons correctly to 1st British Airborne, losing thirteen aircraft.

On Arnhem bridge, the day began with a German air raid, followed by shells and mortars from SS-Kampfgruppe 'Knaust' to the north and SS-Kampfgruppe 'Brinkmann' to the east. Frost now had only 250 unwounded men in ten of the eighteen houses he had first occupied. Protecting the wounded and prisoners was becoming a critical problem, as were food, water and ammunition. The battle for Arnhem bridge had become a waking nightmare in which the troops lost track of time. The Germans continued to blast the British out of their positions, but every time they attacked they were driven back, and the bridge remained closed. A summons to Frost to surrender was contemptuously rejected.

On the left flank of XXX Corps' drive towards Arnhem, 53rd Division of XII Corps had exhausted itself reaching the Turnhout-Eindhoven road. 7th

Armoured Division took over the Aart bridgehead, and 15th Division sidestepped eastward to pass through 53rd Division next day. On the right flank, 3rd Division of VIII Corps had almost reached Weert, and 11th Armoured Division had passed through towards Helmond, reaching just south-east of Eindhoven. The pressure on 101st Airborne led Dempsey to reinforce Taylor with a further armoured battalion from VIII Corps' 4th Armoured Brigade.

As dusk fell, the Luftwaffe bombed Eindhoven with 120 Ju 87s and Ju 88s (its only long-range bombing raid of autumn 1944 in Western Europe), causing at least 1,000 civilian casualties. Brereton and Ridgway, who had just arrived in the town by jeep, were caught up in the bombing and separated. Next morning Ridgway pressed on northwards to meet Taylor and Gavin at their respective headquarters. Brereton went separately to see Taylor at Son before turning back, and flew next day to SHAEF Headquarters to attend a planning conference, making no further effort to influence the battle.

▼ *A PzKpfw V Ausf. G Panther, probably of 9th SS Panzer Regiment, 9th SS Panzer Division 'Hohenstauffen', during the retreat through France to Arnhem. The tank is heavily camouflaged against Allied air attack, with a lot of external stowage, and two of the crew are performing aircraft sentry duty. A quick camouflage scheme of brown and green patches has been painted over the factory yellow, and no markings are visible except for the prominent (and puzzling) '6' on the turret.*

THE STALEMATE, 20 SEPTEMBER

The fog and rain continued into Wednesday (D plus 3), grounding the Poles and 325th Glider Infantry in England once again. Only resupply drops were possible, and 82nd Airborne received 80 per cent of its supplies. By dawn Urquhart had pulled 4th Parachute Brigade back and assembled his division into a thumb-shaped pocket at Oosterbeek with its base on the Lower Rhine. Using the Phantom radio equipment, Urquhart agreed with I Airborne Corps that the Poles should now land at Driel, opposite the Heveadorp ferry, to establish a bridgehead. Urquhart got through on the BBC radio to change 1st British Airborne's supply drop zones, but dropping canisters into the woods and streets of Oosterbeek against the intense German anti-aircraft fire was haphazard, and only thirteen per cent of its intended supplies reached 1st British Airborne.

Uncoordinated German attacks continued all the way around the British perimeter at Oosterbeek, with the forces intermingled in the woods and houses. An attack shortly after dawn by Kampfgruppe 'von Tettau' and SS-Kampfgruppe 'Krafft' against the perimeter was heavily repulsed. With neither side strong enough to make a decisive attack the fighting began to slow down, largely from exhaustion, into an affair of snipers and mortars. In at least one house the British and Germans held different floors and passed rations to each other, while 1st British Airborne found time during the battle to produce a one-sheet newspaper.

But this slowing of the pace did nothing to diminish the casualties. By the end of the day no Parachute Regiment battalion numbered more than 100 men, and only 1st Battalion of the Border Regiment was still intact. Within the perimeter both movement and care of the wounded became impossible, with the Main Dressing Stations coming under fire. By agreement the British pulled back slightly at mid-day to give the Germans possession of these buildings, allowing them to tend the

▶ *Soldiers of 101st Airborne take cover as a convoy of XXX Corps trucks comes under German fire on 'Hell's Highway' north of Eindhoven, Wednesday 20 September. The American defence was handicapped by all their movement being cross-country, as the road was reserved for the British. Although they were mostly unsuccessful, the delays imposed by these German attacks on XXX Corps' movement up the road helped decide the battle. (IWM photograph BU1062)*

wounded properly. This was one of several incidents of cooperation between enemies in a very hard-fought battle. Model further ordered that all civilians in Arnhem and Oosterbeek, which were now in a battle zone, were to be evacuated, which took four days to complete. The 'Orange Battalion' of the PAN with 1st British Airborne, some of whom fought at Arnhem bridge, quietly disbanded next day.

North of Eindhoven, on what 101st Airborne had started to call 'Hell's Highway', the German attacks began again at dawn. 107th Panzer Brigade advanced once more from the east against Son but was beaten back by 101st Airborne with British armoured support. Taylor then switched to a limited offensive, and 1/501st Parachute Infantry at Heeswijk took 418 German prisoners.

While 101st Airborne and 8th Armoured Brigade fought, XXX Corps continued up the road as best it could, including the delayed assault boats and 43rd (Wessex) Division moving from Hechtel. The first troops of the division's 130th Brigade reached Grave at noon, but on the congested road the full division took even longer than the Guards Armoured to reach Nijmegen.

At I Airborne Corps Headquarters the delays on Hell's Highway together with the news from Arnhem caused Gavin to snap at Horrocks' slowness, while the normally icy Browning threw an ink bottle at a picture of a German general on the wall. Help was offered by 52nd (Lowland) Division, which volunteered to fly into an airstrip near Nijmegen next day. Browning, still expecting the Poles and 325th Glider Infantry, turned the offer down.

Because of 82nd Airborne's weakness and the expected major attack at Groesbeek, the Guards Armoured was broken up to provide support. While the Grenadiers and Irish Guards prepared for the assault crossing, the Welsh Guards covered Grave bridge, and the Coldstream supported the Groesbeek position. Meanwhile the Household Cavalry patrolled west as far as the main supply depot for First Parachute Army at Oss, where the pragmatic storekeepers issued supplies to both sides (German rations from Oss reached as far south as British 3rd Division at Weert during the battle).

That morning, the Irish Guards and 504th Parachute Infantry started to clear the suburbs of Nijmegen for the river crossing, while the Grenadiers and 505th Parachute Infantry moved towards the bridge. The assault crossing began at 1440, just after the arrival of the boats, with an attack by Typhoons of RAF 83 Group, followed by a ten-minute artillery and smoke bombardment from 100 guns of XXX Corps and the tanks of the Irish Guards. At 1500 two companies of 3/504th Parachute Infantry crossed the Waal west of the bridges in 19ft assault boats under heavy German artillery fire. Half the boats reached the far shore, and six successive journeys brought the rest of 3/504th Parachute Infantry and 1/504th Parachute Infantry across. Once ashore, 3/504th Parachute Infantry attacked eastwards, clearing first the railway bridge

▶ *Cromwell tanks of the Guards Armoured Division, heavily festooned with external baggage, driving up 'Hell's Highway' just south of Nijmegen, Wednesday 20 September. The windmills in the area were used to pump water along the nearby drainage ditches. Throughout the battle, the last vehicles of a division moving up the road to Arnhem were at least 24 hours behind its leading troops. (IWM photograph B10131)*

then the road bridge at the cost of 107 casualties. Some 417 German bodies were later recovered from the railway bridge area alone. At the same time, 505th Parachute Infantry and the Grenadiers attacked through the town towards the road bridge, the first Grenadier tanks crossing at 1910. In defiance of Model's orders, Brigadeführer Harmel ordered the bridge blown as the Grenadiers crossed, but the charges failed to go off. Later that night Model, not realizing he was too late, authorised Bittrich to blow Nijmegen bridge if necessary.

On Groesbeek heights, Corps 'Feldt' resumed its attack at dawn with 406th Landesschützen Division to the north and the newly arrived II Parachute Corps to the south. Serving under General Feldt, this consisted of the Training Battalions of 3rd and 5th Parachute Divisions, both of which had been destroyed in Normandy. By mid-morning 82nd Airborne had identified this attack as coming from both full strength parachute divisions and alerted Gavin, who returned to his command post from Nijmegen. At first II Parachute Corps' drive met considerable success, and by evening it had almost reached the bridge at Heumen, threatening to cut the road behind 82nd Airborne. But counter-attacks by 508th Parachute Infantry, supported by the Coldstream, gradually restored the position.

At Arnhem bridge, Frost had water for only one more day, and Urquhart advised I Airborne Corps

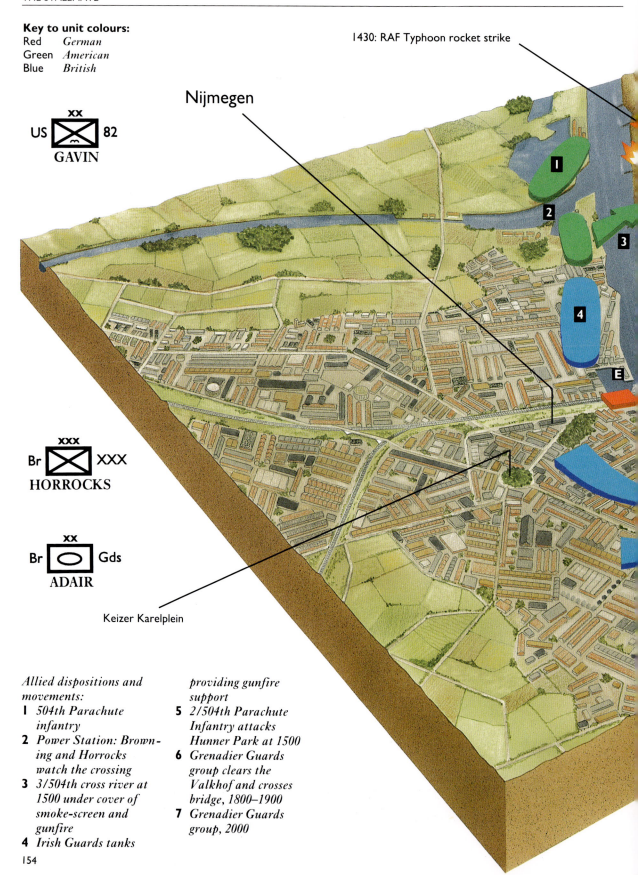

Key to unit colours:
Red *German*
Green *American*
Blue *British*

1430: RAF Typhoon rocket strike

Nijmegen

US ⊠ 82 GAVIN

Br ⊠ XXX HORROCKS

Br ⬭ Gds ADAIR

Keizer Karelplein

Allied dispositions and movements:
1 *504th Parachute infantry*
2 *Power Station: Browning and Horrocks watch the crossing*
3 *3/504th cross river at 1500 under cover of smoke-screen and gunfire*
4 *Irish Guards tanks*
   providing gunfire support
5 *2/504th Parachute Infantry attacks Hunner Park at 1500*
6 *Grenadier Guards group clears the Valkhof and crosses bridge, 1800–1900*
7 *Grenadier Guards group, 2000*

154

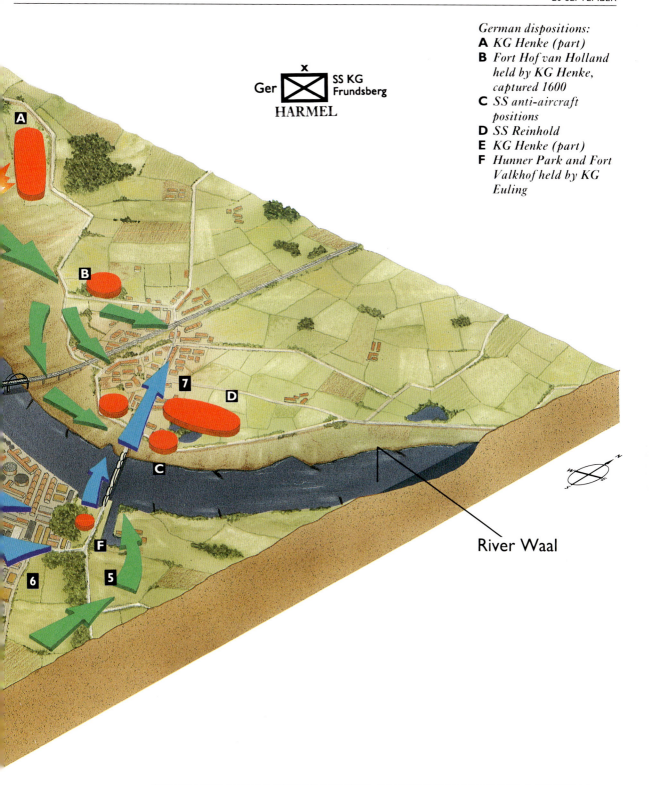

Ger **SS KG Frundsberg**

HARMEL

German dispositions:
A *KG Henke (part)*
B *Fort Hof van Holland held by KG Henke, captured 1600*
C *SS anti-aircraft positions*
D *SS Reinhold*
E *KG Henke (part)*
F *Hunner Park and Fort Valkhof held by KG Euling*

River Waal

THE RIVER CROSSING AT NIJMEGEN

1500–2000 20 Sept 1944, as seen from the Groesbeek Heights

that relief of the bridge by Guards Armoured was now critical. The German bombardment continued, blasting down the buildings still held by the British and using flamethrowers to clear them from the rubble. At noon Frost himself was badly wounded by a mortar blast, and Major Gough took over command of the remaining troops. Almost out of ammunition, with wounded crowded into cellars, the British held on to their shrinking perimeter. Shortly after 1800 four PzKpfw VI Tiger tanks at last crashed their way across Arnhem bridge from north to south, but nothing else could follow them. At 2100 Gough negotiated a truce enabling the Germans to collect over 200 wounded of both sides from the cellars, including Frost who became a prisoner.

Much farther south, the British flanking operations remained painfully slow. In a last effort by XII Corps, 15th Division forced the line of the Wilhelmina Canal at Best, but still the village itself remained in German hands. VIII Corps began moving 69th Brigade of 50th Division northward to reinforce 101st Airborne, while 11th Armoured Division made some progress towards Helmond. With the German flanks growing stronger, these attacks across country stood little chance.

At Oosterbeek, far from expecting to crush 1st British Airborne, Model put Kampfgruppe 'von Tettau' under II SS Panzer Corps in order to check an expected breakout by Urquhart's troops. More German reinforcements continued to arrive, and XII SS Corps was expected with the new 180th Infantry Division and 190th Infantry Division within a week. In keeping with German doctrine rather than expecting any chance of success, Bittrich also ordered Harmel to counter-attack and retake Nijmegen next morning.

With only three battalions of the 'Frundsberg' between Nijmegen and Arnhem, it seemed that nothing could stop the Allies reaching Arnhem bridge that night. But on the other side Adair's Guards Armoured, fought to a standstill, would not advance at night into the *polder* of the 'island' without infantry, and Horrocks let them halt.

Meanwhile, far away from the battlefield, SHAEF Headquarters completed its move from Granville to Versailles, just west of Paris, drastically improving its communications. After four days, it was becoming clear to the senior Allied commanders that the original 'Market-Garden' plan had failed, and that the war against Germany was by no means over yet. The first hint of a change in attitude

◄ *Troops of 1st British Airborne with Sten submachine-guns, dug in to defend the Oosterbeek pocket beside their jeeps, late on Monday 18 September. Note that one is a signaller, still wearing his earphones and using the 22 radio set in the jeep beside him. This picture gives a good impression of the limited view from ground level of both sides when fighting in the pocket. (IWM photograph BU1143)*

► *Above right: On the other side of the Oosterbeek pocket, German infantry dug in among the trees. From their general appearance, these troops seem to be from one of the*

came when Montgomery at 21st Army Group Headquarters received a message from Eisenhower denying that SHAEF had ever intended a broad front advance and reaffirming priority for the northern thrust. With 'Market-Garden' a failure and both sides temporarily locked in an exhausted stalemate, the whole nature of the Battle of Arnhem was about to change.

various improvised formations which made up Kampfgruppe 'Von Tettau'. (IWM photograph MH3956)

▶ *A British casualty, with a leg wound, being carried by stretcher-bearers into one of the hotels or large houses used by 1st British Airborne as Main Dressing Stations. Later in the battle conditions became very overcrowded, and despite Red Cross markings it was almost impossible, among the houses and trees of Oosterbeek, for both sides to avoid firing at these positions before they were finally passed to German control. (IWM photograph BU1158)*

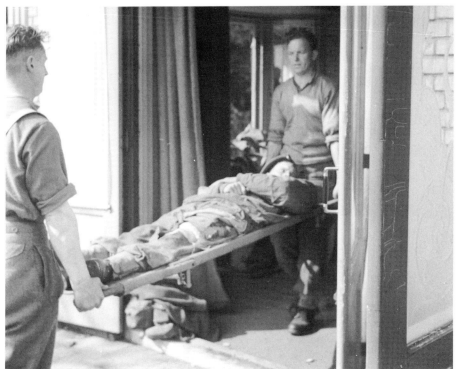

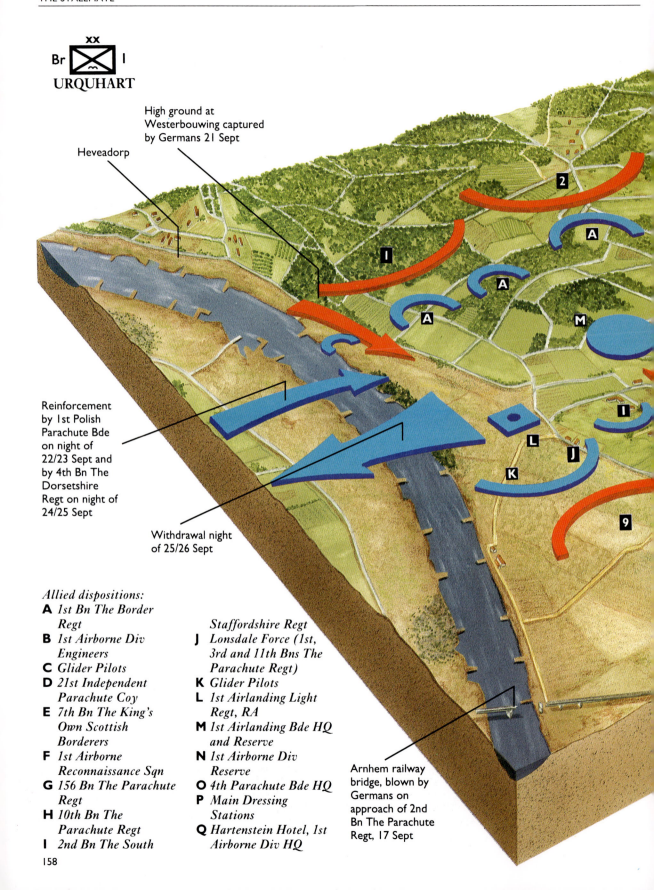

Br **⊠** I
URQUHART

High ground at
Westerbouwing captured
by Germans 21 Sept

Heveadorp

Reinforcement
by 1st Polish
Parachute Bde
on night of
22/23 Sept and
by 4th Bn The
Dorsetshire
Regt on night of
24/25 Sept

Withdrawal night
of 25/26 Sept

Arnhem railway
bridge, blown by
Germans on
approach of 2nd
Bn The Parachute
Regt, 17 Sept

Allied dispositions:
A *1st Bn The Border
Regt*
B *1st Airborne Div
Engineers*
C *Glider Pilots*
D *21st Independent
Parachute Coy*
E *7th Bn The King's
Own Scottish
Borderers*
F *1st Airborne
Reconnaissance Sqn*
G *156 Bn The Parachute
Regt*
H *10th Bn The
Parachute Regt*
I *2nd Bn The South*

Staffordshire Regt
J *Lonsdale Force (1st,
3rd and 11th Bns The
Parachute Regt)*
K *Glider Pilots*
L *1st Airlanding Light
Regt, RA*
M *1st Airlanding Bde HQ
and Reserve*
N *1st Airborne Div
Reserve*
O *4th Parachute Bde HQ*
P *Main Dressing
Stations*
Q *Hartenstein Hotel, 1st
Airborne Div HQ*

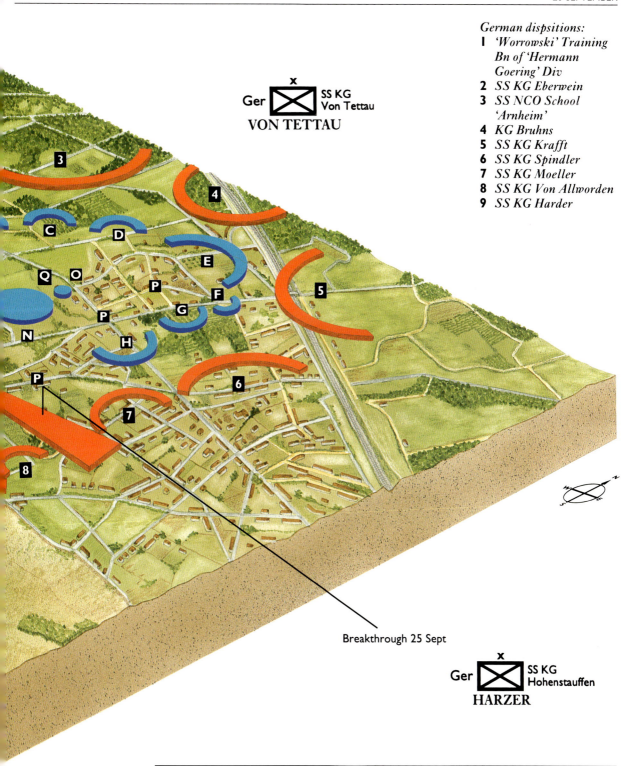

German dispsitions:
1 'Worrowski' Training Bn of 'Hermann Goering' Div
2 SS KG Eberwein
3 SS NCO School 'Arnheim'
4 KG Bruhns
5 SS KG Krafft
6 SS KG Spindler
7 SS KG Moeller
8 SS KG Von Allworden
9 SS KG Harder

Ger SS KG Von Tettau
VON TETTAU

Breakthrough 25 Sept

Ger SS KG Hohenstauffen
HARZER

1ST AIRBORNE DIVISION PERIMETER, OOSTERBEEK

20–26 Sept 1944, as seen from the direction of Arnhem Bridge

THE NEW ALLIED PLAN, 21 – 22 SEPTEMBER

The fog and rain continued into Thursday (D plus 4), which was bitingly cold. As dawn arrived, Generalfeldmarschall Model at Army Group B issued fresh orders. Corps 'Feldt' was to hold its position. It had spent itself in the attack over the Groesbeek heights, and with Nijmegen bridge now in Allied hands there was little that it could do. Model placed all troops as far south as Elst under II SS Panzer Corps, which was to wipe out the British at Arnhem while containing any drive north of Nijmegen. Student's First Parachute Army was to organize a coordinated pincer attack by LXXXVIII Corps and LXXXVI Corps against Hell's Highway for next day.

At Arnhem bridge, the last fight began at about 0900, as Gough and his men tried to break out northwards against SS-Kampfgruppe 'Knaust'. There was no formal surrender or end to the fighting. In small groups, the British either ran out of ammunition or were overwhelmed. Some refused to give up or fought on with knives, and the last shots were not fired at Arnhem bridge for another two days. But at 1200, SS-Kampfgruppe 'Knaust' at last crossed Arnhem bridge. Frost's men had fought for 88 hours without relief, the last twelve of them without food or water.

In the Oosterbeek pocket, Urquhart re-organized his defence, placing Hicks in charge of

the western face against Kampfgruppe 'von Tettau', and Hackett in charge of the eastern face against SS-Kampfgruppe 'Hohenstauffen'. At 0900 an attack by Kampfgruppe 'von Tettau' drove 1st Battalion of the Border Regiment back off the Westerbouwing hill (30m high), the crucial high ground that overlooked the Heveadorp ferry, and away from the ferry itself, which was destroyed in the fighting. From the Westerbouwing, German fire could dominate any attempted river crossing. In their confusion and exhaustion, neither side had appreciated the vital significance of this ground. Kampfgruppe 'von Tettau' pushed Hick's troops back about 800m during the day, but Model's orders to eliminate the British pocket could not be carried out with the available forces. Instead, the Germans set up loudspeakers to play music to the British, along with invitations to surrender, while the sniping and mortaring continued.

At Nijmegen, the way across the two bridges was finally cleared of German snipers by 1000. Two hours later, while the Grenadiers recovered, the

◀ *Arnhem bridge, taken by a German photographer from the north side of the ramp looking south, shortly after the last stand of Frost's men, Thursday 21 September. The burnt out German pillbox can be seen to the right of the bridge, together with the rubble of buildings destroyed in the fighting. The vehicles wrecked in 9th SS Reconnaissance Battalion's attack have been cleared away to the left and the bridge is now open. (IWM photograph HU2127)*

Irish Guards led off northwards with the Welsh Guards following. The attack started just as SS-Kampfgruppe 'Knaust' was crossing Arnhem bridge. Short of ammunition, artillery and air cover, the tanks of the Guards Armoured pushed up the exposed causeway road as far as Elst, and halted in the face of German fire. By 1600, SS-Kampfgruppe 'Knaust' had reached Elst from Arnhem to establish a firm block.

Meanwhile, 43rd Division, which was still waiting for its last brigade to get through from Eindhoven, was busy clearing the remaining pockets of German resistance from Nijmegen. Horrocks ordered the division, under Major General G. I. Thomas, to take over the lead from the spent Guards Armoured, advance through Driel and link up with 1st British Airborne at Heveadorp. Relieved of much of the responsibility for Nijmegen, 82nd Airborne began a general attack late in the afternoon with 504th Parachute Infantry and 508th Parachute Infantry, which cleared Corps 'Feldt' off the Groesbeek heights before establishing a solid defence.

During the afternoon, 1st British Airborne established firm radio contact with XXX Corps through the Royal Artillery's 64th Medium Regiment. The distance from Nijmegen to Arnhem is only 17km (eleven miles), and through this link Urquart could call for fire support from the whole of XXX Corps' artillery, drastically reducing the German advantage north of the Lower Rhine. Without this fire support the Oosterbeek pocket could not have been held, and after the battle Urquhart tried unsuccessfully to have 64th Medium Regiment awarded British Airborne insignia. In response to this stiffening resistance, Model ordered specialist troops and equipment for street fighting to be flown into Deelen by Junkers Ju 52 transport aircraft, and was promised 506th Heavy Tank Battalion, freshly equipped with 45 of the formidable PzKpfw VIB King Tiger tanks, from eastern Germany.

Back in England, 1st Polish Parachute Brigade's three infantry battalions took off at 1400, flying on the northern route. Of its 114 Dakotas, 41 turned back in the bad weather (including virtually the whole of 1st Battalion) and three landed in Brussels. Over Driel more than 100 Luftwaffe fighters were

◀ *Paratroops of 1st Polish Parachute Brigade at last preparing to take off on Thursday 21 September. This picture gives an unusually good view of the manner in which British-style equipment was fitted over the Denison smock before donning the parachute harness. The soldier on the right is rearranging his face veil before fitting his helmet.*

◄ *Paratroopers of 82nd Airborne Division watch as Cromwell tanks of the Guards Armoured Division, probably from 2nd (Armoured Reconnaissance) Battalion of the Welsh Guards, move across Nijmegen bridge northward towards Arnhem on the morning of Thursday 21 September. The low, flat ground of the 'island' can be seen in the distance on the right. (IWM photograph B10172)*

waiting for the Poles, of which 25 broke through and together with anti-aircraft fire claimed thirteen more Dakotas. At 1700, Major-General Sosabowski landed at Driel with 750 men and no heavy equipment, which had been lost in the gliders two days before.

To the Germans, the Polish landing, coinciding with the move south to Elst by SS-Kampfgruppe 'Knaust' to confront the Guards Armoured, appeared as an attempt to outflank them and capture Arnhem bridge once more from the south. Obersturmbahnführer Harzer rapidly organized 2,500 sailors, airmen, coastal defence troops, Dutch SS police and German infantry as a blocking force (known as 'Sperrverband Harzer') between the Poles and the bridge, west of the Nijmegen road. Flying resupply after the Poles, 115 transport aircraft of RAF 38 Group were intercepted by ten Fw 190s which broke through the fighter screen again. Some 23 resupply aircraft were shot down and 38 damaged by fighters or flak, and only 41 out of 300

A Sherman V tank of the Guards Armoured Division. This tank, 'Monck', is the command tank of Lieutenant Colonel R. F. S. Gooch, MC, 1st (Armoured) Battalion, Coldstream Guards, identifiable from the 'All Seeing Eye' formation sign of the Guards Division, the regimental number '52', and the HQ squadron diamond, all on the stowage box fitted to the nose of the tank, and the regimental flag displayed. The hull machine-gun has been removed to accommodate an extra radio operator, and there is an extra aerial fitted at the right hull position.

▲ *500ft (160 metres) above Driel at 1700 on Thursday 21 September, the leading paratroopers of 1st Polish Parachute Brigade prepare to leave the jump door of their C-47 Dakota. The Dakota had only one jump door, which some pilots preferred to leave open during the flight. It was known for the leading paratrooper of the 'stick' of fifteen men to become wedged in the door if the pilot manoeuvred suddenly to avoid enemy fire. After the jump signal was given, the actual moment of jumping was often left to the 'stick' leader, who would watch for obstacles.*

tons got through to the British at Oosterbeek. After nightfall, the Poles began planning to cross the Lower Rhine, but no boats arrived from XXX Corps before dawn.

North of Eindhoven, 101st Airborne continued to push the Germans back on either side of Hell's Highway in a series of limited attacks supported by British armour. The drives by VIII Corps and XII Corps, which had fought their way across country

roughly level with the line of the Wilhelmina Canal, had come virtually to a halt. Lieutenant General Dempsey began to move Second Army Headquarters to St Oedenrode, and Field Marshal Montgomery established 21st Army Group Tactical Headquarters just south of Eindhoven to be in closer touch with the battle.

In response to General Eisenhower's earlier message, Montgomery sent a signal to SHAEF demanding that Eisenhower make good his commitment to the northern thrust by halting Patton's Third US Army and placing Hodges' First US Army at least under some form of British control. On the same day, Patton arrived at Versailles with Bradley's blessing, demanding more troops for his thrust across the Rhine. Eisenhower's response was to summon a major conference of his Army Group and Army commanders – the first since before the D-Day landings on 6 June – for the next day.

Friday 22 September (D plus 5) was very misty, and there were no resupply flights from England, but the weather was beginning to lift. At 0900 General Student's attack on Hell's Highway began with Kampfgruppe 'Huber' (part of 59th Infantry Divison) from the west and Kampfgruppe 'Walther' (now mainly 107th Panzer Brigade) from the east, breaking through to cut the largely undefended section of road between Uden and Grave. This also split 69th Brigade of British 50th Division, which was moving up to cover the gap between 101st Airborne and 82nd Airborne. In response, 101st Airborne, now under XXX Corps with its long familiarity with air support procedures, obtained 119 rocket-firing Typhoon sorties from RAF 83 Group along Hell's Highway during the day.

Not far away over Kleve, completely divorced from the Arnhem battle, 9th Air Force fighters dominated the skies, while 8th Air Force and Bomber Command, whose bombers might have influenced the battle considerably, flew raids against German cities. Only at Arnhem and Nijmegen did the Germans continue to enjoy air superiority. Lieutenant General Dempsey's chief of staff, attempting to reach Horrocks at Nijmegen by aircraft, was shot down but survived.

Major General Taylor received some warning of the German pincer attack through the PAN, and rushed 150 men of 506th Parachute Infantry to Uden by 1100, only minutes before the German tanks arrived. A limited attack north-west by 501st and 502nd Parachute Infantry had to be abandoned as Kampfgruppe 'Huber' reached Veghel by 1400, putting the bridge under fire, and in the course of the fighting Colonel John H. Michaelis, commanding 501st Parachute Infantry, was seriously wounded. Brigadier General Anthony McAuliffe, the division's artillery commander, began with 2/501st Parachute Infantry defending Veghel and finished with eight battalions as American and British reinforcements arrived. Horrocks was forced to turn the whole of 32nd Guards Brigade (the Grenadiers and Coldstream) around to drive back south down Hell's Highway from Grave to Uden, clearing the road of Germans. For a crucial day, supplies and equipment, above all river crossing equipment, could not travel beyond Veghel.

The renewed attempt by XXX Corps to reach 1st British Airborne began shortly after dawn with orders from Horrocks to take all risks. 43rd Divison attacked north from Nijmegen, with 214th Brigade moving towards Driel, while 129th Brigade and the Irish Guards Group attacked at Elst. On the exposed 'island' movement within sight of the enemy was almost impossible for either side, and unsupported vehicles were open targets. But at 0830 a few armoured cars of the Household Cavalry found a route through to the Poles at Driel. Strictly, this completed the link between XXX Corps and 1st British Airborne, four days and eighteen hours since the start of 'Market-Garden'. That afternoon Lieutenant Colonel Mackenzie crossed the Lower Rhine and used the Households' radios to send a long signal to Horrocks and Browning before driving off to Nijmegen. By late afternoon a single infantry battalion, 5th Battalion of the Duke of Cornwall's Light Infantry with some tanks, had reached the Poles.

At 2100 Sosabowski, acting on Horrocks' orders, attempted a river crossing towards Heveadorp with four rubber boats, all that were available. Under intense German fire, about 50 Poles crossed, of whom 35 survived to join the Border Regiment. A plan for 5th Battalion of the Duke of Cornwall's Light Infantry to follow them later that night was called off as no further boats or DUKW amphibious craft had arrived. German attacks continued all around the Oosterbeek pocket, and at 2144 Urquhart signalled Browning that relief within 24 hours was vital. Bittrich meanwhile conferred with Harzer and von Tettau to plan the final destruction of 1st British Airborne next day.

▶ *The PAN (Dutch) resistance made a major contribution to 'Market-Garden', although they were shot by the Germans if caught fighting on the Allied side. Here two PAN men, wearing identifying orange armbands, pass information to officers on the Intelligence staff of 50th (Northumbrian) Division near Valkenswaard on Monday 25 September (note the 'Tyne-Tees' shoulder flash of the two British officers). Failure to make proper use of PAN information contributed to 1st British Airborne Division's problems at Arnhem. (IWM photograph B10313)*

While the fighting raged all day from Veghel to Oosterbeek, Eisenhower's Army Group and Army commanders assembled at Versailles. Even for this vital meeting, Montgomery stuck to his custom and sent Major General de Guingand to represent him, reportedly because he did not trust himself to speak to the American generals. This meeeting began to repair the mistakes in the original 'Market-Garden' plan, as Eisenhower asserted the authority that had drifted for the last month. Instead of individual actions against a defeated enemy, Eisenhower now insisted on a coordinated advance to the Rhine by all his Armies, stressing the importance of First Canadian Army's attack to clear the Scheldt and open Antwerp now that the war was going to last beyond September. Bradley was instructed to halt Patton (the formal order to Third US Army was issued next day), while First US Army was ordered to swing northwards towards Aachen, sending XIX Corps under Major General Charles H. Corlett (temporarily reduced by Bradley to two divisions) northwards to cooperate with British VIII Corps. In return, Second British Army would change its axis of advance, with VIII Corps leading north-east across country towards Venlo and Kleve, instead of XXX Corps heading north past Arnhem. Although First US Army remained under Bradley, Montgomery was allowed direct communication with it.

That afternoon Montgomery visited 3rd Division at Weert, the first of a series of visits to explain the new plan throughout Second British Army. Although a bridgehead at Arnhem might be useful, and there were humanitarian reasons for saving 1st British Airborne, from this point XXX Corps' efforts north of Nijmegen became a secondary operation, and any idea of an advance past Arnhem was given up. It says much for Montgomery's state of mind that he seems to have believed that this new plan was feasible, and that Lieutenant General O'Connor might yet rescue his battle for him.

Next day, Lieutenant General Dempsey placed 101st Airborne under VIII Corps, while 50th Division was reinforced by 131st Brigade of 7th Armoured from XII Corps, and – together with the Royal Netherlands Brigade 'Prinses Irene' – took over Nijmegen from 43rd Division. VIII Corps now had to fight on two fronts: while 101st Airborne and 50th Division defended against attacks from the west and north-west, 3rd Division and 11th Armoured Division were to drive north-east to the Rhine, keeping step with US XIX Corps. Horrocks' XXX Corps was left with the troops north of Grave – 43rd Division, 82nd Airborne and the fragmented Guards Armoured – while I Airborne Corps continued to command the survivors of 1st British Airborne. After meetings between Montgomery, Dempsey, their Army Corps and divisional commanders, Second British Army signalled I Airborne Corps at 2020 that it had permission to withdraw 1st British Airborne if necessary, just over 24 hours after Urquhart's appeal.

▲ *Major General 'Roy' Urquhart on the back lawn of his headquarters at the Hartenstein Hotel, Friday 22 September, with 1st British Airborne Division's pennon beside him. Except for his red beret and rank badges, Urquhart is dressed in the regulation battledress uniform for all British officers. Previously a* brigadier in the 51st (Highland) Division, he *was promoted to lead 1st British Airborne in January 1944 without previous airborne experience. Despite his very orthodox approach, Urquhart was regarded by many in the division as an outstanding leader. (IWM photograph BU1136)*

THE END AT ARNHEM, 23 – 26 SEPTEMBER

Saturday 23 September (D plus 6) produced the first good weather since the start of 'Market-Garden', despite the morning fog and the rain that night, and 2nd Tactical Air Force was heavily active over Oosterbeek. With artillery and air support, 1st British Airborne held on to its foxholes and houses, and once more Harzer and von Tettau could not break through the perimeter. In the afternoon, an angry Model visited II SS Panzer Corps Head-quarters and gave Bittrich 24 more hours to wipe 1st British Airborne out. Model also changed Army Group B's command structure, placing all forces west of the 'Market-Garden' salient under Fifteenth Army, and all those to the east under First Parachute Army, at last relieving Armed Forces Command Netherlands and Wehrkreiss VI of their fighting responsibilities. So far, Model's defensive scheme had largely succeeded, stopping 'Market--Garden' only two-thirds of the way to its objective on the Zuider Zee. Now, in the classic manner of German counterstrokes on the Eastern Front, he planned to destroy both I Airborne Corps and XXX Corps north of Nijmegen and regain the line of the Waal.

Farther south, the Germans renewed their attacks against Veghel in the morning with 6th Parachute Regiment (now part of Kampfgruppe 'Chill') from the west and Kampfgruppe 'Walther' from the east, but they were both driven off by noon. Three hours later, 506th Parachute Infantry with British armour linked with 32nd Guards Brigade at Uden, reopening Hell's Highway.

At 1300, the delayed last wave of airborne reinforcements took off from England in the largest 'Market-Garden' airlift since its first day. Escorted by fighters of 8th Air Force, 654 troop carriers and 490 gliders flew on the northern route almost without incident to land at 1500. 82nd Airborne received 3,385 troops in 428 gliders, mainly the delayed 325th Glider Infantry Regiment, which

A captain in the Royal Netherlands Brigade 'Prinses Irene', wearing British battledress and equipment with Dutch rank badges, including brigade shoulder flash, 'Lion' cap badge and Dutch national 'Lion and Netherlands' sleeve badge.

▲ *Major General Sosabowski, in Denison smock and paratrooper's uniform, at his head-quarters in the woods east of Driel with Major General G. I. Thomas commanding 43rd (Wessex) Division, probably on Saturday 23 September. Thomas is wearing an unusual uniform of pre-war style boots, puttees and breeches with a battle-dress blouse worn over a sleeveless sweater and motoring goggles around his general's cap. With a reputation for offering unwelcome advice, Thomas did not get on well with Sosabowski and was heavily criticized for his division's slowness during 'Market-Garden'.*

dropped at Oude Keent, a disused airfield just outside Grave which I Airborne Corps planned to use for resupply. The battalion then marched northwards to join its brigade, which had been placed under 130th Brigade of 43rd Division by Horrocks. At Driel, 41 USAAF Dakotas dropped supplies and equipment to Sosabowski, who was increasingly ready to show his disgust with his treatment and that of his brigade by the British.

On the 'island', XXX Corps' advance against SS-Kampfgruppe 'Frundsberg' made little prog-ress, delayed until supplies and equipment could reach it while Hell's Highway was cleared farther south. Late in the morning Lieutenant Colonel Mackenzie finally reached Browning at I Airborne Corps Headquarters. Browning gave Mackenzie a message of greeting to take back to Urquhart, but other than expressing his anger with 43rd Division's slow progress he had nothing to offer. That afternoon 130th Brigade with more river crossing equipment linked up with the Poles at Driel, and after nightfall Sosabowksi sent 200 men of his 1st Battalion across the Lower Rhine in assault boats to join 1st British Airborne. Next morning Mackenzie also recrossed the Lower Rhine to rejoin his division.

On Sunday 24 September (D plus 7) the weather remained reasonable after some morning fog, and 2nd Tactical Air Force flew 22 close air support sorties for 1st British Airborne from mid-afternoon, despite problems in identifying targets in the shrinking Oosterbeek pocket. Through XXX Corps artillery support and its own fighting qualities, 1st British Airborne continued to hold the perimeter, although Brigadier Hackett was wounded by a shellburst that morning. Urquhart's men were now threatened with the same fate that had overwhelmed Frost, a collapse from exhaustion and lack of ammunition. At 1500 a medical truce came into force, carefully negotiated between 1st British Airborne and II SS Panzer Corps, which allowed the transfer of 700 wounded to the Germans, followed by 500 more next day. This left Urquhart with about 1,800 troops organized in small groups to defend the pocket.

Both sides at Arnhem had now been fighting for a week without rest, almost without sleep, and a single fresh formation might swing the battle. This

should have arrived four days before. 101st Airborne received 907th Glider Field Artillery Battalion and the last of 327th Glider Infantry. The seaborne tails of both divisions also arrived from England through the Normandy beaches, com-pleting their deployment.

1st Battalion of 1st Polish Parachute Brigade, which had turned back on Thursday 21 September,

▲ Two British paratroops, one of them wearing the sleeveless 'jump jacket', fit a Mark 1 Weapons Container underneath an aircraft before take-off in England. Fitted with its own parachute, this container was used to carry a variety of stores and equipment. Other stores were dropped directly from the open doors of the cargo aircraft. (IWM photograph H37727)

▼ Troops of 1st Airborne Division in the grounds of the Hartenstein Hotel displaying yellow parachutes as a guide to Allied aircraft dropping supplies, probably on Saturday 23 September. As this picture shows, even when the Allied pilots were aware of the intended supply drop zones, picking them out from among the trees and houses was extremely difficult. (IWM photograph BU1119)

◀ Top: German infantry in the Oosterbeek pocket, late in the fighting. The mixture of uniforms worn and weapons carried by these men tells its own story. The German ability to assemble improvised forces at short notice was much admired by the Allies, but although these could be strong in defence, they had great difficulty making coordinated attacks. (IWM photograph HU2126)

◀ Men of the Glider Pilot Regiment, carrying Sten submachine-guns and pistols, fight their way through the rubble of a building in Oosterbeek, Saturday 23 September. The 1,200 men of the Gilder Pilot Regiment at Arhem formed two 'Wings', each the equivalent of a battalion, and played a major part in the defence of the perimeter. (IWM photograph BU1121)

▲ A British ammunition truck explodes, scattering incendiaries on to the road, having been hit by fire from Parachute Battalion 'Jungwirth' near Koevering on 'Hell's Highway', on the evening of Sunday 24 September. Much of the road at this point was lined with trees, making ambush easier for the Germans. (IWM photograph B10124A)

arrived on the German side in the form of the King Tigers of 506th Heavy Tank Battalion, of which two companies (30 tanks) were sent to the 'Frundsberg' near Elst and one company to the east side of the Oosterbeek pocket. Even before these tanks arrived, XXX Corps had made only slow progress north of Nijmegen against the German defence. The only success that day was the capture of Bemmel by 69th Brigade and the Welsh Guards.

At 0930 Horrocks, together with Thomas and Sosabowski, surveyed the far side of the Lower Rhine from the steeple of Driel church. Thomas came away believing that Horrocks had issued orders for the withdrawal of 1st British Airborne that night, and began planning a crossing to seize the Westerbouwing and help Urquhart. Horrocks, who later denied he had issued these orders, then went to Second British Army Headquarters to consult Dempsey. Who actually gave the order to withdraw from Arnhem cannot be established, but Montgomery notified London of the decision, and the forthcoming thrust north-east by VIII Corps, that evening. As news of the planned withdrawal spread there was a late flurry of activity from the airborne commanders. First Allied Airborne Army

◀ *Officers of 1st Polish Parchute Brigade, 1st Airborne Division and 43rd Division at Sosabowksi's headquarters east of Driel, probably Saturday 23 September, planning the river crossing by 4th Battalion of the Dorsetshire Regiment. Note the 'Wessex Wyvern' divisional patch of the Dorsets' officer left, and that like many officers Sosabowski wears no rank or identifying badges on his Denison smock. This often makes precise identification of airborne troops from photographs extremely difficult.*

tried to arrange for 8th Air Force fighters to drop belly tanks full of supplies to 1st British Airborne, while Browning now wanted 52nd (Lowland) Division flown in, a suggestion vetoed by Dempsey and Montgomery.

In response to Generalfeldmarschall von Rundstedt's suggestion that all German troops in Holland should fall back to the Maas in the face of Second British Army's offensive, Hitler demanded instead a renewed offensive at Nijmegen and Veghel. Model took full advantage of this by requesting even more reinforcements, including the full strength 363rd Volksgrenadier Division, which could not arrive until after the battle.

The renewed attack on Hell's Highway by Kampfgruppe 'Chill' began shortly after dawn, looking for weak spots in 101st Airborne's line. Most of the Germans were heavily repulsed, but as dusk fell the weak Parachute Battalion 'Jungwirth', reinforced by a company of Jagdpanthers of 559th Assault Battalion, cut the road once again at Koevering, just south of Veghel. Horrocks at St Oedenrode with Dempsey found that he was cut off from XXX Corps HQ for the day. No attack took place from KG 'Walther', which was finally forced to retreat by 11th Armoured Division's capture of Deurne, east of Helmond, opening the way for VIII Corps' advance. Nevertheless, with Hell's Highway closed to supply traffic once more, Dempsey ordered O'Connor to hold in place.

▶ *Wounded survivors of 1st British Airborne captured by the Germans as they occupied the Oosterbeek pocket on Tuesday 26 September. One of these men appears to have been given a German greatcoat to wear. As in virtually all battles, there were incidents on both sides at Arnhem of surrendering soldiers being shot. But, aware of the reputation of the Waffen-SS for brutality, the wounded soldiers were surprised at how well they were treated by the Germans. (IWM photograph HU2131)*

At 0200 on Monday 25 September (D plus 8), 43rd Division made its crossing of the Lower Rhine to help 1st British Airborne in darkness, heavy rain and strong winds. But there were boats and DUKW amphibious craft only for two companies, or 350 men, of 4th Battalion of the Dorsetshire Regiment, of whom 315 reached the far bank to be pinned down at once by German fire. Kampfgruppe 'von Tettau' took 140 prisoners including the battalion commander, and although the Dorsets briefly held part of the Westerbouwing they achieved little else. At 0808 Urquhart signalled Thomas that the evacuation, codenamed Operation 'Berlin', must take place that night. As if to emphasize the point, SS-Kampfgruppe 'von Allworden' with the new

King Tigers of 506th Heavy Tank Battalion attacked that afternoon from the east, driving deep into Urquhart's position and threatening to encircle 1st British Airborne. Artillery and 81 close-support sorties from 2nd Tactical Air Force helped the British troops hold out for another day.

During the morning, as XXX Corps finally secured Elst as well as Boxmeer, Horrocks and Browning met at I Airborne Corps Headquarters to discuss 'Berlin', while Montgomery and Dempsey met at Eindhoven. With so many Germans concentrated at Oosterbeek, the Household Cavalry patrols revealed that the Lower Rhine west of Arnhem was almost undefended, and Horrocks briefly considered making another crossing. Instead,

43rd Division mounted a simulated crossing at Renkum, 6km (four miles) west of Oosterbeek, that night to help the withdrawal.

With assistance from British 50th Division and 7th Armoured, 506th and 502nd Parachute Infantry moved against Hoevering during the day, and at nightfall the surrounded Germans abandoned their position, having mined the road first. This was LXXXVIII Corps' last effort, and next day 101st Airborne cleared the mines and re-opened Hell's Highway for good.

Farther east, VIII Corps drove forward against the retreating Kampfgruppe 'Walther' and 180th Infantry Division. By nightfall, 11th Armoured had reached the Maas at Boxmeer, linking up with XXX Corps. But with only two divisions attacking north-eastward, O'Connor was now completely over-extended. On the Willems Canal line, 3rd Division, already holding 35km (22 miles) of front, was faced with the prospect of holding 51km (32 miles) next day. It was only saved by the arrival of 7th US Armored Division, newly returned to Corlett's US XIX Corps, which came into line beside it.

At 2100 on the Lower Rhine 'Berlin' began with a sustained bombardment by 43rd Division and XXX Corps artillery that lasted eleven hours. At 2140 two companies of Royal Canadian Engineers with 21 stormboats (each holding fourteen men) and two Royal Engineer companies with sixteen assault boats started to cross the river. Leaving behind their wounded with some volunteers, 1st British Airborne started to withdraw in the pouring rain through a gap barely 700m wide to the river bank. The

Germans continued heavy mortaring and took 170 prisoners, but there was no attempt to rush the British troops, and by 0130 the withdrawal north of the Hartenstein Hotel was complete. At 0200 the division's ammunition was blown up and its guns disabled, and at first light the ferrying ended. The survivors of 1st British Airborne marched from

A sergeant of 508th Parachute Infantry, 82nd Airborne Division, wearing the new M1943 field uniform, given to the Airborne troops after Normandy to replace the light khaki M1942 paratrooper's uniform. Note the 'All American' divisional sign on one sleeve and the American flag on the other. He wears jump boots and an M1C paratrooper's helmet, and carries an M3 'Grease Gun' submachine-gun. The AL-141 Signal Panel (white on one side, orange on the other) was used to mark drop and landing zones.

◀ *Top: A German officer (with cap) identified as Brigadeführer Heinz Harmel, accompanied by some formidable-looking members of his SS-Kampfgruppe 'Frundsberg', talks to a Polish prisoner, probably in Arnhem on Tuesday 26 September. The Pole may be acting as an interpreter for the other prisoners visible in the building behind them. (IWM photograph HU2133)*

◀ *Survivors of 1st British Airborne recovering from Operation 'Berlin' in the grounds of the Missionary College in Nijmegen on Tuesday 26 September. Between them these privates and NCOs represent almost every regiment of 1st British Airborne which fought at Arnhem, but most are from 1st Battalion of the Border Regiment. (IWM photograph HU3722).*

Driel to Nijmegen, where their divisional seaborne tail was waiting with clean uniforms and equipment. By 1400 the Germans had occupied the remains of the Oosterbeek pocket, capturing the wounded troops who could not be moved.

With the end of 'Berlin' at 0550 on Tuesday 26 September (D plus 9), 'Market-Garden' also ended. Since the start of the operation, First Allied Airborne Army had dispatched 4,852 troop-carrying aircraft successfully to their destinations, of which 1,293 delivered paratroops, 2,277 gliders, and 1,282 resupply. Altogether 164 aircraft and 132 gliders were lost. USAAF IX Troop Carrier Command suffered 454 casualties, RAF 38 and 46 Groups a further 294 casualties. Some 39,620 troops were delivered by air to their targets (21,074 by parachute and 18,546 by glider) with 4,595 tons of stores. However, only 7.4 per cent of the stores intended for 1st British Airborne actually reached it.

A further 6,172 aircraft sorties were flown in support of 'Market-Garden', more than half of them by 8th Air Force, for the loss of 125 aircraft. It is significant that 2nd Tactical Air Force flew only 534 of these sorties, and 9th Air Force 209 sorties. Browning complained that 2nd Tactical Air Force had turned down 46 out of 95 requests for air support from I Airborne Corps Headquarters, chiefly on grounds of poor target identification. The Allied airforces claimed 160 enemy aircraft shot down, and rescued 205 men from the North Sea during the operation.

At Arnhem itself, 10,300 men of 1st British Airborne Division and 1st Polish Parachute Brigade landed from the air. Some 2,587 men escaped across the Rhine in Operation 'Berlin' (1,741 of 1st British Airborne, 422 of the Glider Pilot Regiment, 160 Poles and 75 from the Dorsetshire Regiment), and 240 more returned later with the aid of the PAN. About 1,600 wounded were left behind in the Oosterbeek pocket, together with 204 medical officers and chaplains who volunteered to stay. The Germans claimed 6,450 prisoners taken, wounded or not, and 1st British Airborne therefore lost about 1,300 killed. The highest proportionate losses were suffered by the Glider Pilot Regiment and Major Gough's Reconnaissance Squadron, each with more than one in five men killed. Three out of nine

◄ *A Sherman tank of the Guards Armoured Division pushes up past a knocked out PzKpfw IV, not far from Uden on Wednesday 27 September. The German tank may well be from 107th Panzer Brigade, which like all German formations at this date had a mixture of vehicles. Note the extra sections of track bolted to the front of the Sherman's hull to give it better armoured protection. (IWM photograph B10375)*

battalion commanders of 1st Airborne Division were killed, four more were wounded and taken prisoner, together with two out of three brigade commanders. Five Victoria Crosses were won at Arnhem, four of them posthumous including one to a resupply aircraft pilot.

In the course of the battle, 1st Polish Parachute Brigade lost 378 casualties. The two American airborne divisions lost 3,664 men together: 1,432 from 82nd Airborne, 2,110 from 101st Airborne and 122 glider pilots. One American battalion commander was killed, another was badly wounded, a regimental commander was also wounded, and two posthumous Medals of Honor were won.

By its own estimate, the total losses for I Airborne Corps were 6,858 men. Second British Army's casualties for 'Market-Garden' alone are harder to calculate, but one estimate places them at 5,354 including 1,480 for XXX Corps, giving a total of 16,805 Allied casualties. German casualties, like their unit strengths, cannot be given accurately for this period of the war. Generalfeldmarschall Model estimated Army Group B casualties in 'Market-Garden' at 3,300, but other calculations place them as high as 2,000 dead and 6,000 wounded.

At 0200, as the last of his men were crossing the Lower Rhine, a soaked and exhausted Major General Urquhart reached I Airborne Corps Headquarters and demanded to see Lieutenant General Browning, who rose and dressed to see Urquhart for a brief conversation before directing him to bed. That evening Browning held a formal dinner party for Horrocks, Urquhart and Thomas, putting his chef to good use. Next morning, Wednesday 27 September, Urquhart went south to 21st Army Group Headquarters at Eindhoven to brief Dempsey and Montgomery himself on the battle.

In the 'Market-Garden' corridor, 21st Army Group was digging in. Its front, already 240km (150 miles) long on 16 September, had been extended by a long thin finger of territory stretching up Hell's Highway from Joe's Bridge to Driel, and from Boxmeer to Oss where 7th Armoured Division of XII Corps had finally linked with the Guards Armoured, adding another 200km (130 miles) to be defended. The fighting to hold this salient would continue, but the Battle of Arnhem was over.

THE AFTERMATH OF THE BATTLE

The end of Operation 'Market-Garden' was no more tidy than its beginning. The new salient held by Second British Army threatened to cut off most of the German troops in western Holland once the attack to clear the Scheldt began, and on 27 September 712th Static Division of LXXXVIII Corps tried to escape through Grave, only to be repulsed by the Coldstream. Next morning two major Luftwaffe air attacks by more than 40 aircraft including Me 262 fighter-bombers damaged both bridges at Nijmegen. This was followed by a suicide attack that night on the bridges by twelve German frogmen, which closed them for 24 hours.

On 1 October Generalfeldmarschall Model began his counter-attack against XXX Corps on the 'island' with II SS Panzer Corps from the north, XII SS Corps from the west and II Parachute Corps from the east across the Groesbeek heights. In five days the German offensive over the open *polder* was heavily defeated by Allied firepower, and on 7 October II SS Panzer Corps gave up its attacks. On the same day USAAF and RAF bombing raids closed Arnhem bridge to traffic, and on 4 February 1945 the Germans themselves blew it into the Lower Rhine.

The survivors of 1st British Airborne returned to a heroes' welcome in Britain within a week of their evacuation from Arnhem, and 1st Polish Parachute Brigade joined them shortly afterwards. But the German threat to the new salient made it

◄ Left to right, Lieut-
enant General Ritchie
commanding XII Corps
(smoking one of his
famous cheroots), Lieut-
enant General O'Connor
commanding VIII Corps,
Major General D. A. H.
Graham commanding
50th (Northumbrian)
Division, Dempsey and
Montgomery review the
situation map at the end
of 'Market-Garden' at
Graham's divisional
headquarters near Best,
Thursday 28 September.
Major General Verne
commanding 7th
Armoured Division was
also present. Despite the
smiles for the camera,
Montgomery would
recommend O'Connor's
replacement that night.
(IWM photograph
B10388).

A private of the Para-
chute Regiment, armed
with a Mark II Sten
submachine-gun and
wearing a Denison
smock over the Airborne
version of battledress
with the famous red
(strictly maroon) beret
and Parachute Regiment
badge, a face veil worn
around the neck as
normal, and ammunition
boots with anklets. The
wounded man is a
lieutenant of the Royal
Army Medical Corps
with a field dressing tied
over his face. Note the
lieutenant's glider badge
and Fairbairn-Sykes
fighting knife, strictly a
breach of the convention
which forbade medical
staff carrying weapons.

impossible to withdraw the two American airborne divisions. On 5 October, 101st Airborne took over 43rd Division's position on the 'island', just in time to repell Model's last attack, made by 363rd Volksgrenadier Division. Over Brereton's protests, Montgomery convinced Eisenhower to let him keep 82nd Airborne in line until 13 November and 101st Airborne until 27 November. The two divisions took more casualties in this period than during 'Market-Garden' itself. Major General Taylor was slightly wounded, and Colonel Howard Johnson, commanding 501st Parachute Infantry, was killed.

The Battle of Antwerp to clear the Scheldt estuary began almost simultaneously with the end of 'Market-Garden'. It lasted until 28 November, when Antwerp was officially opened to cargo ships, and cost 21st Army Group 30,000 casualties. In response to the Dutch transport strike called to coincide with 'Market-Garden', the Germans halted all civilian transport in the country, and 18,000 Dutch civilians died in the 'hunger winter' that followed. Nevertheless, the PAN continued to help

Allied soldiers on the run in northern Holland. Brigadier Lathbury with 142 men escaped to safety in October, and Brigadier Hackett the following February.

The failure at Arnhem and the need to open the Scheldt condemned the troops of both 21st Army Group and Army Group B to a miserable winter fighting in the flat and flooded terrain of Holland. In the spring, Allied attention turned to crossing the Rhine into Germany rather than clearing Holland, and Arnhem was not finally liberated by British troops of First Canadian Army until 14 April 1945.

The OB West report on 'Market-Garden', produced in October 1944, gave the decision to spread the airborne landings over more than one day as the main reason for the Allied failure. A Luftwaffe analysis added that the airborne landings were spread too thinly and made too far from the Allied front line. General Student regarded the Allied airborne landings as an immense success and blamed the final failure to reach Arnhem on XXX Corps' slow progress. In this respect, General-

◀ At the end of 'Market-Garden', an Intelligence officer of 1st Polish Parachute Brigade asks questions of his men while an officer of 1st British Airborne Division (with his back to the camera) listens. 1st British Airborne flew back to England on 30 September, followed by the Poles on 7 October, three days before Browning's after-action report on the battle was submitted.

feldmarschall Model deserves credit for his skill in defending against 'Market-Garden', particularly given the state of Army Group B in September 1944, and for grasping at once the vital importance of the Nijmegen bridges. Although it is known as the Battle of Arnhem (or Arnhem-Oosterbeek to the Dutch), there is a case for calling 'Market-Garden' the Battle of Nijmegen, as some Americans have done.

In October 1944, Lieutenant General Brereton reported to General Marshall and General Arnold in Washington that 'Market' had been a brilliant success, which in his own terms was quite true. Lieutenant General Bradley attributed the defeat of 'Market-Garden' entirely to Montgomery, and to the British slowness on the 'island' north of Nijmegen. Major General Urquhart, who led 1 British Airborne for the last time to help liberate Norway at the end of the war, blamed the failure at Arnhem partly on the choice of landing sites too far from the bridges, and partly on his own conduct on the first day. Lieutenant General Browning's report blamed XXX Corps' underestimation of the strength of German resistance and its slowness moving up Hell's Highway, along with the weather, his own communications staff and 2nd Tactical Air Force for failing to provide air support. He also succeeded in getting Major General Sosabowski dismissed from command of 1st Polish Parachute Brigade for his increasingly hostile attitude.

Field Marshal Montgomery's immediate reaction to 'Market-Garden' was to blame Lieutenant General O'Connor for failing to deliver his expected miracle. On 28 September Montgomery recommended that Browning should replace O'Connor commanding VIII Corps, and Urquhart should replace Browning. In fact, Browning left England in November, having been appointed chief of staff to his old patron, Admiral Lord Louis Mountbatten, now heading South-East Asia Command. He rose no higher in the Army but became Comptroller of the Royal Household after the war. O'Connor left VIII Corps voluntarily in November 1944, having been promoted to command Eastern Army in India.

On further reflection, Montgomery blamed himself for part of the failure of 'Market-Garden', and Eisenhower for the rest. He also argued that the

▲ *Brigadier Gerald Lathbury commanding 1st Parachute Brigade, taken in Britain after his remarkable escape from the Germans following 'Market-Garden'. Recovering from his wounds under German guard in the St Elizabeth Hospital in Arnhem,* *Lathbury escaped with PAN help and led his party (including four American glider crew) back across the Lower Rhine on 22 October, being collected by storm boats of 506th Parachute Infantry Regiment. (IWM photograph H41640)*

salient along Hell's Highway provided a base for the attacks eastward across the Rhine in 1945, describing 'Market-Garden' as 90 per cent successful. Again, in Montgomery's own terms this was true, since the battle had forced Bradley to redeploy First US Army northwards and halt Patton. But, in October, Bradley placed Ninth US Army in charge of XIX Corps on the boundary with 21st Army Group, leaving First US Army with two Army Corps grouped around Aachen and a single Army Corps over-extended through the Ardennes forest to keep touch with Third US Army, which resumed its own attacks eastward in November. On 16 December the Germans took advantage of this error in deployment to launch their offensive through the Ardennes. The direct legacy of the Battle of Arnhem was the Battle of the Bulge (described in *Ardennes 1944*, number 5 in this series). On 28 December, Lieutenant General Horrocks, whose XXX Corps was being committed to the battle to support the Americans, suffered another collapse. Montgomery continued to protect Horrocks, sending him home to rest before returning him to XXX Corps for the final victory.

The next major Allied airborne operation, and the last of the Second World War, sought to rectify the faults evident in 'Market-Garden'. In Operation 'Varsity' on 24 March 1945, 1,696 aircraft and gliders landed 21,680 troops of US XVIII Airborne Corps under Lieutenant General Ridgway (17th US Airborne Division and 6th British Airborne Division), east of the Rhine as part of a river crossing by British XII Corps near Wesel. The whole airborne force landed in two hours barely 8km (five miles) ahead of XII Corps, which made contact on the same day. To the end of the war, 'Market-Garden' remained the only attempt by the Allies to use large airborne forces in deep penetration in Europe.

◀ *Paratroopers of 507th Parachute Infantry Regiment, 17th ('Golden Tallon') Airborne Division, boarding a C-47 Dakota for Operation 'Varsity' on 24 March 1945. By landing two complete airborne divisions (each with two, rather than three, parachute brigades/ regiments) in one lift, 'Varsity' became the largest and most congested single airborne drop ever mounted, larger than the first day of 'Market-Garden'. Although successful, it was also the most costly airborne drop ever mounted, with almost a quarter of the aircraft being hit or shot down by ground fire. Together with 'Market-Garden', this cast serious doubts on the future of airborne operations after the war.*

CHRONOLOGY

1944
13 August Montgomery suggests his 'single thrust' plan to Eisenhower.
16 August First Allied Airborne Army formed.
23 August Eisenhower gives priority to Montgomery's northern thrust.
26 August XXX British Corps starts its drive from the Seine.
29 August Third US Army starts to run out of fuel.
1 September Eisenhower takes command of the ground battle from Montgomery.
2 September Eisenhower adopts the 'two-thrust' plan.
3 September Browning threatens resignation. Von Rundstedt recalled to OB West. XXX Corps liberates Brussels.
4 September XXX Corps liberates Antwerp and halts. German First Parachute Army created under Student.
5 September 'Mad Tuesday' in Holland.
10 September Brussels conference between Eisenhower and Montgomery approves 'Market-Garden'. Guards Armoured Division captures 'Joe's Bridge'.
16 September First air attacks for 'Market-Garden' start after nightfall.

17 September D-DAY FOR OPERATION 'MARKET-GARDEN', THE START OF THE BATTLE OF ARNHEM. I British Airborne Corps, XXX Corps, XII Corps attacks start.
18 September Second airborne lift. VIII Corps attack starts.
19 September Third airborne lift. XXX Corps reaches Nijmegen.
20 September Assault crossing at Nijmegen. Main German attack on the Groesbeek heights.
21 September Fourth airborne lift. Germans recapture Arnhem bridge.
22 September Eisenhower abandons the 'Market-Garden' plan.
23 September Fifth airborne lift.
26 September Operation 'Berlin', the withdrawal of 1st British Airborne. END OF THE BATTLE OF ARNHEM.

5 October Last German attacks on the 'Market-Garden' corridor end.
7 October Allied air raids close Arnhem bridge.
27 November Last troops of First Allied Airborne Army leave the 'Market-Garden' corridor.
16 December The German Ardennes offensive (the Battle of the Bulge).

1945
4 February Germans destroy Arnhem bridge.
24 March Operation 'Varsity'.
14 April Allied liberation of Arnhem.
8 May V-E Day, the unconditional surrender of Germany.

A GUIDE TO FURTHER READING

Although the Battle of Arnhem was quite well known before 1974, it was largely Cornelius Ryan's book, *A Bridge Too Far*, and the feature film based upon it that brought the battle to a wider audience. Since then, there has been a small flood of books of varying quality on 'Market-Garden', together with the publication of intelligence sources and higher commanders' memoirs for both sides. Most of these books are not easily available outside specialist libraries, and a new full-length study of the battle is now needed.

GOLDEN, L. *Echoes From Arnhem*, London, 1984. A personal memoir from a survivor of Arnhem, full of technical information on the signalling problems.

HUDSON, J.A. *Out of the Blue*, Indiana, 1972. A scholarly account of the American airborne forces, starting with an outstanding case study of 'Market-Garden'.

KERSHAW, R. *It Never Snows In September*, London, 1990. An excellent account of the battle from the German viewpoint.

POWELL, G. *The Devil's Birthday*, London, 1984. Despite some flaws, the best account of 'Market-Garden' now available, with a good bibliography.

RYAN, C. *A Bridge Too Far*, New York and London, 1974. The classic, journalist's account of the battle, also with a good bibliography.

SIMS, J. *Arnhem Spearhead*, London, 1978. A 'worm's eye view' of Arnhem bridge from a private solider.

URQUHART, R. *Arnhem*, London, 1958 (paperback 1960). The British divisional commander's own account.

WEIGHLEY, R. *Eisenhower's Lieutenants*, Indiana and London, 1981. The higher strategy of the campaign in North-West Europe, with a good section on 'Market-Garden'.

THE BATTLEFIELD TODAY

The 'Market-Garden' area has not changed greatly since the Second World War, although there are more major roads and built-up areas. The main A67/E34 road now runs west to east from Antwerp to Venlo just south of Eindhoven, which is significantly larger than in 1944. Nijmegen and Arnhem have also grown in size, and both have rebuilt their town centres, which were heavily damaged in the fighting.

The starting place for visiting the Arnhem battlefield is the Airborne Museum at the old Hartenstein Hotel in Oosterbeek. Commemorative marker columns, some with a 'Pegasus' symbol, identify important sites on the battlefield. The road and rail bridges at Arnhem were rebuilt after the war. A new road bridge was opened in 1977 just west of the original bridge, which was renamed the 'John Frost Bridge'. The main A48 road now by-passes Arnhem to the east, also bridging the Lower Rhine, and leads eventually to Deventer, where the bridge over the Ijssel was used to represent Arnhem bridge for the motion picture *A Bridge Too Far*.

Along the Club Route, Joe's Bridge and the bridges at Grave and Heumen are still intact. Among the memorials to the 101st Airborne and 82nd Airborne are those at Son, Best, Veghel, and at St Anthony's Church at Breedeweg on the southern end of the Groesbeek heights. At Nijmegen a new road bridge has been built on the site of the old one, and the main features of the battle are easily identifiable.

BACKGROUND TO CRISIS: THE PLAN IS BORN

The Normandy breakout and subsequent blitz-krieg across north-western Europe ended when the Allies confronted the concrete fortifications of the West Wall along the German border. Henceforth, each tactical event dramatically altered Allied high command confidence in the war's outcome. The US 12th Army Group commander, Lieutenant General Omar Bradley, recalls that in early September 1944 – following the glory days of the pursuit across France – most generals believed victory was imminent. The amazing revitalization of the German Army in October, what the Germans called 'the Miracle of the West', stabilized the front and sobered many. Then, the bloody failure of the November offensive to crack the West Wall plunged Eisenhower and his staff into depressed planning for a winter stalemate. Yet when intelligence officers sifted through November results they decided matters were not so bleak. They believed that continuous Allied pressure was inflicting 9,000 German casualties per day, a manpower drain of five divisions per week. Resurgent optimism swept from Supreme Headquarters Allied Expeditionary Force (SHAEF) downward. Bradley's G-2 (Intelligence) wrote: 'the breaking point may develop suddenly and without warning.' Montgomery's G-2 echoed this belief: 'The enemy is in a bad way . . . he cannot stage a major offensive operation.'

This optimism hid a worsening schism within the Allied camp. Montgomery unrelentingly continued his campaign to boot Eisenhower upstairs so he could be replaced by one supreme land general, namely himself. The Field Marshal believed that all offensive operations south of the Ardennes should be halted so that all resources could be massed north of there in support of a single, 'full-blooded' thrust into the Ruhr. American generals, led by Bradley and Patton, bitterly resisted Montgomery's plan. Regardless of its

military merit – and the Americans believed that Montgomery had repeatedly demonstrated his incapacity to direct bold offensive movements – it placed American units in a subordinate role while reserving to the British the prestige of leading the final assault into Germany. Given that the number of American divisions in northern Europe greatly exceeded the number of British and Commonwealth divisions (42 to 19 at the height of the Ardennes offensive), Montgomery's plan was politically impossible. Yet he continued to advance it at all opportunities, forcing Eisenhower into one of the many unfortunate compromises in which he specialized. Eisenhower decreed that the Allies would close up on the Rhine by attacking on both sides of the Ardennes and then decide what to do. The middle, in the Ardennes itself – an area believed unproductive for either Allied or German offensive action – would be thinly held by battered veteran divisions and recently arrived green divisions.

As early as 19 August, Adolf Hitler began laying the groundwork for what would become the Ardennes offensive. It was remarkable strategic effrontery to consider a major offensive even as the German Army was in the midst of its most punishing losses in five years of war: August saw it lose nearly half a million men, raising the five-year total to some 3.3 million casualties. Yet with the front collapsing, and major units such as the Panzer Lehr Division reduced to a handful of men and five tanks, he ordered units assembled and held in reserve for a decisive counterstroke. In the German view, a successful attack in the East might eliminate 20-30 Russian divisions, but this would hardly alter the strategic situation. Similar results in the West would have decisive impact.

Henceforth, Hitler's strategy called for holding firm on all fronts until offensive preparations were complete. He believed that the British and Americans would be forced to halt after outrunning their supplies. Then the defenders could regroup behind the formidable West Wall fortifications. It was an intuitive conclusion that proved accurate. Furthermore, Hitler believed that the Allied coalition was an unnatural grouping of rival interests. A solid blow would cause the coalition to collapse. Hitler patterned his beliefs on Frederick the Great's experience at the end of the Seven Years War – when, by stubbornly continuing the war against all advice, Fredrick had outlasted the coalition ranked against him. Hitler believed he could do the same. In his view, the key was offensive action. By attacking he would prove to the Western allies that Germany could not be conquered.

On 16 September, Hitler interrupted a staff meeting to announce his 'momentous decision . . . to go over to the counterattack! Here, out of the Ardennes, with the objective – Antwerp!' Such a thrust would sever the American and British armies and lead to 'another Dunkirk'. The attack would take place in bad weather to neutralize the overwhelming Allied air superiority. Western countermeasures would be slow, Hitler believed, because of the Allies' need to coordinate plans. Therefore, German tanks should be able to bounce the River Meuse before Allied reserves entered the fray. Furthermore, Hitler had no

respect for the American fighting man. He felt sure that a surprise blitzkreig assault, backed by special commando units to spread confusion and terror, and pursued ruthlessly, would quickly crack the American line in the Ardennes.

▼*From the east the Russians closed in on the borders of the Reich. Ignoring the advice of Guderian and others, Hitler chose to send reinforcements west. In November and December, 2,277 new armoured fighting vehicles went west and only 919 went east. This left German lines in the east thinly stretched, with infantry forced to fend for themselves against Russian tanks. Here soldiers armed with two stick-grenades, on front lip of foxhole, wait as a Russian T-34 comes into view from the left. (Wood Collection, US Army Military History Institute)*

▶ *By late 1944, Bradley was using the Ardennes sector to refit battered units. To defend the long front, most battalions had to employ some of their specialist troops such as mortar men, gunners and anti-tank company men, as riflemen. Patton noted in his diary in early December that the theatre-wide shortage of infantry replacements meant 'we are stretched pretty thin'. Here GIs line up for a movie at the quiet backwater town of Malmédy, five days before the German counter-offensive begins. (US National Archives)*

ARMY THEATRE

THE OPPOSING FORCES

American Infantry

Pre-war American planners designed the infantry division for mobility rather than power. It had an authorized strength of 14,253, divided into three regiments of three battalions with three rifle companies each. The division's core strength resided in its 27 rifle companies which totalled, along with headquarters personnel, 5,211 officers and men. The balance of the division's manpower was in support units. Experience showed that the divisional structure lacked enough riflemen for sustained combat and thus a unit's striking edge quickly dulled in the furnace of battle.

Like all other armies, the display of firepower during the First World War changed American infantry doctrine to emphasize fire and man-oeuvre. On the squad and platoon level this required aggressive, intelligent action. Yet the US Army filled its combat infantry ranks with the uneducated, unskilled, and unenthusiastic re-cruits, leaving the better quality recruits for the technical branches. Post-war studies found that only fifteen percent of riflemen in average units ever fired a shot during combat. In élite formations such as the paratroopers, the percentage doubled.

▼ *Compared with his opponent, the GI was a superior marksman and fired the best rifle of the war, the M1 Garand semi-automatic. The standard German rifles were bolt-action. Both sides employed comparable light machine-guns. The Americans carried two First World War vintage weapons: a Browning automatic rifle, one per squad; and a heavy .50-calibre water-cooled machine-gun, a weapon type the Germans had abandoned. Here 30th Division GIs relax behind the front on 16 December. They would soon be fighting Peiper. The seated figure has a BAR in his right hand and an M1 in his left, plus .50-calibre machine-gun bullets draped across his shoulders. (US Army Military History Institute)*

▶ *Most defenders in the Ardennes had too few bazookas and were short of ammunition. Typical of the battle, on 17 December a platoon facing five Tiger tanks on a key trail leading to Rocherath-Krinkelt had three rounds of bazooka ammunition. Here bazooka instruction is carried out against a knocked out Mark IV. (US Army Military History Institute)*

▲ *Two-thirds of an infantry division's strength was in support units. According to Patton: '92% of all casualties occur in the infantry rifle companies, and that when the infantry division has lost 4,000 men, it has practically no riflemen left.' The 28th Infantry Division, holding the central Ardennes sector, had lost 6,100 men in the Huertgen Forest. The American Army was also officer heavy; officers represented 7 per cent of manpower, while the German percentage was 2.86. Shown here are some of the few at the sharp end: an infantry-tank team of the 4th Armored Division near Bastogne. (Charles B. MacDonald Collection, US Army Military History Institute)*

All this meant that American infantry lacked aggressiveness in the attack, a characteristic that manifested itself during the counterattack phase of the Battle of the Bulge.

In defence, the GI could more than hold his own against his generally poorly trained counterparts who filled the German ranks. When confronting hostile armour, as would be the case during the critical first days of the coming battle, the infantry suffered a crippling lack of effective anti-tank weapons. As far back as 1943 in Sicily, the GIs had found that their standard hand-held 2.36in rocket launcher, the bazooka, failed against late-model panzers. Yet the Ordnance Department did not develop and supply an alternative.

In theory each US infantry regiment relied on its anti-tank company with six 57mm anti-tank guns. This was a pitiful, obsolete weapon. Sim-

US infantryman, armed with an M1 carbine.

ilarly, the GIs were at a qualitative disadvantage with their close-support artillery. Each regiment had a cannon company comprising six towed, short-barrelled 105mm howitzers. They simply lacked the mobility, particularly in the Ardennes mud and snow, to be useful. In contrast, the Germans had developed a special category of weapon to assist their attacking infantry through the fire zone: self-propelled 75mm assault guns.

The saving weapon for the American infantry was undoubtedly the artillery. The divisional artillery had three twelve-piece 105mm howitzer battalions and one twelve-piece 155mm battalion. Because the mechanics of serving an artillery piece are similar to training exercises – the men do the same thing in training as in combat, laying fire on targets they do not see – green artillery crews performed about as well as veterans. Thus the inexperienced divisions fighting in the Ardennes could expect good artillery support. Since 1942 the Germans had looked down on the American infantry but praised its artillery. Along the entire Ardennes front the defenders employed 228 artillery pieces in 13 general support battalions, and 276 pieces organic to the division. Across the lines the Germans massed some 1,900 artillery and rocket tubes.

In refutation of pre-war doctrine, by 1944 each American infantry division had an attached tank battalion with a 13-tank light company and three medium companies with 53 tanks. When confronted by charging panzers, the mediums in the attached battalions seemed to lack the willingness to support the infantry in the front line. This is understandable given the great qualitative superiority of the German tanks.

The picture that emerges of the standard 1944 US infantry division is not a happy one. Fallacious doctrine had led to poor organizational structure. Worse, in the vital area of anti-tank combat, the men had obsolete weapons. The Ardennes has been called the American Army's 'nursery and the old folk's home'. Here veteran formations absorbed thousands of 'reinforcements' – for psychological reasons the brass had decreed that the former term 'replacements' no longer be used – and were held together by a hard cadre of survivors. The new divisions were untested, yet

▶ The standard American anti-tank weapon was the obsolete 57mm gun. It could stop Mark IVs and light armour but was next to useless against heavier panzers. For years the Germans and Russians had used more powerful 75mm or larger guns for anti-tank weapons. Somehow the American Army, having the world's largest industrial base to draw on, could not provide its infantry with an adequate tank-killing weapon. Men of the 84th Division man a 57mm anti-tank gun in a snowstorm on 4 January. (US National Archives)

▶ US gunners enjoyed the advantage of advanced communications and fire control equipment, which allowed them to engage new targets rapidly. They had perfected the deadly 'TOT' (time on target) tactic that permitted multiple batteries to fire on selected targets for designated periods of time. The resultant volume of fire accurately delivered to a small area awed the Germans. Here a 105mm self-propelled howitzer of Battery C, 274 Field Artillery Battalion fires a mission on 1 January near Bastogne. (US National Archives)

▶ The basis for attaching a tank battalion to the infantry was to provide slugging power for frontal attacks; however, including light tanks, a design made especially for exploitation and pursuit, made no sense. Once or twice during the Ardennes battle the light companies caught German infantry in the open. Otherwise they proved useless. (US National Archives)

▲ The infantry division had an attached tank destroyer (TD) battalion. Pre-war planners believed that tanks would avoid combat with opposing tanks. Experience showed that tanks were the most effective tank killers. The standard M10 featured a 3in high-velocity gun in an open turret (to save weight and increase mobility) mounted on a Sherman chassis. The need to upgrade became apparent, so that by 1944 some were redesigned to accommodate a 90mm gun. Other models in the Ardennes included the M18 with a 76mm gun in an open turret on a light tank chassis. The design effort to unite mobility and gun power at the expense of armour proved a failure. Here a TD provides support to dug-in infantry. (US National Archives)

▶ German tank guns outranged and had higher muzzle velocity than the Sherman's short 75mm gun. The Sherman's gun could penetrate neither the Mark V Panther's nor the Mark VI Tiger's frontal armour, while its own frontal armour could not withstand the German tank and anti-tank guns. The Sherman's only viable tactic was to work for a side or rear shot. During the Ardennes campaign, muddy conditions often restricted combat to the road, thus eliminating the theoretical American counter. In any event, to take out a Panther or Tiger usually required the expenditure of several Shermans, a fact, Bradley noted, that 'offered little comfort to the crews who were forced to expend themselves'. A Tiger's rounds have twice penetrated this Sherman, killing driver and setting tank afire. (US National Archives)

◀ In 1942 the standard American tank, the 33-tonne M4 General Sherman, had entered combat with the British Eighth Army. It proved a good match for the then current German main battle tank, the Mark IV. While Germany and Russia, with inferior industrial bases, managed annually to upgrade tank design, American design stood frozen in time. What worked in 1942 was badly obsolete in 1944. A 3rd Armored Division Sherman guards the road near Manhay. (US National Archives)

Bradley and others knew that green divisions almost invariably failed in Europe in their first battle and took heavy losses while doing so.

American Armour

US armoured divisions typically had three battalions with 177 medium tanks, 77 light tanks equipped with the useless 37mm gun, a self-propelled tank destroyer battalion, three self-propelled medium artillery battalions and three so-called armoured infantry battalions. In fact, once the latter dismounted from their half-tracks, they fought in just the same way as other infantry. The division divided into three combat commands. Tank crews in the armoured divisions consistently showed a willingness to engage enemy tanks. Their Shermans were slightly superior to the German Mark IVs. Against the heavier panzers, they fought at an enormous disadvantage.

Given the American technical inferiority, it is not surprising that nearly every reported German tank was a 'Tiger' and every anti-tank gun an '88'. What surprises across time is the American willingness to fight when they well understood the enemy advantages. In Normandy and during the pursuit across France, the Shermans relied upon superior numbers and bountiful air support to beat the panzers. On 16 December, VIII Corps had 242 Shermans and 182 self-propelled TDs to face about 1,000 German tanks and assault guns, in weather conditions that kept most aircraft grounded.

Given the American problems, it is fortunate that their German counterparts also suffered severe deficiencies.

German Infantry

Heavy losses forced the Germans to restructure their infantry divisions in 1944. To appeal for the patriotic defence of the Fatherland, Hitler created the Volksgrenadier Division (VGD). Formerly this title had to be won in battle. Under new decrees, young recruits, 16- and 17-year-olds in the VGD, and younger 'volunteers' in the SS, joined older men now liable for service to fill the ranks of the refitting formations designated for the Ardennes

▲*The German light machine-gun had such a high rate of fire that soldiers called it the 'Hitler-Sage' (Hitler's* *Saw). Captured film shows machine-gunner (in middle) on 17 December. (US National Archives)*

attack. Many more soldiers came from rear area comb-outs and Luftwaffe and Navy personnel. While their morale remained high – only five soldiers deserted along the entire Western front in the first twelve days of December – they had been hastily trained and knew little of infantry tactics. They tended to advance in clumps, herded forward by veteran NCOs and officers and suffered horrible losses to automatic weapons and artillery fire. Authorized manpower declined from just over 17,000 in the old style divisions to 12,769, divided into three regiments of two battalions each. An élite fusilier battalion gave the division an additional manoeuvre element.

Accompanying the decline in German manpower was an increase in individual firepower. The machine pistol, lavishly distributed to the Volksgrenadiers, proved very successful, particularly when wielded by each regiment's special assault company. The Germans also had what an Ameri-

German Volksgrenadier, armed with Panzerfaust and a Soviet PPSh41 submachine-gun.

▲ *Among various machine-pistols was the famous Schmeisser, whose high cyclic rate of fire made a 'b-r-r-r-r-p' sound, thus winning the name 'burp gun' to the GIs. In spite of the fact that a German division contained 1,200 fewer infantrymen than an American infantry division, the German wealth of automatic weapons gave them superior firepower. Here captured film shows a cyclist delivering a message to infantry riding on the rear of a panzer during the advance. Note the man standing on the left carries a captured Sten gun. (US National Archives)*

can paratroop general called 'the best hand-carried anti-tank weapon of the war', the one-shot Panzerfaust rocket launcher.

Infantry division artillery allocations were similar to those of the Americans. However, most artillery still relied upon horse-drawn transport, a fact that made the artillery slow to displace forward to support the advance and led to tremendous, momentum-numbing traffic jams along the German rear. Higher command echelons had nine

Volksartillerie corps ranging in number of guns from 50 to 100. They included many captured foreign weapons, thus greatly complicating ammunition supply. High command also directed seven new Volkswerfer brigades equipped with rocket-firing Nebelwerfers. Once the spearhead formations outstripped the range of the horse-drawn tube artillery, they relied upon the fully motorized rocket brigades for artillery support. Typically, Goering promised massive Luftwaffe

▶ *The Germans distributed their version of the rocket launcher, the panzerfaust, in lavish numbers. They were easily carried in a shoulder sling that allowed the individual to operate other weapons. The commander of the 82nd Airborne Division noted that his men only acquired an adequate anti-tank weapon after it captured numerous panzerfausts. An anti-tank gunner of the 26th VGD drew this sketch showing his unit advancing near Bastogne on 20 December. The front two marching soldiers are carrying panzerfausts. (Charles B. MacDonald Collection, US Army Military History Institute)*

▶ *German rocket brigades could deliver terrifying saturation fire. The GIs called them 'screaming meemies' because of the sound an incoming rocket made. Fully motorized Nebelwerfer units allowed the Germans to bring forward firepower to support the offensive. They were also used to beef up special assault units. SS Panzer divisions had an attached Nebelwerfer battalion, an extra tank or panzerjaeger battalion, and a heavy 170mm artillery battery. (Military Archive & Research Services)*

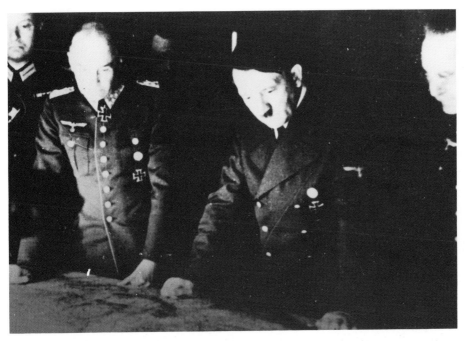

▲ *By autumn 1944, Adolf Hitler exercised total control over the German military. Von Manteuffel recalls that Hitler never possessed 'the form of concentration used by our General Staff officers. He just didn't have the mental faculties to consider any plan up to the minutest details.' Hitler regarded his own military leadership as 'A matter of intellect, tenacity and nerves of steel! Will power was all!'*

Hitler distanced himself from the professional Prussian staff officers and surrounded himself with sycophants. He was thus ignorant of, and divorced from, the most basic principles of war. The 20 July failed assassination attempt took a heavy physical and psychological toll and made him ever more suspicious of the officer corps: 'He came into the map room bent and shuffling. His glassy eyes

gave a sign of recognition only to those who stood closest to him.' He slumped into his chair 'bent almost double with his head sunk between his shoulders'. Pointing to the map, his hand trembled. 'On the slightest occasion he would demand shrilly that "the guilty" be hunted down.' He was the principal German strategist for the Ardennes offensive. (Personality Pictures Library)

▶ *Generalfeldmarschall Walter Model was one of the architects of the 'Miracle of the West'. Apprised in late October of the pending offensive, he responded: 'This plan hasn't got a damned leg to stand on.' He unsuccessfully advanced a more practical, limited alternative, the so-called 'small solution'. He commanded Army Group B, comprising the armies taking part in the Ardennes offensive. Model's attack order read: 'We will not disappoint the Führer and the Fatherland, who created the sword of retribution. Forward in the spirit of Leuthen!' (Military Archive & Research Services)*

Generaloberst Alfred Jodl (not shown) was foremost among Hitler's toadies in the planning of the Ardennes offensive. As chief of the OKW operations staff, he had lived in Hitler's presence for years. Isolated and out of touch, he assumed planning direction for the counter-offensive. The Ardennes operation was the first time in six years of war that OKW took direct control of a major offensive. Jodl saw this as his great opportunity. His inability to stand up to Hitler, coupled with his own and his staff's inexperience, led to many planning blunders. When von Manteuffel tried to advance his opinions on how to conduct the offensive on 3 November, Jodl kept interrupting by shouting: 'That is an order of the Führer! Nothing is to change – all irrevocable!' (US National ◀ *Archives)*

▲*General der Panzertruppen Hasso von Manteuffel, the commander of Fifth Panzer Army, was the kind of aggressive, brainy leader who earned worldwide military respect for the 'Prussian tradition'. A mere battalion commander during the invasion of Russia in 1941, he performed with such distinction that he caught the eye of Hitler himself. At a time when few officers dared argue with the Führer, von Manteuffel managed to persuade Hitler about significant assault tactics, yet he worried that years of Hitler's operational control had 'brought about the death of the German art of flexible command'. Liddell Hart called him 'a master of the art of mobility and surprise'. Von Manteuffel's attack order: 'Forward, march, march! In remembrance of our dead comrades, and therefore on their order, and in remembrance of the tradition of our proud Wehrmacht!' (Military Archive & Research Services)*

◄ *Generaloberst Josef 'Sepp' Dietrich was a long-time Hitler crony, hand-picked to command Sixth Panzer Army. Given the best equipment and all the SS forces, his task was to lead the breakthrough. Of limited ability, he had little impact on the battle. His chief of staff made most army-level decisions. (US National Archives)*

197

▼*Sturmgeschutz III Ausf G of Skorzeny's 150th Panzer Brigade.*

◀ *For the assault, infantry relied increasingly on self-propelled assault guns to escort them through the fire zone. Their battle drill emphasized use of these weapons. Afterwards, commanders blamed them when infantry assaults failed. Assigned 18 to a division, as well as organized into separate support detachments, these weapons also gave the German infantry an effective anti-tank weapon. There was a shortage of these weapons: the entire Seventh Army had only 30. Here infantry ride an assault gun as it attacks on 17 December. (US National Archives)*

support; but, except for one last spectacular day when the Luftwaffe performed its death flight – the Great Blow – the Luftwaffe exerted little influence on ground combat.

The panzergrenadier (PG) and parachute divisions retained their structure and so still had nine infantry battalions. The PG divisions resembled American infantry divisions. They were fully motorized and had organic medium tank and TD

battalions. The two parachute divisions kept their name as an honorific, for they were no longer the élite units of past campaigns.

German Armour

German panzer and SS panzer divisions had one panzer regiment and two panzergrenadier regiments. The divisions averaged 90 to 100 medium

▶ *Even this late in the war, German tank crews maintained a high standard of driving, firing and radio signal functions. According to some experts, the latest model Panther, equipped with infra-red night sight optics, remained the world's best tank through the early 1950s. In December 1944, it far outclassed its American opponents. (US National Archives)*

▼*Panzerkampfwagen VI Tiger II Ausf B of Panzer Abteilung 501.*

tanks. Each type of division had a self-propelled anti-tank battalion. Equivalent to the American armoured infantry, the panzergrenadiers lacked their American counterparts' mobility. Only one-quarter of them rode half-tracks, and material shortages reduced the balance to riding a motley collection of captured vehicles reflecting the flow and ebb of German fortunes since the beginning of the war. The army PG regiments had two battalions each, the SS three. Of the three artillery battalions assigned to the Army divisions, only one was self-propelled. In the SS, one in four was self-propelled. Since the plan for the Ardennes offensive called for the SS to carry the main effort, each SS panzer division had attached units to provide enhanced firepower.

The two panzer battalions in the panzer regiment provided the power for a blitzkreig. Generally, one battalion comprised the 'workhorse' tank, the 75mm gun-armed, 27-tonne Mark IV. It was vulnerable to bazookas and other American anti-tank weapons. The other battalion employed the 43-tonne Mark V or Panther. The Panther had a long 75mm gun – 70 calibres larger than the Sherman's short 75mm gun – that was decisively superior in range and muzzle velocity to American

tanks. It had considerably thicker armour and better cross-country mobility in mud and snow.

Even more formidable appearing was the Mark VI or Tiger tank. Weighing 63 tonnes, armed with the deadly 88mm gun, it carried enough armour to render its front and sides all but invulnerable. The newest model, the Royal, or King, Tiger, weighed 68 tonnes – the heaviest operational tank of the war – and had turret armour more than seven inches thick. Its high-velocity, long 88mm gun fired a 22-pound shell capable of destroying a Sherman at a half mile range. Fortunately for the Americans, the closed terrain and frequently poor visibility partially negated the German tank gun range superiority.

Hitler ordered the Tigers distributed in independent formations, generally company and battalion size, and used to beef up important attacks. About 45 Royal Tigers and 200 Tigers participated in the Ardennes offensive. Dietrich's Sixth Panzer Army received 21 experimental Jagdtigers, a 82-tonne panzerjaeger with the huge 128mm gun, a weapon that had been the mainstay of German anti-aircraft defence. Overall the Germans brought about 1,000 tanks or tank-type vehicles to the opening assault.

◀ *Weather determined the offensive's timing. 'Führer weather' featuring rain, fog and snow would ground Allied air power. Here a 2nd Armored Division mortar carrier fires during a blizzard in preparation for a counterattack at the tip of the Bulge. (US Army Military History Institute)*

▶Lieutenant General Omar Bradley, here decorating Lieutenant General Courtney Hodges after the battle, commanded the mostly American 12th Army Group. Beneath his quiet exterior he was an aggressive leader. Frustration over Eisenhower's seeming preference for British strategies consumed his headquarters. Bradley viewed the Ardennes sector as 'a calculated risk'; the German offensive greatly surprised him. He responded with soldierly skill but was dismayed when Montgomery assumed command of American forces north of the breakthrough. Hodges commanded the US First Army, the army hit by the German offensive. Slow to appreciate German intentions, his limited grand-tactical skills were exhausted by the first days. (US Army Military History Institute)

▶ General Dwight Eisenhower was Supreme Allied Commander in · Europe. While nearly everyone liked the amiable 'Ike,' neither his American nor his British subordinates respected his military prowess. The Anglo-American competition for scarce resources plagued his headquarters, forcing him to make many decisions on a political rather than a military basis. The Ardennes offensive witnessed his finest hour as military leader. Here Ike tours Bastogne with Bradley (left) and Patton. Lieutenant General George Patton commanded US Third Army south of the bulge

and, alone among top Allied generals, he worried about a German Ardennes attack. However, absorbed with his own pending offensive, he unwillingly recognized the moment when it came. Once convinced, he rapidly sent his army to attack the German flank.

Undoubtedly he was the most aggressive Allied army commander and the one most respected by the Germans. (US National Archives)

▲Left to right: Lieutenant General George Patton, commanding officer of the US Third Army; General Dwight D. Eisenhower, Supreme Commander, Allied Forces Europe; and Lieutenant General Omar Bradley, commanding officer of the US First Army.

Eastern front armoured combat featured tremendous armour concentrations on a narrow front. In the west, Allied air superiority prohibited these tactics. Fighter-bombers ('Jabos' in German army slang) dominated mechanized ground combat. Lacking an effective counter, Hitler promised poor weather conditions that would ground the Allied air forces. What passes for intuition was actually based on the careful analysis of long range weather reports by his meteorological expert Dr Karl Recknagel.

In the early months of autumn 1944, U-boats deposited weather teams around the Arctic Circle. There they fought an amazing cat and mouse

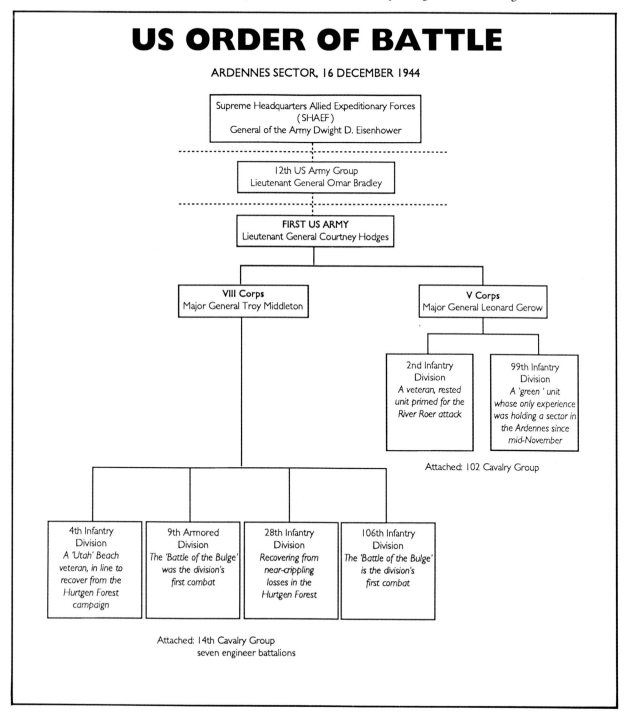

US ORDER OF BATTLE

ARDENNES SECTOR, 16 DECEMBER 1944

Supreme Headquarters Allied Expeditionary Forces
(SHAEF)
General of the Army Dwight D. Eisenhower

12th US Army Group
Lieutenant General Omar Bradley

FIRST US ARMY
Lieutenant General Courtney Hodges

VIII Corps
Major General Troy Middleton

V Corps
Major General Leonard Gerow

2nd Infantry
Division
A veteran, rested unit primed for the River Roer attack

99th Infantry
Division
A 'green' unit whose only experience was holding a sector in the Ardennes since mid-November

Attached: 102 Cavalry Group

4th Infantry
Division
A 'Utah' Beach veteran, in line to recover from the Hurtgen Forest campaign

9th Armored
Division
The 'Battle of the Bulge' was the division's first combat

28th Infantry
Division
Recovering from near-crippling losses in the Hurtgen Forest

106th Infantry
Division
The 'Battle of the Bulge' is the division's first combat

Attached: 14th Cavalry Group
seven engineer battalions

combat against Allied patrols sent to ferret out their secret radio stations. One team, sent to the Spitzbergen area, narrowly avoided British destroyers which had been alerted by Ultra intercepts to expect their landing. They established a weather station that continued in operation four months after the Wehrmacht's capitulation, the last German unit to surrender in the war. In Berlin, Recknagel analyzed these remote reports and predicted that the last two weeks of December would see rain, fog and heavy snow. He said that these conditions would begin on 16 December, a date German planners accepted for beginning the attack.

◀ *Field Marshal Sir Bernard Montgomery commanded 21st Army Group, comprising all British and dominion as well as many American formations. A self-described Great Captain, the near total depletion of British manpower reserves thwarted his offensive concepts. Fortune beckoned when he took over command of American units north of the Bulge. He promptly ran foul of American doctrine and sensibilities. Most American generals disliked the pompous Monty, yet those who worked closest with him respected his abilities. He is seen here with two of his American subordinates; Collins on left and Ridgeway. (US National Archives)*

◀ *Major General Troy Middleton (left) commanded VIII Corps where the German blow fell. A First World War veteran, he was described by Marshall as 'the outstanding infantry regimental commander' on the French battlefield. Both Bradley (right) and Eisenhower (far right) sought him for corps command. Patton wrote that Middleton acquitted himself 'exceptionally well' during the campaign. Yet his complacency before the attack, failure to patrol and failure to fortify, proved costly. (US Army Military History Institute)*

Deception and Intelligence

Hitler believed that the German enciphering system for wireless communications was absolutely secure. It relied upon an ingenious machine known as Enigma, and by 1944 the Allies routinely decoded nearly all of its transmissions. The Germans had begun to realize that somehow the Western Allies had penetrated their secrets. Confident that Enigma was uncrackable, Hitler attributed the leaks to spies and traitors. However, to prevent exposure of the coming offensive, he forbade all electronic transmission of plans connected with it. Instead, officer couriers – escorted by Gestapo agents – hand-delivered all communications. Unbeknown to the Allies, their most dependable source of intelligence would have little relevance for the coming attack.

The Germans took several other steps to hide their intentions. In a stroke of brilliance, Hitler assigned a deceptive, defensive sounding codename: 'Wacht am Rhein' (Watch on the Rhine). Most movement orders designed to mass troops for the attack began with the words 'in preparation for the anticipated enemy offensive'. Oberkommando der Wehrmacht (OKW) planners intentionally exposed one of the two assault armies, Sixth Panzer, to Allied aerial reconnaissance in the Cologne area, where it seemed poised to counterattack the American drive on the Rhine. Just three days before the attack it moved into its real staging area. The other assault army, Fifth Panzer, took over the defensive fighting near Aachen as cover for its offensive deployment. It then withdrew from the defensive fighting, seemingly to refit, as its commander planned the attack while hiding under the name 'Military Police Command for Special Assignment'. This labyrinth of deception confounded Allied intelligence officers.

The Germans achieved amazing success in massing their forces under skies thoroughly dominated by enemy aircraft. Key to this success was the Reichsbahn (the German State Railway). Rail lines leading to the Eifel (the German extension of the Ardennes) had been located based on anticipated military needs for the First World War. Reinforced for the 1940 campaign, they again proved themselves a model of efficiency in 1944.

Trains hauling the vast store of supplies needed for the offensive moved only at night, hiding by day in tunnels or dispersing along rear-area marshalling yards. In November alone trains dumped 3,982 wagon-loads of supplies into assembly areas. Allied air power destroyed a mere four wagon-loads of fuel during the entire month.

So the secret build-up continued, bringing divisions from all over Hitler's empire. Ethnic Germans from border regions were sent to the rear lest they desert and reveal the plan. For the final massing at the front, staff officers orchestrated a three-day forward movement along prescribed staging lines. Three days before the attack they moved up no closer than twelve miles from the front; two days, six miles; the last day, two miles. It utilized time-tested methods dating back to the German offensives in the First World War. They moved only at night, hiding during the day in the Eifel forests, cooking only with smokeless charcoal fires in fear of the special security detachments who roamed in search of anyone violating camouflage discipline. The troops knew nothing of the

▼ *Germans operate an Enigma machine in France in 1940. (US National Archives)*

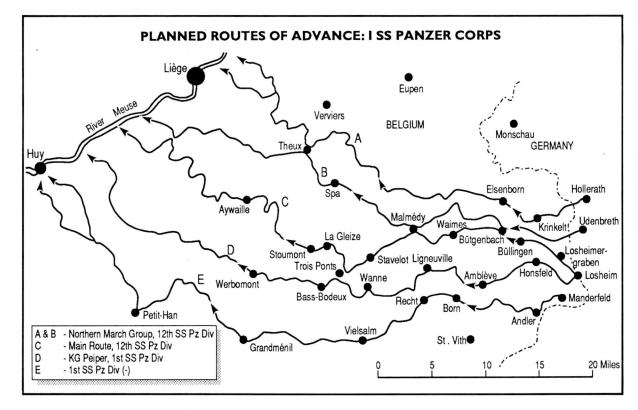

PLANNED ROUTES OF ADVANCE: I SS PANZER CORPS

A & B - Northern March Group, 12th SS Pz Div
C   - Main Route, 12th SS Pz Div
D   - KG Peiper, 1st SS Pz Div
E   - 1st SS Pz Div (-)

assault until the night before the attack. The preparations were carried out with the brilliance for which the German General Staff was renowned – and yet the Americans had ample clues to detect the attack.

The main problem was that everyone believed the Germans were beaten. Beyond that, intelligence officers had grown too reliant on Enigma intercepts. These intercepts informed them of a westward shift of German fighters and of the creation of a large panzer reserve, but that was all. In the past, intercepts had specified when and where attacks would occur. Without such additional information, few believed the Germans were about to launch a major offensive. No one could explain Enigma intercepts of German requests for photo reconnaissance of the River Meuse crossing sites. Yet trusting that von Rundstedt commanded the German defence, and thus that the Germans would behave logically and husband their strength to counterattack the coming Allied offensive, few became alarmed.

The twin beliefs that the Germans were desperately short of resources and that von Rundstedt was in charge coloured the interpretation of aerial

reconnaissance missions which sighted major movements around the Eifel and front-line reports of traffic noise. Intelligence officers decided that von Rundstedt was so hard-pressed that he was shuttling forces behind the Eifel to oppose American attacks. The train movements in the Cologne area were thought to support Sixth Panzer Army as it massed for its counterattack role. Had someone carefully examined the map, he might have seen that rail spur lines ran from the Cologne area to the Eifel.

In the final analysis, Allied intelligence officers possessed a core of hard information to deduce the German plan. They failed, and so the attackers achieved total surprise.

The Plan

Four American divisions held the 85-mile-long Ardennes front. American generals focused on the left-most flank where the 2nd Infantry Division prepared to attack the Roer dams. On the remainder of the front the Americans were content to remain passive. While the southern half of the line followed the course of the Rivers Our and

'Wacht am Rhein' - The German Plan

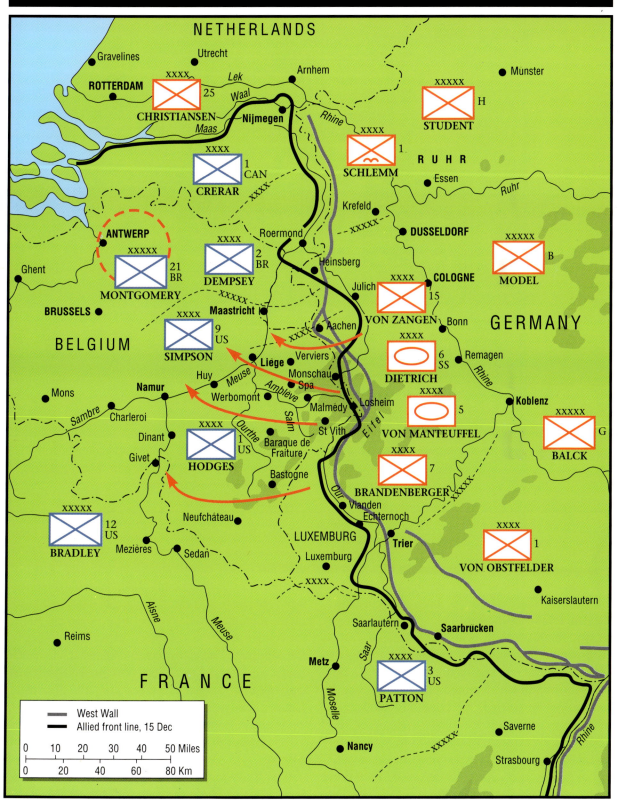

NETHERLANDS

Gravelines
Utrecht
Arnhem
Munster

ROTTERDAM
XXXX 25
CHRISTIANSEN
Lek
Waal
Maas
Nijmegen
Rhine

XXXXX H
STUDENT

XXXX 1
SCHLEMM

RUHR
Essen
Ruhr

Krefeld
XXXXX
DUSSELDORF

XXXX 1 CAN
CRERAR

XXXXX

Roermond
Heinsberg
Julich
COLOGNE
XXXX 15
VON ZANGEN

XXXXX B
MODEL

ANTWERP
XXXXX 21 BR
MONTGOMERY
Ghent

XXXX 2 BR
DEMPSEY

Maastricht
Aachen
Bonn
GERMANY
Remagen
Rhine

BRUSSELS
BELGIUM
XXXX 9 US
SIMPSON
XXXXX
Huy
Liège
Verviers
Monschau
Spa
Meuse
Ambleve
Salm

XXXX 6 SS
DIETRICH

Namur
Mons
Werbomont
Malmedy
Losheim
St Vith
Eifel
Koblenz

XXXX 5
VON MANTEUFFEL

XXXXX G
BALCK

Sambre
Charleroi
Dinant
Givet
XXXX 1 US
HODGES
Ourthe
Baraque de Fraiture
Bastogne
Ourthe

XXXX 7
BRANDENBERGER

XXXXX 12 US
BRADLEY
Mezières
Sedan
Neufchâteau

Vianden
Echternoch

LUXEMBURG
Luxemburg
Trier

XXXX 1
VON OBSTFELDER
Kaiserslautern

Alsne
Meuse
XXXX

Saarlautern
Saarbrücken

Reims
Metz
Saar
Moselle

XXXX 3 US
PATTON

F R A N C E

Nancy
Saverne
Rhine
Strasbourg

Legend:
West Wall
Allied front line, 15 Dec

| 0 | 10 | 20 | 30 | 40 | 50 Miles |
| 0 | 20 | 40 | 60 | 80 Km |

207

GERMAN ORDER OF BATTLE

GERMAN FIFTH PANZER ARMY, FIRST ASSAULT WAVE

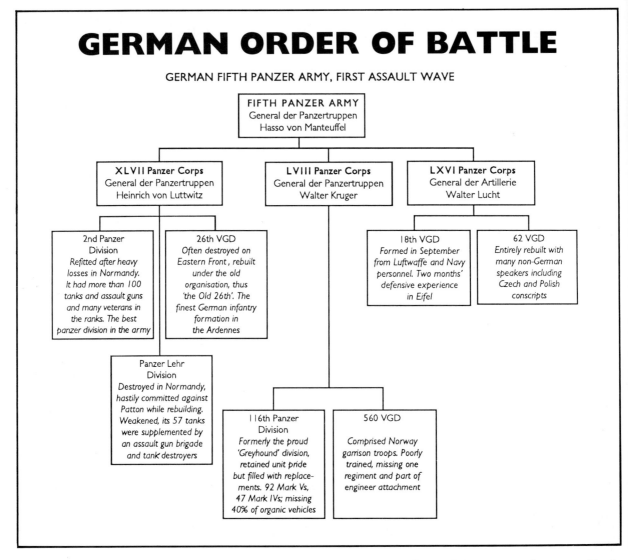

FIFTH PANZER ARMY
General der Panzertruppen
Hasso von Manteuffel

XLVII Panzer Corps
General der Panzertruppen
Heinrich von Luttwitz

LVIII Panzer Corps
General der Panzertruppen
Walter Kruger

LXVI Panzer Corps
General der Artillerie
Walter Lucht

2nd Panzer Division
Refitted after heavy losses in Normandy. It had more than 100 tanks and assault guns and many veterans in the ranks. The best panzer division in the army

26th VGD
Often destroyed on Eastern Front, rebuilt under the old organisation, thus 'the Old 26th'. The finest German infantry formation in the Ardennes

18th VGD
Formed in September from Luftwaffe and Navy personnel. Two months' defensive experience in Eifel

62 VGD
Entirely rebuilt with many non-German speakers including Czech and Polish conscripts

Panzer Lehr Division
Destroyed in Normandy, hastily committed against Patton while rebuilding. Weakened, its 57 tanks were supplemented by an assault gun brigade and tank destroyers

116th Panzer Division
Formerly the proud 'Greyhound' division, retained unit pride but filled with replacements. 92 Mark Vs, 47 Mark IVs; missing 40% of organic vehicles

560 VGD
Comprised Norway garrison troops. Poorly trained, missing one regiment and part of engineer attachment

Sauer, the northern half had no such natural advantages. It represented the easternmost line reached by advancing forces back in the autumn. The line bulged forward to encompass the Schnee Eifel (Snow Plateau) where, back in September, the 4th Infantry Division had achieved a lodgement in the West Wall. This penetration led to no worthwhile objectives and so American planners turned elsewhere, but army and corps commanders mindlessly retained the salient. On 10 December, the green 106th Division took over the position.

Holding the entire Ardennes front with so few troops was a risk – Bradley and others later called it 'a calculated risk', but in fact it was no such thing – necessitated by the critical theatre-wide shortage of front-line infantry. There was a shortage of both divisions and manpower within divisions. Allied planners had badly miscalculated the rate of attrition 'at the sharp end'. They had allocated too few replacement infantry and too many replacement technical and service troops. Inept long-range planning was combined with heavy losses in the autumn. The unexpected onslaught of trench foot caused by slow delivery of poorly designed cold-weather footwear exacerbated the shortage. Consequently, Bradley had committed every division to the front line. Only the refitting 82nd and 101st Airborne Divisions remained in SHAEF reserve.

On 8 November, Bradley and Eisenhower visited Major General Troy Middleton, the com-

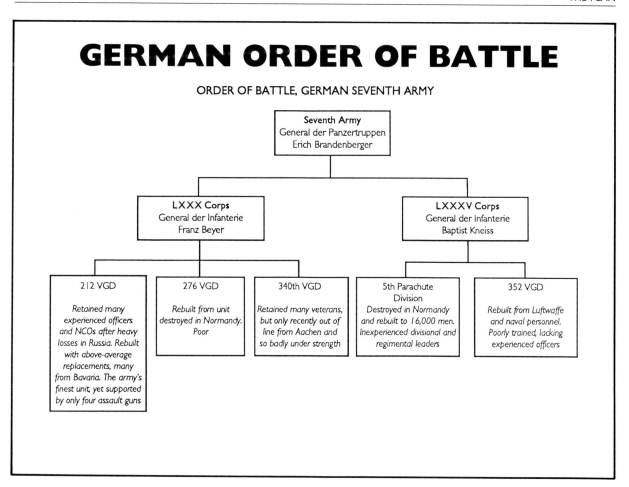

GERMAN ORDER OF BATTLE

ORDER OF BATTLE, GERMAN SEVENTH ARMY

Seventh Army
General der Panzertruppen
Erich Brandenberger

LXXX Corps
General der Infanterie
Franz Beyer

LXXXV Corps
General der Infanterie
Baptist Kneiss

212 VGD

Retained many experienced officers and NCOs after heavy losses in Russia. Rebuilt with above-average replacements, many from Bavaria. The army's finest unit, yet supported by only four assault guns

276 VGD

Rebuilt from unit destroyed in Normandy. Poor

340th VGD

Retained many veterans, but only recently out of line from Aachen and so badly under strength

5th Parachute Division
Destroyed in Normandy and rebuilt to 16,000 men. Inexperienced divisional and regimental leaders

352 VGD

Rebuilt from Luftwaffe and naval personnel. Poorly trained, lacking experienced officers

▶ *Panthers de-train on a spur line running to Eifel – one of the pieces of the puzzle Allied intelligence officers failed to use wisely. (US National Archives)*

GERMAN ORDER OF BATTLE

GERMAN SIXTH PANZER ARMY, FIRST ASSAULT WAVE

Sixth Panzer Army
Oberstgruppenführer
der Waffen-SS
Josef Dietrich

I SS Panzer Corps
SS-Gruppenführer
Hermann Priess

LXVII Corps
Generaleutnant Otto Hitzfeld

Ist SS Panzer Division
'Liebstandarte Adolf Hitler'
With 22,000 men and about 140 tanks or tank-type vehicles, the most powerful division in the Ardennes

12th SS Panzer Division
'Hitler Jugend'
Suffered terrible losses in Normandy. Rebuilt to 22,000 men but short of experienced junior officers

277th VGD
Comprised only some 1,000 veterans. Filled with ethnic Germans from conquered border areas. A weak unit

150th Panzer Brigade
Hurriedly assembled commando unit led by Otto Skorzeny. A makeshift unit in every way

3rd Parachute Division
Destroyed in Normandy. Rebuilt with rear-area Luftwaffe ground personnel. Inexperienced, not parachute-capable

12th VGD
Suffered heavy losses in Russia in summer 1944. Rebuilt and engaged around Aachen earning the honorific 'Volksgrenadier'

326th VGD
Rebuilt with low-quality replacements

▼ *Jagdpanzer IV/70 of SS Panzerjager Abteilung 1.*

mander of VIII Corps charged with holding the Ardennes. During their discussion all realized that the front was thinly held but that it seemed a reasonable risk. No one believed that the hastily trained Volksgrenadier units the Germans used to man the front were capable of offensive action. Furthermore, no one thought a German thrust in the Ardennes could reach an important objective. Only Patton, preparing his own offensive south of the Ardennes, noted in his diary on 24 November: 'The First Army is making a terrible mistake in leaving VIII Corps static, as it is highly probable that the Germans are building up east of them.'

Bradley later claimed that, although he believed a German attack unlikely, he discussed appropriate defensive plans with Middleton: 'If the Germans hit his sector, Middleton was to make a fighting withdrawal – all the way back to the Meuse River if necessary.' The plan relied upon the proven American superiority in mobility whereby reserve armoured divisions would lend assistance from adjacent armies. Planning presumed a limited German spoiling attack of four to six divisions and no one took even this plan too seriously. Had anyone believed an attack possible, the defenders could have fortified. Responding to a post-war question about why this was not done, Middleton said: 'Have you any idea how much manpower and effort would have been required to dig a trench eighty-eight miles long?' While a continuous line was clearly impossible given VIII Corps strength, heavier fortifications at key road intersections and river crossings would have saved many American lives. In the event, the defenders occupied hastily dug foxholes and were without contingency plans for a major German attack.

When von Rundstedt learned of Hitler's plan he was 'staggered' and immediately realized that it was too ambitious for the available resources. He, Model, and von Manteuffel proposed an alternative, which became known as the 'small solution', a pincers attack – one prong of which would strike from the Eifel – with the objective of trapping American forces against the Meuse. Even Dietrich argued against Hitler's plan, but to no avail. Insulated from the incredible hardships and sacrifices German soldiers had made on both the Eastern and Western fronts, Hitler and his en-

tourage lived in a fantasy land. Typical of their unprofessional approach to planning was the question of air support. At one meeting Hitler asked Goering how many aircraft could support the offensive? Goering responded: 'Three thousand.' Hitler turned to von Manteuffel and winked: 'You know Goering. I think we shall have 2,000.' Such laughable planning seriously undermined the chances for the attack.

As ultimately constructed, 'Wacht am Rhein' envisaged a 5.30am assault by three armies striking through the Ardennes from Monschau to Echternach. After crossing the Meuse between Liège and Namur, they would bypass Brussels and capture Antwerp within a week. Cut in two, the western Allies would never recover from the shock, causing their alliance to dissolve and forcing them to sue for a separate peace.

Dietrich's Sixth Panzer Army carried the main effort along the northern flank. Concentrated on a narrow front from Monschau to the Losheim Gap, his first wave comprised four infantry and two élite SS panzer divisions. Curiously, at this stage of the war the Germans had not resolved the doctrinal dispute about whether infantry or armour should attack first. On the Sixth Panzer Army front planners decided that infantry would lead the way to open the sparse road net. The staff expected them to advance three to five miles by noon of the first day. Then the panzers would pass through to begin their race to the Meuse, following the shortest route straight over the Elsenborn Ridge. The powerful 1st SS Panzer Division served as the army's spearhead. Model's plan called for the Meuse crossing on the fourth day.

Von Manteuffel's Fifth Panzer Army, the next army south, had a supporting mission with two major first objectives. Two infantry divisions were to encircle the Schnee Eifel to trap the two forward US 106th Infantry Division regiments. Then the ambitious plan called for them to advance west to capture the key road town of St Vith. Further south, two infantry and three panzer divisions had to secure crossings over the River Our and then race west parallel to Sixth Panzer Army all the way to Antwerp. To begin with, the problem would be bridging the Our. Consequently, here too infantry would lead the way in order to screen engineers who would lay bridges for the panzers heading west. Both panzer armies were to drive relentlessly westward without regard for their flanks.

The weakest of the assault armies, Seventh Army – more a reinforced corps than an army – had a more limited mission somewhat in keeping with its limited mobility and strength. It would conduct a river assault in the Vianden-Echternach area and then march west to protect von Manteuffel's left flank. Planners from Jodl downwards expected the fiercest counterattacks to come from Patton's Third Army, and thus they assigned Seventh Army a largely defensive role. Much hinged upon its ability to advance to key blocking positions along the southern sector.

Hitler hoped to bolster the assault by emulating the winning formula of 1940-1: rapid, deep armoured penetration, paratroop attacks in the rear and infiltration by disguised troops. As an adjunct to the 1st SS Panzer Division's advance, he also laid on Operation 'Greif' (Condor). 'Greif commandos', wearing American uniforms and aided by English-speaking Germans, intended to seize intact at least two Meuse bridges and to spread confusion in the rear by sabotage. In addition, commando extraordinaire Otto Skorzeny commanded a hastily formed, special mechanized brigade of captured or disguised equipment. He was to reinforce the commandos at the Meuse. In the event, however, Operation 'Greif' was to have a very modest impact on the campaign.

Similarly, a proposed parachute drop behind Elsenborn Ridge, Sixth Panzer Army's target, deteriorated from inception to practice when unskilled pilots scattered ill-equipped parachutists all the way from Bonn east of the Rhine to the drop zone. Ten of the 105 Junkers transports delivered the parachutists to the drop area where, once on the ground, they accomplished nothing beyond alarming American rear-echelon soldiers.

Terrain

In the words of the official historian, the Ardennes geography 'leads inevitably to the channelization of large troop movements east to west'. Without excellent traffic control, units would pile up on each other. Once units fixed their direction of

attack they faced restricted freedom of manoeuvre since there were few cross-country alternatives. Most roads ran along narrow valley floors. This provided natural blocking points at the valley entrances and exits when the road curved through the slopes. Where the limited roads converged at market towns – Bastogne, St Vith and Manhay, to name a notable three – combat was sure to occur. In addition to the Our and Sauer river lines held by the defenders at the start, the River Ourthe provided a significant mid-point barrier between the start line and the Meuse, while the Rivers Salm and Amblève cut across very rugged terrain perpendicular to Sixth Panzer Army's line of advance. Small-scale tactics, at battalion level and down, confronted severe command and control problems. Rolling, sometimes rugged terrain featured numerous forests and woods. More than is usually the case, combat became a collection of small, independent actions with the combatants and often their leaders having little appreciation of what was really happening. Having passed this way in 1914 and 1940, the Germans understood the terrain restrictions. Terrain obstacles decreased from east to west, so if a rapid breakthrough occurred the panzers could run free. In 1940 reconnaissance elements had reached the Meuse in 24 hours.

For 'Wacht am Rhein', Hitler dictated the strategy, the choice of ground, the allocation of forces and choice of tactics. Traditional Prussian planning and analysis had little role, and thus many German professional officers felt estranged from the concept. Jodl, in planning his first offensive, made a mistake common to inexperienced staff officers: his rigid plans left little room for subordinate initiative and even less to the chance fortunes of war. More than anything, the plan overlooked the difficulty of heavy tanks manoeuvring across wooded ridge lines, along narrow roads and over numerous rivers and streams. These flaws, which meant that the entire counteroffensive was hostage to the possibility that a blown bridge or the determined defence of a road junction could wreck careful timetables, became clear in hindsight. Yet such was the prestige of the German Army, even in 1944, that when the panzers advanced all seemed possible to both attacker and defender.

ASSAULT

Repulse of Sixth Panzer Army

In the pre-dawn light of 16 December, shells and rockets began landing on American positions. The defenders awoke to the greatest American battle of the Second World War. While the Germans attacked all along the 85-mile front, events in three key sectors tell the story of the first 24 hours. Hitler expected Sixth Panzer Army to carry the brunt of the attack. The army's entire scheme of manoeuvre depended upon I SS Panzer Corps achieving a quick breakthrough of the Elsenborn Ridge. The plan called for two Volksgrenadier divisions to crack the American front and then for the SS armour to drive through the gap and on to the Meuse. The odds greatly favoured the Volksgrenadiers. A mere five battalions of the green US

99th Infantry Division covered the sector. But the attackers would need to hurry; sunset was at 4.35.

The key position was the gloomy pine forest in front of the twin villages of Rocherath-Krinkelt, which lay on the forward slopes of the Elsenborn Ridge. Here the initial attack came against K Company, 3rd Battalion, 393rd Infantry. The Germans skilfully followed the opening barrage so that two battalions appeared at Company K's foxhole line before the defenders had a chance to brace themselves for the impact. The attackers quickly overwhelmed all but one platoon. Yet this platoon and the two adjacent companies managed a fighting withdrawal to a line around the battalion command post. Here they held off all comers. Their stout recovery greatly annoyed the com-

▶ *Morale was high among the Germans on the eve of the assault, particularly among the SS such as those shown here. An exuberant SS trooper penned a note to his sister: 'I write during one of the great hours before we attack . . . full of expectation for what the next days will bring . . . we attack and will throw the enemy from our homeland. That is a holy task!' On the back of the envelope he added: 'Ruth! Ruth! Ruth! WE MARCH!' (US National Archives)*

mander of I SS Panzer Corps. In order to force an opening he committed a battalion of SS panzergrenadiers. They managed to surround the 3rd Battalion but, by failing to eliminate the position, could not open the vital road leading west. At steep cost – the defending battalion lost about 300 men – the Americans held.

In an adjacent position, 1st Battalion, 393rd Infantry, confronted the same overwhelming odds. Since its position was more in the open it had excellent fields of fire. The first German assault collapsed in a hurricane of machine-gun, mortar, and artillery fire. Pressured to achieve an im-

mediate breakthrough, the Germans committed another regiment to the assault. But here the attackers' inexperience showed. They assaulted in dense formations with soldiers literally being herded forward by their officers and NCOs. Eventually weight of numbers forced a breach. The last American reserve, 25 men led by a lieutenant from the regimental anti-tank company and 13 men from the headquarters company, counterattacked into the teeth of the German breakthrough. Showing great fighting spirit, this rag-tail group fixed bayonets, charged, killed 28 Germans, and restored the battalion's line. At a

◀ *This rare, scratchy photo shows German self-propelled 150mm artillery in the pre-dawn light of 16 December. (US National Archives)*

◀ *The opening bombardment caught the Americans by surprise and destroyed wire communications, the primary means of tactical communication. Early in the offensive, artillery officers from all three German armies decided to leave behind half the guns and Nebelwerfers because they could not bring ammunition forward. This left subsequent attacks with greatly reduced artillery support. (Wood Collection, US Army Military History Institute)*

The German Assault, to 20 December

US Front line 15 December		
US Front line 20 December		

0   5   10   15 Miles

0 5 10 15 20 25 Kms

cost of some 400 men the battalion held its position.

During the 38-minute twilight preceding nightfall the Germans began infiltrating gaps in the US position. Strong fighting patrols cut communications. They called out in English hoping to make the defenders reveal themselves. When this failed they sprayed the American position with sub-machine-gun fire. For any unit it would have been an unnerving experience, yet the green 99th Division stood firm. Hungry, cold, and frightened they awaited the dawn.

Some of the American higher ranking officers did not match the valour of the men they commanded. V Corps' acting commander had anticipated a German counterstroke once his attack on the Roer dams began. The sketchy information he received initially convinced him this was what was taking place. As the day wore on he became more alarmed and set off to visit the 99th Division headquarters. He arrived to find the divisional staff milling about in confusion with everyone shouting at the same time. Leading by example was the divisional commander, playing a piano in the middle of his command post to try to settle his nerves. He insisted that everything was under control.

Forcing the Our

Some 25 miles south, Fifth Panzer Army faced the Americans across the River Our. Army commander von Manteuffel had persuaded Hitler to substitute a short bombardment for the planned two- to three-hour artillery preparation in order to reduce the American alert time. Instead of attacking at 10am, which would leave a mere six daylight hours to gain ground, he proposed to begin before dawn under the illumination of giant searchlights bouncing their light off the clouds. Having spent a night in a front-line pillbox overlooking the American positions, he had learned that the defending 110th Infantry Regiment, 28th Infantry Division (110/28) withdrew its outposts at night. Thus he proposed that his assault troops infiltrate selected areas without any artillery assistance. Hitler agreed with all of this.

At 5.30am, an American lookout in Hosingen on the Skyline Drive (the ridge road running parallel to the Our) called his company commander to report a strange phenomenon: in the distance he saw numerous flickerings of light. Seconds later shells starting bursting all along the Skyline Drive to explain this startling observation.

A former Pennsylvania National Guard unit, the 28th Division had earned a good reputation beginning at Normandy; the terrible fighting in the Huertgen Forest, where it lost some 6,100 men, had nearly crippled it. Soldiers had taken to calling its red, bucket-shaped shoulder patch the 'Bloody Bucket'. Sent for rest and refit in the quiet Ardennes sector, the 28th sat squarely in the path of Fifth Panzer Army.

The three regiments comprising the division held a 25-mile front. The left regiment defended good ground and would manage to block the entire LVIII Panzer Corps for a solid 24 hours. The right-hand regiment fought against the under-manned, under-equipped Seventh Army, and it too managed to conduct an organized fighting withdrawal. The centre regiment, 110th Infantry, guarded 15 miles behind the River Our. It faced three German divisions, at odds of more than 10 to 1. Unable to man a continuous defensive line, the regiment occupied company-sized roadblocks on the roads leading up from the Our. Particularly important were the villages of Marnach and Hosingen, through which ran the best roads to Bastogne. Via these roads 19 miles separated the Germans from the critical Bastogne road hub.

The units comprising the assault force included some of the best remaining in the German Army. The veteran 2nd Panzer had 86 tanks, mostly the latest model Panthers, and 20 assault guns. The 26th VGD counted some 17,000 men in its ranks. Unlike other Volksgrenadier units, it had won its honorific title in battle and was one of the few to be rebuilt in the old organization of three infantry battalions per regiment. Both divisions had been brought up to strength with superior replacements, yet both shared the army-wide lack of mechanized transport. In contrast, the experienced Panzer Lehr Division, the corps' third assault division, had been sucked into the defensive fighting against Patton's Third Army in November. It had not recovered from its heavy losses and numbered a mere 57 Mark IV and Panther tanks. Most important, such was the German material poverty at this stage of the war that although Fifth Panzer Army held a formidable qualitative and quantitative edge in equipment, it lacked good bridging equipment for spanning the Our. Until its engineers manhandled pontoons down narrow, slippery roads and fastened them into place, the infantry of 26th VGD would have to carry the fight alone without supporting heavy weapons or tanks.

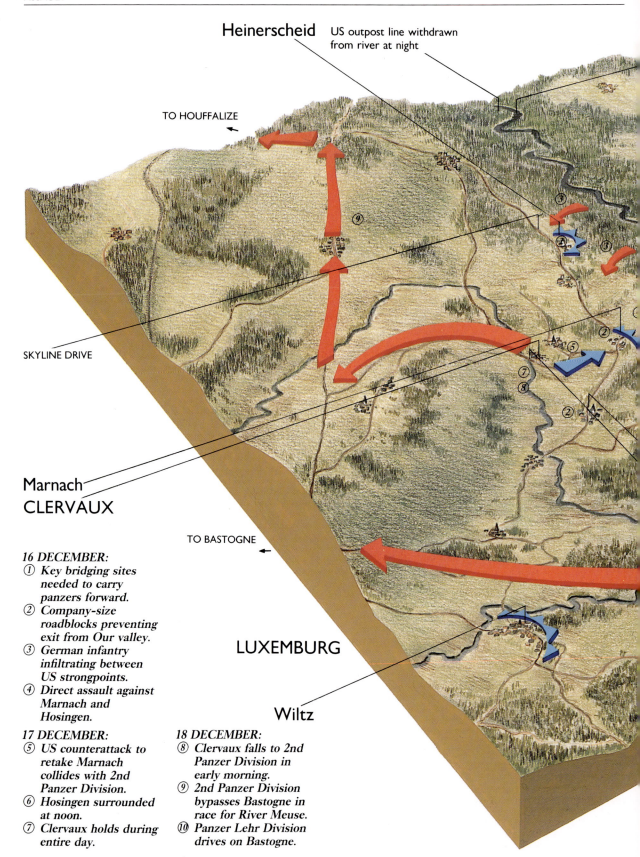

Heinerscheid

US outpost line withdrawn
from river at night

TO HOUFFALIZE

SKYLINE DRIVE

Marnach

CLERVAUX

TO BASTOGNE

LUXEMBURG

Wiltz

16 DECEMBER:
① *Key bridging sites needed to carry panzers forward.*
② *Company-size roadblocks preventing exit from Our valley.*
③ *German infantry infiltrating between US strongpoints.*
④ *Direct assault against Marnach and Hosingen.*

17 DECEMBER:
⑤ *US counterattack to retake Marnach collides with 2nd Panzer Division.*
⑥ *Hosingen surrounded at noon.*
⑦ *Clervaux holds during entire day.*

18 DECEMBER:
⑧ *Clervaux falls to 2nd Panzer Division in early morning.*
⑨ *2nd Panzer Division bypasses Bastogne in race for River Meuse.*
⑩ *Panzer Lehr Division drives on Bastogne.*

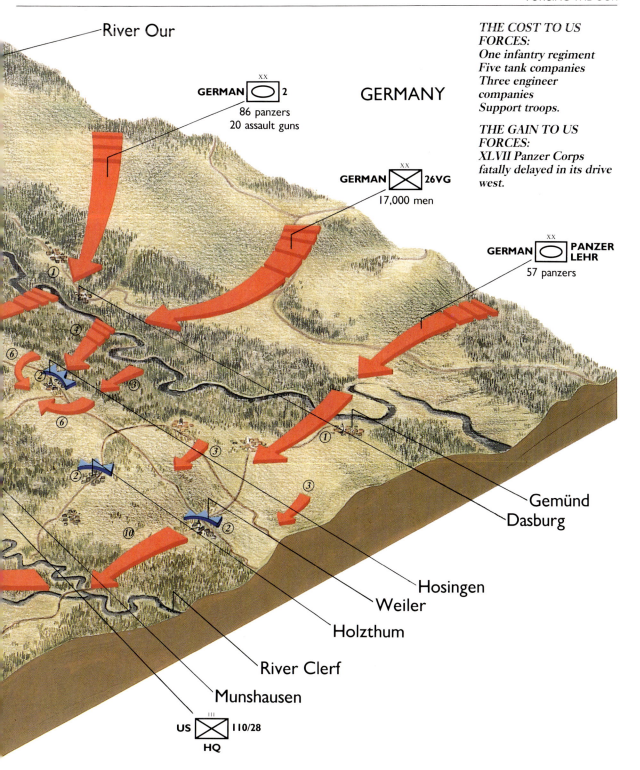

River Our

GERMAN ⬭ XX 2
86 panzers
20 assault guns

GERMANY

THE COST TO US
FORCES:
One infantry regiment
Five tank companies
Three engineer
companies
Support troops.

THE GAIN TO US
FORCES:
XLVII Panzer Corps
fatally delayed in its drive
west.

GERMAN ⊠ XX 26VG
17,000 men

GERMAN ⬭ XX PANZER LEHR
57 panzers

Gemünd
Dasburg

Hosingen
Weiler
Holzthum
River Clerf
Munshausen

US ⊠ III 110/28
HQ

US 110/28TH DIVISION'S DELAYING ACTIONS

16 to 18 December 1944.

219

Some of the shells and rockets from XLVII Panzer Corps' 554 artillery pieces and Nebelwerfers landed amid the 110th's headquarters at Clervaux and awakened the regimental commander, Colonel Hurley Fuller. Turning to his assistant Fuller asked: 'What do you make of it?' The officer replied: 'All this big stuff is a sure sign we're in for a fight.'

To ensure rapid progress, von Manteuffel had directed his men to emulate First World War infiltration tactics ('Hutier tactics') and bypass most pockets of resistance. However, since Marnach and Hosingen blocked the two major westward roads, von Manteuffel demanded that they should be seized quickly by a direct assault.

▲ *Once armoured support, such as this assault gun, crossed the Our, they spearheaded the attack against the 110/28. Lacking effective anti-tank support, the American defence collapsed. (US National Archives)*

◄ *The dispersal of American tanks into 'penny packets' led to futile armoured counterattacks. This Sherman turret shows the all too common result. In 10 minutes, an American light tank company attempting to counterattack to support the 110/28th lost eight tanks to concealed German high-velocity guns and three to panzerfausts. (US National Archives)*

Surprise, coupled with dense fog, allowed the German assault companies to advance to almost on top of the American positions before detection. In some cases the attackers annihilated entire platoons before they could react. Yet many defenders responded with veteran aplomb. Surprised at their guns, Battery C, 109th Field Artillery Battalion, lowered their muzzles to deliver point-blank shells in the attackers' faces. Outside Consthum, an anti-aircraft gunner spotted the attackers, waved them forward in friendly fashion, fingered the button of his quad-50 machine-guns and knocked down nearly 100 Germans in a matter of seconds.

In many places American mortar and artillery fire pinned assault columns to the ground for the balance of the day. In others, such as at Hosingen where the first wave overran a platoon south of the village, the Germans failed to press their advantage. This key village held all day. Nearby, after blundering through a minefield, the panzergrenadiers of the 2nd Panzer Division assaulted Marnach. Thoroughly alerted, B Company shot the attack apart. But as the day progressed, many surviving defenders began to realize that significant numbers of Germans were bypassing their positions and marching west.

Unlike most higher ranking officers, the regimental commander quickly realized that a major attack was under way. Fighting short-handed from the beginning, with one of his three infantry battalions providing the divisional reserve, Fuller requested reinforcements as soon as the communication line was restored at about 9am. The divisional commander, Major General Norman Cota, refused to commit his only infantry reserve so early in the battle. Instead he sent two tank companies, 34 Shermans. Confronting breakthroughs all along his front, Fuller split the tanks into the type of 'penny packets' that so attracted the scorn of experienced German panzer leaders. While this perhaps necessary tactic bolstered many of the beleaguered defenders, the tanks failed to exert a decisive influence. Worse, in the marching and counter-marching no one realized that the two platoons that had been ordered to Marnach did not stay there.

The German infantry suffered heavily in their unsupported attacks against the 110/28th. By afternoon German engineers had finally completed the critical bridges at Dasburg and Gemund. German armour slowly debouched up the narrow, muddy roads of the Our valley towards Skyline Drive. One by one American positions began to face new infantry assaults backed by armour. A platoon at Wahlhausen called in artillery on its own position to try to stop the German armour. The tactic failed and only one American escaped.

Desperate, Fuller organized and armed rear-echelon personnel and established roadblocks to try to halt the attack. Cooks, clerks, and MPs were given a carbine or a bazooka and told to hold at all costs. Middleton, the corps commander, had abandoned his pre-battle plan to conduct a fighting withdrawal in the event of a German attack. Instead he ordered everyone to defend in place until their positions were 'completely untenable'.

In spite of the overwhelming odds and the confused commitment of reserves, by the end of 16 December the 110th Regiment had lost only three defended positions. Partially the success came from the unsuccessful 'Hutier tactics': time and again, while trying to pass between the American outposts, the Germans found themselves raked in flank by vigilant defenders. And partially success resulted from the slow German bridge-laying together with the poor roads that kept the supporting armour from joining battle. Mostly, however, success stemmed from the intrepid fighting of the isolated infantry, handfuls of veterans stiffening numerous green replacements and jointly refusing to yield. Already the Germans were falling seriously behind schedule.

Through the Losheim Gap

At only one point did the Germans achieve the type of clean breakthrough that 'Wacht am Rhein' required. The seven-mile-wide Losheim Gap provided an east to west invasion route that the Germans had used in 1870, 1914, and 1940. Remarkably, it was the sector on the Ardennes front most lightly held by the Americans. One-half of the 14th Cavalry Group, about 900 men, was responsible for the southern five miles. Nominally, they were attached to the adjacent 106th Infantry

221

◀ *In mud and snow, towed anti-tank guns such as this 3in model, photographed by the Germans on 17 December, could not be moved fast enough. Direct fire or infantry assault made the task of limbering the gun difficult and often knocked out the tow vehicle. (US National Archives)*

Division. But the 106th had only entered the line four days previously, and its commander had yet to meet the 14th Cavalry commander. Moreover, the inter-corps boundary between V and VIII Corps was in the middle of the gap, and thus: 'Though two soldiers can shake hands across this boundary, the chain of command separates them by a hundred miles.' Assigned a static position, the lightly armed cavalry sacrificed their one strength, mobility. Beyond the 14th's sector, no soldiers occupied the two northern miles of the gap. Here hourly jeep patrols provided the only security.

The boundary between Sixth and Fifth Panzer Armies also ran through the southern portion of the gap. OKW drew this boundary to provide a swift route west for the 1st SS Panzer Division, giving von Manteuffel's men only enough room to slice around the northern end of the Schnee Eifel to encircle the two American regiments stationed on the high ground. As elsewhere, German infantry had to open the route for the panzers. Accordingly, following the opening bombardment came the 3rd Parachute Division against the northern portion of the 14th Cavalry.

Elements of the 3rd Parachute Division reinforced with tanks faced two cavalry platoons, two reconnaissance platoons, a TD company and headquarters units. In effect, the attackers confronted small islands of defence featuring two to four towed anti-tank guns with a handful of riflemen and machine-gunners. The defenders recovered quickly from their surprise and German inexperience showed itself as the 3rd Parachute's attack dissolved into a series of stumbling, uncoordinated lurches forward. But slowly numbers told. The regular jeep patrol crossing the two-mile-wide void north of the 14th Cavalry reported the area 'crawling with Krauts!' Further south, two regiments of von Manteuffel's 18th VGD backed by 40 75mm assault guns and numerous self-propelled tank destroyers attacked Troop A (a company-sized formation) and one platoon of Troop C, 18th Cavalry Squadron. The attackers suffered heavy losses, trading casualties for speed, but inexorably they overpowered the defenders.

Most defenders fought well, but there were exceptions. At one small village a last radio message reported enemy assault guns 'seventy-five yards from CP, firing direct fire. Out.' After losing three killed, the remaining 87-man garrison surrendered. Reserve cavalry elements failed to stabilize the situation, their intervention weakened by their colonel's cowardice. He fled to the rear 'in search of extra ammunition'. By noon the Germans had either captured, surrounded, or were about to assault every village in the Losheim Gap. And by nightfall the situation had badly deteriorated, with the 14th Cavalry scattered and out of touch with headquarters. However well they had fought during the day, at night the 14th's dispersed elements grew nervous, shuffled positions, and were thrown off balance. Long columns of vehicles with rear-area soldiers clinging to their decks began to hasten to the rear. The situation verged on panic. The appearance of Tiger tanks at dawn on 17 December produced an accordion-like series of retreats and gave the attackers their breakthrough. The cavalry's failure to hold placed the GIs on the Schnee Eifel in great peril.

While one German pincer moved through the Losheim Gap the other advanced south of the Schnee Eifel. The threatened link-up would surround the two regiments defending the high ground. The defenders did not comprehend the true situation. Secure in good positions, they spent an easy day repulsing an occasional German patrol. Proud of their ability to hold their ground in this, their first combat, they did not realize that they confronted an exceptionally thin screen from a German replacement battalion and that the real decision was taking place deep on either flank.

In St Vith the divisional commander, Major General Alan Jones, looked at his situation map and saw the danger. Around noon he telephoned his corps commander to ask permission to withdraw the units atop the Schnee Eifel. Middleton demurred (later saying that he had worried that if the two green regiments started to the rear they 'might go half-way to Paris') and Jones, anxious not to appear jumpy with his first command, did not press the case.

▼ A US M4A3E8 heavily protected by sandbags.

By nightfall the situation had worsened, so Jones called again. The generals spoke on an unsecured, improvised telephone line. Fearful of German eavesdropping, they talked using stilted riddles and code words. Consequently, when Middleton hung up he told his staff that he had told Jones: 'to pull his regiments off the Schnee Eifel'. At the other end Jones reported to his staff that Middleton required the division to hold in place. Some of the 106th's officers realized the implications of the decision to remain in position. Jones' G-2 wrote that evening: 'The enemy is capable of pinching off the Schnee Eifel area. . . at any time.' The stage was set for the largest American surrender in the Second World War.

Reactions at the Top

Spread thinly on the ground, with communications knocked out by the initial German bombardment, the front-line defenders had little knowledge of anything beyond their immediate sector. Their reports seeping up the chain of command gave a fragmentary picture of the situation at the end of 16 December. Some reports from divisional com-

▲ The 3rd Parachute Division used panzerjaegers such as this one to spearhead its drive through the Losheim Gap. In the words of the official historian: 'On no other part of the American front would the enemy so outnumber the defenders at the start of the Ardennes counteroffensive.' (US National Archives)

manders did not help. As late as 4.15pm, 28th Division reported that 'the situation for the division is well in hand'. By nightfall, proud of his inexperienced unit's conduct during the day, the commander of the 99th Division told V Corps 'that the situation was in hand and all quiet'.

As early as 7am the First Army commander, Lieutenant General Courtney Hodges, learned of German attacks. He placed a regimental combat team on alert. At 10.30am he ordered that CCA/9th Armored Division be released from the Roer dams attack and sent to support Middleton. After these commendable initial reactions, a curious torpor overcame Hodges. He believed he faced a German spoiling attack and was reluctant to cancel the Roer drive. He clung to this view into the night even after both V and VIII Corps headquarters had in hand captured German orders announcing that a great counteroffensive was under way. Hodges' V Corps commander wavered between concern over events on his right flank – his lone supply route and potential avenue of withdrawal was through the twin villages of Rocherath-Krinkelt – and a desire to press the Roer attack. VIII Corps commander, Middleton, was in no such quandary. He realized that the German effort was much more than a spoiling attack and that he faced impending crisis. Accordingly, early in the day he had issued Hitler-like orders to all units, with the exception, he thought, of the 106th Division, to stand firm and defend in place. To a certain extent the American higher command was working at cross purposes. The surprise assault had confused them.

Buffered from events at the front, the day saw the army group commander in transit to SHAEF at Versailles. Bradley arrived to press his case to Eisenhower for additional infantry replacements. An officer interrupted the meeting with news from Middleton. First reports indicated German attacks at five points. Most American officers, including Bradley, thought here was the anticipated spoiling attack launched in response to the First Army drive on the Roer dams and Patton's impending offensive. They did not want to play into German hands by diverting troops from those offensives. As the evening wore on, additional reports informed SHAEF that eight divisions previously not identified on the Ardennes front were attacking Middleton. A staff officer commented to the now thoroughly alarmed Bradley: 'Well, Brad, you've been wishing for a counterattack. Now it looks as though you've got it.' Bradley replied: 'A counterattack, yes. But I'll be damned if I wanted one this big.'

Upon first news of the attack, Eisenhower alone sensed it was something big. Although there were only four uncommitted American divisions on the entire Western front, the Supreme Commander recommended Bradley send two armoured divisions, the 7th from the north and the 10th from the south, to help Middleton. Bradley agreed. This quick response proved one of the campaign's key decisions. Still the situation did not appear overly grave. Bradley and Eisenhower spent the evening celebrating Ike's recent promotion by playing five rubbers of bridge over a bottle of champagne.

Across the lines at German army level, the most confident general was the commander of Seventh Army. He had expected little from his weak army, yet as he surveyed the map pins marking his progress he felt he was on the verge of a breakthrough. His forces had managed to cross the River Sauer and establish several lodgements within the American position and had forced the defending 4th Infantry Division to request reinforcements from the embattled Middleton. In contrast, the first day's progress disappointed von Manteuffel. He hoped that by continuing the attack during the night he could return to his ambitious schedule. At the neighbouring Sixth Panzer Army, Sepp Dietrich's chief of staff, who did most of the strategic thinking for his commanding officer, worried that failure to break through would allow American reinforcements to flow rapidly south. He ordered the ill-prepared German parachutists to jump that night to block this flow. Here was wishful thinking in the extreme. It was left to the old veteran von Rundstedt to describe the true situation. He briefed Hitler that while the attack had achieved total surprise, Sixth Panzer Army had failed to achieve a breakthrough and this jeopardized the army's chances of reaching the Meuse.

Hitler typically did not listen to pessimistic news. Believing his troops were on the verge of a breakthrough, delighted that the weather was supposed to remain bad and thus ground Allied aircraft, he exalted: 'Everything has changed in the West! Success – complete success – is now in our grasp.'

But by the end of the first day the Germans had failed to achieve the expected breakthrough. Even green American units had stood firm in the face of surprise while slowing the German advance and inflicting irreplaceable losses. Contrary to Hitler's cherished belief, the Allied High Command, in the person of Eisenhower, was responding in a co-ordinated manner by immediately drawing upon armoured reserves from two adjacent armies. However, tomorrow would tell all. The first day's attacks had disclosed weaknesses in the American position. Bridges had been seized or built, the panzers stood poised to roll.

▲Men of 1st SS
Panzergrenadier
Regiment.

BREAKTHROUGH

Collapse in the Centre

While the American generals worked, according to their varying capacities, to comprehend the German offensive, along the Fifth Panzer Army front von Manteuffel sought to get back on schedule by continuing the attack through the night. Infiltration tactics worked much better in the dark. Assault groups penetrated between American positions and began picking off the artillery positions supporting the front-line village garrisons. They overran some artillery and forced others to displace hurriedly to the rear.

By dawn, tanks of the 2nd Panzer Division were moving forward to attack the Clerf river crossings at Clervaux. Simultaneously, Fuller committed his reserves to retake Marnach. It was an amazing spectacle: a couple of infantry companies and one company of light tanks versus substantial elements of an entire panzer corps. Without artillery support, the American infantry could make no headway. Eighteen light tanks advancing from Heinerscheid ran into concealed German assault guns and lost eight vehicles. Panzerfausts knocked out three more as the effort collapsed. Remarkably, a

▼ *Although front-line defenders quickly captured copies of the German attack order, not until the morning of 17 December did Bradley and Eisenhower learn of these orders. The morning's Ultra decodes provided von Rundstedt's attack order: 'The hour of destiny has struck. Mighty offensive armies face the Allies. Everything is at stake. More than mortal deeds are required as a holy duty to the Fatherland.' Here a posed German photograph taken in the Ardennes on 17 December shows assaulting infantry. (US National Archives)*

third attack featuring a platoon of Shermans carrying an infantry platoon moved from Munshausen and reconquered part of Marnach. But they could not hold alone against counterattacking tanks and panzergrenadiers, so Fuller ordered them to retreat.

At 10.30am a tank company from CCR/9 Armored Division unexpectedly reinforced Fuller in Clervaux. The aggressive colonel split the 17 Shermans into three platoons and used them to reinforce his crumbling positions. Entering combat for the first time, the tanks ran straight into the growing might of the 2nd Panzer Division and were nearly annihilated.

Spearheaded by assault guns and tanks that had finally extricated themselves from the Our valley, Fifth Panzer Army began to overwhelm the 110/28. By noon on the 17th the Germans had surrounded the key roadblock at Hosingen. Frustrated at his lack of progress, the commander of XLVII Panzer Corps committed the Panzer Lehr's advanced guard to the fray. The defenders' five remaining tanks moved to counter one attack after another, but by the evening the Germans had forced K Company into a small perimeter around company headquarters and the regimental engineers into another small pocket across the village. After an epic defence, the Hosingen defenders finally surrendered.

Also during the 17th the attackers brought increasing weight to bear directly against regimental headquarters in Clervaux. Fuller's remaining platoon of Shermans duelled with the German Mark IVs on the heights and managed to block the road by destroying one tank. But by now the attackers had multiple routes to enter the town and Fuller's situation became desperate. He requested permission to withdraw; but Middleton's 'hold at all costs' order remained in effect. The final stand came in an old castle that dominated the town. From its crenellated walls American snipers picked off unwary Germans in the streets below. However, after exhausting their supply of bazooka ammunition, they were helpless to prevent the flood of German armour moving west. At noon on the 18th, a German tank battered down the wooden doors of the castle and forced the surviving defenders to surrender.

The fall of Clervaux and the parallel collapse of the remainder of the 28th Division's positions ended the unit's delaying actions before Bastogne. At a time in the war when American units did not expect to suffer heavy losses, the 110th Infantry Regiment along with the men and vehicles of five tank companies, the equivalent of three combat engineer companies, and supporting tank destroyers, artillery and service troops had all been virtually destroyed. In the words of the official historian: 'without the gallant bargain struck by the 110th Infantry and its allied units – men for time – the German plans for a coup-de-main at Bastogne would have turned to accomplished fact.'

The pressure was now transferred to other American troops who had to determine whether the hours and minutes won by the tremendous fighting spirit displayed by the 28th Division would be sufficient to preserve Bastogne from the advancing German tanks.

The Defence of the Twin Villages

Unlike Fifth Panzer Army, Sixth Panzer Army did not press its attack during the night. When it resumed its attacks at dawn, for the second day the combat around the twin villages of Rocherath-Krinkelt was of the utmost importance. It was a position the Americans had to hold. It had the only usable escape route for the 2nd and 99th Divisions. Attacked frontally by three divisions of I SS Corps, flanked by the breakthrough in the Losheim Gap, Major General Walter Robertson first had to extract his units concentrated in the north-east for the Roer dams offensive. Fortunately, the day before he had disobeyed Hodges' order to continue the 2nd Division's attack against the dams. Furthermore, Robertson had made the key decision to send two battalions to reinforce the defenders in front of the twin villages.

Stiffened by the 2nd Division veterans, the 99th Division managed to hold its position. Behind its protective screen vast vehicular columns clogged the road westwards. Once the 2nd Division arrived to provide a backstop, the 99th Division had to disengage and withdraw. This exceedingly difficult feat of disengaging through the twin villages bottleneck while under attack is described by an

American company commander: 'Wave after wave of fanatically screaming German infantry stormed the slight tree-covered rise held by the three platoons. A continuous hail of fire exuded from their weapons, answered by volley after volley from the defenders. Germans fell right and left. The few rounds of artillery we did succeed in bringing down caught the attackers in the draw to our front, and we could hear their screams of pain when the small-arms fire would slacken. But still they came!'

When five Tiger tanks joined the assault, the company's two supporting Shermans 'bugged out' – in vain an American officer tried to convince the Shermans to stand, but the tank crews replied that it would be suicide to face the Tigers. Meanwhile, the German tanks began methodically to pound

▶ *The 150th Brigade employed a variety of ruses using captured or disguised equipment. American soldiers brush the snow away from the false side panel of a disabled German Jagdpanther disguised as a M10 tank destroyer to reveal the U.S. circle-in-star insignia. (US National Archives)*

▶ *One of the war's famous photographs, captured from the Germans, showing one of Peiper's amphibious cars during the advance. The faint lines on the signs are from the pen of the American censor who obscured the place names on the originals before releasing them. (US National Archives)*

the American foxhole line at 75 yards' range. With their few bazookas knocked out or out of ammunition, the defenders had no counter. Slowly at first, and then with some panic the company broke.

Fortuitously, the Sixth Panzer Army commander was unhappy with his rate of progress and chose this moment to order the 12th SS Panzer Division to redeploy through the Losheim Gap. His decision eased the pressure on the hard-pressed defenders. The Americans milled in disorder at the twin villages front on the night of 17 December, but the Germans did not break through. On the 19th the 2nd Division pulled back to the Elsenborn Ridge position. Here the two divisions joined the 1st Division to form a formidable defence backed by bountiful artillery. The crushing defensive artillery kept the Germans at bay for the remainder of the campaign. On Hitler's

◄ On both sides a prisoner's fate often depended upon the mood of his captors. If enraged, having just seen their buddies killed, or if it were deemed inconvenient to escort prisoners to the rear, they shot them. Patton noted in his diary on 4 January: 'There were also some unfortunate incidents in the shooting of prisoners (I hope we can conceal this).' However, only the Germans executed prisoners as a matter of policy. Here lie American victims of the infamous Malmédy massacre. (US National Archives)

◄ The puny 57mm gun provided the main anti-tank weapon the Americans deployed against Peiper. Some 250 Tigers, including 45 Royal Tigers, participated in the offensive. The only realistic American tactic was to attack the tank's rear. However, the mud and snow limited off-road mobility, thus reducing many tank encounters to frontal slugging matches. Here the inferior American weapons and armaments had no chance. Aware of their inferiority, all too often US tankers 'bugged out' leaving the hapless GI to fend for himself. (US National Archives)

▼ *Panzerkampfwagen IV Ausf J of the 1st SS Panzer Regiment.*

orders, the Germans continued futile attacks here until 24 December.

Robertson's battlefield leadership coupled with the 99th Division's valour allowed the formation of a barrier on the northern shoulder squarely blocking Sixth Panzer Army's intended drive west. As described by Sandhurst historian John Pimlott: 'It was a major contribution to eventual American victory.'

Peiper

From the beginning, some of the keener German officers appreciated the importance of the delayed breakthrough. One in particular was deeply disturbed. Obersturmbannführer Joachim Peiper expected to be driving through the break in American lines in the early morning of the 16th. Instead, he had spent the day in a fuel-consuming traffic jam as his regiment waited for the leading 3rd Parachute Division to clear the way. At last he ordered his tankers to plough through the clogged roads and arrived around midnight in the Losheim

Gap to visit the spearheading paratroopers. He found them resting, awaiting the dawn before advancing, worried about mined roads. Peiper asked if the colonel had personally scouted the route of advance. 'No,' came the reply. Peiper told the colonel to put one of his battalions on the back of the SS tanks. Henceforth his SS men would make their own breakthrough.

At dawn in the Losheim Gap, a scouting American armoured car watched American vehicles with blackout lights stream to the rear. Suddenly appeared a walking soldier carrying a white handkerchief to guide the 'biggest damn tank' the car commander had ever seen. It was Peiper's command.

Peiper had earned a ruthless reputation for leading his tank unit on the Eastern Front. Known as the 'Blowtorch Battalion' after the destruction of two Russian villages and their inhabitants, having once claimed 2,000 enemy killed and only three captured, Peiper now brought his unit west to spearhead the drive to the Meuse. His division, the 1st SS Panzer, was undiluted by large numbers of poorly trained Luftwaffe or Navy replacements, and was the strongest in Sixth Panzer Army. Yet the lack of roads prevented its commitment as a division. Accordingly, the divisional commander divided his unit into four marching groups. Peiper's powerful Kampfgruppe (battlegroup) comprised 100 Mark IVs and Panthers, along with a fully motorized panzergrenadier unit. During their advance they would be joined by Royal Tigers belonging to the 501st SS Panzer Detachment. Peiper, as the armoured spearhead, had strict instructions to follow a prescribed route west and to keep moving without regard to his flanks. He would both spearhead the breakthrough while creating chaos in the American rear. The German high command believed such chaos, augmented by terror tactics, would cause a quick collapse among the 'soft' Americans.

From Buchholz Station, near where the American armoured car spotted him, Peiper trailed behind an American column as it retreated westward. His high fuel consumption in the previous day's traffic jams forced Peiper to divert north to capture a fuel dump at Bullingen. At this point Peiper faced a choice. He could continue west to the Meuse or turn to cut off the 2nd and 99th Infantry Divisions on the Elsenborn Ridge. These divisions had only a single, narrow, muddy farm

track by which to retreat. No defenders stood between Peiper and this escape route – conceivably he could cut off some 30,000 men. The 99th's commander realized the situation: Peiper 'had the key to success within his hands but did not know it'.

Restocked, the SS colonel split his column and turned west. The panzergrenadiers under his subordinate proceeded to commit the most infamous atrocity of the war in western Europe. Mindful of their mission to sow terror, they shot some 85 prisoners just south of Malmédy. Kampfgruppe Peiper had already shot prisoners in Bullingen and were to kill more along with Belgian civilians in the ensuing days. But it was the discovery of these bodies strewn in a field that taught the defenders what kind of soldiers they faced. Word spread quickly about the massacre and considerably stiffened American resolve in the

▼ *Between 16 and 22 December, engineers formed the backbone of the US rear-area defence. Their activities delayed the spearheading panzers time and again. According to the official historian, 'a squad equipped with sufficient TNT could, in the right spot, do more to* *slow the enemy advance than a company armed with rifles and machine guns'. Peiper put it more succinctly. Gazing at the engineers' work, such as this blown bridge at Stavelot, he muttered: 'Those damned engineers.' (US Army Military History Institute)*

days ahead. The Malmédy massacre had the opposite effect Hitler had anticipated.

Peiper's column was now operating in the American rear. Some combat engineers, hastily collected by their colonel, were all that blocked his route west. Shortly after 4pm the colonel reported to First Army at Spa that a strong German column was as far west as Malmédy. The news shocked Hodges' headquarters. Up to this point, Hodges had believed the gravest threats were at St Vith and Bastogne. If the Germans captured Malmédy they could strike north against army headquarters and across First Army's line of communications or north-west towards Liège, the biggest Allied supply dump on the continent. For the first time, Hodges appreciated the dimensions of the German effort. He ordered the 30th Infantry Division to head for Malmédy, but they could not arrive until the following morning. He scraped together the only troops he could find including his headquarters security detachments and sent them to block Peiper. In the meantime, everything depended upon the ability of a series of combat engineer roadblocks to delay Peiper.

About 5pm Peiper departed Ligneuville to seize the bridge at Stavelot. The execrable roads – Peiper later complained that the route was suitable 'not for tanks but for bicycles' - - restricted his advance to a narrow path along a cliff. In the dark, thirteen combat engineers armed with a few mines, a .30-cal. machine-gun, and a bazooka confronted Peiper's advance guard. They belonged to the 291st Engineer Combat Battalion and until a few hours ago had expected to perform their routine work at a local saw-mill. Then came the electrifying order to head for Stavelot and establish a roadblock against a possible German advance. As they worked, Private Bernard Goldstein stood guard by the road. He heard engine noises and tightened his grasp on his M1 rifle. As the vehicles approached, Goldstein made out German voices: they were the paratroopers Peiper had commandeered to ride aboard his tanks. The private shouted: 'Halt!' The return fire sent him scurrying over the hill, but he had alerted his comrades that the Germans were here. Two engineers went forward to investigate, snapped off a few rifle shots, and retired. The bazooka team fired,

although they had no target. And then it was over. The tanks retired while the engineers hurried off in the opposite direction to Stavelot.

After a rapid advance deep into First Army's rear, Peiper's column had met the weakest of opposition and inexplicably coiled up for the night. Peiper himself was probably not with the leading tanks when they halted. He accepted his subordinate's appraisal that the Americans held the hill in strength. His own fatigue undoubtedly clouded his judgment. His column was strung out over 25 miles of poor, sodden roads and his men were tired. These factors partially explain Peiper's decision to halt. The delay, by the narrowest, enabled Hodges to bring the 30th Division from the north to block Peiper's penetration.

Peiper resumed his advance at 8am on the 18th. He rushed the Stavelot bridge – the demolition wires apparently sabotaged by a Greif commando unit – and headed for the next river crossing at Trois Ponts. Again combat engineers intervened, this time by blowing two bridges and forcing Peiper from his direct route. Losing precious time and consuming irreplaceable fuel, Peiper turned north towards La Gleize. He captured an intact bridge but his success was short-lived. A rare weather break brought US fighter-bombers and forced his command to take cover. Simultaneously elements of the 30th Division blocked further westward movement. Peiper withdrew at nightfall on the 18th into La Gleize and Stoumont. Operating in near total isolation, his rearward radio link failed during the day, Peiper experienced enough reverses on 18 December to sense stiffening opposition. He did not know that the ring around his unit was tightening.

Early on the 19th a battalion of the 30th Division recaptured Stavelot, thus isolating Peiper from the balance of the 1st SS Division. Over the next three days the Germans tried desperately to carve a supply route to Peiper's isolated spearhead. They failed. Meanwhile, employing overwhelming force, the American vice around Peiper squeezed. On 23 December Peiper abandoned his mission and led a remnant of his unit on foot back to German lines. Kampfgruppe Peiper, the unit that had come closest to fulfilling Hitler's scheme, had failed.

▼ *SdKfz 251/3 Ausf D of the 2nd SS Panzergrenadier Regiment.*

▼ *Panzerkampfwagen V Panther Ausf G of 1st SS Panzer Regiment.*

RACE TO BASTOGNE

To the Outskirts

The market town of Bastogne was the hub for seven major roads. When the 1940 blitzkrieg had exploded through the Ardennes, Bastogne had been one of the first German objectives. In 1944, OKW planners well recognized Bastogne's importance. Believing that its early occupation was critical, they managed to persuade Hitler to modify his plan in order to seize the town. Then OKW's operational inexperience showed: planners failed to assign a force commensurate with the objective's importance. Unless it found Bastogne lightly defended, XLVII Panzer Corps intended to bypass Bastogne and head west. The 26th VGD received the mission of capturing Bastogne by the third day. This was much to ask, even of a unit as good as 'the Old 26th', since the division first had to seize river crossings at the Our

and Clerf to open the way for the panzers and then march unsupported to Bastogne.

From the American perspective Bastogne seemed terribly vulnerable. Thirty-six hours after the offensive began, Hodges had seen VIII Corps' centre give way. He had thrown all available reinforcements into the battle, so now he was compelled to request help from the SHAEF reserve. On the morning of 18 December, Eisenhower's last reserves, the 101st and 82nd Airborne Divisions, began racing to block the German breakthrough. But it would take time for them to arrive, and it was not at all clear whether the Germans would grant the time.

The delaying action in front of Bastogne had begun the previous evening. Ten minutes after word reached VIII Corps headquarters that the Germans had crossed the Clerf, Middleton ordered his sole armoured reserve, CCR/9th

▶ *Confusion continued in the American high command on 17 December. However, Patton comprehended the situation and entered in his diary that day: 'The German attack is on a wide front and moving fast . . . This may be a feint . . . although at the moment it looks like the real thing.' This posed propaganda photograph shows German troops passing a knocked out American armoured car. (US National Archives)*

Armored Division, to move 'without delay', establish two roadblocks on the main paved road to Bastogne, and hold 'at all costs'. By midnight, 17 December, CCR/9 was in position between Clervaux and Bastogne. By mid-morning of 18 December, panzers had appeared to probe Task Force Rose's roadblock, which comprised 17 Shermans, a company of armoured infantry and an engineer platoon. The inexperienced American infantry broke under German tank fire and headed for the rear.

By 2pm, Middleton had learned that: 'TF Rose . . . is as good as surrounded. . . have counted 16 German tanks. . . TF is being hit from 3 sides . . . Recommend that they fight their way out. They could use 2 platoons of A/52d Armd Inf Bn [the last CCR infantry reserve], everything else is committed.' It is indicative of the paucity of American strength that a hard-pressed captain who faced a charging panzer division had to radio corps headquarters to secure release of reserves and that the only reserves available were two armoured infantry platoons. Middleton, desperate to buy time for reinforcements to arrive at Bastogne, refused Task Force Rose's request to retreat. A handful of Americans broke free at dusk only to stumble into an ambush further west. Only a few vehicles and crews reached Bastogne.

The other, larger roadblock suffered an even more dismal fate. At dusk Mark IVs and Panthers attacked. Equipped with new infra-red night-sight devices, the Panthers picked off the outclassed Shermans. When the roadblock commander was killed, the defence collapsed. At this point, on the evening of 18 December, no formed troops stood between the 2nd Panzer Division and Bastogne. However, according to plan, this division's business lay further west. At a road junction near Longvilly, Colonel Lauchert turned his unit north to bypass Bastogne and headed for the Meuse.

The 2nd Panzer Division's running mate, the Panzer Lehr Division, also had an excellent chance to capture the crucial crossroads. Major General Fritz Bayerlein had finally extracted his division from the clogged traffic of the Clerf valley by the mid-afternoon of 18 December. By that evening his Panzer Lehr was a mere six miles from Bastogne. Here Bayerlein faced a choice. He could turn south to gain a hard surfaced road or could use secondary roads to avoid possible enemy roadblocks. Although he did not know it, no organized defenders guarded either route. Misled by a farmer, Bayerlein led his advanced guard along the side road. It quickly dissolved into a muddy cart path. Bayerlein spent four hours travelling an unopposed three miles to Mageret. There another Belgian told him that a large American force commanded by a major general had just passed through. Knowing such an officer commanded a full division, Bayerlein turned cautious, halted, planted a minefield and waited for dawn. This was hardly the aggressive leadership expected of a spearhead armoured division commander.

The Roadblock Battles

A combination of chance and German blunders had preserved Bastogne and allowed American reinforcements to win the race to the crossroads by the narrowest margin. About 4pm on 18 December, Colonel William Roberts arrived at the head of his CCA/10th Armored Division. This was one of the units Eisenhower had directed to come to Middleton's help back on the evening of 16 December. Middleton wanted Roberts to form three task forces to block three routes leading to the town. 'That's no way to use armour,' objected Roberts. 'Robbie,' replied Middleton, 'I may not know as much about the employment of armour as you, but that's the way I have to use them. . . Move with the utmost speed. And Robbie, hold these positions at all costs.' Again American armour was being deployed in penny packets to form hasty roadblocks. Two teams went east; Team Cherry to Longvilly and Team O'Hara to Wardin, while the third moved north-east to Noville. With Roberts still present, Middleton received another visitor, the acting commander of the 101st Airborne Division, Brigadier General Anthony McAuliffe. Knowing neither the situation nor where his unit was bound, on his own initiative McAuliffe had sped ahead to confer with Middleton. Forcing his way through the westwards-fleeing traffic, McAuliffe had become alarmed. Middleton's calm appraisal hardly reassured him: 'There has been a

▶ *Still exuberant in the advance, German soldiers ride forward on a panzer's deck. (US National Archives)*

The counter to blitzkrieg was defence in depth. By small-unit initiative and stubborn refusal to retreat, the US defenders unwittingly achieved a defence in depth. Unaware as to events on either flank, many units held at critical road junctions. This forced the attackers to use secondary tracks and to infiltrate through the woods in order to bypass the defenders and head west. Frequently they then encountered reserve formations – supply and service troops, artillery and anti-aircraft personnel, engineers and headquarters units. The willingness of these rear-area formations to use their abundant weapons and mobility gave the Americans a deep defence. Note the shot-up windscreen on this jeep. (Charles B. MacDonald Collection, US Army Military History Institute) ▶

major penetration. Certain of my units, especially the 106th and 28th Divisions, are broken.' McAuliffe's 101st would be diverted to Bastogne and hold the key road junction against all comers.

19 December was the last day during which the Germans stood any chance of seizing Bastogne by coup de main. If so, the blow would have to be delivered by the Panzer Lehr Division. At 5.30am, Bayerlein ordered his panzers to advance on Neffe, a village just east of Bastogne. His advance guard reached the village at 7am and then inexplicably halted for an hour. This delay cost Bayerlein his final chance to capture Bastogne before the 101st Airborne intervened.

◀ *German gunners swab the barrel of their 75mm anti-tank gun outside Bastogne while panzers and infantry advance nearby. This is another sketch by the 26th VGD anti-tank gunner. (Charles B. MacDonald Collection, US Army Military History Institute)*

◀ *The converging German attack destroyed Team Cherry. Bastogne could have fallen to both the Panzer Lehr and the 2nd Panzer Divisions. Von Manteuffel later blamed Bayerlein for failing to act independently and thus capturing Bastogne. He committed 'a breach in the regulations applying to the leadership of a panzer division'. Yet von Manteuffel explained his own decision to order the 2nd Panzer to ignore Bastogne as justified on the basis of the need to adhere to the plan. (US Army Military History Institute)*

In a further example of the tremendous value of unchallenged air supremacy, the 101st Airborne had raced much of the way to Bastogne aboard trucks displaying full headlights – an unmistakeable target to hostile aircraft had there been any. McAuliffe again conferred with Middleton. The paratroop general had to decide what to do amid an extremely fluid situation without having access to hard information. In characteristic Airborne style, he aggressively sent the first unit to arrive, the 501st Parachute Infantry Regiment, east. The regiment's advanced battalion collided with the Germans at Neffe. What in reality was an encounter skirmish was misperceived by both sides. The paratroopers thought they had struck an enemy roadblock. The Germans believed that they faced a combined-arms counterattack. German tanks, to which the lightly armed paratroopers had no answer, prevented further American advance. The 501st extended its lines to probe for a German weakness. Meanwhile it called on its rapid-firing light howitzers to shell Neffe.

Unfamiliar with this weapon's sound, Bayerlein believed he was hearing American heavy tank fire. Thinking he faced a large counterattack, and worried about the American armour to his rear on the Longvilly road (Team Cherry, one of Roberts' roadblocks), Bayerlein lost his nerve. Up to this point, the Germans had been encountering small, disorganized units during their race to Bastogne. Collision with formed, aggressive infantry threw them off their stride. Shortly after the war Bayerlein explained: 'The movement of the infantry regiment which had come out of Bastogne to attack me had reacted decisively on my thinking.' S.L.A. Marshal puts it more succinctly. By the advance on Neffe: 'a few American platoons hardened the fate of armies.'

By mid-afternoon, 19 December, German generals from XLVII Panzer Corps down felt that Bastogne could not be captured without committing the entire corps to the effort. For the remainder of the day, German efforts east of Bastogne focused on the elimination of Team Cherry.

The team had been struggling to extricate itself since morning. Its vehicles had become intermixed with elements of CCR/9th Armored fleeing back to Bastogne. When Team Cherry tried to turn around, its lead Sherman fell victim to a German anti-tank gun. Then two anti-aircraft half-tracks, attached to CCR/9th, had raced to the front of the column in an effort to escape. Heedless of shouts to stop, they rounded a curve, spotted the burning tank, and bailed out to avoid a crash. The resultant pile-up plugged the narrow road leading back to Bastogne. At this point three German columns converged on Team Cherry and opened fire.

On the 19th, after destroying the Longvilly roadblock, Luttwitz suggested using his entire corps to capture Bastogne. Von Manteuffel could not believe the Americans would risk annihilation and let themselves become surrounded. Calculating that he could capture Bastogne by default, he adhered to his primary mission and ordered Luttwitz to leave Bastogne for the infantry, to follow the plan and continue west. It was a key mistake.

Trapped motionless, Team Cherry disintegrated under the plunging German fire. Its long column of light tanks, tank destroyers, ambulances and armoured cars filled the air with oily black smoke as one vehicle after another was hit. The team fought back when it could and managed to knock out eight German tanks. But by and large the helpless crews and accompanying infantry could do nothing more than line the ditches, endure and wait for darkness. The action on the Longvilly road saw the virtual destruction of the remnant of CCR/9th Armored, including its entire armoured field artillery battalion. Team Cherry lost 175 officers and men, a quarter of its command, along with seven light, ten medium tanks, and seventeen half-tracks. Substantial elements of other units were also caught in the Longvilly trap. Yet the Americans had absorbed the attention of a German corps and two German divisional generals along with elements from two panzer divisions when all should have been focusing on other objectives.

Summarizing events through the offensive's first three days, the perceptive commentator Pimlott writes that by the end of the 19th: 'The period of American confusion, during which the major German advances should have been made, was already coming to an end.'

THE DEFENCE OF ST VITH

Surrender on the Schnee Eifel

Like Bastogne, St Vith was a key road net and a potential bottleneck. Also like Bastogne, with an ample panzer force at hand German planners had assigned an infantry unit for its capture. This unit, the 18th VGD, first had to form one of the pincers around the Schnee Eifel and then advance on St Vith. On 17 December, St Vith was open to a coup de main since few defenders were in place. But the 18th lacked the mobility for such a coup. Its mobile battalion, comprising three assault gun platoons, a company of engineers and another of fusiliers, was inadequate to accomplish the task. Jodl and his OKW planners again had committed

a capital blunder by failing to match force and mission.

The period from 17 to 19 December passed without significant pressure coming to bear against St Vith. Conversely, the Americans were unable to counterattack to relieve the defenders on the Schnee Eifel. Before dawn on 17 December CCB/9th Armored Division arrived in St Vith. The commander of the 106th Infantry Division, as senior general at St Vith, absorbed it within his command and promptly split its infantry and tank components. He sent the 27th Armored Infantry Battalion forward to attack the German force slicing around the right flank of the Schnee Eifel. The counterattack achieved nothing except to run up the casualty list until the surprise appearance of a supporting American tank platoon shook the Germans. The German reaction is an indication of what might have been had American generals used their armour en masse. Ninety German infantry surrendered in a situation the German divisional commander later referred to as a 'serious crisis'. While this and other American counterattacks helped preserve St Vith, they did not retrieve the fortunes of the isolated regiments on the Schnee Eifel.

With hopes of relief by early counterattack dashed, the Schnee Eifel defenders faced a crippling supply shortage. Aerial re-supply should have solved this problem, but the effort was badly botched. Remarkably, although Allied land forces had been on the continent for over half a year, the only supply containers prepared for parachuting remained in England. Bringing them forward in admittedly poor weather proved beyond Allied

◀ *American prisoners photographed in a German village in the Eifel area. (US National Archives)*

▶ *The gun crew of a 3in tank destroyer struggles to manoeuvre it into position. (US National Archives)*

capability. The two isolated regiments made a last effort to cut their way free on 19 December, but the effort collapsed in the face of withering German artillery fire. That afternoon most surviving defenders – some seven to eight thousand (the exact figure is debated to this day) – surrendered, thus bringing to a conclusion the costliest American defeat during the war in Europe and, next to Bataan, the greatest mass surrender in American history.

After the war American interrogators asked von Manteuffel a leading question: had the cut-off troops resisted as strongly as he had anticipated? Von Manteuffel answered: 'No.'

Breakwater

The German failure to advance on St Vith during the first three days allowed the defence of the St Vith-Vielsalm area to assume a recognizable form. According to the official army historian, by the night of 19 December: 'The troops within the perimeter occupied an "island" within a German tide rushing past on the north and south and rising against its eastern face.' The most advanced German troops had bypassed their position and were 25 miles south-west. The defenders were out of touch with headquarters and the command situation did not improve when, unnerved by the

disintegration of his division, the 106th's commanding officer gave a lower ranking officer, General Bruce Clarke, CCA/7th Armored Division, responsibility for conducting the defence.

The commander of the 7th Armored Division, Brigadier General Robert Hasbrouck, described the situation in a letter to First Army headquarters: 'Both infantry regiments are in bad shape. My right flank is wide open except for some reconnaissance elements, TDs, and stragglers we have collected and organized into defence teams at road centres . . . I can delay them [the Germans] the rest of today maybe but will be cut off by tomorrow. VIII Corps has ordered me to hold and I will do so but need help.' Here was a remarkable display of calm determination.

St Vith also loomed large in German planning. The stubborn defence of the twin villages and the Elsenborn Ridge forced Sixth Panzer Army to shift southward to seek a route to the Meuse. Whereas Peiper could and did slip between American positions, an entire army required a road net to support its advance. On 20 December, the single free road the Germans held served as the main supply route for two armoured and two infantry divisions. All other roads west ran through St Vith. The colossal traffic jam caused by the stubborn retention of St Vith was felt all the way up the German chain of command. Both Model and von

◀ Congested roads leading to St Vith impaired the German advance and forced the top commanders to walk to their meeting. Given that the mud even bogged down light staff cars, like the one shown here, it is easy to understand why the panzers had difficulty. (US National Archives)

Manteuffel had to abandon their staff cars on the clogged roads and walk in order to arrive at a strategic planning meeting. This session between Model and von Manteuffel, army group and army commander respectively, close to the front contrasts sharply with the American operating style. Not for a lack of courage, neither Bradley nor Hodges toured the front during the critical first days.

When von Manteuffel confidently responded to Model's question about Fifth Panzer Army's progress, the latter expressed some doubt: 'I got the impression you were lagging, especially in the St Vith sector.' 'Yes,' acknowledged von Manteuffel, 'but we'll take it tomorrow.' 'I expect you to. And so that you'll take it quicker, tomorrow I'm letting you use the Führer Escort Brigade.'

The German generals expected that 20 December would see an attack featuring the forces released by the American surrender on the Schnee Eifel, the 62nd and 18th VGDs, and the fresh, powerful, Führer Begleit (Escort) Brigade commanded by Colonel Otto Remer. In the event the day passed with surprising calm. The attackers simply could not organize themselves for the assault. In particular, the horse-drawn artillery experienced great difficulty extricating batteries along muddy, forest paths and repositioning them against St Vith.

Impatient, von Manteuffel ordered Remer to attack with his advance guard, but Remer was more interested in the glory drive west than dealing with the troublesome St Vith defenders. Accordingly, Remer made a half-hearted effort. When 90mm guns of an American TD battalion knocked out his four leading Mark IVs, he disobeyed and halted his attack.

On 21 December, Remer again disregarded von Manteuffel's orders and headed west. This left St Vith to the two Volksgrenadier divisions. Their main attack came from the east and was directed against a rugged ridge known as the Prumerberg. Defending was an ad-hoc force commanded by Lieutenant Colonel William Fuller. This force included four 7th Armored Division armoured infantry companies, 400 engineers, two TD companies and 11 Sherman tanks. A 45-minute artillery barrage began the German attack in late afternoon. Tree bursts rained deadly splinters on the American foxholes. Nebelwerfers added their terrifying din. Veterans claimed it was the worst bombardment they had ever experienced. The shelling wounded a tank company commander and sent one of his platoon leaders into shock.

The German Assault, from 20 to 24 December

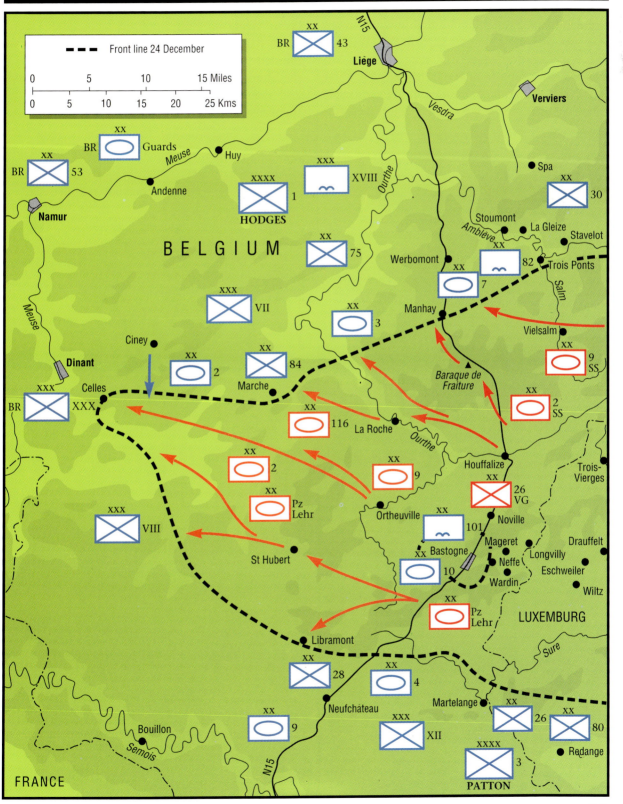

At dusk the German infantry advanced. American artillery severely punished them, breaking up one entire regimental assault. The German commander threw everything he had into the attack. Infantry skilfully infiltrated gaps in the American line and began roaming the rear to isolate the forward defenders. In near darkness six SS Tigers rolled up the front slopes of the Prumerberg. Blocking their advance were five Shermans. The

Americans positioned their tanks beneath the crestline. The commander ordered them to fire simultaneously when the Tigers appeared over the crest. Using an Eastern Front tactic, the Tigers fired flares as they reached the crest. These blinded the American tank crews and silhouetted the Shermans. In seconds the big 88mm guns fired and destroyed all five Shermans at no cost to themselves. Then they began to shoot up the

◀CCA/7th Armored Division fought the all-important delaying action at St Vith. Here a white-camouflaged Sherman and its infantry escort manoeuvre through the woods. (US Army Military History Institute)

Traffic jams that afflicted the German advance around St Vith also delayed American reinforcements. Rushing to reinforce the defenders, a tank general of the 7th Armored Division took five hours to fight through rearward flowing traffic to travel from Vielsalm to St Vith, a distance of some 10 miles. Once CCA/7th Armored arrived, it dug-in and delayed the German advance. Here machine-gunners man a snow-encrusted .30-calibre Browning. (US National ◀Archives)

American foxhole line. The defending infantry had no counter and broke to the rear. Some adjacent units held; others, in the words of the official historian, 'stampeded blindly through the woods in search of an exit to the west'.

Overcome by the attack, Fuller panicked, turned over command to an engineer officer and fled to headquarters 'to plan alternate positions'. Hard on his heels, spearheaded by the Tigers, the intrepid Volksgrenadiers rolled into St Vith. In the town all was confusion, with German and American soldiers and vehicles intermingled. A heavy nocturnal snowstorm began. An artilleryman radioed headquarters for orders. 'Go West! Go West!' came the reply. In a chaotic situation ripe for panic, St Vith's commander, Clarke, coolly led the withdrawal and managed to improvise a new defensive line 1,000 yards behind the town. Converging from several directions, the advancing Germans became hopelessly entangled in St Vith's streets. Men broke ranks to seek warmth, shelter, and to loot the abundant American supplies. Thus, there was no pursuit. So clogged were the roads leading to St Vith that once again Model had to abandon his car and walk.

Afterwards the Americans could compile only partial casualty lists. The 7th Armored Division and 14th Cavalry Group listed 3,397 casualties. In addition, the armoured division lost 59 Shermans, 29 light tanks and 25 armoured cars. Against these losses must be measured their accomplishment. Again the words of the official historian: 'They had met an entire German corps flushed with easy victory and halted it in its tracks. They had firmly choked one of the main enemy lines of communication and forced days of delay on the western movement of troops, guns, tanks, and supplies belonging to two German armies.'

The American success on the Elsenborn ridge had prevented a German advance to the Meuse via the shortest route. The second best path was Route N15, which ran from Bastogne through Manhay, Werbomont and on to Liège. Without possession of Bastogne, this route became feasible only with the capture of St Vith. But St Vith's fall proved too late for the Germans. The American defence had time to consolidate across the projected path of advance. Further advance would require tough fighting with exhausted troops. In the event the German conquerors of St Vith could not exploit their victory. Further success hinged upon the conduct of those forces that had earlier bypassed this pocket of resistance and advanced along portions of Route 15.

There was a 13-mile gap between the American outposts behind St Vith and the Bastogne perimeter. If the German units rolling through this gap could join the most advanced spearheads, together they could crack the American flank bending back from St Vith to Malmédy and Manhay. Then they could continue west. Since a substantial portion of the American strength was involved in checking Peiper, the American line along this front was thin, with defences as yet uncoordinated. Henceforth, the battle featured a race to acquire key road junctions and river crossings leading to the Meuse.

▼ *Formerly charged with providing anti-aircraft defence for Hitler's headquarters, the Führer Begleit Brigade comprised a flak regiment with 24 88mm guns (shown here on the Eastern front), three mobile grenadier battalions, a 105mm artillery battalion, a panzer battalion with 45 Mark IVs and 35 assault guns, plus anti-tank and engineer attachments. In a manner typical of many German élite formations, its commander proved disobedient to army directives, preferring his personal, glory-seeking agenda. Von Manteuffel felt that committing this formidable reserve unit, which was intended to exploit a breakthrough, at St Vith instead of in support of his spearhead elements was a major blunder. (Wood Collection, US Army Military History Institute)*

▲Congested roads placed a premium on traffic control. Aided by air supremacy, the Americans generally out-performed the Germans in this overlooked but important function. Here a victim of too much haste, an M-36 TD has slipped on an icy road and overturned. (US National Archives)

▲The paratroopers of the 82nd and 101st Airborne were the best soldiers in the American Army. They were much more aggressive than line infantry. Here gunners of the 101st man a 3in anti-tank weapon, the barrel of which is camouflaged with fence posts. (US National Archives)

THE DEFENCE OF BASTOGNE

Command Decisions

The Supreme Allied Commander had been watching the Ardennes situation unfold with growing alarm. On the evening of 19 December he convened an emergency meeting that featured decisions vitally affecting Bastogne's fate. On the situation map it appeared that Peiper had achieved a clean breakthrough. Other enemy forces were racing through the gap between Bastogne and St Vith. Rising to the occasion, Eisenhower struck exactly the right note with his opening remarks: 'The present situation is to be regarded as one of opportunity for us and not of disaster. There will be only cheerful faces at this conference table.'

Patton boldly replied: 'Hell, let's have the guts

◄ *Artillery provided Bastogne's defensive backbone. A participant observed a German assault: 'Here and there, among the mushrooming clouds of artillery smoke, the tiny black figures stumbled and fell. Behind them one of the heavy tanks turned back towards its own lines – then rolled and halted . . . The tiny figures of the Germans began to run. More and more of them fell. For twenty minutes the rolling barrage continued to pursue them. When it lifted, the only Germans who remained on the open field were the scores of still bodies.' Here knocked out German vehicles and a dead panzergrenadier lie outside Bastogne. (US National Archives)*

to let the sons of bitches go all the way to Paris. Then we'll really cut 'em up and chew 'em up.' Patton's astonishing, but none the less insightful suggestion had much merit. It would fully capitalize on the great American asset of mobility. It meshed with Bradley's original scheme calling for a fighting withdrawal. But Eisenhower and Bradley typically preferred a more cautious approach.

Ike responded to Patton: 'No, the enemy will never be allowed to cross the Meuse.' His plan was American textbook doctrine based on the lessons of the First World War: firmly hold the shoulders of the penetration. The rush west would be slowed by blocking the road hubs at St Vith and Bastogne while defences were manned behind the Meuse. A major counterattack would be launched as soon as possible.

Hodges' battered units could not participate, so everything hinged on Patton. Eisenhower asked him: 'When can you attack?' Before attending the meeting Patton had carefully examined the situation and had drawn up three contingency attack plans. Consequently, he confidently answered: 'On December 22, with three divisions.'

Patton's bravado irked Eisenhower. In any event he did not particularly like Patton and, not knowing Patton had already considered the problem in detail, believed that this was a typical flippant answer to a serious question. Furthermore, he doubted anyone could turn his army 90 degrees, make an approach march in winter against the grain of his communications and strike the German flank. After dressing down the Third Army commander, Eisenhower authorized a delay of 24-48 extra hours to prepare the attack.

Belying Ike's contempt, as soon as he departed the meeting, Patton telephoned his headquarters to speak in pre-arranged code to his staff. His message informed them which offensive option to employ. According to Patton's biographer, his response to Eisenhower's question was 'the sublime moment of his career'.

Unaware of these decisions, von Manteuffel claimed that on the night of 19 December 'serious doubts arose for the first time' as to the ultimate success of his Fifth Army's operations.

The Ordeal Begins

By 20 December all the units that were to defend Bastogne were in place. Smaller than a conventional infantry division, the 101st Airborne had 11,840 men divided into four infantry regiments. This 'square' formation better lent itself to four-sided defence than the more common three-regiment structure. Three battalions of light, 75mm pack howitzers (the type that had fooled Bayerlein) and one standard 105mm battalion provided the organic artillery support. The other major defending unit was Robert's CCB/10th Armored Division already deployed into task forces to block important roads. By day's end CCB had some 30 medium tanks left. The remnant of CCR/9th Armored probably contributed another 10 Shermans. The 705th Tank Destroyer Battalion armed with new, high-velocity 76mm guns, gave the defenders 36 self-propelled TDs. Also present were four corps artillery battalions whose 155mm howitzers provided McAuliffe (who, after all, was formally his division's artillery commander) long-range firepower. About 130 artillery tubes were inside Bastogne. In addition, the defenders had numerous stragglers and partial units which had filtered back to Bastogne during the chaotic first days. McAuliffe positioned his men along a circular perimeter centred on Bastogne with his artillery centrally grouped to fire in any direction.

On the night of 20 December, McAuliffe visited Middleton in Neufchâteau. He told Middleton that he was certain his men could hold on for at least 48 hours if they became surrounded. The VIII Corps commander apprised him of the latest intelligence, including news that the 116th Panzer Division appeared to be coming in on McAuliffe's flank to add to the three divisions already attacking Bastogne. McAuliffe replied: 'I think we can take care of them.' The airborne commander returned to Bastogne. Some 30 minutes later, German armour cut the road behind him. Bastogne was isolated.

'Nuts!'

Bastogne's isolation came about because of a change in German tactics. Having been stopped cold at Neffe, and unable to slip into Bastogne via

◀ The Bastogne defenders fought with a special determination. A 10th Armored soldier entered a building to see a hand-scrawled message on the wall left by a departing VIII Corps soldier. It read: 'We'll be back – The Yanks.' The reader snorted: 'We'll be back – Hell! We're here to stay.' Here a foxhole with a .50-calibre machine-gun removed from a vehicle and a bazooka (to right of machine-gun) defends the perimeter. The freshly turned earth against the white background provides an unmistakeable target. (US National Archives)

▶ *A colonel on the ground, witnessing the pilots of these C-47s flying straight and level amid heavy anti-aircraft fire so as to deliver their supply bundles accurately, commented: 'Their courage was tremendous, and I believe that their example did a great deal to encourage my infantry.' (US Air Force photograph; print from Military Archive & Research Services)*

Marvie, the Germans concluded that they lacked the strength to capture Bastogne. Instead, they decided to encircle the town. The next two days, 21-2 December, witnessed numerous probes but no full-scale combat, as the Germans manoeuvred around Bastogne's perimeter. This respite gave McAuliffe invaluable time to knit together his paratroopers and armour, who previously had cooperated in uneasy alliance, each arm believing that they alone carried the burden of defence.

At 11.30am on 22 December, four Germans approached the American outpost line carrying a large white flag. Their appearance triggered one of the most memorable incidents of the Battle of the Bulge. They carried a paper demanding Bastogne's surrender and threatening dire consequences if the garrison failed to do so. When the surrender demand reached McAuliffe he laughed and said: 'Aw, nuts!' He believed his men were giving the attackers 'one hell of a beating' and that the demand was ridiculously inappropriate. He sat down to draft a written response and came up blank.

He asked his staff what they thought and one officer replied: 'That first remark of yours would be hard to beat.' So the Germans received the celebrated one word answer, 'Nuts!' But the untranslatable reply was not understood by the German negotiators. An American colonel assisted: 'If you don't understand what "Nuts" means, in plain English it is the same as "Go to hell". And I will tell you something else – if you continue to attack we will kill every goddam German that tries to break into this city.'

Although the defenders' spirits were undaunted, they now faced a serious matériel problem – ammunition. For the first three days Bastogne's ample artillery had decisively intervened whenever a massed target appeared. As elsewhere in the Ardennes, American artillery provided the defensive backbone. By midday on 22 December, McAuliffe had to restrict artillery fire severely in order to conserve ammunition. Guns received a ten round per day ration. This allowed the Germans to manoeuvre openly all around Bastogne's perimeter. The paratroopers were also running low on small-arms ammunition. Everyone wondered if ammunition would give out before relief came.

The day before the airdrop, McAuliffe received a brief, encouraging radio message: 'Hugh [General Gaffey of Patton's 4th Armored Division] is coming.' This manoeuvre was part of the promised Third Army counterattack. The Third Army advanced along a broad front between Echternach and Martelange. German planners had assigned Seventh Army the role of providing flank protection against exactly this type of attack. However, the counterattack came much sooner than the Germans had expected. None the less, difficult terrain and tenacious resistance led to as grim a fight as occurred during the entire battle and slowed Patton's advance to a crawl.

The highly regarded 4th Armored Division had been assigned the mission of relieving Bastogne. During the breakout from Normandy, led by a superb commander, the 4th Armored had earned a reputation for slashing attacks and had become Patton's favourite. But in late December, one of Patton's former staff officers, Gaffey, led the unit. Many of its tanks were the same vehicles that had crossed France and were thus mechanically unreliable. All too many vehicles were being driven by replacement crews. Originally one of the division's combat commands had been well-positioned at Neufchâteau to attack towards Bastogne, but a command foul-up led to a counter-march and forced the division to attack towards Martelange. In spite of Patton's urgings to 'drive like hell', the 4th was making slow progress.

▲ The élite 4th Armored Division began its drive to relieve Bastogne without its superb commander, with ranks only partially replenished with green soldiers, and driving tanks issued in England before D-Day. Some ran only at medium speed, others had turrets without electrical traverse, and most had worn motors and tracks. One tank battalion lost 33 tanks to mechanical failure during its 160-mile rush to the Ardennes. On 24 December, Patton wrote in his diary: 'This has been a very bad Christmas Eve. All along our line we have received violent counterattacks, one of which forced . . . the 4th Armored back.' None the less, Patton concluded that the Germans 'are far behind schedule and, I believe, beaten'. This illustration shows a white-camouflaged 4th Armored Division tank. (US Army Military History Institute)

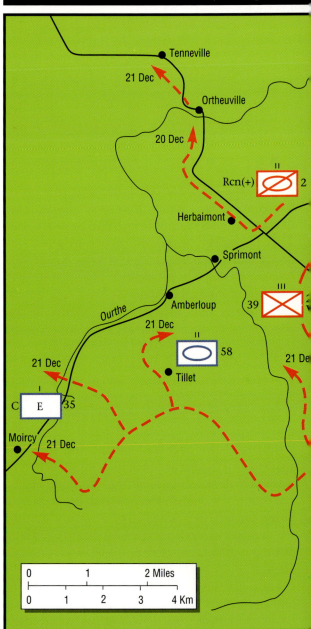

The Defence of Bastogne

Inside Bastogne the defenders felt let down. 'Hugh' simply was not coming fast enough. Small tank-infantry teams were continually striking the perimeter and beginning to wear the defenders down. 23 December dawned bright and clear. The Ninth Air Force's medium B-26 bombers and P-38 and P-47 fighter-bombers dominated the day. An observer saw them 'like shoals of silver minnows in the bright winter sun'. The 'Jabos' hunted for tell-tale vehicle tracks in the snow and followed them to the target. Generally, the German vehicles sheltered in the numerous small woods. The 'Jabos' used rockets, bombs and napalm to ferret them out. During the day the Ninth flew close to 1,300 sorties.

Better than the combat aircraft was the arrival of the lumbering transport aircraft. With practised skill, pathfinders parachuted into Bastogne in the

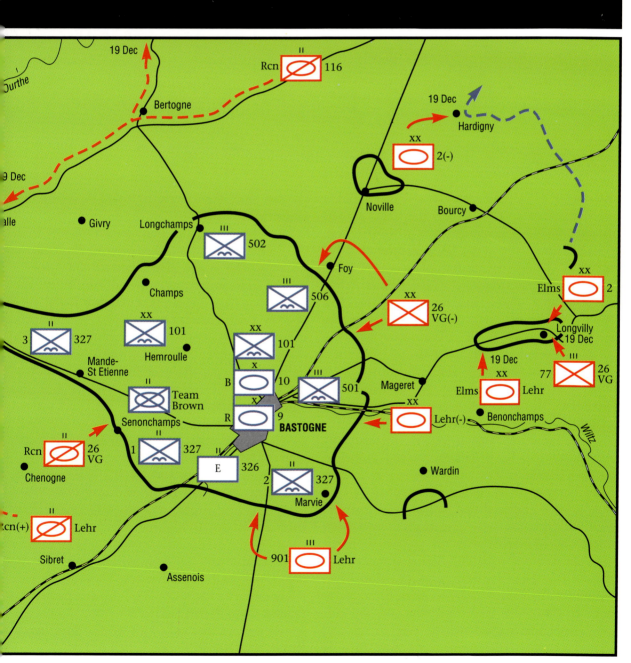

◄ Veteran American tank crews feared German anti-tank guns more than tanks. They felt they would usually hear or see opposing tanks. They seldom saw an anti-tank gun until it opened fire. This sketch by the 26th VGD gunner shows why; his 75mm gun is in perfect enfilade as US half-tracks pass his sights on 24 December. He failed to knock the target out. (Charles B. MacDonald Collection, US Army Military History Institute)

morning of 23 December and set up radar to direct incoming C-47s. During the day 241 aircraft dropped their supply bundles with great precision. Ground forces recovered 95 per cent of these supplies. The next day the transports returned, but this time the Germans were ready for them. While the Germans' fierce anti-aircraft fire knocked down a number of C-47s, the pilots refused to take evasive action so as to deliver accurately the precious supplies. Their gallantry delivered Bastogne from perhaps its severest crisis.

At 3am on Christmas Day, the Germans delivered an all-out attack against Bastogne. The assault was supposed to feature an entire fresh division, the 15th Panzergrenadier. Instead only two panzergrenadier battalions, two self-propelled artillery battalions and eighteen tanks arrived in time. The 15th PGD colonel who commanded the assault force protested that he had been given no time for reconnaissance and that he had been unable to coordinate with his panzer supports. German planning regarding Bastogne was beginning to take on a desperate urgency. Model had ordered Fifth Panzer Army to seize Bastogne at once to 'lance this boil'. Consequently, the colonel's superiors replied that he must attack and should count on the tremendous advantage of

surprise since the Americans would be celebrating Christmas.

Elements of the 15th PGD joined infantry from the 26th VGD and attacked west of Bastogne at Champs. The assault plan called for the attackers to enter Bastogne between 8 and 9am, before the fighter-bombers appeared. Following initial success, by 10am Kokott knew his plan was doomed. He requested permission to withdraw, but his corps commander refused, saying it was vital to capture Bastogne. Reluctantly, Kokott persisted. He knew further effort would only increase the butcher's bill. So the Christmas Day attack against Bastogne petered out. As at Neffe on 19 December, the Germans had penetrated to within one mile of Bastogne. They would never get closer.

Meanwhile, south-west of Bastogne, the US CCR/4th Armored Division faced demolished bridges, cratered roads and tough German resistance as it drove towards the town. By late afternoon the command's leaders doubted whether they could break through if they followed the prescribed route of advance. They asked permission to try a short-cut. The division passed the request up to Patton, asking if he would authorize a bold venture that risked a German flank attack. Patton responded: 'I sure as hell will!'

In CCR's van was a lieutenant colonel destined to make a name for himself. Twenty-eight years in the future, Creighton Abrams would become supreme ground commander of the US forces in Vietnam. Outside Bastogne, he commanded a mere under-strength battalion with 20 Shermans, but he was determined to make the most of it. Sticking a cigar in his mouth he told his command: 'We're going in now. Let 'er roll!'

Leading the way were a handful of the new, upgraded 40-tonne Sherman tanks called Cobra Kings. Hard on the heels of a brief but intense artillery bombardment, Abrams charged into Assenois. Leaping from aboard the tanks, infantry cleared the village in bitter house-to-house fighting. None surpassed a 19-year old private, James Hendrix. Armed with only a rifle, Hendrix attacked two 88mm anti-tank guns. 'Come on out!' he shouted. A German soldier lifted his head from a foxhole and Hendrix shot him. Running to the next hole, Hendrix clubbed its occupant with his rifle butt. Then he charged straight at the two big guns. Dismayed by this beserker-like warrior display, the crews surrendered. It was a one-man assault worthy of the Medal of Honor it won.

Propelled by such valour, the Cobra Kings sped on. They broke through to the 101st's lines, where McAuliffe greeted them: 'Gee, I am mighty glad to see you.' Bastogne's 'siege' was over.

▲ *The Americans had some upgraded Shermans called 'Cobra Kings' armed with 76mm guns with muzzle brakes and having thicker frontal armour. Patton ordered that they lead the effort to break through to Bastogne. (US Army Military History Institute)*

▼ *Armoured infantry of 4th Armored Division attack to widen the corridor into Bastogne on 27 December. The men are widely dispersed to limit casualties in case they are shelled. (US Army Military History Institute)*

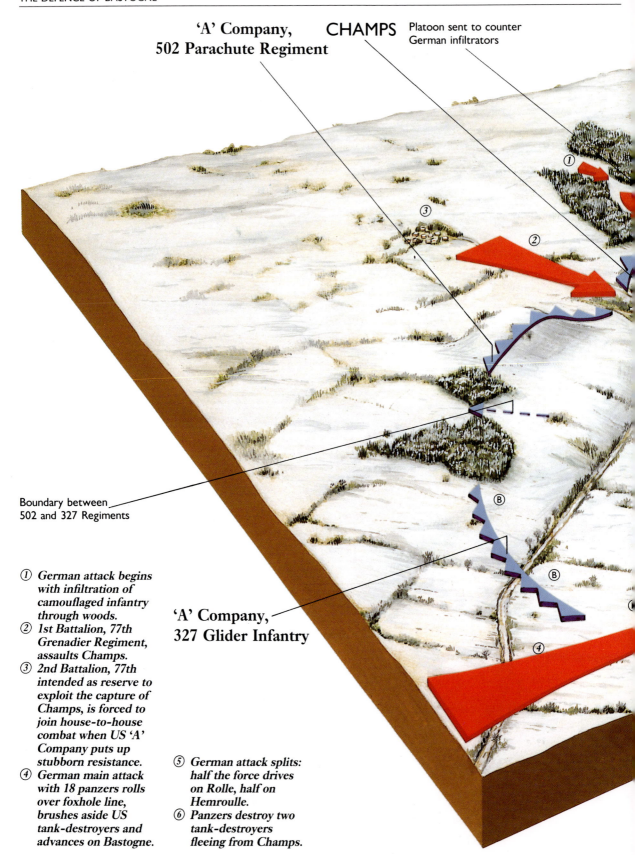

'A' Company,
502 Parachute Regiment

CHAMPS

Platoon sent to counter
German infiltrators

Boundary between
502 and 327 Regiments

'A' Company,
327 Glider Infantry

① German attack begins
with infiltration of
camouflaged infantry
through woods.
② 1st Battalion, 77th
Grenadier Regiment,
assaults Champs.
③ 2nd Battalion, 77th
intended as reserve to
exploit the capture of
Champs, is forced to
join house-to-house
combat when US 'A'
Company puts up
stubborn resistance.
④ German main attack
with 18 panzers rolls
over foxhole line,
brushes aside US
tank-destroyers and
advances on Bastogne.

⑤ German attack splits:
half the force drives
on Rolle, half on
Hemroulle.
⑥ Panzers destroy two
tank-destroyers
fleeing from Champs.

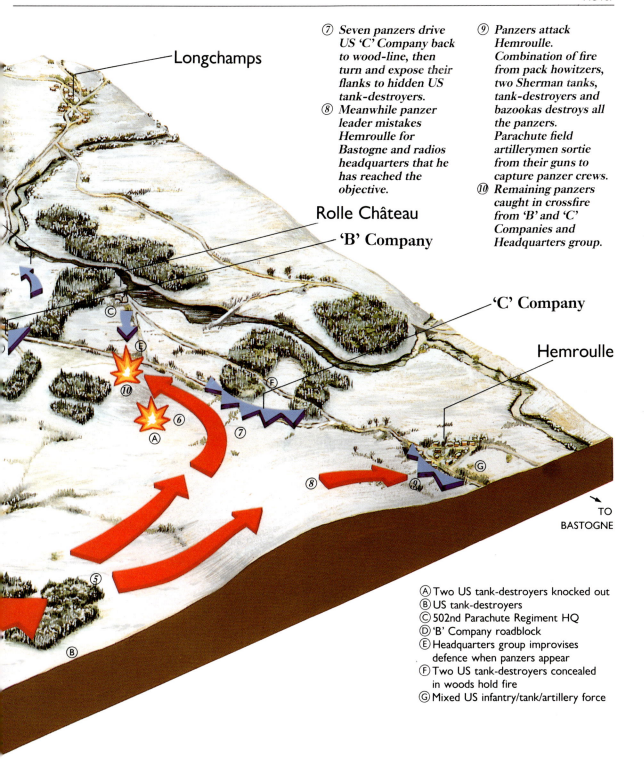

Longchamps

⑦ Seven panzers drive US 'C' Company back to wood-line, then turn and expose their flanks to hidden US tank-destroyers.

⑧ Meanwhile panzer leader mistakes Hemroulle for Bastogne and radios headquarters that he has reached the objective.

⑨ Panzers attack Hemroulle. Combination of fire from pack howitzers, two Sherman tanks, tank-destroyers and bazookas destroys all the panzers. Parachute field artillerymen sortie from their guns to capture panzer crews.

⑩ Remaining panzers caught in crossfire from 'B' and 'C' Companies and Headquarters group.

Rolle Château

'B' Company

'C' Company

Hemroulle

TO BASTOGNE

Ⓐ Two US tank-destroyers knocked out
Ⓑ US tank-destroyers
Ⓒ 502nd Parachute Regiment HQ
Ⓓ 'B' Company roadblock
Ⓔ Headquarters group improvises defence when panzers appear
Ⓕ Two US tank-destroyers concealed in woods hold fire
Ⓖ Mixed US infantry/tank/artillery force

THE BATTLE FOR CHAMPS

25 December 1944.

TO THE MEUSE

The Drive Falters

When the 2nd Panzer Division's advance guards captured a bridge over the Ourthe at Ortheuville on 21 December, they stood less than 40 road miles from Dinant and the Meuse. Before embarking on a final sprint to the Meuse, von Manteuffel had to solve several problems. The 2nd's spearhead was extremely narrow, extending no further than the range of its 75mm tank guns. Part of his left panzer corps was stuck at Bastogne; elements of his right had to conduct time-consuming counter-marches because of American opposition. When the Panzer Lehr and 116th Panzer Divisions came up on the left and right respectively, von Manteuffel would have sufficient force for a broad-based advance to the Meuse. Even then, he would have to leave forces behind to guard his northern flank with each mile he advanced west. All his units were tired, having fought without rest for six solid days. Fatigue's consequences would be seen the next day when the 2nd Panzer's main column halted upon rumour of American tanks. The corps commander hastened to the front, relieved the colonel in command, sent in fresh troops, and the advance resumed – but valuable hours had been lost. Finally, and as it turned out most importantly, fuel deliveries to the forward elements were not getting through. Already major manoeuvre elements had been immobilized for lack of it.

Von Manteuffel's drive to the Meuse was a consequence of decisions made higher in the chain of command. As early as 18 December, Model had phoned von Rundstedt and Jodl to say the offensive had failed. By 24 December he hoped that the 2nd Panzer Division's position could be used to trap and destroy American forces against the Meuse – a return to the 'small solution'. Von Rundstedt was even more pessimistic. On Christ-

mas Day he requested that the attack be halted since even the 'small solution' was now impossible. According to an officer at Hitler's headquarters: 'In spite of all this Hitler not merely clung to the major plan but began to toy with even more ambitious ideas.'

Regardless of von Manteuffel's plans to broaden the 2nd Panzer Division's spearhead and to open a wider supporting road net, during 22-4 December the westernmost elements of Fifth Panzer Army achieved little. Much of the problem was due to the inability of the neighbouring Sixth Panzer Army to create a blocking line east of Liège. It had tried to slip past the Elsenborn position, but American artillery interdicted nearby east-west roads, leaving the remaining roads clogged with traffic. Typical was the experience of the 9th SS Panzer Division: committed on 18 December as part of the second wave, it did not reach the front until four days later. Consequently, Sixth Panzer Army failed to develop the momentum and achieve room to manoeuvre sufficient to perform its blocking mission. Left to its own resources, Fifth Panzer Army's advance slowed to a crawl. Such was its sorry state – its spearhead scattered all the way back to Bastogne, its most advanced units without fuel – that on 24 December Model ordered its advance guard 'to proceed on foot' to the Meuse. The dream of a blitzkrieg had died.

Change of Command

On 20 December, Eisenhower made a decision that shocked senior American generals. He divided American forces into northern and southern components. Those to the north were to be commanded by Field Marshal Montgomery. Ike's controversial decision stemmed from Montgomery's own suggestion to divide the battlefield. Bradley's stubborn refusal to relocate his headquarters rearward once the Germans penetrated between his First and Third Armies played right into Monty's hands. SHAEF staff planners worried that the German advance imperilled Bradley's communications with First Army. Noting that his headquarters had never retreated, Bradley claimed the resultant loss of prestige associated with its first retreat might instil panic in his men. This belief exhibits a ridiculous lack of confidence in his men and inappropriate concern with an unimportant symbol. Had Bradley been less stiff necked, much trouble could have been avoided because Montgomery planned to use the American setback to renew his campaign to become supreme land general of the Allied forces. In his memoirs, Bradley acknowledged that consenting to the command change was 'one of my biggest mistakes of the war'.

The Americans believed a second good reason for putting Monty in charge was that it would hasten British reinforcements to the front. While Montgomery did quickly bring his excellent XXX Corps to the River Meuse, once there it merely provided rear-area security and hardly became engaged. The entire battle cost the British slightly more than 200 killed. In addition to the crisis in command that stemmed from Ike's 20 December decision, a second important consequence was that Montgomery permitted his self-justifying argument for one overall ground commander to colour his view of the strategic opportunities for American counterattack.

Montgomery arrived at Hodges' headquarters, according to a British observer, 'like Christ come to cleanse the Temple'. He ordered the Americans to withdraw to straighten their lines. Giving up ground was outside the American experience. Hodges argued against yielding an inch. For the time being Monty demurred. But he soon became convinced that he should sack Hodges. Indeed, SHAEF had lost confidence in Hodges, who was admittedly exhausted after four exceedingly tough days. Ike retained confidence in Hodges, an opinion bolstered by the fact that even at this moment Hodges planned a counterattack at the base of the German penetration. Coupled with Patton's attack, the dual pincers had the chance of cutting off the bulk of the German forces still

involved in a struggle to reach the Meuse. Montgomery preferred the more cautious approach of 'tidying up' the battlefield before counterattacking.

Last Crisis on the Ground

While the American withdrawal from the St Vith area took place on the night of 23 December, the 82nd Airborne defended a 15-mile long sector blocking the German advance towards Liège. It was a poorly sited position, one which the 82nd had manned by circumstance rather than design. On 24 December, Montgomery arrived at XVIII Airborne Corps headquarters to order a 'tidying' of the front. The Americans typically argued vehemently, explaining that the 82nd had never retreated in its history and should not begin now. In one of his most important positive contributions to the battle, Montgomery demanded a withdrawal north to a better position. Here was military science displayed by a master grand tactician overcoming the unthinking, bulldog tenacity that characterized most American combat decisions. When a ferocious German attack hit the 82nd two days later, it was repulsed after bitter fighting. The outcome would have been different had not Monty insisted upon the retreat.

Decisively blocked at the Elsenborn Ridge and with Peiper's spearhead lost, on 20 December Model had changed Sixth Panzer Army's mission. Henceforth Fifth Panzer Army would make the main effort and the Sixth would be relegated to providing flank protection. Model sent the uncommitted II SS Panzer Corps forward in pursuit of this mission. By the night of 22 December, American patrols had captured an SS officer and learned that an attack on Baraque de Fraiture, on the main road between Houffalize and Manhay, was forthcoming.

General James Gavin, commander of the 82nd, worried that if the Germans seized the crossroads they could drive up the highway and trap both the 82nd and the troops evacuating St Vith against the angle formed by the Rivers Amblève and Salm. Gavin went to the crossroads, realized the position's weakness, and sent his only reserve, the 2nd Battalion/325 Glider Infantry.

Following a night of heavy snow, at dawn on 23 December, SS panzergrenadiers attacked Baraque de Fraiture. The attack caught the defenders carelessly inside the buildings eating breakfast. The glider commander led a counterattack to restore the position. The next hours passed with German mortar and artillery fire shelling the crossroads. Alarmed, the glidermen asked for help. From Manhay came a platoon of Shermans, a platoon of armoured infantry belonging to the 3rd Armored Division and a company of paratroopers from a separate parachute infantry battalion. They ran into a German roadblock that forced the infantry to dismount. The five Shermans 'buttoned up' and drove through the road-

block to arrive at the crossroads at 1pm. Three hours later, following a 20-minute artillery barrage, the 2nd SS Panzer Division delivered a powerful attack.

With the fall of Baraque de Fraiture, the route to Liège, Sixth Panzer Army's formal objective, lay open. Gavin scraped together what he could to block the road. Mostly they were the battered, exhausted St Vith survivors. Whether they could have held is unknown, for the Germans did not press their advantage. A break in the weather the next day allowed the 'Jabos' to dominate. The victors at the crossroads, the 2nd SS Panzer Division, had to hide in the woods. This was the first day the Germans had use of the St Vith road

Late on Christmas night, Hitler held a far-reaching staff discussion. After reviewing Model's report, Jodl paused and then spoke: 'Mein Führer, we must face the facts squarely and openly. We cannot force the Meuse River.' The photograph shows a Panther G knocked out by the 2nd Armored's counterattack near Celles. (US National Archives)

A 'Big Red One' Sherman, from the US 1st Infantry Division, which was part of the force that held the Elsenborn Ridge and forced Model to change Sixth Panzer Army's mission. (US National Archives)

▶ *The 82nd Airborne held a 15-mile sector between the Germans and Liège. Over-extended, elements of its glider regiment were overrun at Baraque de Fraiture. Here men of the 325th Glider Regiment haul an ammunition sled through the snow-covered forest. (US National Archives)*

▼ *US M16 MGMC self-propelled anti-aircraft gun.*

net. Model ordered units forward to support the 2nd SS, but until they arrived he doubted the division's ability to continue.

Counterattack

When Montgomery took charge of the northern sector of the bulge, he demanded one particular American commander to support him: Major General Joseph 'Lightning Joe' Collins. Collins was the most able and aggressive American corps commander in Europe. Originally Montgomery wanted Collins's VII Corps held out of battle until it could deliver a massive counterstroke. But the German attack through Baraque de Fraiture had sucked the corps piecemeal into the defensive fighting. On the afternoon of 24 December, the commander of the 2nd Armored Division, Major General Ernest Harmon, phoned Collins's VII Corps headquarters to ask permission to attack the 2nd Panzer spearhead east of Dinant. Harmon had learned that the Germans were out of fuel and therefore vulnerable. Collins was absent, which led to a fortuitous command mix-up involving his subordinate and higher headquarters. The result was that Harmon believed he had won permission to prepare for an attack and so proceeded. When

Collins returned and learned of Harmon's plan, he decided to interpret Montgomery's and Hodges' restraining orders very broadly. He authorized an attack. On Christmas Day 2nd Armored Division advanced south-west from Ciney. Aided tremendously by Allied fighter-bombers, the crushing weight of American artillery and the panzers' lack of mobility owing to depleted fuel stocks, the division achieved spectacular results. It destroyed the 2nd Panzer's reconnaissance battalion and encircled the balance of the German force around Celles. The division destroyed or captured 82 tanks, 83 anti-tank and artillery pieces, 500 other assorted vehicles, and captured 1,213 men, while killing close to another 1,000. As had been Peiper's experience, the German division died at the point of its furthest penetration. The defeat of the 2nd Panzer Division forced the German High Command to re-evaluate all operations. The Germans had lost the initiative, although Hitler refused to accept this.

Command Crisis

The 2nd Armored Division's success brought into sharp relief the contrast between the American style of war and the Montgomery method. Two

◀ *After the fall of Baraque de Fraiture, the road to Liège briefly lay open. The Germans were unable to capitalize on this advantage, and soon tanks of the 3rd Armored Division had the route blocked. Here Shermans of 3rd Armored train their guns on the woods near Manhay. Narrow roads such as this one prevented all manoeuvre. (US National Archives)*

▶ *When Harmon learned that the 2nd Panzer had run out of fuel, he requested permission to attack. Here a Panther G, having run out of fuel, is captured by advancing Americans. (US National Archives)*

▶ *During the sixteen December days of the offensive, only five featured clear weather that permitted the Allies' full aerial arsenal to fly. Christmas Day was one clear day. The dreaded 'Jabos', fighter-bombers including ones like this P-47N, armed with eight .50-calibre machine-guns and two 1,000lb bombs or ten 5in rockets, joined the P-38 Lightnings and P-51 Mustangs to dominate ground combat. It was, according to the official historian, 'one of the greatest demonstrations of tactical ground support ever witnessed by American troops'. (US National Air & Space Museum)*

▶ *Harmon's 2nd Armored Division captured much booty during its attack against the 2nd Panzer Division, such as these artillery pieces. (US National Archives)*

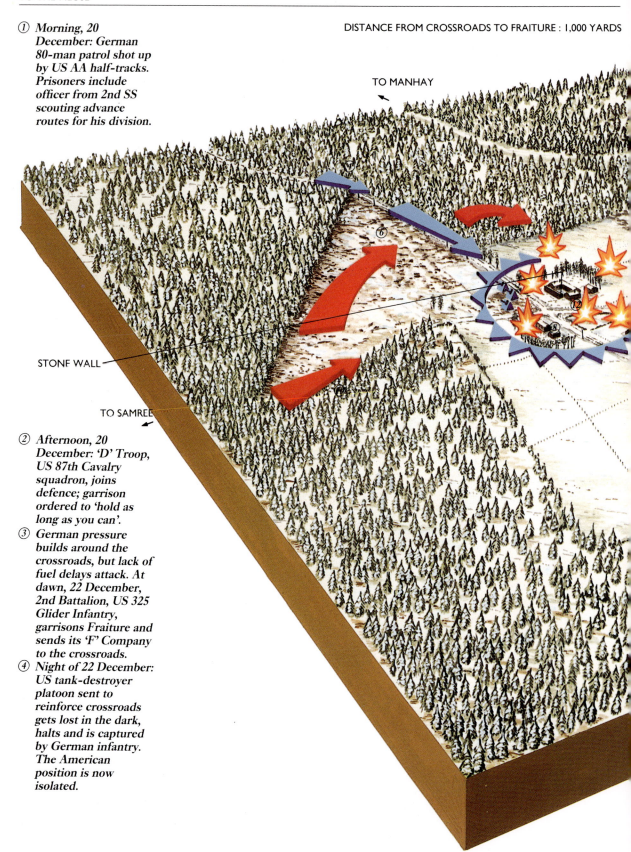

① *Morning, 20 December: German 80-man patrol shot up by US AA half-tracks. Prisoners include officer from 2nd SS scouting advance routes for his division.*

DISTANCE FROM CROSSROADS TO FRAITURE : 1,000 YARDS

TO MANHAY

STONE WALL

TO SAMREE

② *Afternoon, 20 December: 'D' Troop, US 87th Cavalry squadron, joins defence; garrison ordered to 'hold as long as you can'.*

③ *German pressure builds around the crossroads, but lack of fuel delays attack. At dawn, 22 December, 2nd Battalion, US 325 Glider Infantry, garrisons Fraiture and sends its 'F' Company to the crossroads.*

④ *Night of 22 December: US tank-destroyer platoon sent to reinforce crossroads gets lost in the dark, halts and is captured by German infantry. The American position is now isolated.*

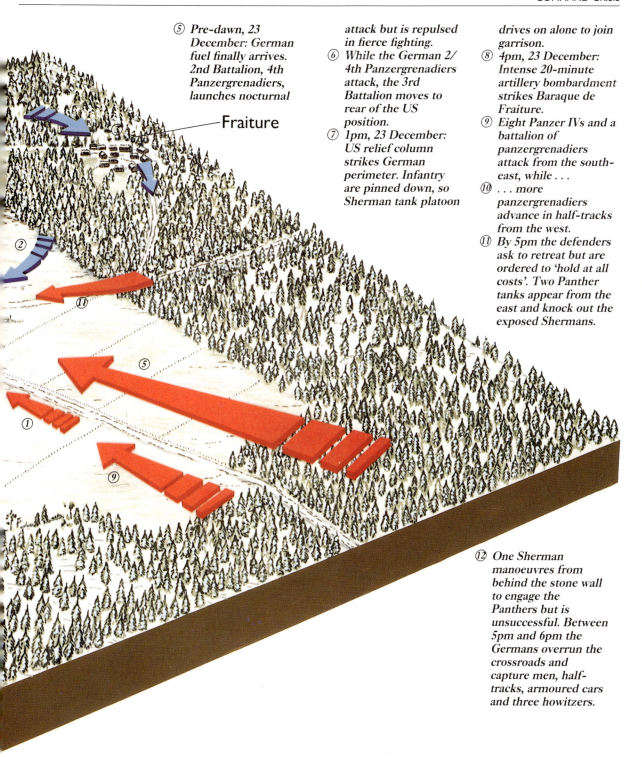

⑤ Pre-dawn, 23 December: German fuel finally arrives. 2nd Battalion, 4th Panzergrenadiers, launches nocturnal attack but is repulsed in fierce fighting.

⑥ While the German 2/4th Panzergrenadiers attack, the 3rd Battalion moves to rear of the US position.

⑦ 1pm, 23 December: US relief column strikes German perimeter. Infantry are pinned down, so Sherman tank platoon drives on alone to join garrison.

⑧ 4pm, 23 December: Intense 20-minute artillery bombardment strikes Baraque de Fraiture.

⑨ Eight Panzer IVs and a battalion of panzergrenadiers attack from the south-east, while . . .

⑩ . . . more panzergrenadiers advance in half-tracks from the west.

⑪ By 5pm the defenders ask to retreat but are ordered to 'hold at all costs'. Two Panther tanks appear from the east and knock out the exposed Shermans.

Fraiture

⑫ One Sherman manoeuvres from behind the stone wall to engage the Panthers but is unsuccessful. Between 5pm and 6pm the Germans overrun the crossroads and capture men, half-tracks, armoured cars and three howitzers.

COMBAT AT BARAQUE DE FRAITURE

20 to 23 December 1944.

days earlier Montgomery had decided to absorb another blow before counterattacking. He studied the maps and saw that the Germans had five panzer divisions lining the western and northern tip of the bulge, with additional major units hastening west. This convinced Montgomery that the Germans were about to deliver their most powerful blow since the first assault. The American commanders saw matters differently.

On the day Harmon smashed the 2nd Panzer Division, Bradley visited Montgomery. The Field Marshal lectured and scolded him like a schoolboy. He exaggerated the extent of the American setback, claiming Hodges' First Army would be unable to attack for three months. Later, in a letter to his British superior he wrote: 'It was useless to pretend that we were going to turn this quickly into a great victory; it was a proper defeat and we had better admit it.' He went on to say if his views had been followed all along this would not have happened.

In fact a great victory had been won. The offensive power of the German army had been smashed. 26 December, two days after Monty's lecture and letter, could be viewed as the high-water mark of the German offensive. While the GIs in the foxholes might not appreciate this fact, Bradley and Patton certainly did. Hodges' northern barrier from Dinant to Elsenborn stood firm. In the south, Bastogne had been relieved. The Americans felt that the over-extended German position invited a decisive counterstroke delivered from the shoulders of the bulge. They pointed to the 2nd Armored Division's success to support their view. Montgomery still adamantly disagreed. That night Bradley phoned Ike's chief of staff: 'Damn it, Bedell, can't you get Monty going in the north? As near as we can tell, the other fellow's reached the high-water mark today.'

This disagreement broadened into a serious rift that came close to fracturing the Anglo-American alliance. Recall that it was this fracture that Hitler had set as his goal when originally planning his 'master stroke'. Montgomery took advantage of the occasion to resume the strategic argument over a narrow versus broad advance into Germany. He used his temporary appointment as commander of American forces north of the bulge as a stepping stone toward his overall goal. On 30 December he baldly stated his demands in a letter to Eisenhower. He wrote that the Allies had just suffered a tremendous defeat. More would occur unless Ike acceded to his demand for 'one commander . . . to direct and control' all land operations in north-west Europe. He insisted that commander be himself.

For Eisenhower this was too much. He drafted a letter to the Combined Chiefs of Staff which presented the choice: Ike or Monty. Given the disparity in manpower, he knew Montgomery would go. Montgomery's dismissal would have enormous consequences. Promoted by an irresponsible press, virulent anti-American sentiment was sweeping England. Sacking Monty might mean an end to Anglo-American cooperation. Fortunately, into the breach stepped Montgomery's gifted chief of staff, Major General Francis de Guingand. After receiving a warning about what was afoot, de Guingand hurried to Eisenhower's headquarters. There the Supreme Commander's own chief of staff told him that it was too late: the decision had been made. Undaunted, de Guingand managed to persuade Eisenhower to delay any action for 24 hours. He returned to Montgomery and in one of the dramatic scenes of the war told his commander he was about to be sacked. The vain, confident Montgomery had no idea this was possible. He nearly collapsed and asked in a small voice: 'What do I do, Freddie?'

De Guingand had already written an abjectly apologetic letter. Monty signed it and sent it off. The letter concluded: 'Very distressed that my letter may have upset you and I would ask you to tear it up. Your very devoted subordinate, Monty.' This placated Eisenhower and the war went on.

▶ *When US First and Third Armies cautiously attacked the tip of the Bulge, von Rundstedt ironically entered in the OB West War Diary 'the small solution'. Here tank crews of the Third Army take a cigarette break. Proud of his men, Patton issued Third Army a general order on 1 January: 'In closing, I can find no fitter expression for my feelings than to apply to you the immortal words spoken by General Scott at Chapultepec when he said, "Brave soldiers, veterans, you have been baptized in fire and blood and have come out steel."' (Charles B. MacDonald Collection, US Army Military History Institute)*

CONCLUSION

Most of the generals on either side recognized 26 December as a turning point; henceforth the Americans held the initiative. Major combats remained. The German effort to again isolate Bastogne produced large-scale armoured actions. However, failure convinced von Manteuffel that it was time to retreat. Typically, Hitler proved slow to adjust to reality. Not until 8 January did he start

Sixth Panzer Army moving east. When, on the Eastern Front, the tremendous Russian winter offensive struck four days later, the defenders lacked tanks and the front collapsed 'like a deck of cards'.

On 16 January, one month after the German assault, Patton's Third Army and Hodges' First Army linked up north-east of Bastogne. It was too

late to trap the mass of Germans. They had conducted a skilful fighting withdrawal under most difficult circumstances. Bradley proposed a 'hurry up offensive' to follow the Germans in hot pursuit through the Eifel and across the Rhine. This was a major departure from previous plans and proved unacceptable to Montgomery and too bold for Eisenhower. Yet ultimately the Rhine crossing at Remagen occurred precisely on this sector and featured the now veteran 9th Armored Division.

The Battle of the Bulge cost the American Army 10,276 killed, 47,493 wounded and a staggering 23,218 missing. German losses are impossible to quantify accurately. It is certain that their casualties exceeded the American total. The Germans lost hundreds of panzers. The Americans quickly replaced their losses. The Germans could not.

Assessment

The German armies never came close to achieving their objectives on the field in the Ardennes. However, according to Bradley, the German offensive caused high-level political and strategic battles that 'violently shook, and very nearly shattered, the Allied high command'. Such a rupture was exactly what Hitler intended. By this measure, 'Wacht am Rhein' came perilously close to success.

In modern war the one way high command can influence events once battle is joined is to allocate reserves. Accordingly, an evaluation of the top generals shows Eisenhower, and to a slightly lesser extent Bradley, to have performed exceedingly well in use of reserves to stop the German drive westwards. After the war, German generals commented that US reserves reacted more quickly than they had expected. Having accomplished this, Ike faltered by only partially following the recommendations of his subordinates – Bradley, Patton and Hodges – to cut off the Germans at the base of the bulge. Instead he pursued Montgomery's more cautious advance against the tip of the bulge. Had Montgomery been willing to use actively the British XXX Corps manning the Meuse to blunt the German advance, and thus use Collins to strike the Germans further east, Bradley writes: 'We could have inflicted an absolute slaughter on the Germans and, ultimately, saved many American lives.'

◀ *The frozen body of a German officer, one of thousands of Germans killed in the campaign. (US National Archives)*

Hitler and Jodl likewise failed to use their reserves wisely. Instead of exploiting Fifth Panzer Army's unexpected success, they reinforced Sixth Panzer Army's failure. By 20 December the German attack had escaped its generals' control. Why had the panzers failed to advance as planned?

The ability of most Americans to stand firm in the face of surprise assault vitally influenced events. The stubborn initial defence disrupted the OKW's carefully prepared plans. It bought enough time for American resistance to harden along more organized defensive lines. With each passing day, coordinated resistance in a region with limited roads made the German task of reaching the Meuse less feasible. It is important to note that merely reaching the Meuse was only the first objective in the plan to capture Antwerp. German tactical support and logistics failed to keep pace with the advance. As early as 19 December, Fifth Panzer Army reported a 'badly strained' fuel supply. The next day the Sixth's 12th SS Panzer Division, supposedly a spearhead unit, ground to a halt for lack of fuel. OKW bungled badly when it failed to ensure that fuel distribution keep pace with the advance, when it miscalculated fuel

expenditures – bad terrain and weather reduced the expected mileage from a tankful of fuel by fifty per cent – and when it optimistically based spearhead advances on captured stocks.

The US Army in the Ardennes Campaign did not serve its soldiers well. It equipped the GI with inferior weapons, trained and organized him according to a faulty doctrine, allowed the enemy to launch a massive surprise offensive against his weakest point and frequently provided poor leadership at army, corps and divisional levels. By and large the American soldier returned valour. Some ran at first shock; most stood firm and fought with what they had.

In his post-war interrogation, von Manteuffel acknowledged the success of the American delaying action. But he proudly noted that 2nd Panzer Division spearheads reached to within four kilometres of the Meuse without a major engagement. While this is true, the division accomplished this feat only at the expense of bypassing all defended positions and leaving it up to supporting units to carve a supply route. Von Manteuffel believed that the second wave's failure was inherent in the original plan. The Germans lacked the strength to

◀ *Two very young Waffen SS troopers captured during the American advance to erase the Bulge. (Charles B. MacDonald Collection, US Army Military History Institute)*

feed the offensive and enough strength to capture the positions bypassed by the first assault wave.

Von Manteuffel also observed that the German High Command failed to convert to the 'small solution' when it became apparent that the all-out drive to Antwerp was impracticable. This observation does raise a most interesting 'what if'? Ridgeway's XVII Airborne Corps' defences facing south were spread exceedingly thinly during the days it focused on screening the withdrawal from St Vith. As late as the fall of Manhay on 24 December, German armour had the opportunity to slice in behind the forces concentrated around St Vith and on the Elsenborn Ridge. They could have trapped this force in a vice, using the Meuse as a barrier, and inflicted a very serious defeat. What impact such a defeat would have had on the Eisenhower-Montgomery feud is difficult to assess, but it is interesting to note that Eisenhower challenged Montgomery knowing that his own standing with the American government was secure. In the event, the partial victory obtainable from the 'small solution' was not in keeping with Hitler's aims. He sought overwhelming victory and was incapable of realizing that his means did not match his hopes. For, in the last analysis, from its

inception the German Ardennes offensive had no reasonable chance of victory.

Before their execution Field Marshals Jodl and Keitel responded to a question about the wisdom of the Ardennes offensive: 'The criticism whether it would have been better to have employed our available reserves in the East rather than in the West, we submit to the judgment of history.' Given that the attack had slight chance of success but did limit Anglo-American penetration east by the end of the war, it can be asserted that one effect of the offensive was to place more Germans and other Europeans under Russian rather than Western occupation after the cessation of hostilities.

Winston Churchill paid eloquent tribute to the American forces in a speech before the House of Commons on 18 January 1945. He concluded that the Battle of the Bulge was 'undoubtedly the greatest American battle of the War, and will, I believe, be regarded as an ever-famous American victory.'

The inscription beneath a statue of a GI in the town of Clervaux, the site of the 110/28 Division's last stand against von Manteuffel's panzers, reminds modern tourists what the American sacrifice and victory meant. It reads: 'To Our Liberators.'

◀ *Guarded by a GI of the 4th Armored Division, captured Germans assist their comrade, suffering from frostbite, to the rear. (US Army Military History Institute)*

THE BATTLEFIELD TODAY

The area is large and the actions were many. Therefore, I recommend selecting a centrally located touring base such as Clervaux. The now-serene castle houses a Battle of the Bulge Museum well worth a visit. Americans will feel welcome in this village, especially when they come upon the memorial to American soldiers.

The Hotel du Parc overlooking Clervaux, and the Vieux Moulin d'Asselborn near the village of Asselborn a few kilometres away, offer quiet lodgings at a reasonable price and excellent food. In the guest-book at the latter inn we saw the names of 101st Airborne veterans.

From either of these bases, one can conveniently visit Bastogne to the south-west and its Battle of the Bulge Museum, or hunt for foxholes and memorials among the woods and villages to the north and east. Foxholes with both German and American relics can be found in a pine wood outside Rocherath-Krinkelt. In villages across the front, such as Echternach, Houffalize and Stavelot, there are preserved German or American tanks. At the edge of a quiet road through a wood outside Meyerode is a memorial to Lieutenant Eric Fisher Wood, an American reputed to have conducted a series of guerrilla actions in the area before he was killed. Here too people remember; on a rainy late-September day, I found fresh cut flowers at the foot of the memorial.

▼ *The 7th Armored Division passes three German tanks on 23 January as it drives to re-enter St Vith. (US Army Military History Institute)*

CHRONOLOGY

1944

6 June D-Day, the Allied invasion of France.

25 July Allied breakout from beachhead begins.

19 August Hitler initiates planning to assemble reserves for counteroffensive in the West.

Early September Allied pursuit across Europe grinds to a halt owing to supply shortages.

10 September US First Army liberates Luxemburg.

16 September Hitler announces intention to launch counteroffensive through Ardennes. Objective: Antwerp.

20 September Soviet forces cross the River Danube.

25 September Montgomery's Operation 'Market Garden' ends in failure.

1 October First Army begins siege of Aachen; Montgomery begins Scheldt campaign to clear Antwerp approaches.

Late October Russians attack into East Prussia.

8 November US Third Army begins drive to breach the German West Wall defence line.

16 November US First Army begins Huertgen Forest campaign.

28 November First Allied ships reach Antwerp; long period of Allied supply shortage eases.

13 December US First Army launches attack to capture River Roer dams; Germans mass in forward staging areas.

16 December, 5.30am Germans open all-out counteroffensive in Ardennes.

Daytime Losheim Gap defences begin to crumble. Sixth Panzer Army assault stalls against US 2nd and 99th Divisions. Fifth Panzer Army makes limited progress against 28th Division.

Night Losheim Gap position crumbles; 106th Division on verge of being surrounded. 110/28 positions fall to German armour. Eisenhower releases 7th and 10th Armored Divisions from reserve.

17 December

Morning Peiper captures Bullingen; 18th VGD captures Schoenberg bridge, isolating US 106th Division.

Afternoon Peiper's SS slaughter unarmed Americans near Malmédy; traffic jams delay German advance on St Vith.

Night Peiper halts before Stavelot; Eisenhower releases airborne divisions.

18 December Peiper repulsed at Trois Ponts; US armour delays German advance on Bastogne.

19 December

Morning 101st checks Panzer Lehr outside Bastogne; Peiper isolated by recapture of Stavelot.

Afternoon 7,000-8,000 American troops surrender on Schnee Eifel; defence of St Vith stiffens.

Night Eisenhower convenes emergency meeting.

20 December Montgomery assumes command of US First Army.

21 December St Vith falls.

22 December McAuliffe rejects surrender demand; Bastogne low on ammunition.

Night St Vith defenders retreat from salient.

23 December Peiper retreats with remnant on foot; defenders of Bastogne re-supplied by air; 2nd SS Division captures Baraque de Fraiture.

25 December Major attack on Bastogne repulsed; 2nd Panzer Division spearhead mauled 4 kilometres short of Meuse; von Rundstedt requests abandoning 'Wacht am Rhein' and substituting the 'small solution'.

26 December US 4th Armored Division relieves Bastogne; initiative passes into Allies' hands.

29 December Allied 'crisis in command' begins with Montgomery's letter to Eisenhower requesting new command arrangement.

30 December Last German effort to close Bastogne corridor fails; von Manteuffel abandons hope for offensive action.

1945

1 January Luftwaffe launches 'Great Blow' in West and suffers irreplaceable losses of nearly 300 aircraft.

8 January Hitler authorizes SS withdrawal from Ardennes.

12 January Soviets begin massive winter offensive across River Vistula in Poland.

16 January US First and Third Armies join at Houffalize.

23 January US CCB/7 Armored Division re-enters St Vith.

28 January Battle of the Bulge officially ends.

7 March US First Army seizes Remagen bridge across River Rhine.

23 March Allied forces under Montgomery cross Rhine north of the Ruhr.

1 April US First and Ninth Armies encircle the Ruhr.

23 April Soviet forces break into Berlin.

25 April US and Soviet patrols meet on either side of River Elbe.

30 April Hitler commits suicide in Berlin.

7 May German High Command unconditionally surrenders all forces.

A GUIDE TO FURTHER READING

BLUMENSON, M. *The Patton Papers 1940-1945*, (vol. 2) Boston, 1974. Patton's diary, revealing his thinking at the time.

BRADLEY, O. and BLAIR, C. *A General's Life*, New York, 1983. Much about grand strategy and the Montgomery feud.

COLE, H. *The Ardennes: Battle of the Bulge*, Washington, 1965. The indispensable official history, but written before declassification of Ultra.

EUROPEAN THEATER HISTORICAL INTERROGATION, Series A Manuscripts 1945; Series B 1946-48, National Archives, Washington. Of particular interest are A872 for OB information, B151 for planning and preparation; and B151A for von Manteuffel's detailed description and critique.

GILES, J. *The Damned Engineers*, Washington, 1985. A detailed account of the engineers' role in delaying the German offensive. Special focus on Peiper's advance.

GOOLRICK, W. and TANNER, O. *The Battle of the Bulge*, Alexandria, VA, 1979. Lavishly illustrated, good general account.

MacDONALD, C. *A Time for Trumpets: The Untold Story of the Battle of the Bulge*, New York, 1985. A recent, exhaustively detailed account. Examines in detail what the Allies knew before the attack.

— *Company Commander*, Washington, 1947. What it was like at the sharp end in front of the twin villages on 17 December.

MARSHALL, S. *Bastogne: The Story of the First Eight Days*, Washington, 1946. Based on combat interviews shortly after battle.

PIMLOTT, J. *Battle of the Bulge*, New York, 1981. An overview with sharp analysis.

WARLIMONT, W. *Inside Hitler's Headquarters 1939-45*, New York, 1964. The view from within by a professional staff officer who was there.

WEIGLEY, R. *Eisenhower's Lieutenants: The Campaign of France and Germany 1944-1945*, Bloomington, IN, 1981. Focuses on leadership and command decisions. Excellent analysis of US Army's weaknesses.

An aerial view of the American 6th Armored Division manoeuvring north-east of Bastogne on 13 January as it drives to link up with First Army near Houffalize. (US National Archives)

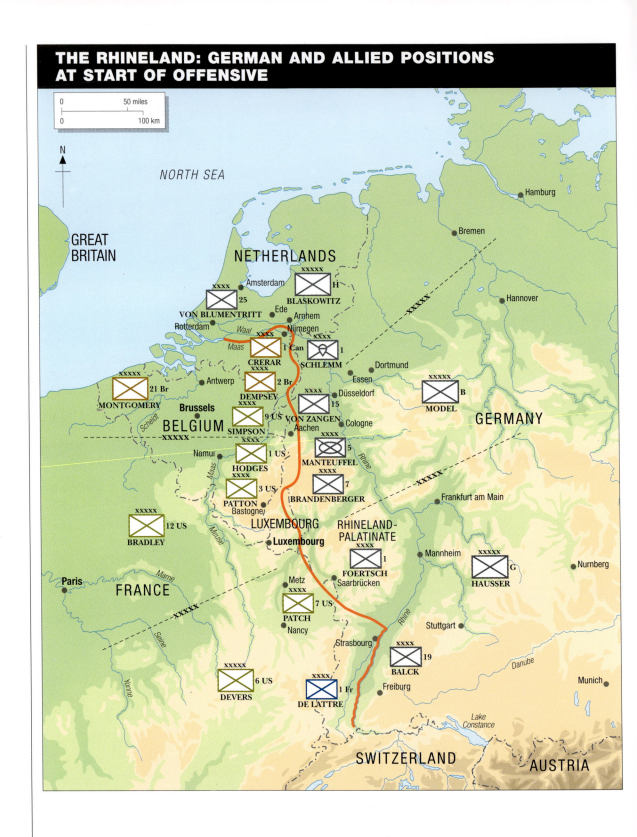

THE RHINELAND: GERMAN AND ALLIED POSITIONS AT START OF OFFENSIVE

0 ——— 50 miles
0 ——— 100 km

N

NORTH SEA

GREAT BRITAIN

NETHERLANDS

Hamburg

Bremen

Hannover

Amsterdam

25
VON BLUMENTRITT
Rotterdam
Ede
Arnhem
Waal
Nijmegen

H
BLASKOWITZ

1 Can
CRERAR
Maas

1
SCHLEMM

Dortmund

Essen

Düsseldorf

B
MODEL

GERMANY

Antwerp

2 Br
DEMPSEY

21 Br
MONTGOMERY

Brussels

9 US
SIMPSON

BELGIUM

15
VON ZANGEN
Aachen
Cologne

Scheldt

Namur

1 US
HODGES

3 US
PATTON
Bastogne

Maas

5
MANTEUFFEL

7
BRANDENBERGER

Rhine

Frankfurt am Main

12 US
BRADLEY

Meuse

LUXEMBOURG

Luxembourg

RHINELAND-PALATINATE

Mannheim

Nurnberg

G
HAUSSER

1
FOERTSCH
Saarbrücken

Marne

Metz

7 US
PATCH
Nancy

Stuttgart

Danube

FRANCE

Paris

Seine

Strasbourg

19
BALCK

Rhine

Munich

Yonne

6 US
DEVERS

1 Fr
DE LATTRE

Freiburg

Lake Constance

SWITZERLAND

AUSTRIA

ORIGINS OF THE BATTLE

On 16 January 1945, the German forces which had undertaken Hitler's last big offensive in western Europe found themselves back at their start line. The massive Ardennes assault was to have pushed the Allies beyond the Meuse and split the British and American forces in half; but it had failed miserably, with losses of over 100,000 men. Hitler's gamble to seize the initiative had failed; all German energy and effort would now have to be geared to the defence of the homeland.

The Allied armies under the supreme command of Gen Dwight D. Eisenhower had, by the start of 1945, arrived at the German border and they stretched from The Netherlands to the Swiss frontier. Below Strasbourg Gen Devers' US 6th Army Group had actually pushed the Germans back to the River Rhine. Elsewhere, the front line either confronted the German Siegfried defensive line (Hitler's Westwall) or rested on other river barriers. North of Aachen, Gen Simpson's US 9th Army had breached the Siegfried Line, but was stalled in front of the River Roer, while Gen Dempsey's British 2nd Army was lined up along the River Maas. In the far north, in Holland, Gen Crerar's Canadian 1st Army held a bridgehead between the Maas and the Rhine overlooking German soil – a legacy of the failed Arnhem campaign – but was confronted with one of the strongest sectors of the Siegfried Line.

To the German people the River Rhine is the mythical border of Germany. It is the river of legend, of Lorelei, of brave Roland and

During the Ardennes operation, this Tiger Mk II from the 501st SS Heavy Tank Battalion was abandoned on the Stavelot road due to a lack of fuel. American engineers inspect the perfectly sound tank. At this time in the war Germany was suffering great shortages of fuel and Hitler's December offensive was designed to overrun American supply dumps and capture new stocks. The plan was not a great success and the lack of fuel was always a great problem for the units involved in the operation.
(Imperial War Museum)

Siegfried. The Rhine is an important symbol of German history and national strength. During Roman times it formed the barrier between the civilised world and the barbarians. In later times, when Germans ruled both sides of the river, it was an important psychological barrier and a vital military objective. As long as the river protected the country from invasion from the west, the German people could keep alive the hope that all was well. In front of the Rhine, between the river and the borders of France, Belgium, Luxembourg and The Netherlands, was the Rhineland. This strip of land had had a chequered past, having been hotly contested throughout history. It had been much disputed during the Thirty Years War, and again in Napoleonic times when the Emperor had pushed the borders of Germany back to the old Roman frontier. Germany retook the territory after the Franco-Prussian War only to have it seized again by France after World War I. In 1940, Germany brought the area back under its domination. In February 1945, the invading Allied armies were poised to take possession of the Rhineland away from the Germans.

The object of the Rhineland campaign of 1945 was to push all German forces back across the Rhine or destroy them in front of the river. Once the river line had been brought under control, preparations could be made for an assault crossing. Eisenhower had decided on a 'broad front' policy in which all of his troops would advance along the whole of his line, rather than focus all of his forces in one particular sector. No crossings would be made of the Rhine until the whole of the Allied Army was in possession of the west bank of the river. It was a policy that was not universally approved, and one which has been called into question by historians ever since. It was, none the less, a strategy that was ultimately successful.

The 'broad front' policy evolved with the progress of the war after the Normandy landings. Initially, pre-invasion planners had envisioned two major thrusts into Germany, each heading for great industrial areas in order to smash the bulk of the German manufacturing capability. One was to pass north of the Ardennes aiming at the Ruhr, while the other was to go south of the Ardennes to eliminate the lesser Saar industrial area. These powerful striking forces would then cross the Rhine and link up behind the Ruhr, thus encircling the powerhouse of the great German war machine. In the event, this did not happen, for in August 1944 the Allied forces broke out of their invasion lodgement in Normandy with such strength that their rapid thrust across France sent the German Army reeling before them. Enemy opposition collapsed everywhere to such a degree that all sectors of the line made rapid advances and were only stopped at the German border by lack of supplies. It was an exhilarating time for the pursuing troops. After being confined within a relatively small bridgehead in Normandy for so long, the open roads and demoralised enemy induced a feeling of invincibility in the Allied armies. The war seemed to be over and the Nazis beaten. But the German Army was not beaten; the Allies' pause in September 1944 allowed a few masterful generals, with experience of organised retreats on the Russian front, to re-establish the much vaunted Siegfried defensive line, reinforce and re-equip battered divisions and stabilise the front. When the advance was ready to begin again, opposition had strengthened to such an extent that Allied progress was difficult, costly and very painful. The Germans had staged a remarkable recovery.

Efforts to get momentum going again ranged from the novel to the predictable. The normally pedantic British field marshal Montgomery, who would only make a move after gaining overwhelming superiority over the enemy in troop numbers, supporting fire and logistical supplies, proposed a swift land-airborne operation to seize a lodgement over the lower Rhine at Arnhem in order to get his British 21st Army Group into northern Germany. Operation Market Garden, as it was called, was a failure, although it did establish British troops across the Maas where their lodgement could look over the border into the German Rhineland. General Bradley, commanding the US 12th Army Group, was somewhat put out when his American advance had to be delayed while men and matériel were switched northwards to help Montgomery's operation. General Patton was also irritated as supplies, especially fuel, were denied to his US 3rd Army and sent northwards. National interests came into play as British troops grabbed the headlines while Americans kicked their heels. This is where Eisenhower's 'broad front' strategy now came into play. With his armies all pressing the frontiers of the German Reich, he now believed that the war could be best won by taking territory all along the line and rolling up German forces everywhere, rather than confining the advance to small, powerful thrusts such as the Arnhem operation. It would also mean that all nationalities would be involved in the main fighting, helping to salve the national pride of the Canadian, British, American and French armies.

Farther south, Gen Bradley's US 12th Army Group spent the autumn attacking the Siegfried Line in a series of offensives, the most important and bloody of which was the capture of Aachen, where they pierced the

Supreme Allied Commander Gen Dwight D. Eisenhower (left) talks to MajGen Alvan Gillem, commander US XIII Corps (centre), and MajGen Raymond McLain, commander US XIX Corps (right). Eisenhower had previously commanded the North African 'Torch' landings and the invasions of both Sicily and Italy. (National Archives, Washington)

defensive line and got to the River Roer. In the far south, Gen Devers' US 6th Army Group had been slowed almost to a halt as they approached the German border through the difficult terrain of the Vosges Mountains. His armies became stalled by a large and troublesome pocket of German resistance at the confluence of the Saar and Moselle rivers known as the Colmar 'Pocket'. By November the deteriorating weather and enemy opposition had contrived to make any advance a slow and costly process.

Montgomery now pressed Eisenhower to modify his strategy to allow the original single major thrust through northern Germany to the Ruhr by a powerful group of British and American armies (with him at the head) to take place. Eisenhower refused and pressed on with his 'broad front', but did give permission for a combined British-American operation to clear the northern Rhineland. Montgomery's plan was to advance through his lodgement east of the River Maas, through the Reichswald and clear the enemy as far as the Rhine, while Gen Simpson's US 9th Army attacked across the River Roer and made for the Rhine. Both of these armies would then meet up and clear the whole of the Rhineland, trapping those German forces still west of the Rhine by encirclement. This operation was scheduled to start on 1 January 1945.

However, events overtook these plans when Hitler launched his Ardennes offensive on 16 December 1944. Generalfeldmarschall Gerd von Rundstedt, Commander-in-Chief West, sent his re-equipped and reconstituted 5th and 6th Panzer Armies through the lightly held Ardennes sector of the front line in Belgium, to the complete surprise of the whole of the Allied command. The battle that followed was protracted and bitter. Gains were made initially as they overran whole American divisions and caused great panic in rear areas, but the advance ran out of steam close to the River Meuse. Then the Allies set to the task of eliminating this 'bulge' in their lines. Inexorably, the great weight of their superior forces was gradually applied to the enemy's flanks, squeezing the life out of the penetration and forcing the long German retreat to begin. Within one month, they were back at their start line. Loss of life had been great on both sides; very little was achieved by the Germans. If Hitler had ever subscribed to the art of tactical defence and kept these two great panzer armies behind the Siegfried Line as a mobile reserve, instead of squandering them in the snow of the Belgian mountains, then the outcome of the final year of the war might have been a little different.

When the effects of the 'Battle of the Bulge' had finally died down, Eisenhower could once again resume his advance. Montgomery's Rhineland offensive could now go ahead with the American 9th Army led by Simpson under his command. Bradley and Devers could move their army groups to the Rhine also. All along the front line, the German Army would be squeezed back into their homeland towards complete destruction.

OPPOSING COMMANDERS

The commanders facing each other on the borders of Germany in February 1945 were each handicapped by their own philosophies. The Allied armies in the West were led by men who answered to the peoples of democratically led governments. The German army answered to one man, Adolf Hitler.

ALLIED COMMANDERS

In the Allied camp, its top commanders had achieved fame beyond the battlefield. The press and newsreels of the day portrayed them in an heroic mould, with many of them achieving the status of movie stars. Eisenhower, Montgomery, Bradley and Patton were all too famous ever to be removed from command because of their mistakes. Such changes would seriously damage morale, and more importantly, national pride. Their generalship therefore, although often questioned by politicians, Chiefs of Staff and, later, historians, was never seriously contested at the time. On the other side, German commanders were often dispatched with indecent haste by their Supreme Commander when the consequences of their actions ran counter to his expectations, even though many of them were very competent individuals.

Leading the Allied team was the Supreme Allied Commander in Europe, Gen Dwight D. Eisenhower. He was the very spirit of Allied co-operation. He was a true professional soldier of great skill with his

FM Montgomery, commander British 21st Army Group, with four Allied army commanders. From left to right: Gen Sir Miles Dempsey (British 2nd Army), LtGen Courtney Hodges (US 1st Army), Montgomery, LtGen Bill Simpson (US 9th Army) and Gen Harry Crerar (Canadian 1st Army). (National Archives, Washington)

most prominent asset being his ability as an administrator, rather than as a great strategist. His role was to weld together the vast armies of American, British, Canadian, Polish, French and Belgian troops into a powerful fighting force. That he achieved this, in spite of the efforts of his strong-willed and often troublesome subordinate commanders, is a testament to his diplomatic and people skills. Eisenhower may have lacked experience as a field commander, but his mastery of the technicalities of war, his exceptional logistical gifts and his exercise of tact and diplomacy, enabled him to achieve all that was expected of him.

Eisenhower's Army Group Commanders lined up along the German frontier were, from north to south, Montgomery, Bradley and Devers; one British and two American. Field Marshal Bernard Montgomery commanded the British 21st Army Group, comprising Canadian 1st Army, British 2nd Army and US 9th Army, with great success. He began the war as a divisional commander, shot to fame with his handling of 8th Army in North Africa and, with command of all land forces during the D-Day landings, became the most prominent British field commander of the war. He was the master of the 'set-piece' battle. Careful planning, calculated strategy and disciplined use of all logistical supplies, marked his approach to warfare. He never acted until he had overwhelming superiority over his enemy in both men and matériel. He showed unconcealed scorn for those commanders who relied on fortune and élan to carry them through. Montgomery was a showman able to exploit media interest at home and inspire great confidence in his men in the field. He was generally disliked by his American allies; his abrasive manner and nationalistic approach to the conduct of the war also irritated many of his contemporaries.

General Omar Bradley was America's counterpart to Montgomery, commanding the massive US 12th Army Group which, in February 1945, consisted of the US 1st and 3rd Armies (Bradley's US 9th Army was on loan to Montgomery for the Rhineland campaign). Bradley was the most important US field general of the war. In 1942, during the 'Torch' invasion of North Africa, he acted in a liaison role for Eisenhower, later commanding a corps at the end of the campaign. Service in Sicily, in a subordinate command to Gen Patton, followed. He was eventually given the US 1st Army for the Normandy invasion. By 1 August he had risen to army group command with almost one-and-a-half million American troops under his control–the largest army ever assembled under the command of a single American general. Bradley had a quiet and unassuming manner, a great respect for his men and a sure grasp of strategy and tactics. His relationship with Eisenhower was one of mutual respect, for although he lacked the flair and drive of Gen Patton, his performance was solid, dependable and effective.

The last of Eisenhower's army group commanders, at the head of US 6th Army Group, was LtGen Jacob Devers. The least well known of all the major commanders, Devers had approached the German border from the south via the landings on the French Riviera. His army group comprised US 7th Army and the French 1st Army. Devers had started the war in charge of a division and by 1943 was in command of all American forces in the UK. He went to the Mediterranean as deputy to the Supreme Allied Commander, Gen Henry Maitland Wilson, and gained experience there of handling large formations. Devers was later selected to head the invasion of southern France. His army group's progress from the Mediterranean had been relatively easy compared to that faced by other Allied units in Normandy, with major enemy opposition only increasing as he approached the German border.

Making up these three army groups were a clutch of army commanders whose performances ranged from the pedantic to the outrageous. In the extreme north Canadian 1st Army had LtGen Henry Crerar at its head. By nature a reserved man, he hated personal publicity. He was also handicapped, not only by having Montgomery as his boss, but by being required to report daily to the Canadian Prime Minister, Mackenzie King, and ultimately to the Canadian Parliament. He suffered by having two masters; his every move was scrutinised directly both by politicians and his army group commander. None the less, his great skill in handling the logistical side of the 'Veritable' campaign and his cool nerves in mastering the largest force ever commanded by a Canadian general – over 475,000 men – more than made up for his cool relationship with Monty.

Heading British 2nd Army was LtGen Miles Dempsey, another very modest general who shied publicity. His role in the Rhineland campaign was secondary as his forces were being kept back for the Rhine Crossing. Mongomery's third army commander was the American LtGen Bill Simpson, whose US 9th Army would handle the southern part of Montgomery's Rhineland operation. Simpson's army was the youngest of them all, having joined the campaign in north-west Europe towards the end of 1944. Tall, bald, amiable, Simpson was a good subordinate to both Montgomery and Bradley, keeping himself above politics and personalities, being content to fight his army to the best of his ability, no matter whom he reported to.

Bradley's army commanders presented two contrasting styles. At the head of the US 1st Army was LtGen Courtney Hodges, who had taken over the formation when Bradley was promoted to army group commander. Hodges had been Bradley's deputy and understudy and slipped into the command of 1st Army with ease, continuing to fight the army in the mould of Bradley: cautious, dependable and thorough. In complete contrast was LtGen George Patton with his US 3rd Army. 'Old Blood and Guts' Patton was certainly the exception of all the major Allied generals. A cavalry man, he was an outstanding practitioner of mobile warfare, believing in employing bold tactics and always being on the offensive. Patton commanded a corps in North Africa and Sicily, and came close to being returned to the USA as a result of his forceful and bullying manner. Eisenhower gave him a chance to redeem himself with the 3rd Army in north-west Europe and his successful performance and wide sweeping thrusts into the German-occupied territory made him immensely popular with the American press. His tactics of pushing forward at any cost certainly caused unease in the enemy camp. Many German commanders considered Patton to be the best of the Allied generals.

The US 7th Army, commanded by LtGen Alexander Patch, was part of Devers' 6th Army Group. Patch had arrived in the European theatre after successfully commanding US forces against the Japanese at Guadalcanal in the Pacific. Together with the French 1st Army under Gen Jean de Lattre de Tassigny, the US 7th Army landed along the coast of southern France in August 1944 and advanced up the Rhone valley in pursuit of the German 19th Army.

GERMAN COMMANDERS

At the head of the German army was Adolf Hitler. He exercised total command over every strategic decision. By 1945 his health had deteriorated and he was a broken man, yet he still kept a very tight hold on the German conduct of the war. As a result, every major decision, and many minor ones, had to be agreed by him. His main strategy at that point was that Germany was to be defended at all costs and the Rhine was to remain inviolate: there was to be no retreat. It mattered little that tactics might demand a realignment of the front, his generals made such withdrawals at their peril. His contribution to the campaign was negative and ultimately aided the Allies more than his own side. Hitler's greatest mistake was to force his generals to squander their strength in front of the Rhine, rather than to get behind the river and use the obstacle as a defensive moat, where his mobile reserves could pinch off any attempted crossing.

At the head of the German forces facing the Allies was GFM Gerd von Rundstedt, Commander-in-Chief West. One of the old school of professional German soldiers, Von Rundstedt commanded army groups during the campaigns in Poland in 1939 and France in 1940. After the victory in France he was promoted to field marshal and commanded Army Group South during the invasion of Russia. He was sacked by Hitler for staging a tactical retreat at Rostov, but was later reinstated to take over Army Group West in France in order to head off the likely Allied invasion. After the July Plot of 1944 he was again dismissed by Hitler, only to be restored to command once again in the West prior to the Ardennes offensive. He was one of the most offensive-minded of the German generals, but by 1945 had realised that the war was lost and could only be prolonged by withdrawing behind the Rhine.

Confronting the Allies along the German border Von Rundstedt had lined up Army Groups H, B and G. At the head of Army Group H, having taken over the formation early in February 1945, was GenObst Johannes Blaskowitz, a veteran commander of armies in Poland and Russia. Blaskowitz was one of the most senior German generals but blighted his career when he ran foul of Hitler with his criticism of the SS in occupied Poland. A professional of the old school like Von Rundstedt, Blaskowitz soldiered on from an obstinate sense of duty. Even though he was discredited by his leader, his professional pride remained intact and he fought his army with all the power that was available.

The commander of Army Group B was, in great contrast to Blaskowitz and Von Rundstedt, a confirmed Nazi. Generalfeldmarshall Walther Model was a favourite general of Hitler's who had risen to fame through his exploits in Russia, being promoted from command of a division to army commander within months. Model was regarded as being one of the major defensive strategists of the war. His handling of army groups during the retreat in Russia and the stabilisation of the Western Front in the autumn of 1944, helped preserve the strength of the dwindling German army. He was on the spot during the Arnhem operation and was able to organise the local units swiftly in order to contain the British attack. Against his better judgement he was ordered to carry out the ill-fated Ardennes offensive and could not be blamed for its failure. Model was one of the best of the younger generation of generals.

GenObst Johannes Blaskowitz, Commander Army Group H, was an infantryman of the old school and one of the most senior German generals. He commanded the German 8th Army in the war against Poland and was later head of the army of occupation there. It was in Poland that he became appalled at the conduct of the SS and sent a note about their conduct to Brauchitsch and Jodl. Hitler got to hear of it and the incident blighted Blaskowitz's career. He was passed over during the grand promotions of 1940, when many generals junior to him were elevated to field marshal. He was not given another fighting command for the next four years until after the Allies landed in Normandy in 1944. (Imperial War Museum)

Commanding Army Group G was GenObst der Waffen-SS Paul Hausser. Another veteran of the old Imperial Army, Hausser retired as a lieutenant general in 1932 but came back into service in 1934 in order to organise the training of the Waffen SS. He gave good account of himself later in the war during the fighting in Russia in command of the SS Panzer Corps at Kursk. He led the II SS Panzer Corps in France against the British and later became the first SS officer ever to command an army when he took over the German 7th Army.

Lined up along the German border facing the Allies were six German armies: 1st Parachute Army, 15th Army, 5th Panzer Army, 7th Army, 1st Army and 19th Army. Commanding the 1st Parachute Army was Gen der Fallschirmtruppen Alfred Schlemm, a veteran with an outstanding fighting record. A divisional field commander in Russia, Schlemm became Student's Chief of Staff in Crete. He was then given I Parachute Corps in Italy. He stoutly defended the Anzio perimeter after the Allied landings and then performed a series of remarkable defensive actions during the retreat up the Italian mainland.

The German 15th Army had Gen der Infanterie Gustav von Zangen at its head. General von Zangen commanded the 17th Infantry Division in Russia in 1942, a corps in France during 1943 and an army detachment in Italy before he moved into the command of 15th Army on the Western Front. General der Panzertruppen Hasso von Manteuffel was in command of 5th Panzer Army. Manteuffel had led Rommel's old 7th Panzer Division in Russia, and was at the head of the 5th Panzer Army during the Ardennes campaign. Another army commander who had been present during Hitler's winter offensive was Gen der Panzertruppen Erich Brandenberger. He still commanded the 7th Army opposite the Americans and had previously led the 8th Panzer Division during the invasion of Russia. Holding the far south of the line, opposite the American 6th Army Group on the upper Rhine, were the German 1st and 19th Armies. The 1st Army was led by Gen der Infanterie Hermann Foertsch, and the German 19th Army was commanded by Gen der Panzertruppen Hermann Balck.

GFM Walther Model, Commander Army Group B, was a confirmed Nazi and one of Hitler's favourite generals. After a successful period in Russia where he rose from head of the 3rd Panzer Division to the command of both Army Group North Ukraine and Army Group Centre, he was recalled to the West to take over Army Group B in France. In December 1944 he undertook Hitler's Ardennes offensive, although he had grave doubts about its objectives. Model was one of the best of the German field generals; he had a great ability as a defence strategist and a sound understanding of the tactics of tank warfare. (Imperial War Museum)

OPPOSING ARMIES

The collapse of the Ardennes offensive in 1945 had left the German Army with an even greater sense of despair than it had felt when the Allies had first arrived at the Reich border. Morale was low; units were dramatically under strength, equipment was poorly maintained and new supplies were meagre, and spasmodic. A fanatical determination still prevailed throughout the forces, but each man knew that the war was almost certainly lost. There was nothing to fight for but the homeland. It was, however, a homeland that was being overrun, not only by the British and Americans, but by an even more terrifying horde from the East: the Russians had begun their new winter campaign and were pressing towards Berlin.

On paper the German forces facing the Allies along the Rhineland and down to the Swiss border still seemed formidable and quite comparable to those of their enemies. Commander-in-Chief West, Gerd von Rundstedt, in principle, controlled nearly 60 divisions. However, most of these German units had become just a pale shadow of their former strength and effectiveness, while the Allies' forces were still remarkably intact, albeit nominally under strength through earlier heavy fighting and reduced numbers of reinforcements. In western Europe Eisenhower had at his disposal 3 army groups, 9 armies, 20 corps and 73 divisions of which 49 were infantry, 20 armoured and 4 airborne. However, not all of these units were on the Western Front. Over three million Allied soldiers had been shipped into the war zone since June 1944. Great as the battles on the Western Front were, Germany had a

Exhausted German infantry captured by the Americans during their drive to the Rhine. The picture shows the desperate plight of the German Army at that time, with much of its number made up of old men and youths. (National Archives, Washington)

LEFT Troops of the 1st Battalion, 120th Regiment, from the US 30th Division near Wesel, in pursuit of the retreating 116th Panzer Division, during US 9th Army's drive to the River Rhine. The infantry are supported by an M24 'Chaffee' light tank, carrying a .3 inch (75mm) M6 gun. (National Archives, Washington)

Troops of the 15th Scottish
Division dug in on the side of the
road in front of Cleve. These men
of the Argyll and Sutherland
Highlanders were consolidating
the gains made during the first
two days of the Reichswald
battle, before launching their
attack on the town.
(Imperial War Museum)

much bigger adversary to deal with to the east. Facing the Russians Hitler had 133 German divisions and, in addition to this, there were 24 German divisions in Italy, 17 in Scandinavia and 10 in Yugoslavia.

The German Army of early 1945 was markedly different from the all-conquering legions that spread out across Europe at the beginning of the conflict. The great losses sustained during the drawn-out campaigns in Russia – on a scale and ferocity that dwarfed that of all other theatres of war – had crippled the German Army. Reinforcements had to be gleaned from a variety of sources, including enlisting Russian and east European prisoners. All this diluted the 'racial purity' of the original army and led to a sharp decline in standards. Fitness ideals had been relaxed and those with definite physical problems, such as loss of hearing and stomach ulcers, had been admitted into fighting units. Many of the German divisions had been raised on a reduced scale, with only two infantry regiments, instead of three, each containing only two infantry and two artillery battalions, instead of three. In contrast, Allied divisions were raised with a full complement of men, equipment, transport and support. The great manufacturing power of the major Allied nations ensured that this was so.

In manpower terms both sides were having to dig deep to provide reinforcements. The British were the most sorely pressed, having had to resort to disbanding units to provide replacements for the fighting divisions. The USA was also under serious pressure having to deal with competing claims for new divisions not only from western Europe, but from those armies fighting in the Italian and Pacific theatres; they also wanted new blood. In late January there were only six divisions left in the USA that had been scheduled to be sent overseas, four of which were

Infantry from US 9th Division watch a demonstration, early in February 1945, of the use of a 2.36 inch (660mm) anti-tank rocket launcher M9A1–the bazooka. The M9A1 fired a 3.4lb (1.53kg) hollow charge rocket and had a maximum range of 400 yards (364m). Almost half-a-million bazookas were built during the war.
(National Archives, Washington)

earmarked for Europe. However, the Germans still had reserves on which to draw, for in January 1945 Hitler decreed that older men up to 45 years of age should be shifted from industry to the armed forces. In February eight new divisions were created, many of them made up of youths just turned 17. So fanatical was their indoctrination, the Germans were able to convert these raw recruits into dangerous and effective defenders in just a few weeks.

The individual soldier fighting for the Allies was well fed, well equipped and well clothed compared to his German opponent. The large supply train that led back across Europe to the sea shipped forward, right to the front line, vast amounts of stores providing for all his needs and a great many of his comforts. The quantity and quality of the supplies sustaining the Allied armies in the field could only be dreamed of by the Germans. In almost every measure, the Allies were superior to their enemy: in numerical terms, they had three times the artillery, ten times the number of tanks, four times the aircraft and two-and-a-half times the number of troops. Their superiority in the design of battle-worthy equipment was not so apparent, with the Germans having two world-beating tanks, the Panther and the Tiger, an excellent multipurpose artillery piece, the notable 0.34 inch (88mm) and very effective lower calibre infantry weapons such as the MG42 and Panzerfaust. The standard Allied tank, the Sherman, was no match head-to-head with the German main battle tank, but it was present on the battlefield in such numbers that it was always the most effective. The British 25-pdr (11.25kg) field gun, supporting every divisional attack, was probably the best in the world.

In the air, the German Luftwaffe still had a large number of aircraft – over 5,000 operational in November 1944 – but was really a spent force. It did manage to put over 1,000 planes into the air on New Year's Day 1945 over northern France, Belgium and The Netherlands, in support of the Ardennes offensive, but the effort proved to be a last show of strength that could never again be repeated. A shortage of trained pilots and difficulties in the supply of aviation fuel grounded all but a few sporadic fighter bombers carrying out hit-and-run attacks. In contrast, the Allies could muster a tremendously powerful air armada. In close support of ground troops were six tactical air commands. The British 2nd Tactical Air Force supported the British and Canadians, whilst the 1st French Air Corps aided the French 1st Army. The Americans had the IX, XI, XIX and XXIX Tactical Air Commands providing support for the US 1st, 7th, 3rd and 9th Armies. All of this was backed by 11 groups of medium and light bombers of the IX US Bomber Command. And behind all this were the mighty US Eighth Air Force and the fighters and bombers of the Royal Air Force; in total 17,500 first-line combat aircraft could be called upon to harass the enemy.

The reality of defeat that permeated the German Army in 1945 dictated that its strategy would have to be one of defence. It had once been the best offensive army that the world has ever seen, but events had overtaken the army of the 'Blitzkrieg' and it now had to employ the same tactics that it had derided its British and French enemies for practising during the glory days of 1940. The initiative is always in the hands of the attacker and it was hard for the Germans to have to react to the moves of its enemies, rather than to order the flow of the battle for themselves. Their goals and options were now simply to try to survive, just like the British did in 1940.

American troops from 102nd Division, US XIII Corps, raid German houses in Lovenich looking for mattresses with which to line their foxholes. Although looting was officially frowned upon, nothing could stop the infantryman acquiring anything that made his spartan life a little more comfortable. (National Archives, Washington)

OPPOSING PLANS

In late January Eisenhower presented his ideas for the further prosecution of the war. Although still maintaining his 'broad front' strategy with his first intention being to destroy the main elements of the German Army west of the Rhine and then to develop mobile operations east of the river, his main emphasis was to engineer the elimination of the great manufacturing area of the Ruhr. The thrust of the Allied advance would then be north-east through the north German Plain. This more or less consigned the decisive battle of the Rhineland to 21st Army Group since it was the nearest group to the Ruhr industrial area.

Eisenhower knew that when Montgomery launched his proposed attack south-east from the Nijmegen area through the narrow passage between the Maas and the Rhine, he would be attacking one of the most heavily fortified sectors of the Siegfried Line. This was the shortest route to the Ruhr, and Hitler knew it. The region was of such importance to the German war effort that any attempt to capture it was bound to provoke a desperate German reaction. Although Hitler had laid down that every metre of German soil was to be defended to the last, some parts had to be defended more than others. This was one of those sectors. Operation Veritable, as the attack was called, was sure to develop into a very costly and difficult one.

A Churchill bridging tank is brought forward through the Reichswald to tackle an anti-tank ditch. In the background is another Churchill with a fascine strapped to its front, ready to drop it into a stream or gully to provide a crossing place for armour. These ready-made bridges and fascines often rendered anti-tank defences immediately obsolete by enabling a crossing to be made of the obstacle within minutes. (Imperial War Museum)

A mortar team from 2nd Battalion Middlesex Regiment fires its 4.2 inch (107mm) mortar in support of the British 3rd Division during the attack on Kervenheim. The 4.2 inch (107mm) mortar was one of the heavy infantry weapons provided by a machine gun battalion to each infantry division. The Middlesex Regiment supplied heavy machine-guns and mortars via the four of its battalions who were attached to the 3rd, 15th, 43rd and 51st Infantry Divisions throughout the war in north-west Europe. (Imperial War Museum)

To help 21st Army Group succeed with 'Veritable' Eisenhower had given Montgomery one of Bradley's armies – Gen Simpson's US 9th Army – from US 12th Army Group. Simpson's forces would attack across the River Roer 60 miles (96km) to the south two days after the launching of 'Veritable', and then turn north to link up with Montgomery and help clear the way to the Rhine opposite the Ruhr. The combined armies would then launch an assault over the Rhine, once all the Allied forces had gained the west bank along its complete length, in order to encircle the great industrial area. The US 9th Army's attack across the Roer and subsequent advance was given the code name 'Grenade'.

While this great attack was taking place in the north, Eisenhower's other forces would continue to push back the enemy in front of the Rhine. Bradley's other two armies, the 1st and the 3rd, were faced by ground that was not suitable for mobile warfare, so the advance was planned to develop in stages. First the heavily forested high ground of the Eifel had to be cleared, then, to the south, the triangle of land between the confluence of the Saar and Moselle rivers had to be captured to bring Patton's 3rd Army up to the main fortifications of the Siegfried Line. But perhaps the most important immediate objective of US 1st Army, was the capture of the Roer dams. The seven dams controlled the flow of water along the River Roer in front of Simpson's US 9th Army. They were capable of flooding the whole of the low ground alongside the Roer producing a formidable water barrier should the Germans choose to destroy them. With the dams in German hands, Simpson could not attack across the river for fear of his rear being cut off by this rising water. The dams had to be captured before 'Grenade' could go ahead. They were, however, a formidable objective. The Americans had been trying to capture them (albeit often in a half-hearted way) since 15 December. Bradley was now told to redouble his efforts and seize them.

Next to Bradley's army group, to the south, was Devers' 6th Army Group. Devers had already reached the Rhine south of Strasbourg, but the Germans still had an expansive bridgehead, measuring 30 by 50 miles, (48 by 80km) on the west bank around the town of Colmar, known to the Allies as the Colmar 'Pocket'. Eliminating this bridgehead was essential to Eisenhower's plans to build a complete line along the Rhine before attempting any crossings of the river. The elimination of this pocket was begun in the final weeks of January by one American and five French divisions of Gen Jean de Lattre de Tassigny's French 1st Army.

The main handicap facing Von Rundstedt and his generals was Hitler's long-standing decree forbidding any voluntary withdrawal. With the bulk of the Siegfried defensive line still intact, Hitler felt that his policy of 'hold till the last' could be implemented by his troops. Not a

American infantry from 334th Infantry Regiment, inspecting a German 4.75 inch (122mm) schwere Feldhaubitze being used in an anti-tank role. The howitzer, a captured Russian artillery piece, had been in service with the Red Army since 1938 and was one of the most successful and reliable guns of the war. This particular gun had been captured on 1 March in a surprise night attack on the town of Boisheim by the US 84th Division, where the 334th's 3rd Battalion caught the whole garrison asleep. Eight of these guns covered the approaches to the town, but none had been manned during the night. (National Archives, Washington)

defensive bunker or pillbox was to be relinquished wittingly; each had to be prised from the defenders at great cost to the attackers. Hitler also delayed granting authority for preparing other defensive positions to the rear, fearing that these new fortifications would act as a fall-back zone of refuge to the forward troops and encourage retreat into them. The German Army would have to stand its ground and absorb the shock of the attack as best it could. It had already demonstrated an adeptness to soak up punishment; it would now have to exercise its proven ability to improvise, block, mend, and delay, just as it had done during the two preceding years in North Africa, Italy, France and Russia.

The German forces facing the Allies west of the Rhine were very thinly spread. They were, however, along much of their front, ensconced inside the fortifications of the Siegfried Line. Unfortunately for the Germans, this line was not as strong as Nazi propaganda had made out, as it had never been properly completed along its whole length, nor did it have the weapons and manpower that it was designed to have. If the strategy for which it had been planned had been implemented – fixed fortifications equipped with their full complement of men and guns, and with a mobile armoured reserve behind the line able to attack any Allied penetration – then the battles to clear the Rhineland might have been more equally balanced. As it was, there were just too few troops to deal with all the attacks along the front.

Von Rundstedt's three army groups barred the way into the Reich: in the north was Army Group H (Blaskowitz), in the middle Army Group B

(Model) and in the south was Army Group G (Hausser). Generaloberst Johannes Blaskowitz had control of two armies: the XXV Army (Von Blumentritt) in Holland which did not take part in the Rhineland battles and the I Parachute Army (Schlemm) holding the line inside Germany west of the Rhine from the ground opposite Nijmegen in the north to Roermond on the River Maas in the south, the ground over which the 'Veritable' and 'Grenade' offensives would strike. General der Fallschirmtruppen Alfred Schlemm's army consisted of four corps, three in the line and one as a mobile reserve. The bulk of these forces were in the northern sector covering the Rhine approaches, with the line most lightly held in the south opposite Venlo and Roermond. Schlemm was keeping his armour in a central position behind a weaker screen of infantrymen.

Generalfeldmarshall Walther Model, commander Army Group B, held the line opposite Bradley's American forces. Model knew that some American units had been shifted to the north and felt that the main American thrust would come in the area of Roermond, with the British 2nd Army attacking across the River Maas near Venlo. He also thought that Bradley would press on with his advance through the Eifel, continuing the moves that he had performed so well in clearing the last of the 'Bulge'. Model's forces consisted of XV Army (Von Zangen) in the North, V Panzer Army (Manteuffel) holding the centre and VII Army (Brandenberger) opposite Patton's US 3rd Army in the south.

Generaloberst der Waffen SS Paul Hausser, commander Army Group G, was using his armies to oppose LtGen Patch's US 7th Army Group. Häusser had two armies of his own: 1st Army (Foertsch) and 19th Army (Balck) to hold the Siegfried Line around Saarbrücken and the eastern banks of the southern Rhine.

The opposing sides then were lined up for a fight: the Allies in attack and the Germans in defence. Both sides knew that the key to the coming offensives was in the north, with the Germans not knowing exactly where the blow would fall, but having a good idea that it would be aimed at an early crossing of the Rhine and the capture of the Ruhr industrial area.

OPERATION VERITABLE

Field Marshal Montgomery had decided that 'Veritable' was to be planned and executed by Canadian 1st Army, under the command of LtGen Henry Crerar. The battle was to be the largest Allied offensive since Normandy. Crerar was to deploy his men along the front line south-east of Nijmegen close to the German border and to attack through the corridor between the Rhine and Maas rivers. Barring the way along this proposed route was the dense forest of the Reichswald, with just a small strip of land on either side available for forward movement: to the north the open land was barely a mile wide and bounded by the flooded River Rhine; to the south it was confined by the flooded Maas. Running across the path of the advance was one of the most difficult sections of the Siegfried Line's fortifications. Crerar's objective was to break through this defensive line and then unleash his armoured troops into the flat area of the Rhineland, heading south to meet up with the Americans and south-eastwards to seize the east bank of the Rhine. At this point the British 2nd Army (Dempsey) would join in the battle, crossing the Maas unopposed into areas already captured by Canadian 1st Army.

Crerar employed five divisions for the initial breakthrough: two Canadian divisions from Canadian II Corps (Simonds), the 2nd and 3rd Infantry Divisions, and three divisions from British XXX Corps (Horrocks), the 15th Scottish, 51st Highland and 53rd Welsh Divisions. The commander of Canadian 1st Army planned for two divisions to attack into the Reichswald (British 51st and 53rd Divisions) while two other divisions (Canadian 2nd and British 15th Divisions) provided flank

This scene of troops moving over frozen ground was taken on 21 January, 18 days before the start of 'Veritable'. During the planning stages of the operation, it was hoped to make the attack over frozen ground so that tanks could advance with the infantry and wheeled traffic could move freely. The thaw that set in just a few days before the start of 'Veritable' resulted in a battle that was handicapped by the mud almost as much as by the enemy. (Imperial War Museum)

Commander British 21st Army Group, FM Montgomery, with the men who ran 'Veritable'. From left to right: MajGen C. Vokes (Canadian 4th Armored Division), Gen Harry Crerar (Canadian 1st Army), Montgomery, LtGen Brian Horrocks (British XXX Corps), LtGen G. Simonds (Canadian II Corps), MajGen Dan Spry (Canadian 3rd Division) and MajGen A. Matthews (Canadian 2nd Division).
(Imperial War Museum)

BELOW Dead German infantryman of the 84th Division killed during the shelling at the start of 'Veritable' on 8 February. The man lies in a communication trench on the edge of the Reichswald which had been captured by the 5th/7th Gordon Highlanders, part of 51st Highland Division.
(Imperial War Museum)

protection outside of the forest to the north. The fifth division (Canadian 3rd Division) was to become waterborne and clear the enemy from the isolated fortified villages which had become stranded by the rising floodwaters, but whose artillery still constituted a sideways threat to those troops outside of the forest. All of the divisions were placed under the immediate command of LtGen Brian Horrocks of British XXX Corps. Once the breakthrough had been accomplished, the British 43rd Wessex Division and the Guards Armoured Division would be introduced into the battle with the intention of securing the line Gennep–Asperden–Cleve. This was the final objective of 'Veritable', from then on the battlefield would open out and a more mobile warfare would take place, albeit still within the confines of an area littered with extemporised fortifications, the most notable of which was the 'Hochwald Layback' which covered the approaches to Xanten and the Rhine bridges at Wesel.

A complicated deception plan had been engineered by the Canadians to mislead the enemy as to the location of the forthcoming attack. Road and radio traffic was increased to the west of Nijmegen along the River Waal and lower River Maas, to give the impression that the troops there were being reinforced in preparation for an attack northwards into Holland, towards Utrecht and Amsterdam. The actual build-up of forces opposite the Reichswald was prepared silently and with great ingenuity without alerting the Germans. When the offensive was finally launched, it was able to achieve total surprise to most of the German high command.

General Schlemm, however, believed that the Allies would take advantage of their presence over the River Maas near Nijmegen and launch an attack through the Reichswald. Blaskowitz would have none of it, for he was convinced that the attack would happen much farther south and refused Schlemm permission to move any extra troops northwards to strengthen the Reichswald area. None the less, Schlemm did slip three battalions of first-class paratroopers from 2nd Parachute Regiment (Lackner) into the forest to help bolster the defences of Gen Fiebig's 84th Infantry Division who were holding the line there.

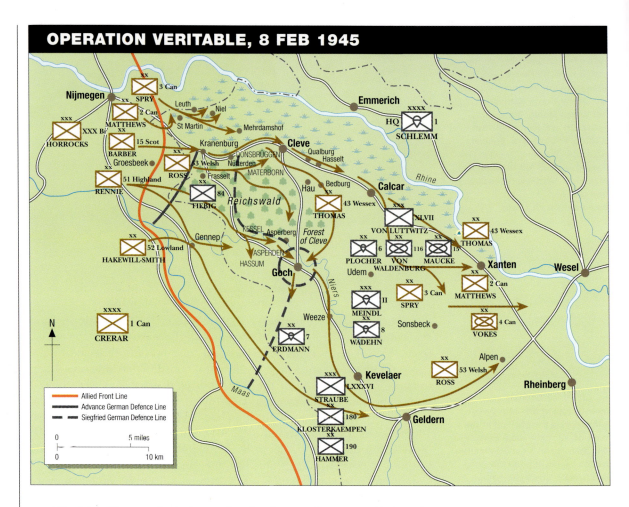

OPERATION VERITABLE, 8 FEB 1945

Allied intelligence had shown that in the northern area facing the Canadians there would be the three corps of Schlemm's 1st Parachute Army. Holding the line from the Rhine to Udem, but held back as the Wehrmacht's only mobile reserve, was the German XLVII Corps of Gen der Panzertruppen Heinrich Freiherr von Luttwitz, consisting of 6th Parachute Division (Plocher), 116th Panzer Division (Von Waldenburg) and the 15th Panzer Grenadiers (Maucke). From Udem to Weeze was II Parachute Corps commanded by GenLt Eugen Meindl with 7th Parachute Division (Erdmann), 8th Parachute Division (Wadehn) and 84th Infantry Division (Fiebig) under his control. General der Infanterie Erich Straube commanded the LXXXVI Corps who were responsible for the line from the south of Weeze to the south of Venlo. The corps comprised 180th Infantry Division (Klosterkemper) and 190th Infantry Division (Hammer).

Many of Schlemm's formations were not at the front but were held back from the line, waiting for any Allied penetration. The whole scheme of the Siegfried Line was that its forward outer line was held by light troops whose purpose was to slow down the attack for long enough for reinforcements to be rushed into the contested area to man the main second-line defences. Thus, although the Reichswald front itself was held by only one division, the 84th, Gen Schlemm could get two parachute, one panzer, and one panzer grenadier divisions to its aid within a day.

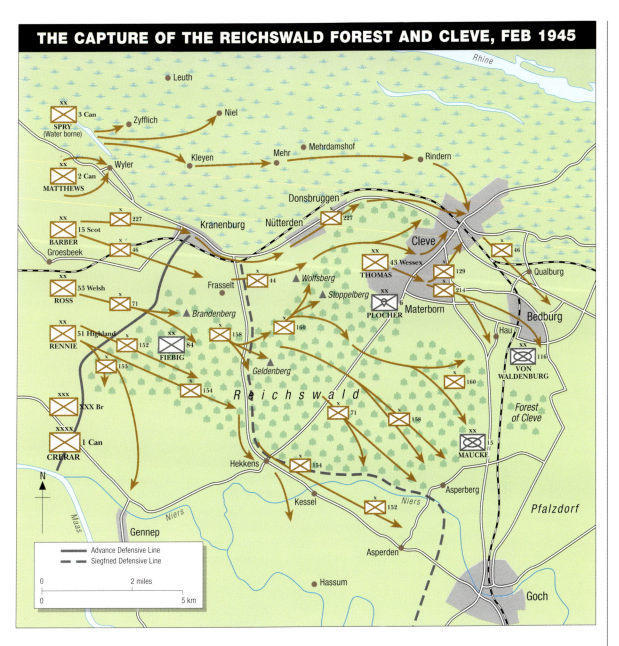

During the planning stages of 'Veritable', Gen Crerar knew that there would be two great questions hanging over the battle. The first concerned the weather. The winter of 1944/45 had been harsh and much of the planning had taken place with a background of frequent snow falls and hard frosts. The ground in northern Germany was frozen solid. This was perfect for operations, but if the weather thawed and the terrain turned to mud, the offensive would be severely hampered. In the event the cold weather did not hold; a rise in temperature a few days before the start of the operation, and the onslaught of heavy rains, turned the battlefield into a quagmire. In delaying the start of the offensive until early February, the advantage provided by the cold frozen ground was lost.

The other worrying question concerned the attack by Simpson's 9th Army. His assault across the River Roer – Operation Grenade – was

scheduled to take place two days after the launch of 'Veritable', just long enough later to throw the Germans off balance. But there could be no crossing of the river until the Roer dams had been captured by US 1st Army and the threat of flooding removed. Simpson could not afford to have the rear of his army cut off from its supply base by rising water. Would the dams be captured in time? It was important that the two offensives be mutually supporting, for if Simpson could not attack, then Montgomery's forces would draw German reinforcements onto their front which would make for a very difficult fight indeed.

Operation Veritable got underway on 8 February, heralded by a night-time bomber raid on Cleve and Goch in which both towns were completely destroyed. Further raids on Emmerich, Calcar, Udem and Weeze contributed to the disruption of enemy communications. As soon as the last bomber headed for home the massed artillery began their bombardment of preselected targets in the path of the Canadian advance, firing the heaviest barrage employed by the British during the war. These guns were later joined by the aimed fire of tanks, anti-tank guns, rocket projectors, mortars and machine guns, concentrating on

targets close to the start line. After five-and-a-half hours' continuous fire, the barrage began to lift and the infantry moved forward.

Facing the troops as they advanced across the open ground were the outer layers of the Siegfried Line, Hitler's great Westwall. These outpost positions consisted of extensive minefields followed by a double line of trenches protected by an anti-tank ditch, just in front of the Reichswald. Every farmhouse and village near the forest had been converted into a strong-point, with reinforced cellars and gun emplacements built into them. These makeshift bunkers were all interconnected with communication trenches stretching back into the woods. Roads were blocked with concrete and steel obstacles, covered by anti-tank guns. Three miles (4.8km) further into the Reichswald were the main defence lines, with concrete pillboxes and reinforced bunkers, barbed-wire entanglements, tank traps and emplaced guns. The lines ran through the forest from north to south and extended beyond the limits of the woods, linking up with the flooded Rhine and Maas rivers, completely barring any passage. Spurs of these lines connected up to the fortified towns of Cleve and Goch creating an area of almost impenetrable fortifications. Manning the defences were the German 84th Infantry Division, commanded by GenMaj Heinz Fiebig. The division consisted of about 10,000 men, but contained many substandard units including men grouped together with specific health problems such as the 'Magen' battalion of men with stomach problems, and the 'Ohren' battalion of troops with poor hearing. Volkssturm units, made up of local men aged from 16 to 60 who were capable of bearing arms, were also present in the division. The brutal fact was that these troops were expendable, manning defences which would inevitably crumple under the weight of an Allied attack, but which would delay the advance long enough for seasoned troops to be brought into the line.

The Canadian attack began with four divisions at 1030hrs, when the artillery barrage lifted and rolled forward in front of the advancing troops. The Canadian 2nd Division, commanded by MajGen A. B. Matthews, attacked on the extreme left flank of XXX Corps, making for the village of Wyler in order to open up the Nijmegen–Cleve road.

OVERLEAF **By blowing dykes and opening dams, the Germans flooded the lower Rhine valley forming a seemingly impenetrable area of low-lying flood land on the border of Holland and Germany. This area linked with the formidable fixed defences of the Siegfried Line effectively blocked the northern route into Germany.**

3rd Canadian Division was given the task of securing the flooded area on the left flank of the main British/Canadian thrust – Operation Veritable. This entailed assaulting enemy-held isolated villages which appeared as islands in the flat waterlogged landscape. Dotted through the still waters were buildings and farms, some of which were fortified by the enemy into well-defended strong points.

Tony Bryan. 04/00

The road was reached without too much difficulty, but it took until 1830hrs in the evening before it was cleared. On their right were the 15th Scottish Division commanded by MajGen Barber, supported by 6th Guards Tank Brigade, with their axis of advance being along the road towards Cleve. As the troops came to grips with the enemy they found the defenders dazed and overwhelmed by the long bombardment. Opposition was at first slight, with the main delay caused by the minefields. Resistance stiffened, however, as the advance progressed.

Because of the narrowness of the front allocated to 15th Division, only a small part of its strength could be employed at first, but progress was maintained which allowed the right-hand of the division – the 46th Brigade – to take the village of Frasselt, overlooking Kranenburg, by early evening. The left-hand of the Scottish Division, the 227th Brigade, fared less well initially when the Germans manning the defences in front of them put up a stubborn resistance. The Argyll and Sutherland

Highlanders lost every officer in its forward company within minutes. Most of the supporting tanks were bogged down in the mud, but relentless pressure applied by the Scotsmen allowed progress to be made and the town of Kranenburg was occupied by 1700hrs. The main road between Kranenburg and Cleve was waterlogged to a depth of several feet and stoutly defended, so the advance temporarily switched inland. The division's new thrust employed its reserve brigade, the 44th, to break through the Siegfried defences and seize the heavily defended area around Nutterden and open the main road into Cleve. It was then intended for the remaining two brigades to attack Cleve itself. Once the town had fallen, the 43rd Wessex Division, commanded by MajGen Ivor Thomas, would pass through and exploit the open ground beyond, wheeling south towards Goch at the rear of the Reichswald, outflanking any German defenders holed up in the forest.

The 44th Brigade intended to attack the fortifications of the Westwall with their armoured breaching force, which consisted of Churchill tanks of the Grenadier Guards, flame-throwing Crocodile tanks and a battery of self-propelled guns. In the event, much of this armour was bogged down either in the mud or in the vast traffic jams that clogged the roads forward. Enough striking force did, however, get forward to join in the attack and Nutterden was reached in the early hours of the next morning after protracted fighting.

To the right of the 15th Division were the two units making the frontal assault on the Reichswald: the 53rd Welsh Division under the command of MajGen R. K. Ross and 51st Highland Division commanded by MajGen T. G. Rennie. These two divisions came out of the smoke at 1030hrs, following closely behind the rolling barrage, and plunged into the forest. The Welsh Division was on the left of this attack next to the Scottish Division and advanced with 71st Brigade up front across an open valley against little opposition. The brigade traversed the anti-tank ditch and swept into the north-west angle of the Reichswald, taking its objective, an area of high ground called the Brandenburg Height, at **301**

1400hrs. Tank support had mostly bogged down in the thick mud during the advance, although some Churchill tanks had got through and kept up with the forward troops. 160th Brigade now took over the front and made it to the main part of the Siegfried defences around midnight.

The Welsh Division's neighbour to the south was the 51st Highland Division. It had the most difficult of all the fighting that day, having to clear a wide sector of the front from a narrow base. Major-General Rennie attacked with a reinforced 154th Brigade, but had the misfortune to meet the paratroopers of the 2nd Parachute Regiment (Lackner) that Schlemm had moved there just days before. The division did not reach the edge of the forest until night was falling. Here 152nd Brigade took over the advance and plunged through the breach and into the woods, spending the rest of the night clearing a path. 153rd Brigade now entered the fight and forced itself onto the high ground at the south-west corner of the Reichswald, although its start had been delayed by the traffic of 152nd Brigade moving forward.

The fighting on the first day of 'Veritable' had not reached all of the initial objectives, but XXX Corps had made a promising start. The Canadian 3rd Division, commanded by MajGen Dan Spry, now began its part in the offensive when it took to the water in Buffaloes and began clearing the fortified villages to the north of the 15th Division. The blown dykes on the Maas and Rhine had created vast inland waterways. These waterlogged areas were obviously a problem to the advance, but they did aid the Canadians in one sense: the depth of water covering the deadly minefields and tank traps allowed the Buffaloes, full of infantry, to sail over the worst of the fixed defences with impunity. Spry's 'water rats' chugged out into the darkness to make waterborne assaults on the marooned islands which were isolated from each other in the floodwater. Many of these villages were well defended and it was a particularly difficult and costly task for the Canadians to clear them of the enemy, but by first light the Canadian infantry had captured all of its objectives and continued with its sweep to clear the flooded flat lands.

All along the front fighting went on throughout the night. In some places the main defenders had fallen back into the prepared bunkers of

A knocked-out Valentine XI tank has succumbed to the rising waters along the Nijmegen–Cleve road just after the opening of 'Veritable'.
(Imperial War Museum)

the Westwall, while elsewhere, especially against the Highland Division, seasoned troops clung on tenaciously to every last piece of ground. When morning came, the advance continued. The Canadian 2nd Division had been 'pinched' out of the attack as the front narrowed around Kranenburg. The 15th Division, with flank protection supplied by the 'naval' forces of Canadian 3rd Division, resumed its advance towards Cleve. Although a few hours behind schedule, Gen Horrocks believed that it was time to call up the 43rd Division to exploit the capture of the town. He put it on one hour's notice to move from midday and signalled for the Scotsmen to 'press forward'.

The Canadian Army's attack had caused consternation in the German camp. Was this the start of the long-awaited offensive in the north or just a spoiling attack made to take attention away from the site of a bigger assault across the Maas in the south? Those commanders in the area – Fiebig, Straube and Schlemm – believed the former, while higher command were not convinced. Schlemm did, however, persuade his army group commander, Blaskowitz, to release the 7th Parachute Division, commanded by GenLt Wolfgang Erdmann, for the battle. Elements of this division were rushed forward to bolster the eastern defences of Cleve, especially the high ground to the west of Materborn.

The Materborn feature was also the objective of the 15th Scottish Division on the second day of the battle. The Scotsmen arrived on the western side of the feature just as the German 7th Parachute Division arrived on the eastern face. The two sides clashed with great force on a spur called the Bresserberg. A severe firefight took place throughout the day which resulted in the Scottish Division achieving control of the whole of the Materborn feature. Reconnaissance patrols found that Cleve seemed to be lightly held by dazed German troops and Horrocks received reports that the 15th Scottish were moving into the outskirts of the town. These optimistic reports convinced the corps commander that it was time to introduce the 43rd Wessex Division into the battle. This was a bad move.

At this point on the second day the whole front was suffering from the complete collapse of the roads in the rear. The main Nijmegen–Cleve road was flooded by the ever rising water from the

blown dykes and was difficult to negotiate, as it was impossible to move off the road due to the surrounding waterlogged ground. Other roads forward were either secondary roads that were lightly metalled and beginning to disintegrate, or sandy tracks which had been reduced to seas of glutinous mud. The heavy rain of the past few days showed little sign of stopping. Great traffic jams began to build up as tanks, troops and supplies tried to make their way forward. The battle was becoming a logistical nightmare. It was into this chaos that 43rd Division now attempted to get forward to exploit the breakthrough. The axis of the 43rd's advance, the Nijmegen–Cleve road, was already in use by the forward units of the 15th Division, who were trying to fight a difficult battle. The arrival of the Wessexmen and their transport led to a foul-up of monumental proportions.

Elsewhere on the battlefield slow progress was being made. The Welsh Division had pushed on with 160th Brigade to take two more features in the Reichswald – the Geldenburg and the Stoppelburg – cutting the minor road which passed through the forest from Kranenburg to Hekkens, and had reached the northern edge of the Reichswald alongside 15th Division with the 158th Brigade. The Highland Division continued its advance within the forest with 152nd Brigade, brushed aside a German counter-attack, and had reached the Kranenburg–Hekkens road. Outside, to the south of the Reichswald, 153rd Brigade moved over open country towards Gennep alongside the River Maas. Thus by the end of the second day, most of the original objectives had been taken. With the Americans due to launch 'Grenade' the next day, 10 February, Horrocks could afford to take some risks to keep the operation on schedule, for the attack across the Roer in the south would at least stop German reinforcements being moved north against him and might well attract some German units away from him.

Before Operation Grenade could start, however, there was the matter of the Roer dams to consider. Simpson had his 9th Army lined up against the River Roer ready to attack across it and link up with Montgomery, but he could not risk committing his troops over the river with the dams still intact or uncaptured. It was clear that should he do so, the Germans would blow the seven dams and release the 3,920 cubic feet

(111 million cubic metres) of water to create a vast floodland which would isolate his forces over the river for days or even weeks. The dams had to be captured.

The problem of the Roer dams had been appreciated since the previous November when 9th Army arrived on the river, but they were located in 1st Army's zone. It was difficult to get anyone to take their capture seriously enough to make it a high priority. Attempts by the RAF were made to bomb the dams, but other than superficial damage to the Erft dam, the raids were not successful. In early December Hodges gave the problem over to Gen Gerow's US V Corps. On 13 December Gerow's troops attacked towards the dams. The assault did not lack strength, consisting as it did of three divisions – 8th, 78th and 99th Infantry Divisions – plus the 102nd Cavalry Group and a combat command from 5th Armored Division, but the whole scheme lacked impetus and failed to get anywhere near the objectives.

The seven dams were located in the heart of the Westwall, with two belts of fortifications guarding the large backwaters behind them. The whole area was a network of steep-sided gorges and small mountains, covered in pine trees and deep with snow. The roads were narrow and winding, with virtually each bend covered by an enemy pillbox. Progress along the mountainsides was extremely slow and hazardous. The three-pronged attack on the dams immediately ran into trouble as it battered the bunkers of the first belt of the Siegfried Line. After three days of fighting, and with the loss of 2,500 men (half of whom were non-battle casualties), the penetration achieved no more than 2 miles (3.2km). On the fourth day of the operation things ground to a complete halt. The attack had the misfortune to run headlong into the opening moves of Hitler's great Ardennes offensive. The 'Battle of the Bulge' had started.

It took until the end of January 1945 for US 1st Army to push the enemy back to the line they held at the start of their offensive. Only then could the problem of the Roer dams be once again considered. By that time planning for the 'Veritable'/'Grenade' attack was well in hand. It was clear to everyone now that the dams had to be captured before the great push in the north could be undertaken. Preliminary moves to achieve this were made on 30 January. On 2 February, Gen Heubner

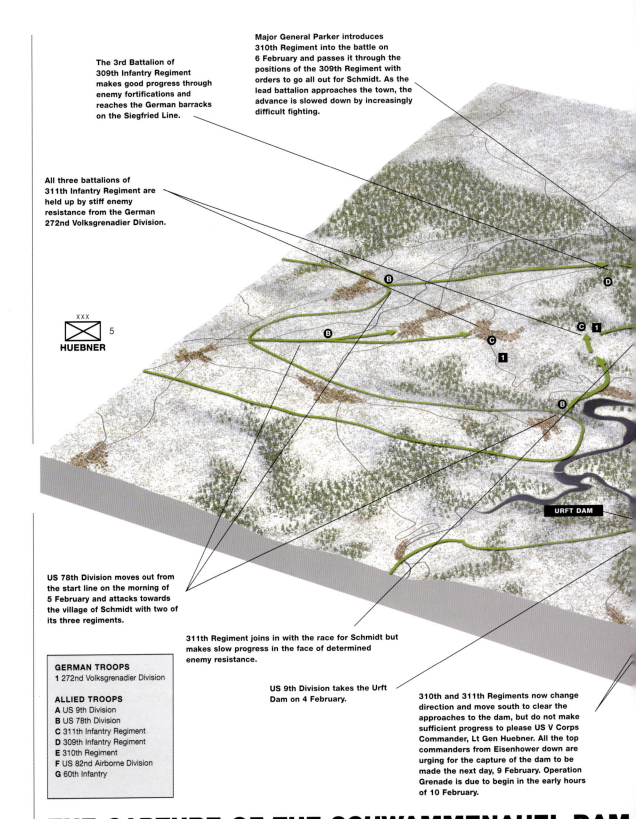

The 3rd Battalion of 309th Infantry Regiment makes good progress through enemy fortifications and reaches the German barracks on the Siegfried Line.

Major General Parker introduces 310th Regiment into the battle on 6 February and passes it through the positions of the 309th Regiment with orders to go all out for Schmidt. As the lead battalion approaches the town, the advance is slowed down by increasingly difficult fighting.

All three battalions of 311th Infantry Regiment are held up by stiff enemy resistance from the German 272nd Volksgrenadier Division.

HUEBNER

URFT DAM

US 78th Division moves out from the start line on the morning of 5 February and attacks towards the village of Schmidt with two of its three regiments.

311th Regiment joins in with the race for Schmidt but makes slow progress in the face of determined enemy resistance.

US 9th Division takes the Urft Dam on 4 February.

310th and 311th Regiments now change direction and move south to clear the approaches to the dam, but do not make sufficient progress to please US V Corps Commander, Lt Gen Huebner. All the top commanders from Eisenhower down are urging for the capture of the dam to be made the next day, 9 February. Operation Grenade is due to begin in the early hours of 10 February.

GERMAN TROOPS
1 272nd Volksgrenadier Division

ALLIED TROOPS
A US 9th Division
B US 78th Division
C 311th Infantry Regiment
D 309th Infantry Regiment
E 310th Regiment
F US 82nd Airborne Division
G 60th Infantry

THE CAPTURE OF THE SCHWAMMENAUEL DAM
5 – 9 FEBRUARY 1945

309th Regiment is sent forward to take the village of Kommerscheidt and hold the left flank of the attack. The village is reached on 7 February, but is not cleared until the next day.

Paratroopers from the US 82nd Airborne Division attack from the north on 7 February in a move to force the Volksgrenadiers back from the area around Schmidt. On 8 February they assist 309th Regiment in taking Kommerscheidt.

On the day that Operation Veritable is launched 80 miles to the north (8 February), the capture of the great dam at Schwammenauel is still a distant objective. Schmidt is finally taken that day in a joint effort by 310th and 311th Regiments. Great pressure is now put on Gen Parker to move on to seize the dam.

KOMMERSCHEIDT

SCHMIDT

RIVER ROER

SCHWAMMENAUEL DAM

KONIG
272

PUECHLER
LXXIV

In desperation, Huebner puts Maj Gen Craig, commander US 9th Division, in charge of the attack and introduces his 60th Infantry Regiment into the battle. On 9 February Craig launches his effort to capture the dam. 60th Regiment sweeps around the dam to the east and 309th Regiment presses down the sides of the backwater directly at the Schwammenauel.

Just as darkness falls on 9 February, the 1st Battalion of 309th Infantry Regiment capture the dam, only to find that the enemy have blown the valves to release a controlled torrent of flood-water into the Roer Valley. Operation Grenade, due to begin in just eight hours time, is postponed.

N

(who had taken over command of US V Corps from Gen Gerow) gave MajGen Edwin Parker orders for his 78th Infantry Division to capture the village of Schmidt together with the largest and most important of all the dams, the Schwammenauel. Parker was told that the operation was the most vital at that time on the entire Western Front, as indeed it was.

The task was a tall order for the 78th Division who had only limited battle experience. Parker's division set out through the close country at 0300hrs on 5 February, just five days before the scheduled start of 'Grenade'. The next day the adjacent division, the 9th Infantry, had managed to capture the Erft dam intact and hopes were high for a successful operation. The 78th Division slipped through the outer pillboxes of the Westwall with little difficulty, then things went bad. The closely wooded country and the lack of any supporting fire made progress extremely slow. In an effort to achieve the breakthrough, Parker put all three of his regiments into the attack, urged on personally by his corps and army commanders. Armour tried to get up with the leading troops but the enemy covered all the routes.

Inexorably, time slipped by and the pressure for success rose. By 8 February – the day that 'Veritable' was launched – the 78th Division had still not taken Schmidt, the village overlooking the Schwammenauel dam. Shortly before noon, Hodges telephoned Heubner and expressed his dissatisfaction: Bradley, Simpson, Montgomery, Crerar and Horrocks were all waiting for news. Heubner piled on the pressure. He shifted a regimental combat team from 9th Division, together with the 9th's divisional commander, MajGen Louis Craig, across to Schmidt and told Craig to take over 78th Division's men and seize the Schwammenauel.

Despite the introduction of a new commander and a veteran unit, the going was slow again on 9 February. It was not until darkness had fallen that the leading regiment, 309th Infantry, approached the Schwammenauel. Sending two groups of the 1st Battalion onto the dam, one to cross over the top and one to move against the lower level, the structure was captured. Engineers searched for demolitions, expecting the Germans to blow the dam at any moment: small arms fire picked off the troops as they scrambled over buildings. Just after midnight, in the early hours of 10 February, they finally penetrated the lower tunnels and began looking for explosives. They found none. Enemy troops had done all the damage they intended to do: they had blown the machinery and destroyed the discharge valves. The damage did not cause a major cascade of water, but a steady and powerful flow that would create a long lasting flood all the way down the River Roer. The Schwammenauel's reservoir would take weeks to empty. Operation Grenade could no longer go ahead that day and was postponed.

Seventy miles (112.7km) to the north, 'Veritable' staggered on. Montgomery knew that with the Americans unable to launch their attack, the Germans would move troops up to the North to counter his attack now that it was safe for Von Rundstedt to do so. It was a setback which would cost the Canadians and British dearly, but in the final analysis, Monty was not too displeased. He was the overall commander for both operations and as long as Crerar could hold the enemy in the north, hammering away at him in a battle of blind attrition, the American operation, when it was launched, would be against much lighter opposition than first envisaged. As Montgomery said at the time: 'When Grenade is finally launched it should produce quicker results'. To bolster the forces available to Crerar, Montgomery gained two American divisions from Eisenhower to take over the line held by British 2nd Army's 52nd Lowland and 11th Armoured Divisions, and release the two units for the Rhineland operation.

So Horrocks pressed on into the Reichswald. On 10 February, the third day of the battle, the Welsh and Highland Divisions pushed on through and alongside the Reichswald. In the north of the battlefield, the 15th Scottish nibbled away at Cleve while the Canadian 3rd Division continued to hold the northern flank as waterborne infantry. The 43rd Wessex Division crawled its way through the traffic jam that had clogged all the routes forward and its leading brigade, 129th Brigade, tried to slip round the south of Cleve. In the darkness, it took a wrong turn, ended up in the town itself and was forced to fight a vicious battle, much to the surprise of the German defenders–and the 15th Scottish Division who were planning their own assault on the town. The Wessexmen were immediately embroiled in difficult street fighting, for the whole town was a smouldering ruin. The air-raids sanctioned by Horrocks at the start of the battle had flattened Cleve. All streets were choked with rubble; fallen buildings blocked every pathway and enormous craters provided perfect positions for the enemy defenders. There was no clear way through Cleve along the blocked highways, the route eastwards was completely closed. Horrocks' bombing of the city had backfired on him.

The capture of Cleve was one of the first and most important of the initial objectives assigned to 'Veritable'. Horrocks had hoped to have the town in his possession on the first day and to be able to exploit its possession in order to wheel southwards and take Goch. Enemy resistance all around the town was making this impossible. On this third day of the battle, new German units were coming into the line to bottle up the Canadian 1st Army in and around the Reichswald. One of the first to arrive was the German 6th Parachute Division commanded by GenLt Hermann Plocher. Advance elements of this division barred the way to the 53rd Welsh Division in the middle of the forest. The remainder of XLVII Corps (Von Luttwitz), the Wehrmacht's mobile reserve, was also committed to the battle. Seasoned panzer troops now began to replace the wrecked remnants of the German 84th Division who had taken the full force of the Allied attack. Resistance began to stiffen considerably.

The next few days saw a stand-up slogging match between the two opposing forces. For XXX Corps there were no quick gains to be had, just a few yards of waterlogged ground taken at a high price. To the men of both sides the battlefield resembled the worst days of World War I. They lived and fought in trenches and pillboxes, suffered tremendous artillery bombardments and struggled to keep dry in the appalling conditions. The rain was incessant. Supplies were difficult to get forward over roads that had collapsed under the pounding of the traffic. Everywhere the cloying mud bogged down the tanks, whilst flame and shot shattered the unwary. And all the while the pressure to get forward, to make progress and to move on did not let up.

Cleve was finally taken and cleared on the 11th by the Scottish Division together with the Canadian 3rd Division who had landed from their Buffaloes and advanced down the west bank of the Spoy Canal into the

Tony Bryan. 04/00

During the mid-afternoon of 11 February under an overcast sky, the 53rd Welsh Division made their attack on this German machine-gun post in the Reichswald Forest. It was the third day of the battle and the German defenders were falling back and moving rapidly to new defensive positions as they were forced to give up their previous ones. The defenders had therefore been in action continuously for three days and were becoming tired, depleted and disorganised.

The new defensive positions included improvised bunkers built of wood and sand bags, covered in earth; few of these such bunkers showed any signs of long occupancy. They were mostly equipped with weapons removed from bunkers on the western side of the forest just before they were overrun. German tactics were to delay the enemy for as long as possible and then retire to the next defensive position.

town. The presence of the 43rd Division to the south of the town was also having the desired effect; German forces were unable to stabilise the line and block the Wessex Division's steady progress around to the east. Fighting was hard, but little by little the Wessexmen gained the upper hand, although their long tail of vehicles, guns and supporting arms only added to the immobilised mass of troops and armour along the flooded road back to Kranenburg. Both the 43rd and 15th Divisions struggled with, and often against, each other to get their formations into a fighting position.

For XXX Corps, the next few days were spent slowly consolidating the ground taken by force, and applying relentless pressure to a stubborn enemy. The 53rd Division crossed the Cleve–Gennep road in the heart of the Reichswald, heading for both the eastern edge of the woods and the southern fringe that opened out onto the River Niers. The 51st Division attacked the important crossroads at Hekkens in the south of the forest, took the little hamlet and headed west for Gennep to clear the open land between the Reichswald and the Maas. The 43rd Division took the villages of Materborn, Hau and Bedburg and established itself clear of the suburbs of Cleve, facing south towards Goch. In the meantime, Von Luttwitz moved his two panzer divisions from XLVII Corps up to counter-attack and retake Cleve. The 15th Panzer Grenadier Division, commanded by GenMaj Wolfgang Maucke, positioned itself south of Cleve between the square Forest of Cleve and the Reichswald and sent a battle group into the woods towards the advancing Welshmen in an attempt to get to Cleve from the south. The clash was spirited and costly; the Welsh battalions held their ground with small arms and mortars while the divisional artillery pounded the attackers. The deluge of high explosives broke up the move and put the 15th Panzer Grenadiers to flight.

Generalmajor Siegfried von Waldenburg advanced with his 116th Panzer Division westwards to Bedburg, the village that had been just recently taken by the British 43rd Division. On 12 February Von Waldenburg hit the 43rd Division, but the attack, although heavy, lacked sufficient strength to break the Wessexmen. Overwhelming artillery fire decimated the Germans and broke up their advance. The German corps commander realised that Cleve could not be retaken and so Von Luttwitz went on the defensive. Schlemm ordered that XLVII Corps should hold a line extending from Hasselt on the Calcar road, along the Eselberg ridge just south of Bedburg to the edge of the north-west corner of the Forest of Cleve. Von Luttwitz deployed his divisions with the remnants of 84th Division on the right, the 15th Panzer Grenadiers on the left and elements of 116th Panzers supporting both of them. The German 346th Division, commanded by

Troops from the Highland Light Infantry of the 15th Scottish Division roll a large wooden swastika along the streets of Kranenburg just after its capture. The men intend to use the trophy as firewood. In the background, a British tank crewman dressed in an oversuit looks on.
(Imperial War Museum)

GenMaj Walter Steinmueller, newly arrived in the area, also joined the battle.

Now began the advance that turned 'Veritable'. Major-General Thomas was given orders to attack south with his 43rd Wessex Division and take Goch. The advance began on 13 February when the 5th Wiltshires, of 129th Brigade, pressed forward to the high ground south-east of Bedburg to secure a start line for their sister battalion, the 4th. This second battalion was ordered to capture the hamlet of Trippenburg and a vital set of crossroads. A heavy counter-barrage laid down by the enemy caught the 5th Wiltshires as they deployed and set off for the ridge, but they pressed on grimly and took the low heights. The 4th Wiltshires now passed through with the main attack. In driving rain the troops moved out across the slopes supported by the Shermans of 8th Armoured Brigade's Nottinghamshire Yeomanry. The heavy tanks with their narrow tracks soon found the thick mud impassable and most were bogged down. The Wiltshiremen struggled on in the face of withering fire from the German defenders. Devoid of armoured protection, the exposed infantry doggedly prodded home their attack. Trippenburg was reached as darkness fell and cleared by midnight. It had taken all day, but the outer crust of the Von Luttwitz defensive line had been pierced. During the night the 4th Wiltshires repulsed a counter-attack by paratroopers backed by Tiger and Mark IV tanks during which a complete company was overrun. In the morning 5th Wiltshires came forward and continued the attack. They struggled throughout the hours of daylight to cover just a few hundred yards to the vital crossroads. In front of them, the 15th Panzer Grenadiers made them pay dearly for every foot of ground taken. All senior officers of the battalion bar one were casualties. Shell-fire continued unabated. Night came and still the Wiltshires fought on, straining their way forward in the dark. Eventually their superhuman effort won the day and they took the crossroads, 400 yards (364m) east of the Forest of Cleve. They had suffered over 200 casualties.

Thomas now committed 130th Brigade into the battle. The lead battalion, 4th Dorsets, formed up under fire and set out for Goch. It was

the same as the previous two days: infantry pressing forward through ferocious defensive fire and tenaciously resisting countless enemy counter-attacks. A fresh new German formation, Battle Group Hutze, now loomed up before the Wessexmen. The infantry battle continued with machine gun, shell and mortar fire criss-crossing the area. As the Dorsets tired, the 7th Hampshires took over the advance. The fighting continued with equal ferocity. Day passed again into night, still the struggle went on, each side pounding the other in a slugging match that would eventually see one or the other collapse. Now the 5th Dorsets came forward and took up the gauntlet. As they struck out for their objective, counter-attacks came from the rear and hit the Hampshires, while withering fire from the enemy in the Forest of Cleve raked the 5th Dorsets' right flank.

Major-General Thomas had decided that all troops engaged on both sides were nearing the limit of their endurance. It was time for a bold stroke. He ordered 130th Brigade to push on its attack with all three battalions and capture a new start line 800 yards (728m) south-east of the Forest of Cleve. He now intended to launch the fresh 214th Brigade on a two-battalion front straight down the road to Goch. It was a masterful move timed to perfection. When, at 1520hrs on 16 February, the two lead battalions of 214 Brigade – 7th Somerset Light Infantry and 1st Worcestershires – arrived at the start line, 130th Brigade had only just captured it. They did not pause; the divisional artillery immediately opened up with a rolling barrage and the two new lead battalions surged out into the flat open countryside. The momentum of the attack, even though some of the armour was initially left behind, took the enemy by surprise. There was no let-up, most sections had the support of a tank from the 4th/7th Dragoon Guards which blasted every building and strong point they came across. Those whose tanks had not yet reached them pressed on regardless. Every German that resisted was shot dead. In the first two hours the 7th Somersets had advanced over 2,000 yards (1,820m), by nightfall they had covered 3,000 yards (2,730m). Alongside them, the 1st Worcestershires kept pace.

BRITISH 43RD (WESSEX) DIVISION ADVANCE TO THE GOCH ESCARPMENT, 13 – 17 FEBRUARY 1945

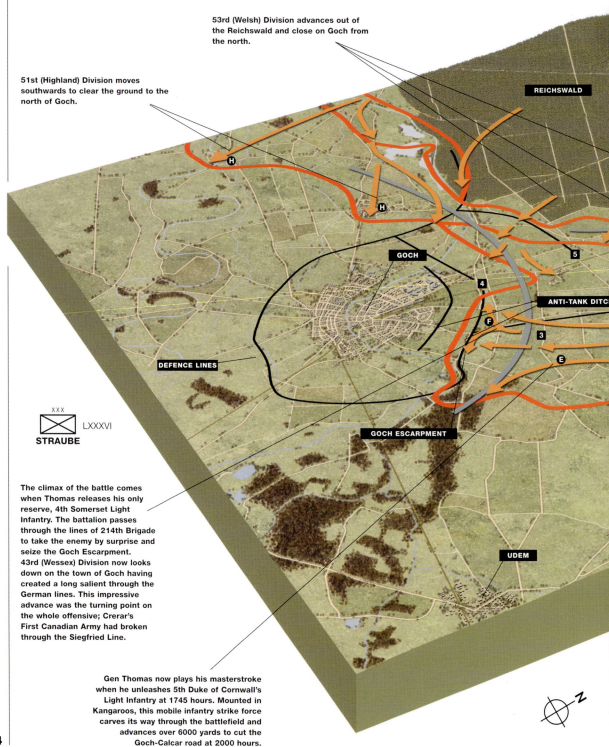

53rd (Welsh) Division advances out of the Reichswald and close on Goch from the north.

51st (Highland) Division moves southwards to clear the ground to the north of Goch.

REICHSWALD

GOCH

5

4

ANTI-TANK DITCH

F

3

E

DEFENCE LINES

XXX
LXXXVI

STRAUBE

GOCH ESCARPMENT

UDEM

The climax of the battle comes when Thomas releases his only reserve, 4th Somerset Light Infantry. The battalion passes through the lines of 214th Brigade to take the enemy by surprise and seize the Goch Escarpment. 43rd (Wessex) Division now looks down on the town of Goch having created a long salient through the German lines. This impressive advance was the turning point on the whole offensive; Crerar's First Canadian Army had broken through the Siegfried Line.

Gen Thomas now plays his masterstroke when he unleashes 5th Duke of Cornwall's Light Infantry at 1745 hours. Mounted in Kangaroos, this mobile infantry strike force carves its way through the battlefield and advances over 6000 yards to cut the Goch-Calcar road at 2000 hours.

N

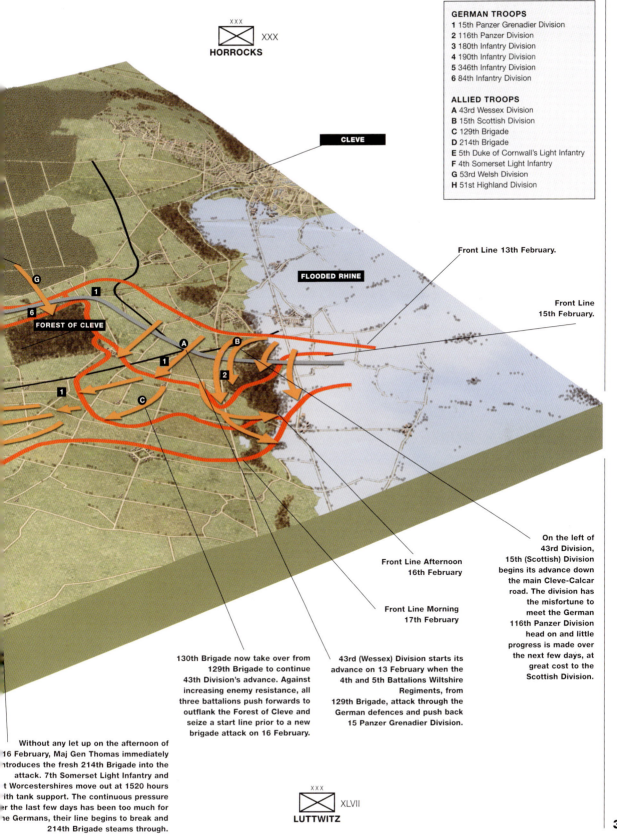

GERMAN TROOPS
1 15th Panzer Grenadier Division
2 116th Panzer Division
3 180th Infantry Division
4 190th Infantry Division
5 346th Infantry Division
6 84th Infantry Division

ALLIED TROOPS
A 43rd Wessex Division
B 15th Scottish Division
C 129th Brigade
D 214th Brigade
E 5th Duke of Cornwall's Light Infantry
F 4th Somerset Light Infantry
G 53rd Welsh Division
H 51st Highland Division

XXX
HORROCKS

CLEVE

FLOODED RHINE

FOREST OF CLEVE

Front Line 13th February.

Front Line 15th February.

Front Line Afternoon 16th February

Front Line Morning 17th February

On the left of 43rd Division, 15th (Scottish) Division begins its advance down the main Cleve-Calcar road. The division has the misfortune to meet the German 116th Panzer Division head on and little progress is made over the next few days, at great cost to the Scottish Division.

130th Brigade now take over from 129th Brigade to continue 43th Division's advance. Against increasing enemy resistance, all three battalions push forwards to outflank the Forest of Cleve and seize a start line prior to a new brigade attack on 16 February.

43rd (Wessex) Division starts its advance on 13 February when the 4th and 5th Battalions Wiltshire Regiments, from 129th Brigade, attack through the German defences and push back 15 Panzer Grenadier Division.

Without any let up on the afternoon of 16 February, Maj Gen Thomas immediately introduces the fresh 214th Brigade into the attack. 7th Somerset Light Infantry and Worcestershires move out at 1520 hours with tank support. The continuous pressure the last few days has been too much for the Germans, their line begins to break and 214th Brigade steams through.

XXX
XLVII
LUTTWITZ

315

Now Thomas played his masterstroke. The 5th Duke of Cornwall Light Infantry, its men mounted in Kangaroos (turretless tanks) and supported by B squadron of the 4th/7th Dragoon Guards, arrived at the village of Blacknik. They then deployed into five columns and headed due south, hell-bent for the villages of Imigshof, Bergmanshoff and Schroenshof, 6,000 yards (5,460m) ahead. In the words of the Brigade Commander, Brigadier Hubert Essame: 'This overwhelming stroke was too much for the enemy. In the dark and confusion, he went to ground.' The DCLI made it to the villages, turned out the defenders and cut the important road from Goch to Calcar, splitting the enemy defences in half. The 43rd Division's only reserve, the 4th Somerset Light Infantry, was now set loose to complete Thomas' plan. In a night attack, they surprised the enemy by slipping through the advance battalions and made for the escarpment overlooking Goch. Catching the German defenders completely by surprise, they seized the escarpment and had consolidated their possession of it by dawn. The 43rd Division now held the commanding ground looking down on Goch, just 1,000 yards (910m) away. It was the turning point in the battle.

The spectacular success of the Wessex Division in carving out a great salient in the German line, caused much consternation to the enemy and split his defences wide open, but he was stubbornly resisting everywhere else he was in contact with the Canadian 1st Army. In the Reichswald the Welsh Division had made it through the forest and broke out into the open overlooking the flank of the 43rd Division. Horrocks now ordered the division to close up with the 43rd and take the escarpment from east of the railway that led from Cleve to Goch. The 51st Highland Division, reinforced with the 32nd Guards Brigade from the Guards Armoured Division, had made steady progress along the ground between the Maas and the Reichswald, crossing the small River Niers and taking Kessel. It now pressed on up the Niers towards Goch. On the extreme right of the Highlanders, the 52nd Lowland Division had been introduced to the battle on 14 February, with instructions to advance alongside the Maas

Infantry from the 2nd Seaforth Highlanders of the British 51st Division advance through the Reichswald. In the background a Churchill Crocodile flame-thrower tank rumbles forward ready to deal with a strong point that the battalion had encountered during the advance. (Imperial War Museum)

from Gennep and take the villages of Afferden and Well and then swing behind Goch towards the east. Four divisions were now pressing Goch and its defence line: the heavily fortified town had now become the western cornerstone of the German defences. The German garrison in Goch included 180th and 190th Infantry Divisions together with the 2nd Parachute Regiment, all part of Gen Straube's LXXXVI Corps.

As the 43rd Division were approaching Goch, the 15th Scottish were pushing forward along the road from Cleve to Calcar. They ran into the 116th Panzer Division and suffered a bloody rebuff. The advance started on 12 February but two days of fighting saw 15th Division halted around the Moyland Woods. On the 14th some changes to the command structure were made by Gen Crerar. The fighting had moved past the narrow confines of the corridor between the Rhine and the Maas and the front was now opening up across the rolling land behind the Reichswald. Crerar now introduced the Canadian II Corps, under the command of LtGen Simonds, as a component force. Comprising the 15th Scottish Division and the Canadian 2nd and 3rd Divisions, Canadian II Corps took over the responsibility for the left wing of Canadian 1st Army. The Canadian 4th Armored Division and the British 11th Armoured Division were held in reserve to exploit any breakthrough.

Simonds withdrew the 15th Scottish from the Calcar road and replaced it with the two Canadian infantry divisions. The 3rd Division tried again for the Moyland Woods and spent several days attempting to take command of the Cleve–Calcar road. The 2nd Division meanwhile put in a set-piece attack on 19 February, striking south-east from Louisendorf to cross the Calcar–Goch road. Two battalions of the division crossed the road and consolidated for the night. Around midnight, they were counter-attacked by Battle Group Hauser, a combat team from the crack Panzer Lehr Division who had been refitting nearby in Marienbaum. Together with the 116th Panzer Division, Battle Group Hauser caught the Canadians just after they had sent their armour back for refuelling and rearming. The two battalions were all but wiped out and survivors were sent reeling. Through the night and into the next day the battle raged and the Germans gradually forced the Canadians back. In the late morning Sherman tanks from the Glengarry Horse and the Queen's Own Cameron Highlanders arrived and restored the balance. Then 17-pdr (7.65kg) anti-tank guns moved into position and attacked the exposed Jagdpanthers and the Germans began to falter. By the end of the afternoon, the Panzer divisions had started to pull back. The

German counter-attack had fizzled out through lack of strength, but the Canadians' advance had also been forced to halt. There was now a pause in the battle while Crerar worked out what the next moves might be.

Whilst the Canadians had been pressing towards Calcar, XXX Corps were poised to take Goch. The 43rd Division ensconced on the escarpment overlooking the town began bridging the anti-tank ditch at the base of the feature and on 8 February sent the 7th Somerset Light Infantry down into the outskirts of the town. The battalion actually got across a second anti-tank ditch in the suburbs and deployed within the town itself, regardless of their own division's artillery fire. But this attack was a diversion for the big event, for the two Scottish divisions, the 15th and the 51st, were assigned to the capture of the town. The next day, the 51st put in a two-brigade attack from west of the River Niers using the 152nd and 153rd, as the 15th Division, recently returned to XXX Corps from the Canadians, used its 44th Brigade to open the attack east of the Niers. Both attacks carried with them a great mechanised train of armoured support in the shape of tanks, bridge-carriers, Kangaroos, bulldozers, flame-throwers and guns. The artillery barrage that shot them forward was tremendous. The opening moves were slow against the concrete defences and dug-in emplacements, with the 15th Scottish meeting especially spirited resistance from the German defenders. The garrison commander, Col Mutussek, had moved the bulk of his forces over the River Niers which ran through the town to counter the 15th Division, leaving the south more open for the 51st Highlanders. Too late he realised his mistake and the Highlanders poured into the town and over the bridge onto the eastern side. Close house-to-house fighting raged on throughout that day and into the next, but the Scottish divisions were in the town and were not going to be evicted. The Germans were caught unprepared for events and eventually succumbed to the all-round pressure. By the 22nd, Goch had fallen and been completely cleared of the enemy. Operation Veritable, the plan to break through the Westwall was over, but the battle was not yet won. All of Montgomery's troops now looked to the Rhine and the bridges at Wesel.

OPERATION GRENADE

Men of the 309th Combat Engineers from the US 84th Division drag an assault boat to the banks of the River Roer at Linnich, prior to the assault in the early hours of 23 February. The steel boats were powered by paddle and carried one section of men. They were ungainly craft, square ended and very difficult to manoeuvre.
(National Archives, Washington)

By 21 February the flooded waters of the River Roer had started to recede. Lieutenant-General Bill Simpson, US 9th Army's commander, had been watching the level carefully for the past 11 days. His engineers had calculated that it would be at its lowest on about 25 February, but Bill Simpson wanted to take the Germans by surprise and so planned to launch his army across the Roer just before that date. He decided that the river level early on the morning of 23 February would be just low enough to make a crossing and, more importantly, bridging operations, possible. The attack would still be risky, for the fast-flowing water would be very lively, but the element of surprise would make it worth the risk.

Simpson's 9th Army was lined up along the River Roer on a front of 30 miles (48.3km), from north of Dueren to the confluence of the Maas and the Roer. The northern corps would head east across the Roer and then swing northwards to link up with Canadian 1st Army before turning eastwards again for the Rhine. The others would head north-east and

**Follow-up infantry of
US 29th Division from XIX Corps,
preparing to be called forward to
cross the River Roer on the first
day of Operation Grenade.
(National Archives, Washington)**

east to close on the Rhine and clear the Rhineland. To protect his southern flank as his forces moved inland from the Roer, VII Corps from US 1st Army, commanded by MajGen J. Lawton Collins, would cross the Roer with its 104th Division (Allen) and 8th Division (Weaver) and advance alongside Simpson's extreme right-hand division.

Simpson had three corps with which to launch the assault. In the south, next to 1st Army's VII Corps, was Simpson's XIX Corps, commanded by MajGen Raymond McLain. On the right of XIX Corps' front was 29th Division (Gerhardt) with 30th Division (Hobbs) holding the river opposite Jülich. These two assaulting divisions had the back-up of 83rd Division (Macon) and 2nd Armored Division (White) behind them to exploit the breakout. The next corps to the north was MajGen Alvan Gillem's XIII Corps. Gillem intended to cross the river with his 102nd Division (Keating) on the right and 84th Division (Bolling) on the left at Linnich. In reserve he had the 5th Armored Division (Oliver). To the north was XVI Corps, commanded by MajGen John Anderson, a new formation as yet untried in battle. Anderson's corps was not to make an assault crossing, but to drive north along the west bank of the Roer and make an unopposed crossing when XIII Corps had cleared the area opposite. XVI Corps was then to take Roermond and drive north to link up with the Canadian 1st Army. The corps consisted of 35th Division (Baade), 79th Division (Wyche) and 8th Armored Division (Devine).

Operation Grenade began early on 23 February when, at 0245hrs, a tremendous artillery barrage lit up the dark skies. The guns of US

1st and 9th Armies, together with those of the British 2nd Army, laid down a massive bombardment on known and suspected German strong points across the River Roer. Over 1,500 guns hammered out all along the front for 45 intensive minutes. Then, as the barrage died away, the infantry of six divisions dragged their assault boats across muddy foreshores and into the river.

The most northerly of all the assault divisions was the 84th Division. It attacked from the centre of Linnich across a relatively narrow section of the river below the smashed road bridge at 0330hrs. The leading troops of the 1st Battalion, 334th Regiment, paddled their way over in 15-man assault craft through the swollen and violent river. The current was swift and merciless, sweeping aside any boat that had the misfortune to catch it broadside on. The first waves made it across with few casualties, but successive waves caught the force of the German defenders as they came up out of their shelters at the end of the artillery barrage. German small arms and mortar fire peppered the tiny craft as they made for the far side, but still the casualties were relatively light.

The orderly initial assault was followed by complete chaos. Many of the first waves of craft were still stuck on the far shore or had drifted downstream. When it came time for the next battalion, the 3rd Battalion, to cross, the footbridges the troops were supposed to have used were all out of action. One was not able to anchor on the far bank because of enemy fire, one was knocked out by a direct hit and the other was demolished by assault boats drifting down the river from the crossing site of the 102nd Division upstream of Linnich. As a result of these delays with the bridges, the 3rd Battalion was not able to start across the Roer

Infantry of the US 84th Division cross the River Roer dry shod on a footbridge at Linnich. The picture was taken on the first day of Operation Grenade. The bridge comprises a wooden treadway anchored to the storm boats used in the assault. (National Archives, Washington)

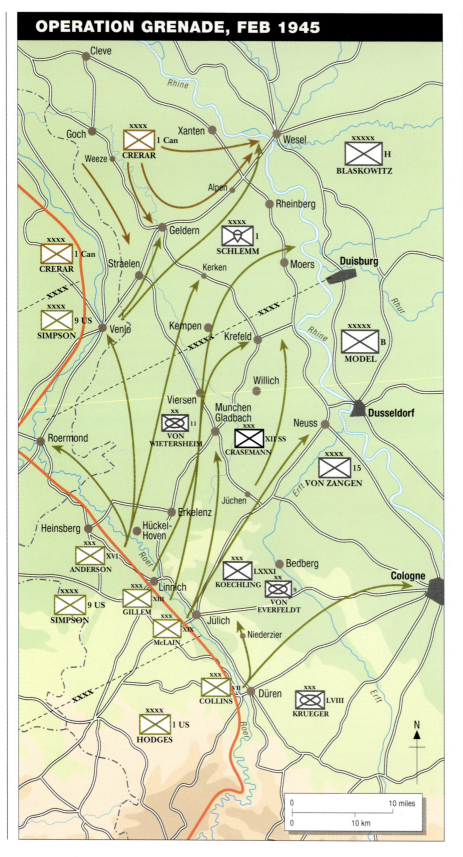

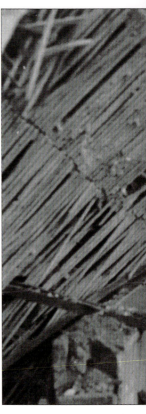

TOP **The road bridge at Linnich, knocked out by artillery fire and bombing. The US 84th Division crossed the Roer just downstream to the right of the picture. (National Archives, Washington)**

RIGHT **Storm boats, used in the crossing of the Roer, have drifted from the crossing sites and have become caught on a blown bridge downstream. Many of the boats from the first waves of the assault were lost like these, forcing the subsequent waves to delay their crossings. This picture was taken in the XIX Corps' sector. (National Archives, Washington)**

until 0645hrs. All was not lost, however, for the 1st Battalion had seized the initiative. The men over the river had not stopped to clear the enemy from the far side, but had wheeled to the left and immediately moved downstream towards the village of Korrenzig. They pressed on regardless, taking the enemy by surprise, and were able to cover 2,000 yards (1,820m) and get into Korrenzig by 0610hrs, well before the follow-up battalion had even started to cross!

The 3rd Battalion completed its crossing using a shuttle service of boats at about 1035hrs. German artillery fire now homed in on the crossing site and pounded the area. The strong points and pockets of isolated German infantry, by-passed by the 1st Battalion, were now cleared by the 3rd Battalion and then it too moved off towards Korrenzig. By 1450hrs the whole of 334th Regiment was over the river.

Meanwhile the 1st battalion was keeping up the pressure and had moved on, by 1405hrs the battalion had advanced another 1,500 yards (1,365m) and taken Rurich. In less than 12 hours, the battalion had carved out a bridgehead 4,000 yards (3,640m) long by 1,000 yards (910m) deep. The next objective was Baal, 2,500 yards (2,275m) away to the north-east. The 3rd Battalion moved up and passed through the leading troops to take the town by 2115hrs that night, bumping into a German counter-attack on the way. At the end of the day two complete regiments were over the Roer, and occupied a bridgehead 3.5 miles (5.6km) long from Linnich to Baal, stretching down the river to the north-east. The German troops facing the 84th Division across the Roer were from the 59th Infantry Division (Poppe) and were disposed to

American 6 inch (155mm) Howitzer belonging to 113th Field Artillery Battalion from US 30th Infantry Division being towed across the River Roer on a floating pontoon bridge. The picture was taken on 24 February, the day after XIX Corps' assault crossing of the swollen river.
(National Archives, Washington)

intercept an American crossing moving east towards the Rhine. In swinging north immediately after the crossing instead of due east where they were expected, the men of the 84th had outfoxed the enemy and turned things to their own advantage. The Americans also clashed with the inferior forces of the badly depleted 183rd Volksgrenadier Division (Lange) who were to the left of the German 59th Division.

South of Major-General Alexander Bolling's US 84th Division was 102nd Division, who crossed the Roer on the upstream side of Linnich. Major-General Frank Keating's 102nd Division formed the other part of XIII Corps' assault. Its crossing was launched after a deception plan using a diversionary smokescreen at an alternative site which drew away some of the German interdictory fire. Prior to the assault a raiding party under the command of Lt Roy Rogers went across the river and silenced four troublesome machine-gun posts. Minutes later the 407th Regiment's assault battalions followed across. The division's crossing was fairly uncomplicated and took few casualties. The villages of Gevenich and Tetz were taken that day, but the division had to withstand counter-attacks from both the German 59th Infantry Division and the 363rd Volksgrenadier Division (Dettling) backed by armour. The German attacks were repulsed with artillery and bazooka fire, there being no heavy weapons over the river at that time because of the lack of bridges.

Upstream from Linnich were the crossing sites allocated to McLain's XIX Corps. The most northerly, next to the 102nd Division, was MajGen Charles Gerhardt's 29th Division. It was due to cross in and above Jülich.

A party of VIPs in front of the Citadel at Jülich, just after they had taken lunch in the ruined fortress. From left to right: MajGen McLain (US XIX Corps), FM Montgomery (British 21st Army Group), Winston Churchill (British Prime Minister), MajGen Gillem (US XIII Corps), FM Brooke (British Chief Imperial Gen Staff) and LtGen Simpson (US 9th Army). (Imperial War Museum)

325

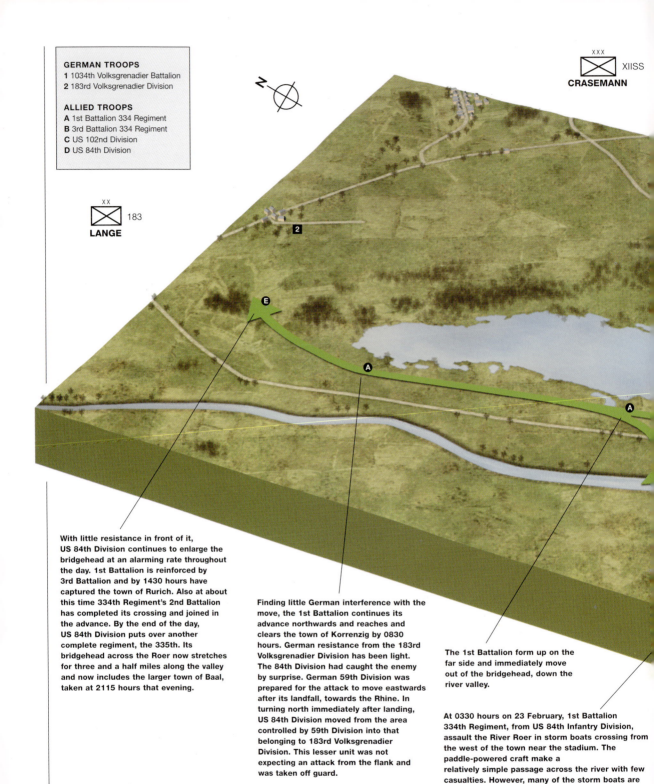

GERMAN TROOPS
1 1034th Volksgrenadier Battalion
2 183rd Volksgrenadier Division

ALLIED TROOPS
A 1st Battalion 334 Regiment
B 3rd Battalion 334 Regiment
C US 102nd Division
D US 84th Division

XXX
XIISS
CRASEMANN

XX
183
LANGE

With little resistance in front of it, US 84th Division continues to enlarge the bridgehead at an alarming rate throughout the day. 1st Battalion is reinforced by 3rd Battalion and by 1430 hours have captured the town of Rurich. Also at about this time 334th Regiment's 2nd Battalion has completed its crossing and joined in the advance. By the end of the day, US 84th Division puts over another complete regiment, the 335th. Its bridgehead across the Roer now stretches for three and a half miles along the valley and now includes the larger town of Baal, taken at 2115 hours that evening.

Finding little German interference with the move, the 1st Battalion continues its advance northwards and reaches and clears the town of Korrenzig by 0830 hours. German resistance from the 183rd Volksgrenadier Division has been light. The 84th Division had caught the enemy by surprise. German 59th Division was prepared for the attack to move eastwards after its landfall, towards the Rhine. In turning north immediately after landing, US 84th Division moved from the area controlled by 59th Division into that belonging to 183rd Volksgrenadier Division. This lesser unit was not expecting an attack from the flank and was taken off guard.

The 1st Battalion form up on the far side and immediately move out of the bridgehead, down the river valley.

At 0330 hours on 23 February, 1st Battalion 334th Regiment, from US 84th Infantry Division, assault the River Roer in storm boats crossing from the west of the town near the stadium. The paddle-powered craft make a relatively simple passage across the river with few casualties. However, many of the storm boats are lost while trying to bring them back to the near shore ready for the second wave.

US 84 DIVISION CROSS THE RIVER ROER AT LINNICH, 24 FEBRUARY 1945

German 1034th Volksgrenadier Battalion, from 59th Infantry Division, holds the river line opposite Linnich. The area back from the river has been mined and wired and concrete pill boxes cover important road junctions.

XX
59
POPPE

The floods which covered the river valley, caused by the sabotaging of the Roer dams, have begun to recede, but areas of trapped water still keep any likely avenues of advance confined to the roads.

1

B

B

D

D

A

B

LINNICH

XX
102
KEATING

XX
84
BOLLING

XXX
XII
ILLEM

334th Regiment's 3rd Battalion cross the Roer immediately after the 1st Battalion, but run into trouble from a now alert 1034th Volksgrenadier Regiment. This second wave is also slowed down by lack of storm boats and growing chaos at the launching sites. One company is sent a few hundred yards inland to form a stop line to prevent the enemy counter attacking the lodgement. Bridging operations start, but are unsuccessful.

III
334

3rd Battalion put out more patrols to seal off the bridgehead and to make contact with US 102nd Division's crossing just upstream of Linnich.

327

German troops captured by the US 102nd Division during the first day of 'Grenade'. The prisoners are all young men, some of them just boys, from the German 59th Division. The German division had suffered dreadful casualties in the previous fighting around Aachen and at one point was down to around 1,000 men. As with all German units, replacements were often just young boys or old men, conscripted into service with little equipment or training. They were often put into the line to help absorb an initial attack, before the more seasoned troops could be brought up to counter-attack any lodgement. (National Archives, Washington)

The river to the north of the town was too wide to bridge and the troops of 115th Infantry Regiment crossed over in assault boats and Landing Vehicle Tracked (LVTs). Just upstream in Jülich itself the river was much narrower with steep banks and the second assault regiment, 175th Regiment, crossed over on footbridges. An advance party had moved over the Roer to protect the sites whilst engineers built the bridges. When they were ready, the assaulting infantry raced across. Although casualties were heavier than elsewhere, they were still relatively light.

Dominating the town of Jülich was the Citadel, a 400-year-old fortress, with huge stone walls. Before the crossing, American bombers had plastered the fort with 1,000lb (450kg) bombs, but it had remained intact. Preparations were made to take the Citadel with tanks, explosives and flame-throwers but they were stranded on the western side of the river during day one. When they finally arrived over the river the next day, there was no costly assault to be endured for the Germans had withdrawn.

The most southerly of XIX Corps crossings was that carried out by the 30th Division, commanded by MajGen Leland Hobbs. Like the 29th Division, the 30th planned to cross dry shod. In fact it went one better, for an advance party of 119th Regiment went across an hour before the artillery bombardment began and provided a screen for engineers to start work on a footbridge. At the same time as the barrage went in, the engineers began building the bridge. By the time the last shells were falling, the regiment was racing across the completed bridge. The other assault unit was the 120th Regiment who crossed further upstream using LVTs.

Opposing XIX Corps was the 363rd Volksgrenadier Division. Its main offensive effort had been launched against 102nd Division downstream and it was unable to organise any counter-attacks against XIX Corps. The crossings had been completely successful with relatively slight casualties.

Not so the crossing in VII Corps' sector. General Collins' group had a much harder task in supporting the efforts of 9th Army. It assaulted the Roer with two divisions: MajGen Terry Allen's 104th Division on the left and MajGen William Weaver's 8th Division on the right, both in the area of Dueren. Collins divided the town between the two divisions. More than any of other crossings, the Roer at Düren proved to be the biggest problem during the D-Day of 'Grenade'. The swollen river running through its narrow course proved to be too swift for footbridges and all the infantry crossed in boats. In the 104th's area, the first waves of the 415th Regiment got across with little difficulty. The 413th Regiment had more trouble. Its first waves were almost completely wiped out as an effective force when it became disorganised by enemy counter fire. German artillery forced the remainder of the regiment to complete its crossing in the 415th's sector. By daylight, the German fire had made bridging operations almost impossible. Long-range artillery bombarded the sites all through the day. Smokescreens were laid but these had little effect, the guns were already registered on the bridge's locations. A direct hit completely demolished a finished road bridge. None the less, those troops over the river pressed inland and took two villages en route to Oberzier. Opposed by a weak 12th Volksgrenadier Division (Engel), the enemy failed to put up much resistance.

The final crossing, and the most southerly, was made by 8th Division. Crossing upstream of the 29th Division, this assault was the most precarious of them all. The crossing places were overlooked by the foothills of the Eifel and the enemy had the whole area registered by its artillery. The Roer was swift and narrow, with no possibility of bridges being built to get the first waves of troops across. All the assaults were made by boat; each of them was a disaster. The 13th and 28th Regiments were supposed to cross with powered assault boats, but virtually every one had engine malfunctions. Paddle-powered storm boats were too flimsy for the fast- flowing river and many of the craft tipped their loads of infantry into the icy waters. As the night became day, German fire increased in intensity limiting all operations on the river bank. Not one bridge was built during the day. Those troops that did make it over the river were disorganised and poorly equipped. Most of their weapons were lost during the crossing. Smashed by the river and pounded by the artillery, the 8th Division would have been an easy target, but the 12th Volksgrenadier Division never counter-attacked with any force.

Even with the problems suffered by VII Corps, the opening round of 'Grenade' could be viewed as a success. The 84th Division's penetration in the North and the lodgements gained by eight divisions had effectively broken the Roer as a defence line. The only real enemy counter-attack had been the one against 102nd Division. The great weight of American firepower and muscle would now inexorably pour across the river against a dispirited and increasingly emasculated opposition. Casualties had been light, the entire 9th Army had suffered 92 killed, 61 missing and 913 wounded, with the losses of VII Corps amounting to 66 killed, 35 missing and 280 wounded, a total of just under 1,500. It was a relatively small price to pay for such a large gain.

News of the American crossing of the Roer was received by Commander of Army Group B with some alarm. Generalfeldmarschall

OVERLEAF **In the early hours of a February morning the US 84th Division crossed the River Roer as part of Operation Grenade. Thirty-five storm boats were used in the first wave, but as they were paddle powered they crossed intermittently, with varying distances between them and at different speeds. The fast current tended to sweep them downstream and so their passing across the river was skewed, rather than straight. Enemy fire was sporadic and slight, but even so there were some casualties.**

Tony Bryan 04/00

Tank crewmen from
US 8th Armored Division help
medics lower an injured
infantryman from the rear of
their tank after having brought
him back to an aid station from
the front line. The tank is a
Sherman M4A3, it has the
larger .3 inch (76mm) gun
and horizontal volute spring
suspension. Picture taken at
Linne on 26 February 1945.
(National Archives, Washington)

Model acted swiftly and placed his reserves, the 9th and 11th Panzer Divisions, at the disposal of the German 15th Army's commander Von Zangen. Model had intended to use the two armoured divisions together as a corps under the command of GenLt Fritz Bayerlain, but not enough of the 11th Panzers had yet arrived from the Saar-Moselle sector where it had been deployed to justify the arrangement, so the divisions were handed over to Von Zangen. He, in turn, allocated those parts that were ready to move on to Koechling's LXXXI Corps. It was a mistake; this valuable armour dribbled into the battle rather than being thrown in as a powerful strike force.

Simpson's forces now turned to exploit the bridgehead. He was anxious to get his army pivoting to the north as early as possible. He knew that as each division wheeled to the left, its right wing would become vulnerable. It was absolutely imperative that everyone kept abreast of each other. XIX Corps was probably the most exposed in view of the trouble that VII Corps was having at its crossing sites.

The 84th Division led the way north clearing the far side of the Roer in order to allow Anderson's XVI Corps to cross unopposed. The division ran into trouble north of Baal and its advance slowed down. Simpson decided that, as opposition was comparatively light, Anderson should find and try to exploit his own crossing places rather than wait for XIII Corps to capture them for him. West of the Roer below Anderson were several German bridgeheads still on the Allied side of the Roer. Anderson now made to capture the one at Hilfarth, complete with the bridge across the river which was supplying the garrison in the town. He gave the task to 35th Division, while the 79th Division staged a feint several miles downstream. To assist the attack on Hilfarth, MajGen Baade

Five days into 'Grenade', infantrymen of the 2nd Battalion, 334th Regiment, from US 84th Division crouch in the shelter of an M3 half-rack personnel carrier to avoid enemy shrapnel and sniper fire. Resistance by this time consisted of small rearguards manning extemporised road blocks and setting ambushes to harry the advancing Americans with their small arms fire. (National Archives, Washington)

put 137th Regiment over the Roer into XIII Corps bridgehead to attack down the eastern side of the river. After a protracted fight, Hilfarth was captured with its bridge intact. By noon on 26 February tanks and other vehicles of XVI Corps now swarmed over the Roer in force, freeing up Gillem's XIII Corps to continue its advance northwards.

Gillem now inserted his 5th Armored Division onto his right flank and set the 84th and 102nd Divisions to take Erklenz and the last anti-tank ditch in front of the Americans. This they did against the feeble opposition put up by the German 338th Infantry Division (Von Oppen) which had just arrived into the sector controlled by XII SS Corps. With Erklenz captured the road network over a wide flat plain now opened up. It was perfect tank country. Now the advance began to gain momentum.

In front of XIX Corps, the introduction of elements of the 9th and 11th Panzer Divisions slowed the advance down, but the hurriedly committed German units could not put up a concerted defence, nor gain enough strength to counter-attack. The 29th and 30th Divisions now began to roll up this opposition between them. McLain then inserted his 2nd Armored Division to take over the lead and the advance motored on. XIX Corps' success was mirrored by Collins' VII Corps. After his sticky start at the river crossings, his troops applied 72 hours of unremitting pressure as successive fresh units went into the line to replace those tired by the fighting. It was too much for the 12th Volksgrenadier Division. Resistance collapsed leaving the bridgehead to expand at an alarming rate as the American corps headed east for the River Erft.

Simpson's army was now getting up to speed. His reserve divisions and armoured formations were introduced into the bridgehead and began to fan out, striking for important communication centres and river crossings. With the 84th Division still heading north, after taking Erklenz, and Anderson's corps pushing down the Roer valley, Model

German troops advance past a burning American half-track during the Ardennes offensive. Hitler's gamble, to attack through the mountainous region of Belgium in December 1944, was a failure and resulted in a great loss of men and matériel that could have been put to better use in the defence of the Reich within and behind the Siegfried Line. After this offensive, the depleted German Army in the west could only hope that a substantial stand against the advancing Allies could be made further back on the River Rhine. But Hitler would not even allow this and insisted that every metre of the ground between the German frontier and the river be defended to the last. By the time the front had been pushed back to the Rhine, there was very little left to defend it with. (Imperial War Museum)

could detect that the possible direction of the attack was aimed at a link-up with the Canadian 1st Army and not eastwards towards Cologne and the Rhine as first supposed. If that were so, Von Zangen's 15th Army and the whole south wing of the German Army Group H was in danger of being caught in a great pincer movement and crushed. The Americans would then take Schlemm's II Parachute Army in the rear. Model informed his C-in-C West, Von Rundstedt, that it was no longer possible to form a defensive line on the east bank of the Rhine. Von Rundstedt consulted with Hitler and urged him to sanction a general retreat back across the Rhine; failure to do so, he warned, would lead to the collapse of the entire Western Front. Hitler dismissed the proposal outright. He even refused to agree to an adjustment to 15th Army's line. The fight to contain the Allies in the Rhineland would continue on its present course. To help prevent the collapse, Von Rundstedt ordered Blaskowitz to release the Panzer Lehr and 15th Panzer Grenadier Divisions to help bolster Von Zangen's defences. It was too little, too late.

The US 9th Army's great breakout made good use of its superiority over the Germans in mechanised warfare. The combination of armour and infantry in such large numbers was powerful enough to break any defence that the enemy was capable of mounting. Bill Simpson exercised a policy of 'relentless pursuit'. When the advance passed from the area controlled by the German 15th Army into that of the II Parachute Army, opposition became much tougher. Schlemm had withdrawn the German 8th Parachute Division from the Canadian sector and placed it in front of XVI Corps. The elite troops put up a dogged resistance whenever they could catch the Americans, but Simpson's leading groups often just by-passed the opposition, cut their rear and left the German defenders for the follow-up troops to deal with. Operation Grenade had become unstoppable.

THE FINAL BATTLE

In contrast to the light opposition encountered and breathtaking gains made by the US 9th Army in the South, the Canadian/British attack in the North continued unabated. Crerar's Army was locked into a battle that had little real scope for mobile warfare until the stubborn defences of the Westwall had been broken. He had to ask his troops for one more great effort and to suffer even more attrition until the Rhine was reached.

On the right of the battleground, XXX Corps advanced along two axes: Gennep–Venlo and Goch–Geldern. The 51st Highland Division had helped in the capture of Goch and was now engaged in crossing the small River Kendal, a tributary of the Niers, south of the town. On 25 February the division crossed the river and took its final objective, a lateral road heading south-east towards Weeze. The 51st Highland Division was then pulled out of the line and sent back to the rear for rest and refitting. It had been earmarked by Montgomery for the proposed Rhine crossings. The 52nd Lowland Division took over the sector held by the Highland Division and continued southwards, clearing the east bank of the Maas.

Men from the 1st Battalion Herefordshire Regiment cross the anti-tank ditch that surrounds Udem. The ditches were a common type of temporary defence which were thrown up throughout the whole of the Siegfried Line. They caused little difficulty to the infantry and could be bridged in seconds with specialised armoured bridging equipment. Covering fire, smoke and a determined attack meant that troops and tanks could be over the ditch in a very short space of time. The secret was in trying to keep the enemy occupied whilst the breach was made. (Imperial War Museum)

LEFT AND BELOW **On the day, 3 March, that the Welsh Division joined up with the US 35th Division at Geldern, completing the linking of the 'Veritable' and 'Grenade' offensives, the Royal Norfolks of the British 3rd Division were capturing the town of Kervenheim, to the left of the Welshmen. The pictures show infantry street fighting and clearing houses in the town. (Imperial War Museum)**

RIGHT **The parish church and stone tower of Goch suffered from the Allied bombardment during the capture of the town. The tower had been standing since the 14th century, but this did not escape its being plastered with a 'Hitler Youth' sign an each of its walls. The picture was taken on 3 March, just a few days after the town's capture by the Scottish and Highland Divisions. (Imperial War Museum)**

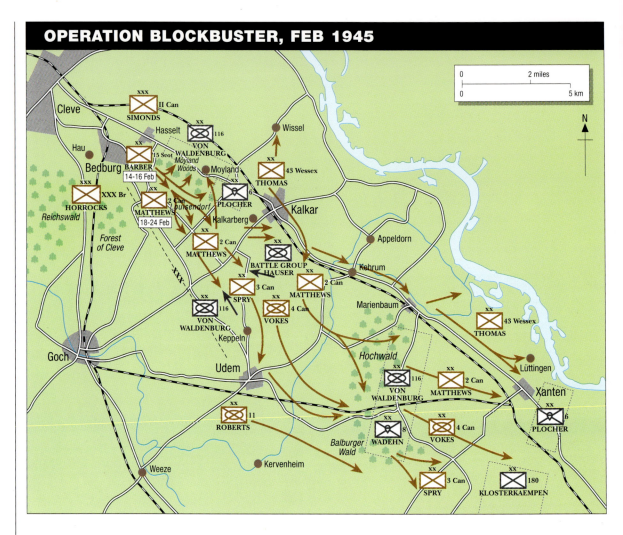

After its welcome release from the confines of the Reichswald and a few days' rest out of the line, the 53rd Welsh Division led the advance from Goch to Geldern. The three towns of Weeze, Kevelaer and Geldern to its front were all fortified. On the left of 53rd Division, the 15th Scottish Division advanced abreast of it for a few more days until it too was relieved by a fresh division. On 25 February the British 3rd Division commanded by MajGen 'Bolo' Whistler crossed the River Maas and took over the sector in front of the Scottish Division, resuming the advance two days later.

Meanwhile the 53rd Division pressed on. The ground was still littered with anti-tank ditches, barbed-wire and concrete fortifications, but the pressure applied by XXX Corps' three divisions was constant and resolute. Weeze fell to the Welshmen in a two-brigade pincer attack, while Kevelaer followed soon after on 2 March, when reconnaissance troops found the town to be unoccupied. The next town, Geldern, was to be the pivot for a change of direction. Once the town had been captured, XXX Corps would swing to the east and head for the bridges at Wesel, meeting up with the Canadians and sealing those German troops that were encircled in the trap. Geldern was also to be the meeting place with the Americans racing up from the south aiming to complete an even greater encirclement.

After XXX Corps had broken up the western side of the battlefield with its capture of Goch, it became the turn of the Canadian II Corps to attack in the East. The corps had been badly mauled when trying to capture the Moyland woods and advance over the Goch–Calcar road and it took a few days to rethink tactics and plan for a new offensive. Crerar decided to add weight to his forces and plan a heavy thrust through the line of fortifications known as the 'Hochwald Layback' which barred the way to Xanten and the Rhine. Instead of advancing with the Cleve–Xanten road as his axis, he planned to take his main force round the south of Calcar and head across the high ground through the gap between the Hochwald Forest and the smaller Balbergerwald, approaching Xanten from west of the town. Once Xanten was captured, Wesel and the bridges over the Rhine were doomed. Xanten was the gateway to the Rhine.

Crerar's troops would be attacking one of the strongest sections of the Rhine defences. General Schlemm had ordered his two corps commanders in the area, Von Luttwitz and Meindl, to reinforce the escarpment that stretched from Calcar to Udem. This ridge of high ground barred the way through the gap south of the Hochwald. Behind the ridge were further tank ditches, pillboxes and wire entanglements. The gap itself was covered by a remarkable number of .3 inch (88mm) guns, salvaged from the Siegfried Line defences.

A German infantry unit command post, overrun by the US 1st Army during the breakout to the Rhine. The camouflaged field HQ is set into the ground with wooden sides and roof giving overhead cover. (National Archives, Washington)

Hot food is unloaded from a mess truck at Wegburg onto a jeep to be taken up to the forward troops of the US 8th Armored Division on 2 March. Progress by the division had been through relatively undefended country, but from this point onwards the 8th Armored, from US XVI Corps, was to come up against the Germans facing the Canadian 1st Army and resistance to its advance stiffened alarmingly. (National Archives, Washington)

The operation was given the name 'Blockbuster'. Simonds had been loaned the British 43rd Infantry and 11th Armoured Divisions to help with the assault. On 26 February, just as the American forces over the Roer had got into their stride, the Canadians attacked. Two infantry divisions, the Canadian 2nd and 3rd, crossed the start line on the Goch–Calcar road and began sweeping the enemy aside. Carried in Kangaroo armoured troop carriers and moving at a brisk tank pace, the infantry advanced behind a rolling barrage. It was not long before they met stiffer opposition as Gen Schlemm's parachute forces began to make their presence felt. Support came from the Canadian 4th Armored Division, commanded by MajGen Chris Vokes, and Udem was taken after a bitter struggle. The axis of the attack then swung eastwards and the Canadians made for the Hochwald Gap, with the 2nd Canadian Division attacking the Hochwald on the left, the 3rd Canadian Division the Balbergerwald on the right and the 4th Canadian Armored Division plunging straight through the middle. This is where the whole offensive came to a shuddering halt. The ground was too exposed, and the enemy too firmly ensconced, for the Canadians to brush the opposition aside.

It took the Canadians five days to break through the gap and the woods. Five days of murderous and costly fighting in conditions that matched the worst days of the war. On the left flank the 43rd Division made an easier advance through Calcar and headed for Xanten down the main road, opposition becoming lighter all the way as German troops pulled back into Xanten lest they be surrounded. To the south of the Balbergerwald, the British 11th Armoured Division joined in the fight and added their weight to the advance. On 2 March, the Canadian II Corps successfully broke through the woods and looked down on Xanten, the last town before the Rhine.

To the south momentous events were unfolding. Simpson's 9th Army was sweeping all before it. Anderson's XVI Corps was pushing down the Maas, closing on the British XXX Corps; Gillem's XIII Corps was wheeling north-east to Krefeld and the Rhine; and McLain's XIX Corps had captured Mönchengladbach, the largest German town to fall so far in the war, and was now plunging eastwards making for the Rhine opposite Düsseldorf. The right flank protection, given by Collins' VII Corps, had expanded into a full-blown advance, having itself joined in the charge and crossed the River Erft, and now bore down on the great city of Cologne. Von Zangen's 15th Army could do little to stop them.

On 3 March, the British XXX Corps' 53rd Welsh Division, together with the 8th Armoured Brigade, continued their advance towards Geldern. Just after midday they met up with the US 35th Division just outside the town; 'Veritable' and 'Grenade' had finally joined together to provide a continuous front. The fate of the Germans west of the lower Rhine was now sealed. British XXX Corps, Canadian II Corps and the American XVI Corps all began heading east for the river, squeezing the enemy into a rapidly diminishing bridgehead. Elements of 15 German divisions were backing up to the Rhine, caught in the vice of the advancing Allied armies. Schlemm pleaded with Von Rundstedt to allow him to withdraw what was left of the 1st Parachute Army over the river,

Knocked-out Sturmpanzer VI (Sturmtiger) assault gun, one of only ten built, being examined by an infantryman from the US 30th Infantry Division. The Sturmtiger housed a 15 inch (380mm) rocket projector, intended for use as a mobile assault howitzer against troop concentrations and fortifications. The picture was taken on 28 February 1945, five days into US 9th Army's advance. (National Archives, Washington)

but Hitler still blocked the move. On 5 March the Americans finally reached the Rhine further to the south and one by one the bridges across the river were blown to prevent them falling into Allied hands.

The remnants of the II Parachute Army were gradually squeezed into a tiny lodgement around the two remaining Rhine bridges at Wesel. By 6 March Schlemm began evacuating some of his troops across the road and rail crossings, in defiance of orders, but he still maintained his vigorous defence of the 'pocket' around Wesel. When the Canadians and the 43rd Division attacked Xanten after a terrific barrage, they still found a determined and tenacious German garrison defending the town. The Americans also found to their great cost just what the Canadian 1st Army had had to contend with when they too met stiff German resistance from the paratroopers holding the Wesel 'pocket'. After the rapid advance from the Roer, the last few miles to the Rhine were some of the most difficult met by the Americans during the whole of the journey.

On 3 March 1945 at around 3pm the British and the Americans met near the canal just outside the small town of Geldern. The British had driven south as part of Operation Veritable, whilst the Americans, as part of Operation Grenade, had pushed north to meet the Anglo-Canadian units. This encounter helped seal the retreating enemy into a pocket with their backs to the River Rhine.

By 8 March the Germans knew that to hold out any longer was pointless. Under strict orders from Hitler not to allow the bridges to fall into Allied hands on pain of death, Gen Schlemm pulled back into Wesel all who could be released to do so. With just a few dogged defenders keeping the advancing Allied armies at bay, everything that could be moved was saved, but masses of equipment had to be abandoned. The end came on 10 March when both bridges at Wesel crashed into the river, leaving just a brave rearguard and a few stragglers to be mopped up by the Americans and British. The butcher's bill for the German campaign to stop the British 21st Army was over 90,000 men. Allied losses amounted to 22,934, of which 7,300 were American, 5,304 Canadian and 10,330 were British. It was the last great stand-up fight between the Germans and the Allies; the rest of the war for the Nazi regime was marked by a long retreat into oblivion.

Tony Bryan 04/00

THE AMERICAN DRIVE TO THE RHINE

Whilst Montgomery's British 21st Army Group struggled with its epic campaign in the north of Germany, Bradley's 12th Army Group and Devers' 6th Army Group continued Eisenhower's 'broad front' policy and were steadily pushing the enemy back to the River Rhine all along the line.

Bradley's initial moves in early February were a continuation of the clearing of the 'bulge' formed by Hitler's Ardennes offensive of December 1944. He knew that the main thrust was to be in the north, but sought Eisenhower's permission to carry on through the Eifel region in an attempt to capitalise on the disorganised German retreat from the Ardennes. Eisenhower gave the go-ahead providing that such an advance resulted in a quick and decisive penetration of the enemy's defences, followed by a rapid drive to the Rhine. Eisenhower warned Bradley not to get bogged down in the mountainous fir-covered forests of the Eifel.

The elimination of the German penetration in the Ardennes had pushed back the German 6th Panzer Army to a point that it was pulled out of the line by Hitler and sent to the Eastern Front. That left the German 5th Panzer and 7th Armies facing Bradley, both of which had been badly mauled during the winter offensive. The German High Command could not believe that the Americans would attack through the Eifel in winter and decided to move some of its strength northwards opposite Simpson's

American troops pass a knocked-out M24 light tank that had been disabled by armour-piercing shot during a German ambush just short of the Rhine. (National Archives, Washington)

9th Army, where they thought an attack would be more likely. This decision led to the shuffling of units opposite Bradley's sector and gave him more confidence that the Eifel was just the place through which to launch his attack. He could not have been more wrong.

On 28 January, Hodges' 1st Army and Patton's 3rd Army advanced into the frontier defences north-east of St. Vith. The going was very slow. It was not so much the enemy in the shape of the German 5th Panzer Army that stalled them, as the weather. The American divisions that launched the attack had to contend with waist-high snow drifts, icy roads, frozen equipment and overcast skies. Movement was slow and precarious; traffic jams and treacherous conditions held progress to a crawl. In the first few days of the advance, the three American corps that undertook the attack had only managed to draw up to the first pillboxes of the Siegfried Line. On 1 February, Eisenhower called a halt to the proceedings and ordered Bradley to release seven divisions to 9th Army to help in Montgomery's offensive. He also gave instructions for the capture of the Roer dams as 1st Army's main priority.

While Bradley's main advance was halted, there was a problem in the south of his sector that required immediate attention. The enemy still held a triangle of land between the Saar and Moselle rivers near Trier that needed to be eliminated. General George Patton's 3rd Army was given the task to clear the area and bring the American line up to the defences of the Westwall. Again, it was bitter fighting in bitter winter weather. The task took the form of successive limited objective attacks culminating in one all-out attack by the 3rd Army on 19 February before the German forces could be eliminated from the triangle.

Still farther south, in the sector controlled by Devers' 6th Army Group, an American-French attack eliminated the German bridgehead across the Rhine known as the 'Colmar Pocket', on 9 February. The combined attack by US 7th Army and French 1st Army pushed Balck's 19th Army back across the river. This brought Allied forces up to the west bank of the Rhine all the way from Strasbourg to the Swiss border. The fighting cost the French and Americans 18,000 casualties; the Germans probably suffered double that number.

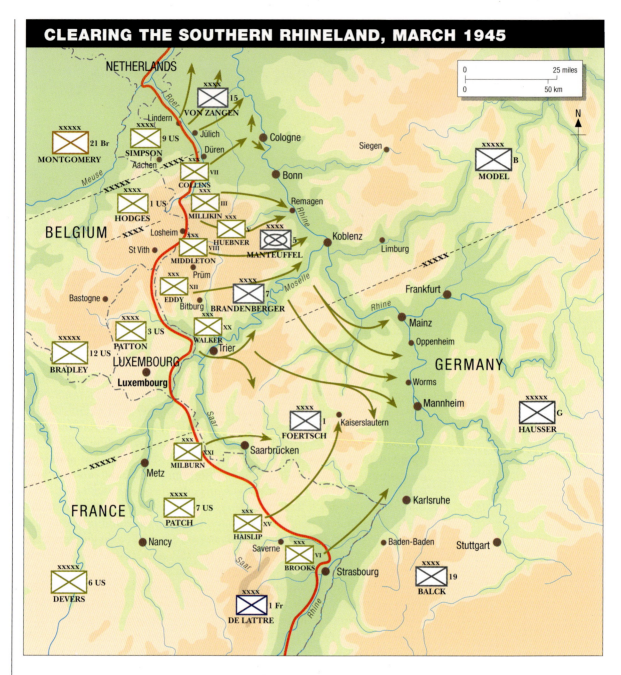

Even though Bradley had had to relinquish nine divisions to Simpson and Montgomery, his 12th Army Group was still a considerable striking force. After the commencement of 'Grenade' Bradley was able to contemplate his general move to the Rhine, code-named 'Lumberjack'. Gen Collins' US VII Corps had already attacked across the River Roer in support of US 9th Army's Operation Grenade. It now became the lead corps for 1st Army's drive to the Rhine, gathering momentum as the 'Grenade' campaign developed. Hodges used the bridgehead created by VII Corps to insert other units into the battle zone. Rather than stage assault crossings of their own, Hodges introduced one division after another each using the bridges of the adjacent division, then shifting

American troops make themselves at home in a captured German bunker on the Siegfried Line. (National Archives, Washington)

south to create other bridging sites for other divisions. US III Corps, under the command of MajGen John Millikin, crossed over VII Corps' bridges before moving south to create sites for the next corps, V Corps, under MajGen Heubner. As Collins' VII Corps reached the city of Cologne it turned south down the Rhine to link up with III Corps. Millikin's corps in turn moved south-east to meet the confluence of the Rivers Ahr and Rhine, to join up with the leading elements of Patton's 3rd Army who were attacking eastwards from the area of the Eifel. With the severe winter weather gradually easing, Patton's men had managed to seize the two main road centres in the western Eifel – Prüm and Bitberg – and had driven east to the River Kyle.

The American armies were now gradually breaking out of the confines of the Westwall. The shifting of troops to the North had weakened German resistance to a point where it was rapidly becoming disorganised. The northern wing of Von Zangen's German 15th Army had been shattered by Simpson's advance and the eastwards drive by Collins. Further south, Hodges' and Patton's moves through the southern Eifel had added to Model's woes by smashing through the German 5th Panzer Army (Manteuffel) and the German 7th Army, now commanded by Gen der Infanterie Hans Felber. In addition, Patton's drive down the Moselle valley was putting pressure on the German 1st Army and unhinging the whole of the German Army Group G and the industrial area of the Saar.

On 3 March, just as VII Corps had reached the Rhine north of Cologne, Patton's 3rd Army made its strike: Troy Middleton's VIII Corps headed eastwards from Prüm and MajGen Manton Eddy's XII Corps crossed the River Kyle east of Bitburg. The going was slow at first, especially near Prüm as the enemy struggled to contain the assault, but on 5 March, Patton unleashed his armour and by nightfall they had advanced over 12 miles (19.3km). The tanks moved against negligible opposition – Manteuffel's 5th Panzer Army could do little to stop them – cutting through hastily organised strong points and heading straight for the Rhine. In just over two-and-a-half days, the US 4th Armored

Division had advanced 44 miles (70km), taking over 5,000 prisoners and spreading alarm and confusion in the German rear. Everywhere, German troops were pulling back on foot, in horse-drawn carts and in commandeered motor vehicles, searching for crossing points over the Rhine whether they be barges, bridges or ferries. One by one the bridges over the Rhine were blown as Hodges' and Patton's forces neared the river. Each German commander knew that the penalty for allowing a bridge to fall into Allied hands was death. But, on 7 March, a catalogue of German mishaps, exploited by brave and determined American troops, allowed elements of MajGen John Leonard's 9th Armored Division from Millikin's III Corps to capture the Remagen bridge intact, although it was severely damaged. A bridgehead was quickly put over the river and reinforced in strength over the next few days. The bridge finally collapsed into the river ten days later, but by then several alternative crossing sites had been established.

No sooner had Patton's forces reached the Rhine than they turned swiftly southwards, sweeping up the valley to get behind the troops of the German 7th and 1st Armies who were manning the Westwall facing Patch's US 7th Army. GenObst Paul Hausser, commander Army Group G, realised that unless reinforcements could be sent to bolster the German 7th Army against Patton, his 1st Army would be surrounded and annihilated. The reply that came from the new Commander-in-Chief West, GFM Albert Kesselring (who had replaced the disgraced Von Rundstedt), was that no reinforcements were available. On 12 March Patton attacked from Trier with XX Corps (Walker), whilst XII Corps (Eddy) crossed the Moselle near the Rhine and drove south-west into the rear of the German 1st Army. Gen Foertsch, the German 1st Army's commander, was gradually being enveloped, for as Patton harried the rear, Patch and De Lattre pounded his front with their US 7th and French 1st Armies. Once again Hausser appealed to Kesselring, this time to be allowed to pull his forces back across the Rhine. Permission was denied, but Kesselring did suggest that any American encirclement that threatened the annihilation of the main body of troops was to be avoided. This was no authority for a full-scale withdrawal, but it was enough of a hint to allow the most seriously threatened units to be pulled back.

The American armies now operated through open country against only sporadic resistance. On 20 March permission was given to Felber to pull his German 7th Army back over the Rhine, while the remnants of German 1st Army held bridgeheads around the three remaining bridges. On 23 March, approval was finally issued for a formal withdrawal across the river. By that time almost all who were going to make it back had already done so. At the end of the next day the last Rhine bridge crashed into the river and only stragglers and abandoned equipment were left on the west bank. The River Rhine, from the North Sea to the Swiss border, now marked the Allied front line.

AFTERMATH

To the Germans the River Rhine was the last shield before the Ruhr and the last practical defensive line before the great north German plain. It was also a great psychological barrier for the German nation. Once it was crossed and the Allies were pouring out into the Nazi Fatherland, every person would, in their hearts, know that the war was lost.

By the end of March 1945, British, Canadian, American and French forces were all lined up along the whole length of the Rhine and their commanders were contemplating how best to cross the great German moat. Even though the Americans had their bridgehead over the river at Remagen, the area on the far side was not suitable for immediate large-scale operations. The Remagen lodgement would be exploited, but until it could be expanded and developed to contain a powerful striking force, it was much more of a symbolic breach of the Rhine than a practical one.

The main effort was once again in the north where Montgomery, true to form, took his 21st Army Group across the Rhine in a ponderous, set-piece, assault supported by air landings on the far side. The crossings, code-named 'Plunder', were an extension of his Rhineland campaign. Montgomery had been conditioned by the harsh opposition he had received in the February/March battles and was intent on ensuring that his overwhelming fighting power was put to good effect. 'Plunder' was heavily supported by air strikes, smoke and artillery on a massive scale. On 24 March, the British 2nd and US 9th Armies, under the command

An American machine-gun crew of the 102nd Division manning a .3 inch (76mm) Browning Model 1917 medium machine gun in a captured factory at Uerdingen. The gun first entered service in 1918 during World War I and remained in use in the American army until the early 1960s. (National Archives, Washington)

of LtGen Miles Dempsey and LtGen Bill Simpson, were put over onto the far side of the Rhine either side of Wesel and quickly established strong bridgeheads. The British moved north-east onto the northern plain, as the Americans began a wide south-easterly encirclement of the Ruhr industrial region.

In contrast to Montgomery, the other American armies chose to improvise their crossing and exploit any tactical situation as it occurred. With US 1st Army already across the river at Remagen, Patton's 3rd Army quickly followed suit at Nierstein when his 5th Division, from XII Corps, jumped the river one day before Monty's set-piece attack. Other crossings swiftly followed: on the 25th the US 87th Division crossed at Boppard and the 89th Division at St. Goar. A day later US 7th Army got across the river at Worms and even the French soon got into the act with their crossing at Gamersheim. In just a few days, the whole of the Rhine barrier had been breached.

Allied forces now fanned out and split the Germans apart. Montgomery's armies drove through Blaskowitz's German Army Group B with the Canadians heading for northern Holland, whilst 2nd Army made for Bremen and Hamburg. Simpson's 9th Army continued its envelopment of the Ruhr to meet up with Hodges' 1st Army and seal the German defenders of Model's 5th Panzer Army in an iron ring. Model's other two armies, the 15th and the 7th, were split wide open by the remaining forces of US 1st Army. Eisenhower then decreed that the main Allied thrust would be by Bradley's armies for the city of Leipzig and that Berlin, always the great objective of the British, was to be left for the Russians to capture. In consequence, Simpson's 9th Army reverted back to Bradley and the giant part of the capture of the remainder of Germany was given over to the Americans. Patton cleared the southern part of the country and moved into Czechoslovakia, Patch swept through Nuremberg and over the Austrian border, and De Lattre de Tassigny took his French 1st Army through the Black Forest, up into the Tyrol.

That these lightning moves were possible was in no small measure due to the Russians. The opposition was disorganised. Hitler was fighting a war on two fronts and the numbers of men involved in the East almost

The road bridge at Wesel, destroyed by the retreating Germans on 10 March 1945, just as the British and American forces reached the heavily defended Wesel 'pocket'. Those defenders who had not made it over the bridge were taken prisoner.
(National Archives, Washington)

German troops race past a burning American vehicle. Even though the retreat to the Rhine was often something of a rout, nothing could be taken for granted by the Americans. The German Army had always been especially proficient at aggressive defence and the advancing Allied troops often ran into spirited ambushes by small groups of the enemy, just strong enough to hold up the advance for long enough to organise the next road block further back. (Imperial War Museum)

dwarfed the Anglo-American operations in the west. The war with Russia was on a massive scale. At the end of 1944 the Red Army had gained a foothold in East Prussia, but then paused in order to build up strength for their final offensive. The Germans did all they could to improvise defences and tried desperately to amass enough units to counter the expected blow, but when it came the attack was of such massive power and ferocity that the Eastern Front, like the Western, was torn wide open. Over a million-and-a-half Russian troops faced just a third of that number of Germans on the East Prussian front alone. The amount of armour at their disposal was equally overwhelming: 3,000 Russian tanks against 700 German. The January offensive drove a deep bulge in the German line and got to within 60 miles (96km) of Berlin. The penetration was then exploited to the full during the campaigns in Silesia and Pomerania during February and March and the front line was gradually pushed back all along the German mainland.

The battles of March and April broke out everywhere and were conducted by everyone. All of the Allies, both in the west and the east harried the Germans at every opportunity. The German collapse, when it came, was total and final. On 30 April Hitler committed suicide in his Berlin bunker; on 4 May German forces in north-west Europe surrendered to the Allies.

THE BATTLEFIELD TODAY

The battles for control of the Rhineland took place in a heavily populated western nation and brought great devastation to its towns and cities. It is therefore only natural that after the war Germany began the great task of rebuilding itself and totally obliterating the permanent reminders of its unhappy past. Virtually every one of the ferro-concrete structures that made up Hitler's great Westwall have been destroyed, most of them by American engineers within days or even hours of their capture, fearful lest they fall once again into German hands. Others became eyesores or were in the way of progress or redevelopment and were removed. Some still exist, tucked away in isolated woods, or built into the side of a hill and overgrown with vegetation, but too few remain to illustrate the power of the Siegfried Line. In a few places, most notably around Aachen, sections of 'dragon's teeth' still survive, marching across fields as if waiting to trap some unsuspecting tank.

The temporary field works, dug in desperation as the Allies approached, disappeared immediately after the war when returning German farmers reclaimed their land and put it to good use helping to feed the nation. There is one notable exception, however, for at the base of the escarpment, just one mile to the north of Goch, the first of the anti-tank ditches dug to protect the town remains intact. Still 20 feet (6m) deep and covered with saplings, it rests at the foot of the low hill so brilliantly captured by the 43rd Wessex Division in the action which turned 'Veritable'.

All of the towns devastated in the battles have been rebuilt, but there are just enough of the original buildings showing scars of the war to recreate the past. It is possible to relive the battle in one's mind as you stand with some action photograph and compare what was then with what is now. At Linnich, just below the rebuilt bridge you can look down on the crossing site of the US 84th Division where its leading troops stormed across the Roer at the opening of 'Grenade', the river unchanged in over 50 years.

Well away from the roads, in areas seldom visited by anyone, you can still come across a long-forgotten battlefield. Slit trenches and dugouts, abandoned as the battle moved on, remain just as they were left, with the accumulation of 50 years of leaves falling into their open sides. The area in front of the trenches is often littered with cartridge cases, buried just 2 inches (50mm) below the surface lying just where they fell, spinning from a soldier's rifle. But perhaps the most evocative site of all is the deep forest of the Reichswald, where the British XXX Corps fought its terrible battle. The thick woods, intersected by long straight rides, remain just as they were. In the winter, in the rain, with mud underfoot and grey skies overhead, it's just as though you were back in the dark days of 1945.

RIGHT **After 24 hours without rest, these two tankers from the US 2nd Armored Division warm their feet by a fire. BrigGen I. D. White's division was part of McLain's XIX Corps, on the right flank of Gen Simpson's US 9th Army. The 2nd Armored Division led the advance with little respite once the corps had broken out from the Roer crossings.**
(National Archives, Washington)

1944

19 November US 9th Army attacks Hitler's Westwall defences (Siegfried Line) and reaches the River Roer.

16 December Hitler launches his great offensive through the Ardennes in an attempt to reach the River Meuse and split the British and American armies.

1945

12 January Russian Red Army launch their great winter offensive against the East German front.

16 January The Ardennes offensive fails and the German forces who had undertaken the attack are forced back to their original start line. The 'bulge' in the American front had been eliminated.

28 January US 1st and 3rd Armies start to move eastwards towards the Rhine through the Eifel region but are halted by Eisenhower three days later due to lack of progress against the Westwall defences.

1 February British XII Corps clears Roermond Triangle to bring Allied forces up to River Maas.

8 February Canadian 1st Army launches Operation Veritable with attacks through and around the Reichswald Forest.

11 February Canadian 1st Army takes the important town of Cleve in the heart of the Westwall defences.

9 February US 6th Army eliminates Colmar 'Pocket' and closes on the upper Rhine.

10 February US 1st Army captures Roer dams, but Germans flood the valley preventing the start of US 9th Army's Operation Grenade.

17 February The 43rd Wessex Division advances to the Goch escarpment and produce an 8,000 yard (7,280m) salient through the Siegfried Line which outflanks the Reichswald defences.

22 February 15th Scottish and 51st Highland Divisions take the town of Goch and finally break through Hitler's Westwall.

23 February US 9th Army begins 'Grenade' and cross the River Roer.

26 February US XVI Corps crosses the River Roer at Hilfarth and sweep down the eastern side of the River Maas towards the Canadian 1st Army.

26 February General Crerar launches Operation Blockbuster with Canadian II Corps in an attempt to break through the 'Hochwald Layback' and take Xanten to reach the Rhine opposite Wesel.

1 March US 9th Army captures Mönchengladbach.

3 March XVI Corps of US 9th Army and British XXX Corps of Canadian 1st Army link up at Geldern to complete the joining of 'Veritable' and 'Grenade'.

7 March US III Corps captures Rhine bridge intact at Remagen and establish a bridgehead for US 1st Army.

10 March Final two bridges at Wesel are blown by the Germans and British 21 Army completes its clearance of west bank of northern Rhine.

14 March US 3rd Army crosses lower River Moselle to outflank Siegfried Line.

22/23 March US 3rd Army crosses Rhine near Nierstein.

23 March Approval given by Hitler for a formal withdrawal across the Rhine of all German forces, but by that time all who were going to make it back had already gone.

23/24 March British 21st Army Group crosses Rhine as part of Operation Plunder.

24/25 March British and American airborne forces land east of the Rhine to link up with British 21st Army Group.

31 March French 1st Army crosses Rhine near Germersheim.

ORDERS OF BATTLE FEBRUARY 1945

German Army

Commander-in-Chief (West) – Gerd von Rundstedt

Army Group H (Blaskowitz)
  25th Army (Von Blumentritt)
    XXX Corps (Fretter-Pico)
      346 Infantry Division (Steinmueller)
      6 Parachute Division (Plocher)
    LXXXVIII Corps (Reinhard)
      2 Parachute Division (Lackner)
  1st Parachute Army (Schlemm)
    LXXXVI Corps (Straube)
      180 Infantry Division (Klosterkemper)
      190 Infantry Division (Hammer)
    II Parachute Corps (Meindl)
      7 Parachute Division (Erdmann)
      8 Parachute Division (Wadehn)
      84 Infantry Division (Feibig)
    XLVII Corps (von Luttwitz)
      15 Panzer Grenadier Division (Maucke)
      116 Panzer Division (Von Waldenburg)

Army Group B (Model)
  15th Army (von Zangen)
    XII SS Corps (Crasemann)
      59 Infantry Division (Poppe)
      176 Infantry Division (Landau)
      183 Infantry Division (Lange)
    LXXXI Corps (Koechling)
      12 Volksgrenadier Division (Engel)
      363 Volksgrenadier Division (Dettling)
      353 Infantry Division (Thieme)
  5th Panzer Army (Manteuffel)
    LXXIV Corps (Puechler)
      85 Infantry Division (Chill)
      62 Volksgrenadier Division (Kittel)
      272 Volksgrenadier Division (Konig)
      3 Parachute Division (Schimpf)
      3 Panzer Grenadier Division (Denkert)
      9 Panzer Division (Von Elverfeldt)
    LXVII Corps (Hitzfeld)
      26 Volksgrenadier Division (Kocott)
      89 Infantry Division (Bruns)
      277 Volksgrenadier Division (Viebig)
    LXVI Corps (Lucht)
      18 Volksgrenadier Division (Hoffmann-Schonborn)
      246 Volksgrenadier Division (Korte)
      326 Volksgrenadier Division (Kaschner)
      2 Panzer Division (Kokott)
      5 Parachute Division (Heilmann)
  7th Army (Brandenberger)
    XIII Corps (Felber)

      167 Volksgrenadier Division (Hocker)
      276 Volksgrenadier Division (Dempwolff)
      340 Volksgrenadier Division (Tolsdorf)
    LIII Corps (Rothkirch und Trach)
      9 Volksgrenadier Division (Kolb)
      79 Volksgrenadier Division (Hummel)
      352 Volksgrenadier Division (Bazing)
    LXXX Corps (Beyer)
      212 Volksgrenadier Division (Sensfuss)
      560 Volksgrenadier Division (Langhauser)

Army Group G (Hausser)
  1st Army (Foertsch)
    LXXXII Corps (Hahm)
      416 Infantry Division (Pflieger)
      11 Panzer Division (Wietersheim)
    LXXXV Corps (Kniess)
      347 Infantry Division (Trierenberg)
      719 Infantry Division (Gade)
    XIII SS Corps (Von Oriola)
      19 Volksgrenadier Division (Britzelmayr)
      559 Volksgrenadier Division (Von Muhlen)
      17 SS Panzer Grenadiers (Klingenberg)
    XC Corps (Peterson)
      6 SS Division (Brenner)
      36 Volksgrenadier Division (Welln)
    LXXXIV Corps (Behlendorff)
      47 Volksgrenadier Division (Bork)
      257 Volksgrenadier Division (Seidel)
      553 Volksgrenadier Division (Huter)
  19th Army (Balck)
    XVIII SS Corps (Meyer)
      405 Replacement Division (Seeger)
      708 Volksgrenadier Division (Bleckwenn)
    LXIII Corps (Abraham)
      16 Volksgrenadier Division (Haeckel)
      159 Infantry Division (Burcky)
      189 Infantry Division (Bauer)
      198 Infantry Division (Schiel)
      338 Infantry Division (Von Oppen)

NOTE: The overall situation on the Western Front in early 1945 was chaotic and meant that many of the above German units were incomplete, often only existed in battle groups and were being shifted from sector to sector at short notice. It would be very difficult to give an exact German 'order of battle' on any front at this period of the war.

Allied Armies

Supreme Allied Commander – Dwight D. Eisenhower.

US 12th Army Group (Bradley)
- US XVIII Airborne Corps (Ridgway)
  - US 17 Airborne Division (Miley)
  - US 82 Airborne Division (Gavin)
  - US 101 Airborne Division (Taylor)
- US 1st Army (Hodges)
  - US III Corps (Millikin)
    - US 1 Infantry Division (Andrus)
    - US 9 Infantry Division (Craig)
    - US 78 Infantry Division (Parker)
    - US 9 Armored Division (Leonard)
  - US V Corps (Heubner)
    - US 2 Infantry Division (Robertson)
    - US 28 Infantry Division (Cota)
    - US 69 Infantry Division (Reinhardt)
    - US 106 Infantry Division (Perrin)
    - US 7 Armored Division (Hasbruck)
  - US VII Corps (Collins)
    - US 8 Infantry Division (Weaver)
    - US 104 Infantry Division (Allen)
    - US 3 Armored Division (Rose)
    - US 99 Infantry Division (Lauer)
- US 3rd Army (Patton)
  - US 14 Armored Division (Smith)
  - US VIII Corps (Middleton)
    - US 4 Infantry Division (Blakely)
    - US 87 Infantry Division (Culin)
    - US 90 Infantry Division (Van Fleet)
    - US 6 Armored Division (Grow)
    - US 11 Armored Division (Kilburn)
  - US XII Corps (Eddy)
    - US 5 Infantry Division (Irwin)
    - US 76 Infantry Division (Schmidt)
    - US 80 Infantry Division (McBride)
    - US 89 Infantry Division (Finley)
    - US 4 Armored Division (Gaffey)
  - US XX Corps (Walker)
    - US 26 Infantry Division (Paul)
    - US 65 Infantry Division (Reinhart)
    - US 94 Infantry Division (Malony)
    - US 10 Armored Division (Morris)

US 6th Army Group (Devers)
- US 7th Army (Patch)
  - US 12 Armored Division (Allen)
  - US VI Corps (Brooks)
    - US 36 Infantry Division (Dahlquist)
    - US 42 Infantry Division (Collins)
    - US 44 Infantry Division (Dean)
    - US 103 Infantry Division (McAulife)
    - Algerian 3 Infantry Division (Gillaume)
  - US XV Corps (Haislip)
    - US 3 Infantry Division (O'Daniel)
    - US 45 Infantry Division (Frederick)
    - US 63 Infantry Division (Hibbs)
    - US 100 Infantry Division (Burress)
- French 1st Army (de Tassigny)
  - French 27 Alpine Division (Molle)
  - French 1 Infantry Division (Garbay)

- French 2 Armored Division (Leclerc)
- French I Corps (Béthouart)
  - French 4 Mountain Division (De Hesdin)
  - French 9 Colonial Infantry Division (Valluy)
  - French 14 Infantry Division (Salan)
  - French 1 Armoured Division (Sudre)
- French II Corps (De Montsabert)
  - Moroccan 2 Infantry Division (Carpentier)
  - French 5 Armored Division (De Vernejoul)

British 21st Army Group (Montgomery)
- British 2nd Army (Dempsey)
  - British 79 Armoured Division (Hobart)
  - British I Corps (Crocker)
    - British 49 Infantry Division (MacMillan)
    - Polish 1 Armoured Division (Maczek)
  - British VIII Corps (Barker)
    - British 3 Infantry Division (Whistler)
    - British 11 Armoured Division (Roberts)
  - British XII Corps (Ritchie)
    - British 52 (Lowland) Division (Hakewill Smith)
    - British 7th Armoured Division (Lyne)

- Canadian 1st Army (Crerar)
  - British XXX Corps (Horrocks)
    - British 15 (Scottish) Division (Barber)
    - British 43 (Wessex) Division (Thomas)
    - British 51 (Highland) Division (Rennie)
    - British 53 (Welsh) Division (Ross)
    - British Guards Armoured Division (Adair)
    - Canadian 2 Infantry Division (Matthews)
    - Canadian 3 Infantry Division (Spry)
  - Canadian II Corps (Simonds)
    - Canadian 4 Armored Division (Vokes)
- US 9th Army (Simpson)
  - US 75 Infantry Division (Porter)
  - US 95 Infantry Division (Twadle)
  - US XVI Corps (Anderson)
    - US 35 Infantry Division (Baade)
    - US 79 Infantry Division (Wyche)
    - US 8 Armored Division (Devine)
  - US XIII Corps (Gillem)
    - US 84 Infantry Division (Bolling)
    - US 102 Infantry Division (Keating)
    - US 5 Armored Division (Oliver)
  - US XIX Corps (McLain)
    - US 29 Infantry Division (Gerhardt)
    - US 30 Infantry Division (Hobbs)
    - US 83 Infantry Division (Macon)
    - US 2 Armored Division (White)

Air support
- British RAF
  - 2nd Tactical Air Force
- French
  - 1st Air Corps
- American
  - IX, XII, XIX, XXIX Tactical Air Command
  - IX US Bomber Command
  - US Eighth Air Force

NOTE: These Allied groupings were as existed for the opening of the 'Veritable' 'Grenade' operations early in February 1945. During this period, many units were being earmarked and shifted to new sectors at short notice as the situation demanded.

SELECTED BIBLIOGRAPHY

Allen, Peter *One More River,* JM Dent, 1980

Barclay, Brig CN *The History of the 53rd (Welsh) Division in the Second World War,* William Clowes, 1956

Blake, George *Mountain and Flood,* Jackson & Son & Company, 1950

Draper, Lt Theodore *The 84th Infantry Division in the Battle Of Germany,* Viking Press, New York, 1946

Elstob, Peter *The Battle Of The Reichswald,* Macdonald, 1970

Essame, MajGen H The 43rd *Wessex Division at War 1939–1945,* William Clowes, 1952

Essame, MajGen H *The Battle For Germany,* Batsford, 1969

Horrocks, LtGen Sir Brian *Corps Commander,* Sidgwick & Jackson, 1977

MacDonald, Charles B *The Last Offensive,* Washington, DC, 1951

MacDonald, Charles B *The Siegfried Line Campaign,* Washington DC, 1963

Martin, LtGen HG *The History of the Fifteenth Scottish Division 1939–1945,* William Blackwood, 1948

Mitcham, Samuel W *Hitler's Legions,* Leo Cooper, 1985

Salmond, JB *The History of the 51st Highland Division 1939–1945,* William Blackwood, 1953

Weigley, Russell F *Eisenhower's Lieutenants,* Sidgwick & Jackson, 1981

Whitaker, WD & S *Rhineland: The Battle To End The War,* Leo Cooper, 1989

Whiting, Charles *Siegfried,* Leo Cooper, 1983

Williams, Jeffery *The Long Left Flank,* Leo Cooper, 1988

A machine-gun crew of the US 9th Army looks out across the River Rhine from a captured barn. The Browning 0.5 inch (12.7mm) M2 (HB) heavy machine gun had been in American service since 1921 and became one of the best anti-personnel weapons ever used. It was also capable of firing armour-piercing rounds. In this picture, the crew were using the gun's effective range of over 2,000 yards (1,820m) to provide interdictory fire against enemy movements across the river. (National Archives, Washington)

WARGAMING THE CAMPAIGN

Most wargamers who recreate the battles of the Western Front on the tabletop tend to concentrate on the larger, more publicised campaigns, such as the battle for Normandy, Operation Market Garden and the Battle of the Bulge. In the past few years a new series of Divisional histories, books covering more obscure battles (such as the Overloon salient, the campaign for the Schelde or the battle for Aachen) and research information via the Internet have helped make minor battles more accessible to wargamers. The battle for the Rhineland is a fascinating source of inspiration for miniature gamers, and this book provides information on dozens of actions which would translate well onto the tabletop.

Gaming with Miniature Figurines

For several years, the most popular set of wargame rules for Divisional or Brigade-sized games was *Command Decision*, which replaced the earlier Wargames Research Group rules as the standard within the hobby. In the last few years *Command Decision* had evolved through three editions, each becoming more elaborate (and complex). At the same time, their position was challenged by *Spearhead*, a set which mirrored the basic simplicity of the *Command Decision* playing system, but which introduced new approaches to wargaming in the period. Both sets are sound, playable rules systems, and although both can be slowed down by the use of additional or special rules, experienced gamers can play a fast-moving and enjoyable game with them. While primarily designed for 1:300 or 1:285 scale figures, they are both equally suitable for 10mm or 15mm scales, although less than ideal for anything larger.

An ideal multi-player game on this scale would be the struggle to capture Goch. Although the attack on 19 February involved three British divisions, only three brigades spearheaded the attack. While the defenders benefited from strong defences and interior lines of communication, the overwhelming artillery firepower of the British proved decisive. A game where each Allied player has set objectives, and an overall commander allocates corps level resources would recreate the command structure of the battle, although for the German player his options are more limited, and his objective would be survival, or even the successful extrication of his forces while causing high casualties to the attacker. At this stage of the war British manpower reserves were drained, and heavy losses were unacceptable, and should be reflected in the victory conditions.

Other suitable games on this scale could be the attack by the 43rd (Wessex) Division towards the Goch–Calcar road, the Roer crossings by Simpson's 9th Army or the reduction of the Xanten pocket. Each has its own interesting features; a classical divisional attack where the British

American dead from the first waves of the 84th Division's assault crossing of the River Roer at Linnich. The paddle-powered storm boat was swept by German machine-gun fire as the infantry tried to reach the far side of the swiftly flowing river. Despite several of the boats being caught by German fire, casualties were relatively light for such a complex operation.
(National Archives, Washington)

commander showed unusual flair in the juggling of his forces, a river crossing under enemy fire and the grinding reduction of an enemy bridgehead, while the defender tries to extricate whatever troops he can. The beauty of this level of gaming is that it allows for logistical considerations to enter into the game. The account of the drive on Cleve where two divisions shared the same muddy road is an example of the importance of logistics, and can be represented by special rules governing the arrival (or non-arrival) of reinforcements and ammunition.

While these larger Divisional actions are best suited for large games involving several players, this level of wargame is perfect for two opponents. As most of the engagements fought during this campaign were fought on the brigade level, this provides the best scope for wargamers. While there are several commercial rules sets available, one of the most popular is *Rapid Fire*, a simple and elegant set of rules which are reminiscent of the Charles Grant *Battle* rules of the 1970s. Designed for 15mm and 20mm figures, games using *Rapid Fire* are consistently fun, fast moving and a pleasure to play. While they lack the detailed command and control rules of the larger sets, a recent *Operation Market Garden* supplement included suggestions for a command structure.

An unusual brigade-level action would be the initial attacks in the Reichswald by the 51st (Highland) Division and 53rd (Welsh) Division; assaults made in atrocious conditions, where contact between the units of the attacking force was almost impossible. Suitable limitations will need to be imposed on the units, virtually fighting 'blind' through the dense Reichswald forest. Other ideal brigade scenarios would be the

ABOVE **A modern view of the edge of the Reichswald at the point where the 53rd (Welsh) Division entered the woods. The road turns sharply to the left in the distance, just in front of the trees, where it is joined by one of the major rides through the forest. This track served as the main axis for the 53rd Division's advance and was code-named 'Maine'. The rising ground of the Brandenberg feature can be made out above the top of the trees. (Norbert Rosin)**

RIGHT **Dragon's teeth marking an anti-tank section of the Siegfried Line stretch across a modern farm to the north of Aachen. Most of Hitler's Westwall defences have disappeared but it is still possible to come across some remnants of the fortifications in the Rhineland area. (Author)**

night battle in the streets of Cleve by a brigade of the 43rd (Wessex) Division, the later drive through the Reichswald, and any of the Roer river crossings by Simpson's 9th Army. The conditions facing the British need to be recreated; mud too thick to allow armour support, continual rain (and consequently poor visibility) and a lack of logistical support. It is precisely these challenges which makes the Rhineland operation so fascinating to refight.

For years there were no commercial rules available which covered this level of gaming. This has now changed, and in the last couple of years *Crossfire* and *Battleground* have both filled the void. Other less commercially popular sets are also available. Of the two, *Crossfire* has the more elegant games system, using a unique method of adjudicating movement and

combat. It produces a tense, enjoyable game, and the system lends itself perfectly to certain aspects of the Rhineland campaign. *Battleground* places a greater emphasis on hardware (tanks, weapons etc.) and although slower, it produces a highly realistic game.

The amphibious operations conducted by the 3rd Canadian Division to the north of the main Operation Veritable battleground provide a highly unusual battalion-level game. German-held villages became island strongpoints, and these were assaulted by battalion-sized Canadian units riding in amphibious carriers. Players may have to adapt special rules to suit the circumstances, reflecting the shock-effect of these amphibious assaults, and the concentrated barrages which preceded them. The assault of the Wiltshire battalions near Tippenburg, or the following day's action by the Somersets are both prime examples of British battalion-level attacks; rigid start-lines, limited objectives and supporting armour and artillery fire. By contrast, the river crossings by units of the American 84th Division and the subsequent exploitation of their bridgehead was a far more impromptu affair, particularly the assault on Korrenzig village by the I/334th Battalion. The terrain which formed the battleground for the latter action makes a refight using rules such as *Crossfire* particularly rewarding.

Skirmish Games

There are too many sets of skirmish-level rules to name, but most Second World War sets place an emphasis on equipment and squad-level tactics. Although excellent for recreating the constant patrolling during any phase of the war, skirmish-level games are also suitable for refighting several of the actions of the Rhineland campaign. For example, the patrol by Lt Roy Rogers across the Roer River to silence German machine guns is a fascinating subject for a skirmish game, as is the race to secure the Roer Dams before they could be destroyed. Similarly, the rapid advance made by Patton's 3rd Army through the Saarland during

March 1945 left numerous groups of German soldiers isolated behind American lines. While many simply surrendered, others tried to rejoin their units, providing a suitably compelling background for a skirmish game. The whole Rhineland campaign contains engagements worthy of refighting at almost every level, from divisional down to the actions of individual squads. The secret is to adapt whatever rules you use to reflect the particular circumstances of the Rhineland battles: mud, rain and a dogged defence.

The Reichswald, unchanged after 54 years. The picture shows one of the major cross tracks in the 51st (Highland) Division's sector. (Author)

Board and Computer Games

Although no board wargames deal directly with the campaign, several portray the larger campaign in north-west Europe. The flavour of the latter stages of the war is admirably caught in the old SPI game *Battle for Germany*, where the player takes either the Russian or the Allied army, plus the German defenders facing the troops of his opponent. In recent years board wargames have been partly eclipsed by computer wargames, and several provide an excellent vehicle for refighting the campaign. Of these the most accurate is *The Operational Art of War, Volume 1*, a clumsy title for a superb wargame. Only one of the initial scenarios included with the game relates to this phase of fighting in north-west Europe, but a scenario design package is also included in the game. Players can also download extra scenarios from several free web sites, and these include ones featuring the Rhineland battles. Although the game is flexible, most scenarios concentrate on the army group level, and the players move battalion-sized units. Another popular computer game is *West Front*, fought at a brigade level, and each unit represents a platoon. Once again, the initial range of scenarios are augmented by additional games which can be downloaded. These include the battle for the Reichswald and the capture of Düren by the US VII Corps. On an even smaller scale, *Steel Panthers* provides a playable game where each infantry squad and individual tank is represented. Like the previous games, downloaded scenarios from the Internet provide a greater range than the designers included with the initial game, and a design package allows gamers to create their own scenarios.

BELOW **Infantry from the Canadian 3rd Division pass through a flooded village whilst securing the extreme left side of the Canadian 1st Army's sector. The rising water from the blown dykes on the Rhine and Maas rivers had inundated miles of open countryside, leaving isolated villages protruding from the water. These groups of houses had often been reinforced by German defenders to form strong points from which they threatened the flanks of Operation 'Veritable'. (Imperial War Museum)**

INDEX

References to illustrations are shown in **bold**.